THE LONG MARCH

Books by Harrison E. Salisbury

The Long March   1985

China: 100 Years of Revolution   1983

A Journey for Our Times   1983

Without Fear or Favor—The New York Times   1980

The Unknown War   1978

Russia in Revolution 1900–1930   1978

Black Night, White Snow: Russia's Revolutions 1905–1917   1977

Travels Around America   1976

The Gates of Hell   1975

To Peking—and Beyond   1973

The Eloquence of Protest—Voices of the 70's *(Editor)*   1972

The Many Americas Shall Be One   1971

War Between Russia and China   1969

The 900 Days—The Siege of Leningrad   1969

The Soviet Union: The Fifty Years *(Editor)*   1967

Behind the Lines—Hanoi   1967

Orbit of China   1967

Russia   1965

The Northern Palmyra Affair   1962

A New Russia?   1962

Moscow Journal: The End of Stalin   1961

To Moscow—and Beyond   1960

The Shook-up Generation   1958

American in Russia   1955

Russia on the Way   1946

THE
LONG MARCH

THE UNTOLD STORY

Harrison E. Salisbury

McGRAW-HILL BOOK COMPANY

New York   St. Louis   San Francisco   Auckland   Bogotá
Hamburg   Johannesburg   London   Madrid   Mexico
Milan   Montreal   New Delhi   Panama   Paris
São Paulo   Singapore   Sydney   Tokyo   Toronto

Reprinted by arrangement with Harper & Row, Publishers, Inc.

First McGraw-Hill Paperback edition, 1987

1 2 3 4 5 6 7 8 9 S E M S E M 8 7

ISBN 0-07-054471-9

LIBRARY OF CONGRESS CATALOGING-IN-PUBLICATION DATA

Salisbury, Harrison Evans, 1908–
  The long march.
  Bibliography: p.
  Includes index.
  1. China—History—Long March, 1934–1935. I. Title.
DS777.5134.S34 1987   951.04'2   86-21159
ISBN 0-07-054471-9 (pbk.)

Designer: Sidney Feinberg

Maps: Andrew Sabbatini

To the heroic men and women of China's Long March and to my companions in our own Long March of 1984—my beloved wife, Charlotte, my friend Jack Service, my two dear Chinese comrades, General Qin Xinghan and Zhang Yuanyuan

CONTENTS

ILLUSTRATIONS

A section of photographs follows page 212

MAPS

THE LONG MARCH

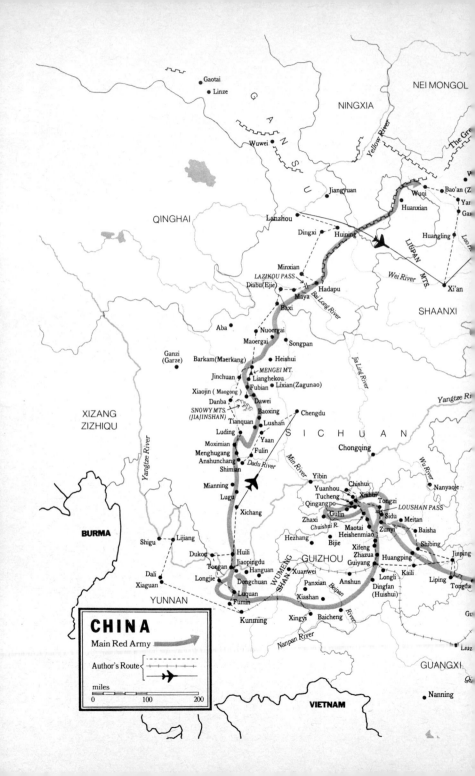

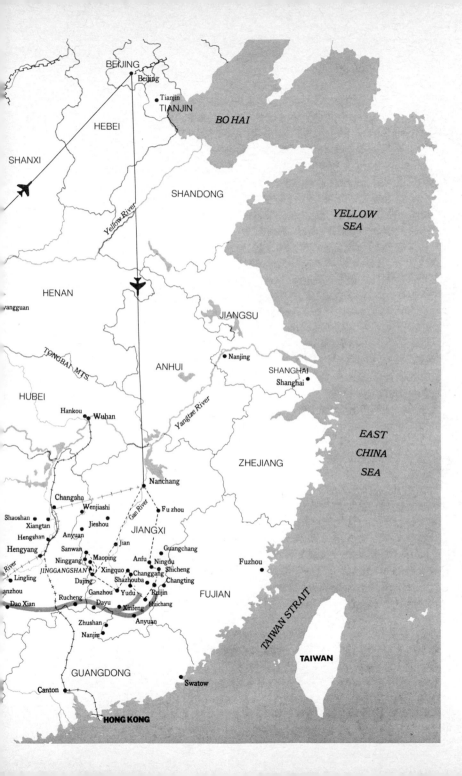

BEHIND THE LONG MARCH

E ACH revolution is carried out under its own legend. The American was fought with Valley Forge engraved in the hearts of the patriots, that ordeal from which George Washington and his men came forth steeled for victory.

The French stormed the Bastille and in Petrograd in 1917 it was the Winter Palace. There were only seven prisoners in the Bastille; the Bolsheviks walked into a Winter Palace defended only by a handful of teenagers and some women. Never mind. These became the symbols of revolution.

China's Long March of 1934 was no symbol. It was a great human epic which tested the will, courage, and strength of the men and women of the Chinese Red Army.

It was not a "march" in the conventional sense, not a military campaign, not a victory. It was a triumph of human survival, a deadly, endless retreat from the claws of Chiang Kai-shek; a battle that again and again came within a hair's breadth of defeat and disaster. It was fought without plan. Mao was excluded from the preparations and was only told at the eleventh hour. In the end, it won China for Mao Zedong and his Communists. No event in this century has so captured the world's imagination and so profoundly affected its future. It led in a straight line from the shallow river of the Yudu in southern China, crossed by the Red Army on October 16, 1934, to the proclamation by Mao, from the rostrum of Tiananmen Square in Beijing on October 1, 1949, of the People's Republic of China—that is, to the triumph of Communism in a land inhabited by one-quarter of the human inhabitants of the earth.

It was a long time coming. The descent of the empire of the Qings was slow and painful, eroded by weakness from within and by brute western military, technological and economic power from without.

1

Revolution took a hundred years to succeed. First there were the Taipings and their mystical pseudo-Christian uprising of the 1850s. Then
the Heavenly Fists, the Boxers, in 1900, again mystical, fanatic, xeno-
phobic. Finally, in 1911 Dr. Sun Yat-sen's democratic, ill-articulated
revolutionaries brought down the old Empire and China plunged into
a chaos as had not been seen since the time of the Warring States 400
years before Christ.

Between October 16, 1934, and October 1, 1949, China's stage was
filled with heroism, tragedy, intrigue, bloodletting, treachery, cheap
opera, military genius, political guile, moral goals, spiritual objectives,
and human hatred. Shakespeare could not have written such a story. It
is not yet finished. Perhaps it never will be.

The first word of this remarkable drama was brought to the world
by Edgar Snow when he visited Mao Zedong and the Communists in
their sanctuary in the loess hills of northern Shaanxi in 1936. They had
arrived there a year earlier after more than six thousand miles of marching, fighting, starving, and freezing through the roughest wrinkles of
the globe—the backcountry of China—crossing twenty-four rivers and,
as Mao calculated, one thousand mountains.

On the main march of the First Front Army, some 86,000 men and
women were said to have started out. Possibly 4,000 arrived with Mao
a year later, October 19, 1935, in northern Shaanxi.

I first read of the Long March on the pages of Edgar Snow's *Red Star
Over China*. Most Chinese heard of it from the Chinese edition of his
book. It captured my imagination as it did the imagination of thousands.
"Some day," Snow wrote then, "someone will write the full epic of this
exciting expedition." He once hoped to write this story, but for many
reasons never did.

After years of effort, I first got to China in 1972. A bit later I put
before the late Zhou Enlai a proposal to retrace the route of Mao's Red
Army and write the story of the Long March. Jack Service, the old
China hand, joined me in this proposal, which was made again and
again over a period of a dozen years.

Nothing came of it. These were the last turbulent years of Mao
Zedong, years of the Cultural Revolution and of the Gang of Four.
Mao's comrades of the Long March, the men who had been tightly
bonded by hardship and sacrifice, were in disarray. Many were dead.
Many had succumbed in the horrors of the Cultural Revolution. Some
had been murdered. Many still languished in jail. In those years, to have
been a hero of the Long March meant that you were labeled an archvil-

lain by those struggling to inherit Mao's power.

Not much chance to write history under those circumstances. Even with Mao's death in 1976, and the arrest and trial of Qiang Jing, Mao's widow, and her associates in the Gang, the path back to the Long March did not swiftly reopen. Only with the gradual ascendency of Deng Xiaoping, the rehabilitation of the old heroes, their assumption of high positions in government, and, most important, the evolution of a new and (relatively) realistic attitude toward history, did retracing the Long March begin to seem plausible.

Much had changed during those years, but not my resolve to record the story of the Long March if humanly possible. In August 1983, word finally came from Beijing: The door to the Long March was open! The resources, the archives, the historical materials, would be put at my disposal. I could travel the *Chang Zheng*, the journey of 25,000 li, every li of it. Two men, I later learned, were largely responsible for this decision: General Yang Shangkun, Vice-Chairman of the Central Military Commission, and Huang Hua, former Foreign Minister.

On March 1, 1984, my wife, Charlotte, and I flew to Beijing and embarked on a whirlwind round of interviews with surviving senior generals, widows of Party figures (some of them victims of the Cultural Revolution), archivists, and historians. Soon Jack Service joined us. After a month in Beijing we set out on the route of the March, accompanied by General Qin Xinghan, deputy director of the National Museum of Military History in Beijing, a specialist in the Long March, and Zhang Yuanyuan, a senior interpreter from the Foreign Office.

We flew to Nanchang, capital of Jiangxi, the province from which the Long March started. We explored the remote mountains where the Communists sank their first roots, and we interviewed dozens of survivors of the March, men and women, soaking into our brains the crises and conflicts that gave birth to what could as well have become the Fatal Retreat.

That was the start. We followed on the route of the Red Army. Not every li of the way. We skipped a bit here and there, particularly some of the zigzags in Guizhou, taking side excursions over the terrain traveled by the secondary armies, tasting the sheer exhaustion of the Red Army's travel by climbing the spiky trail that leads from the crossing of the Golden Sands River past Fire Mountain and Lion's Head not far from Tibet, emerging from the mountains by mule and horseback, and moving up to the Great Snowies, the roads in late May leading through fields of snow, on to the terrible Grasslands, where, as at Passchendaele, men had slipped into the bottomless muck and dragged down to eternity anyone who tried to lend a helping hand.

The journey covered 7,400 miles on the roads and trails—jeep, minibus, command car—and took two and a half months. Then more and more interviews, and another trip to China, in autumn 1984.

Only the journey over the actual ground could convey a feeling of what Mao and his men and women endured. This is still backcountry. No cities. No foreigners. In town after town, no one could remember a foreigner ever visiting.

No one, foreign or Chinese, had made the trip. No one is likely soon to repeat it as we did.

Here, then, is the record of the Long March of fifty years ago, pieced together from hundreds of interviews, documents, archives. I put to the Chinese every hard question I could think of. They did their best to answer, sometimes going back again and again to the records until they ferreted out the missing fact.

The story is an epic. Not only because of the heroism of the simple soldiers and their commanders but because it became, in effect, the crucible of the Chinese Revolution. It forged the brotherhood that fought Chiang Kai-shek to a standstill and came to power under Mao's leadership.

That this brotherhood disintegrated in the madness of Mao's final years adds a note of tragedy to the heroic drama. But now, amazingly, the survivors have come to the top. Under the leadership of Deng Xiaoping they have moved China onto what they call a "new Long March," one as difficult as the original and one which may become the great social and political experiment of our times. But that and the debacle of the Cultural Revolution and the Gang of Four constitute another tale. This is the story of the Long March—all of it that I could assemble together with the help of Chinese historians and the survivors themselves.

Here and there, more episodes may float to the surface. But enough is told here to demonstrate that this human undertaking has no parallel. In it there is a little, perhaps, of the exodus of the Jews, a little of Hannibal's crossing of the Alps, of Napoleon's march on Moscow, and, to my surprise, some echoes of America's winning of the West, the great cavalcade over mountain and prairie.

But no comparison fits. The Long March is sui generis. Its heroism has fired the dreams of a nation of 1.1 billion people and set China moving toward a destiny no man can yet divine.

1

A WALK BY MOONLIGHT

THE October sun flooded the whitewashed hospital room and outside in the compound under the broad-leafed camphor trees there was a flurry of movement, shouted orders, the sound of a bugle, and a tramp of feet that sent small spirals of dust into the still air. Within the room, the patient, emaciated, his left leg in a cast, craned his neck, trying to see what was going on. Something was up, that was plain, some new movement of the Red Army about which he had not been informed. A nurse was passing his door and he called out: "What's happening?"

"I don't know, Commander," she replied, glancing outside. "We haven't been told."

Chen Yi cursed as he had a hundred times since he had been carried from the front in Xingguo county six weeks ago with a bullet wound in his hip which refused to heal. Splinters of bone kept working out and when he asked for an X-ray the doctors put him off with excuses: the X-ray machine was out of order, there was no power for it, the batteries were too weak.

Chen Yi was a sanguine man of thirty-three, a native of Sichuan, outgoing, known for his sense of humor, a senior commander of the Red Army, but today he was out of sorts, irritable, restless, worried. Something was going on and he couldn't figure out what. He twisted in bed, frustrated by his wound. A few minutes later the nurse appeared again. "There is someone to see you, Commander," she said, hurrying to punch up his pillows and straighten the sheets. Chen Yi looked over her shoulder and saw his old friend and comrade Zhou Enlai entering the room. Later on, Chen Yi would recall the date of Zhou's visit. It was October 9, 1934—the second day in the tenth lunar moon in the Year of the Dog—the day he was told about what was to become the Long March.[1]

Yudu was a drowsy town of less than ten thousand in southern Jiangxi on the banks of the Yudu River. Not much happened there: a ferry across the river, a market. In October of 1934 there was a feeling of well-being about the place, tempered with a little nervousness. The weather was pleasant: warm days, cooler nights, hardly any rain. Most of the crops were in and only the late rice, some buckwheat, and sweet potatoes still awaited harvest. The soybeans—vines, roots, and all—were drying on the gray-tile roofs, twisting over the winged roof ends. Red earthen jars stood against the courtyard walls, filled with bean paste. In the corners were heaps of bitter melons, green with red seeds, orange pumpkins, and strings of drying red peppers. The peasants knew now that there would be enough food until the next crop began to come in, but there was an edge of unease in Yudu. The Red Army had imposed heavy requisitions of rice in the summer and there had been an unusual drive for recruits. The harvest had been generous and people were taking a breather in the eternal cycle of planting and harvesting, of harrowing and transplanting, but something seemed to be in the air. No one knew just what. The autumn moon festival was behind them and the red fortune paper over the door lintels and the guardian door posters, fierce and frightening, had tattered a bit. People hoped they would still protect them against bad luck.[2]

Liu Ying was spending a few weeks in Yudu rounding up new recruits for the Red Army, one of the many young women engaged in the work. Liu Ying was twenty-six years old and a tiny woman, a scant five feet tall, petite as a child's doll. Helen Snow once said that she could not imagine how Liu Ying avoided being blown away during the Long March.[3] Later on, when Liu Ying married Luo Fu, a top Party leader, he said the same thing. Small Liu Ying was, but she possessed a spirit of spun steel, and Mao Zedong had taken her under his wing. One day he came to the Communist youth league office, a bodyguard at his side. He spoke to the little army recruiter privately and told her she must leave Yudu immediately and report for duty at Ruijin, headquarters of the Central Soviet Area in southern Jiangxi, for a very special job.

"I told him that I couldn't leave," she recalled fifty years later. "I hadn't finished my job. I had to get more recruits to fill my quota."

But Mao was firm. She must return. Liu Ying was puzzled, but she made her way back to Ruijin. It was a forty-mile walk and it took her two days, just a short stroll compared with those she would soon be taking.[4]

A short, stylish man with a bullet-shaven head sat behind a fine teakwood desk in an imposing building overlooking a lake in Nanchang, capital of Jiangxi province. A smile of satisfaction played over his thin lips as he picked up *Minguo Ribao,* the local Nationalist daily. His eye roved past the main news story about the award of contracts for constructing a railroad bridge, past the welter of advertisements for sex tonics, "female" remedies, and jewelry, and focused on the main editorial. The date was October 10, 1934, Double Ten, the anniversary of the founding of the Nationalist regime, and the editorial was dedicated to the problems of the day. It warned of natural calamities, of the imminence of a second World War. The Communist bandits had taken advantage of China's plight to run rampant. People should turn to morality, stop drinking and dancing, and strive for the survival of the homeland, of China. Fortunately, the situation here in Jiangxi was improving rapidly. The Communist bandits would be wiped out within the year. They were surrounded on all sides and had to rope their soldiers together to keep them from running away. "The day of their collapse is not far away."

The reader of the newspaper lightly licked his lips. These were words of which he approved. In fact, they were words that he himself had dictated. His name was Chiang Kai-shek. He was forty-eight years old and he had come to Nanchang to direct his Nationalist Army in the mopping up of the "Red bandits." Things were going well. A couple of days later, Chiang ordered up his personal plane and prepared to take off on a quick inspection trip to Shaanxi, Ningxia, and Sichuan.[5]

The Communist Third Army Group was encamped in the area of Shicheng, a bit north of Ruijin, the Central Soviet Area's capital. A compact, salty man named Kong, then twenty-three, who all his life would remain a plainspoken revolutionary soldier, was head of the Third Army's scouting detachment. The Army was resting. It had been pulled out of line two weeks earlier after a hard and not very successful battle. Now it was being prepared for new operations. These were very secret. Kong's comrades only knew that soon they would be on the march again. (Later on, this secrecy would be much criticized as counterproductive.) Kong knew a good deal more, because he was a scout, but he wasn't talking about it. Like so many of his comrades, Kong came from a very poor peasant family, one of five brothers and seven sisters. His family had opposed his joining the Red Army. His parents upheld the traditional Chinese precept that you did not use good iron to make nails, nor send good men into the army. But Kong joined anyway. He wanted land; the Red Army promised it.

In Kong's first battle the Red Army smashed the Eighteenth Nationalist Division and captured its general, a big, red-faced, hated man from Hunan named Zhang Huizhan. Fifty years later, Kong recalled every detail of it: the rally on the mountain slope (no town square was big enough) where Zhang was hauled up before a crowd of peasants, poor townsfolk, young Red Guards with red-tasseled spears, and angry, battle-weary Red Army soldiers. Zhang stood on the platform wearing a dunce cap, arms bound behind his back, and the crowd shouted for his head. Presently it was chopped off, put on a raft, and floated down the river Gan as a warning to other Nationalist generals. The memory of the event so stirred Kong that as he told his story he burst into doggerel that had been sung on the occasion: "We're so happy. We fought at Longshen and captured the head of the tyrant Zhang.'"[6]

There was almost nothing that the tall, soft-spoken, rather elegant young man named Wu did not know about what was afoot with the Red Army in that October of mysterious comings and goings and growing excitement in the soviet base area and its capital at Ruijin. The base had been set up five years earlier by Communist forces led by Mao Zedong and his ally Zhu De. Their association was so close that the army was known to the peasants as the "Zhu-Mao" army and many, many firmly believed Zhu-Mao was one man. This was not entirely illogical. In fact, on one occasion Zhu De, the big, slow-moving, earthy Communist general, explained that you could not separate Zhu from Mao. This was a rather elaborate Chinese pun, because *zhu* means pig (in another ideograph) and *mao* means hair.[7]

Wu knew everything or almost everything that was going on, because he was serving as interpreter for a man called Li De, the representative of Moscow's Comintern to the Chinese Revolution. Li was now and had been for more than a year directing the Chinese Red Army with a dismaying absence of success.

Wu Xiuquan was twenty-eight years old. At nineteen, he had gone with a hundred other young Chinese to the Soviet Union, there to remain five or six years, studying the language, studying revolution, and studying military science. He had been back in China for three years and had been serving as interpreter since Li De's arrival in the soviet area, in October 1933.

Now Wu had a problem on his hands—culinary, not military. When Li De came to the soviet area the Chinese went to great trouble to make him comfortable. He lived in a new three-room house, specially built, located in a field of rice paddies about a mile from GHQ and not quite so distant from Party headquarters. The house was rather isolated and something about its setting impelled Wu and others to call it "Bleak House." In time, Bleak House became Li De's private nickname.

Wu's problem arose indirectly from the rice paddies. He and Li De's staff had raised a dozen ducks in these frog-filled paddies. The ducks had grown fat. By no means was Wu going to leave them behind. So it was duck for dinner every night, and to the end of his days Wu remembered that the last duck, crisp-fried, was served up in succulent pieces on October 10, 1934. Wu always associated that day with the Red Army's departure even though later on there came to be general agreement that the Long March did not formally begin until October 16, 1934.[8]

As the autumn days rolled on, talk among the Party cadres grew a bit more open. There was even a published hint of what lay ahead, for those who knew how to read between the lines. Luo Fu (Zhang Wentian) published an editorial in the Party newspaper, *Red China*, on September 29, 1934, in which he said that in order to defend the soviet and crush the Fifth Encirclement Campaign of Chiang Kai-shek, "We cannot but temporarily abandon some Soviet districts and cities. . . . In some places, because of the layer upon layer of lines of enemy blockhouses, [we must] smash the line of blockade and move the district, and preserve the vital force of the Army's main strength."

Everyone among the higher echelons knew that a move was under way, but they did not know to where. Some guessed Hunan, some another part of Jiangxi, some Guizhou, and some Yunnan or Sichuan. No one knew except the people at the very top. When cadres met one another within the sanctuary of Yunshishan, north of Ruijin, where headquarters had been moved to escape Chiang Kai-shek's fighter-bombers (he now had two or three hundred of them), they would say knowingly: "The time to move is coming." Sometimes they would ask: "Are you going?" The answers would vary. Some would say: "Sure." Others would say: "I don't know." Usually, "I don't know" meant that they weren't going. Actually, as Cai Xiaoqian recalled: "The news was like a large rock being thrown into the water." There was lots of uneasiness. Lists began to be made up. Some relatives appeared back in their native villages with boxes and trunks, explaining: "He is going away" (but not saying where). Some of the wounded were evacuated from the hospital back to their units. Gossip rose about who would go and who would stay. At first it was said that the elderly Xu, that is, Xu Teli, who had been Mao's teacher at Changsha Normal School, was being left behind, too old for the arduous ordeal ahead. Then it was said that he would go; had been assigned to the convalescent column; a horse had been found for him but no groom as yet.[9] What the gossips didn't know was that Mao Zedong had been shown a list of those who were slated to stay behind. There were many names on it of persons close to him —his brother Zetan, and Zetan's wife, He Yi, Mao's double sister-in-law (she was the sister of He Zizhen, to whom Mao was married); He Shuheng, Mao's friend, fellow Hunanese, and fellow co-founder of the Communist Party; Qu Qiubai, an early general secretary of the Communist Party, now deposed (too ill with tuberculosis, it was said, to be brought along); Commander Chen Yi; He Chang, a very early member of the Communist Party and a Mao supporter; Liu Bojian, another Mao adherent, and leader of the Ningdu Uprising; and many, many others. It seemed that not one of Mao's recommendations was accepted. Not even his plea that Qu Qiubai be brought along. A connection with Mao was a ticket for staying in the soviet area at a time when the chances of survival there were, in the opinion of General Chen Pixian, who was left behind, about one in ten.[10]

Mao Zedong was forty years old in the autumn of 1934: hollow-cheeked, gaunt, straight dark hair almost to his shoulders, thin, eyes burning, high cheekbones, about him an aura of pain. He had been ill for several months with recurrent malaria, and despite the best efforts of his missionary-trained doctor, Nelson Fu, he was still semiconvalescent, weak and frustrated. He knew what the Red Army was going to do. He had been told of it by Zhou Enlai after the decision had been made. Zhou was, in effect, chief of staff and participated in the discussions, but the orders were given by Li De, automatically supported by Bo Gu, the Party secretary. Even if Zhou differed, there was always a two-to-one vote against him. His task was to implement, then, as a good officer, the decisions of the high command.

Mao had not been consulted, nor had his advice been sought. This was not surprising. Within the dominant "Russian" faction there was a strong movement to expel Mao from the Party.[11] Mao had been removed from power over military and political decisions two years earlier. He was left with what amounted to the ceremonial title of Chairman of the Central Soviet Area; he presided over local meetings and for some weeks had been engaged in nominal inquiries into local conditions in Yudu, the riverine market town where he now lived in a comfortable gray-brick courtyard house up a narrow lane almost at the base of Yudu's north gate. He lived there with his wife, He Zizhen, twenty-four, pregnant for the fourth time. The child was due in February.[12]

Some gossips said then, and the tale has been repeated over the years, that Mao was under house arrest at Yudu; that he was not free to go to Ruijin, to consult with the Politburo, of which he was a member; that he had been cut off from all contact with the military and political leadership. It seems clear that he was not under house arrest. This is affirmed by all of the important Long March survivors with whom the author spoke and by contemporary Chinese Party historians and archivists. However, the idea of sending Mao to Yudu in the weeks when the decision to leave the Central Area was being made and implemented seems curious. The need for personal "research and studies" by Mao in Yudu could hardly have been pressing. In the opinion of Interpreter Wu Xiuquan, who was in a position to know, there were those who did not want Mao to come on the Long March. "Mao was deliberately excluded," Wu said. "This was just an excuse to keep him out."[13]

An effort had been made in the spring of 1934 to ship Mao off to the Soviet Union for "medical treatment." A proposal to this effect was sent to Moscow by Bo Gu and Li De. Apparently it was Li De's idea (although he says nothing in his memoirs about it). But Moscow rejected the idea. The Comintern believed that despite its troubles with Mao, his prestige and name were needed. Moreover, in the words of Interpreter Wu Xiuquan, Mao had declared: "I will not go. I will not leave the country."[14]

Feelings were heated. There is a thirdhand account that Mao once said to Edgar Snow as they passed Bo Gu on a street in Paoan: "You know that man once tried to kill me."[15] It would hardly be surprising if an effort was made in late summer or early autumn of 1934 to get rid of Mao. But no positive evidence of a plot to compel him to stay behind has turned up.

Once he had gone to Yudu, he was not in a position easily to visit government, Party, and political offices located a day or two of travel away. But he did not lose his personal bodyguards and he moved freely about Yudu and its neighborhood.

Living in Yudu was different from living at Cloud Stone Mountain, as he did in September 1934. His house had been a beautiful small temple up two flights of stone steps at the top of a stone escarpment. He was not more than a mile from GHQ. Luo Fu, Mao's Politburo colleague and thus far a supporter of Li De, lived in one wing. There was opportunity for cozy talks and this turned out to be very important. Mao could easily visit GHQ although he seldom did because his advice was ignored. Often they did not tell him about Politburo meetings. But he visited his offices in the Central Area government, of which he was chairman. These were located a short distance away, at a place called Shazhouba. The government offices occupied a rather splendid ancestral hall built in 1922 by the Yang family clan. Mao lived here for about a year. The Yang hall possessed an elegant two-story meeting chamber, fine dark wood rooms, cut-stone floors. This was also the residence of Zhu De and his wife, Kang Keqing, of Chen Yi and of Zhou Enlai. However, Zhu De and his wife were usually at the front, as were Chen Yi (until he was wounded) and Zhou.[16]

The deliberate exclusion of Mao from decision-making was not the full picture.[17] At this period, as in some other periods of stress, Mao was ill. From midsummer into October 1934 he was confined to bed with malaria or was barely convalescent. His energy levels were low and he may have been in a state of depression.

This seems natural. The revolutionary movement that was largely his creation, the military machine that he and Zhu De had built up, the Communist area that he had established five or six years earlier, the whole apparatus that he had put into operation, had fallen into the hands of the enigmatic representative from Moscow's Comintern, Li De, and Li's Chinese sycophant, Bo Gu, a very thin man in thick spectacles whom the British ambassador, Sir Archibald Clark Kerr, once called a golliwog because that was what he looked like. Mao had been stripped of all important instruments of power. The Politburo was solidly against him. So was the Central Committee, and he had been frozen out of the military agencies. Mao was outwardly quiet, but inside he seethed. He was not ignorant of the balance of forces and he knew there were strong currents running against Li De and Bo Gu. He understood what it meant when two leading commanders, Lin Biao, his personal protégé, and Nie Rongzhen, one of his old faithful, slipped into his small courtyard at Yudu, sat down on the benches, and said they had come for advice. He knew what they meant when they asked him cautiously: "Where shall we go?" He knew how to answer them with equally cryptic words: "Go where your orders take you." He knew their orders and he knew the orders were a military secret. He would not violate that secrecy. This was not the time to speak. That time would come, and, he was certain, before very long.

Nearly fifty years later, Nie Rongzhen recalled how eager he and Lin Biao had been to get more information about the new move, especially where they would be going, and how firmly Mao shut them off. He didn't want to stir speculation that he was plotting with his old generals. He brought the talk to an end and suggested that they go visit a newly opened library.[18]

Just after noon on October 10, a crowd began to collect at a crossroads just outside Meikeng, where the Central Red Army headquarters was located. It was a warm, pleasant day. Those who gathered were not military-looking. There were a hundred or more men and twenty or twenty-five women. They had been assigned to the convalescent unit— the old, the feeble, the wounded, the ill, the female. Each had a blanket, a bag of food, ten jin of rice—enough, it was hoped, for ten days—a knapsack with a change of clothing, a comb, a brush, a notebook, possibly a flashlight (these were the hardest to find), some spare batteries, soap, a book or two, and any other essentials. Each had strapped to his belt a big enamel cup with a toothbrush and a towel stuffed into it. The oldest in the group was Xie Juezai, Secretary-General of the Government. He was more than sixty and a horse had been provided for him. Dong Biwu, like Mao a founding member of the Communist Party, was forty-eight and in the opinion of his comrades would never have survived had he been left behind. Xu Teli, Mao's former schoolteacher, lean, leathery, humorous, with a whispy beard, was fifty-seven. He had a horse. There was a horse, too, for Cai Chang, a fearless woman comrade, and for He Zizhen, Mao's pregnant wife.

Soon the ragtag group was formed into platoons and squads and each member, man and woman, was issued a spear with a festive red tassel. These were for defense if the column was attacked. Just before sunset Deng Fa, the Party's security chief, head of the secret police, and commander of the whole administrative noncombat column, a onetime sailor, showed up. He dropped his usual seriousness and joked with the assembly, speaking Mandarin with a heavy Cantonese accent. He was trying to cheer them up. "This is a great company," he said. "We have musicians, playwrights, writers. If we want to put on a show we have all we need." The atmosphere lightened a bit and the column started off in the dusk for Yudu. It was part of the Red Star Brigade, and along the path red stars had been posted at intervals so they would not lose their way.[19]

Mao did not start until later. First he had tasks to perform. One of the most difficult was a speech on October 15 to the Party cadres in Yudu, the people who were staying behind. Mao had to tell them that the Red Army was pulling out and give them some notion of what to expect and how to operate once the main forces had left. By this time no one in Yudu could doubt that something extraordinary was going on. Thousands of troops were moving in and then out of Yudu, across the river or southward toward Anyuan.

To be sure, most of the young men in the Red Army had not been told. They believed they were going to fight a big battle. They understood they were breaking out of the encirclement. Many of them had been issued padded clothing for winter (to their surprise) and all were supposed to have ten days' ration in their rice bags. But care had been taken not to expose the real object of the operation.

Mao, ill and sallow, still being treated by Dr. Nelson Fu, spoke to the Party gathering with as much confidence as he could muster. His actual words have not been preserved, but there is no doubt that he conveyed the instructions of the Central Committee. The troops were going to break the encirclement, to set up a new base, to frustrate Chiang's plans for a sixth campaign. The cadres were to carry on as usual. The armies were being divided. The Red Army was leaving behind substantial forces to protect the soviet area. They were not going for good. They would be back. Mao was confident of the ultimate victory of the Revolution.

As Mao spoke—it was called a three-tier meeting: high, middle, and low cadres—Zhou Enlai, Zhu De, Bo Gu, Li De, the chiefs of all the armies, the whole top Party apparatus, were already on the move. The central organs had reached Yudu October 12. They were passing through under the cover of night. There were thousands of bearers (at one silver dollar a day),[20] carrying the worldly goods of the soviet—the printing presses, the engraving plates for paper money, the machinery for making shells, the press for reloading and arming spent cartridges, the X-ray machine, chests of important (and unimportant) official papers and documents, the reserves of silver dollars, gold bars, rice, medicines, spare guns, cannon, radio and telephone equipment, great rolls of telephone wire. "It was like a house-moving operation," Mao said later. Edgar Snow called it "a nation on the march." That was over-blown. Mao's words hit the mark.

In late afternoon on October 18, Mao and an entourage of about twenty, including bodyguards, his secretary and staff, assembled in the small stone court of the house beside the north gate of Yudu. They moved out of the court and joined other units of the Central Column. Mao brought along a bag of books, a broken umbrella, two blankets, a worn overcoat, an oilcloth. He left his nine-compartment knapsack behind.

So began what Mao knew would be a dangerous and possibly fatal retreat from the comfortable base where the Communists had pros-pered those past few years. They were moving in stealth in the hope that Chiang Kai-shek's bombers would not spot them and rain explo-sives on the long and complicated columns that snaked out sixty miles from end to end. It was a time of grim faces, cold determination, and not a little questioning. No one knew where they were going or where it all might lead. Not Mao, not Bo Gu, not Li De or Zhou Enlai. None could guess how long it might be before Chiang detected the slow-moving columns. No commander could fail but be cc :erned at the overburdened bearers, many of whom, with the heaviest loads, could hardly maintain a pace of two miles a day.

A battalion of engineers had thrown five pontoon bridges across the Yudu River. Its waters were low at this season. The width was not more than 250 or 300 feet at Yudu, and where the river was broader it was so shallow men and horses had no trouble wading across. The five pontoons were scattered up and down the river a few miles in each direction from Yudu.

Mao and his company walked along the bank of the river for no great distance. The moon came out. The river was placid. The air was still. Presently they arrived at their crossing and clattered over the broad planks. It was an easy crossing and soon the company was moving westward on the far side. The quiet, the moonlight, the splash of water along the pontoons, all this raised the spirits of the men and women, and many began to sing softly, old Red Army chants, as they walked in single or double file on the narrow paths of their unknown route to a goal none of them could guess.[21]

2

THE RISE OF THE RED BANDITS

THINGS were going well, very well, Chiang Kai-shek must have thought as he boarded his plane at Nanchang on October 15, 1934, and took off for a firsthand look at China's uneasy northwest. As always, his wife, Meiling, the beautiful youngest daughter of Charlie Soong, was with him. Seldom had Meiling been far from Chiang's side since they were married on December 1, 1927, in Shanghai's Majestic Hotel before fifteen hundred invited guests, with a Methodist YMCA pastor to pronounce them man and wife, a Russian band playing "Here Comes the Bride" and an American tenor singing "O Promise Me." Chiang's first stop would be Xi'an, the capital of Shaanxi province.

Chiang had spent much time in Nanchang during the four years of his First, Second, Third, Fourth, and now his Fifth, "annihilation" campaigns against the "Red bandits." At last, he believed, the Communists had been cornered, thanks to the new tactics of his German military advisers.

Chiang had brought in the Germans when the Russians pulled out after he turned on his Communist allies in 1927 in Shanghai. Chiang's butchers chopped off so many Communist heads their weary arms could hardly raise the great scimitars from their sides.

The Russian advisers had come in the days of Dr. Sun Yat-sen, the founder of the Chinese republic, whose mantle Chiang was trying to drape over his own narrow shoulders. General Galen and the others had won Chiang's respect at Whampoa Military Academy in Canton when he was commandant.[1] Nonetheless, in 1927 he would have killed them all, and Mikhail Borodin, Stalin's special agent in China, as well, had he been able to lay hands on them. Chiang was ready to slaughter every Communist in China in his drive to win power for himself.

But that was another story. Chiang had some professional respect for the Communist commanders fighting him in Jiangxi. He knew many of them from the days when they had all marched together under the banner of Dr. Sun. One of the leading "bandits," Zhou Enlai, had been Chiang's number two, the political chief, at Whampoa. Many others had passed through the Academy. Not Mao Zedong. Chiang hadn't encountered Mao but he knew a lot about him and, of course, he knew that other leading "Red," tough old (forty-eight) Zhu De. Zhu De had been a warlord general and an opium smoker before he joined the Communists.

Chiang had no reason to underestimate these men, no matter how he sneered at them as "bandits." They had survived for seven years despite everything he had been able to do. Now, thanks to Adolf Hitler, he felt the end was near. It was Hitler who had detached one of his best generals, Hans von Seeckt, to come to China and it was von Seeckt who had developed the blockhouse strategy that was strangling the Communists.

Von Seeckt moved the Nationalist troops forward very slowly, very carefully, and as they advanced they constructed blockhouses and pill-boxes (three thousand in the past year) which controlled every road and path. Slowly but surely these blockhouses forged a chain around the Communists. Von Seeckt drew the chain tighter and tighter. He stifled their trade. They could not sell their rice or maize. No one got into their territory. No one got out. The peasants had no salt for months, no kerosene, no cotton cloth.

Something else had changed. Until Chiang's Fifth Campaign the Communists had played hit-and-run. They sucked the Nationalists deep into their territory and sandbagged them in deadly ambushes. The Communists captured huge quantities of guns and ammunition and from the thousands of Nationalist prisoners they replenished the losses in their ranks.

No more. Now the Communists were confronting Chiang in costly head-to-head battles, defending their territory as if every inch was precious. In the battle of Guangchang in April 1934, they had stood and fought the Nationalists to a standstill. It had cost them at least eight thousand casualties, maybe more. It had cost Chiang the same. But Chiang could replace his losses by impressing more men. The Communists could not. Even if they won this kind of battle, they suffered losses they could not afford.[2]

As Chiang flew north in his new Ford trimotor plane with its gleaming aluminum wings, he could look forward to the future with some satisfaction. The Communists had prevented him from consolidating his strength with the regional warlords who were forever conspiring against him. With the Communists out of the way, he might even win a foreign ally to give him greater bargaining power with the Japanese, who had seized Manchuria and were threatening China proper. Hitler was helping him against the Communists; perhaps he might lend a quiet hand. Or possibly the Russians. Stalin was not going to help while Chiang was fighting the Communists, but he was a realist. A unified China under Chiang should be worth a good deal to Stalin in facing the Japanese threat.

Chiang flew north from Nanchang, high above the Yangtze, over the great rice fields of the south, and on across the yellowed hills of the loess country. Behind him in that difficult corner of southern Jiangxi remained the Communists, holed up within an ever-tightening band. Let them struggle. They would not get away this time. As *Minguo Ribao* put it: "They will be finished this year. They are surrounded on all sides. The day of their collapse is not far away." When Chiang returned, he would give the order for the final assault.

Not many in Nanchang would have seriously challenged Chiang Kai-shek's conviction that the Communist days in Jiangxi were numbered. To the rest of China the Communists might be a vague presence only dimly perceived but Nanchang knew better. It had known the Communists since August 1, 1927, when they seized the city and then marched south hoping to revive the revolution that Chiang Kai-shek had drowned in the blood of Shanghai.

The key figure in the Nanchang Uprising was a handsome, brilliant, extraordinarily persuasive young man of twenty-nine whose whole life would be spent in the high ranks of the Communist Party of China. This was Zhou Enlai. He once described himself as the product of a "bankrupt Mandarin family," and like many young Chinese of his generation he had taken the first opportunity to join the radical student movement, sail to Europe for work (the Renault plant in France), study (Paris and Berlin), and become a founding member (in Europe) of the Chinese Communist Party.

The year 1927 was a watershed in China's political evolution. It was marked by the climax of the great northward expedition, which started in 1926 from Canton, led by Chiang Kai-shek, in which the Nationalists and the Communists marched as allies. The objective was Wuhan and then, it was hoped, Shanghai and Peking. Zhou Enlai raced ahead to aid a rising of the workers of Shanghai. The first two rising proved premature and were crushed. The third succeeded. Hundreds of thousands of workers took to the streets, grasped power, and prepared to welcome Chiang and the Nationalist troops.

But when a single bugle sounded in Shanghai on the morning of April 12, 1927, it ushered in not the era of revolutionary triumph that Zhou and his comrades had expected but a "feast of heads." While the workers had hoisted banners proclaiming "Hail the National Revolutionary Army" and "Hail Chiang Kai-shek," the Generalissimo had struck a deal with his old underworld connections. The bugle was a signal to Shanghai's gangsters. The gangs of "Pockmarked" Huang, Huang Chingyuan, simultaneously chief of detectives of the French Concession and head of the Green Gang, tore loose. Chiang's troops stood by as the gangs descended on the workers in the districts of Zhabei, Nanshi, Wusong, and Pudong. Broadswords swung. Machine guns chattered.

Thousands perished. Some were shot; some beheaded; some hurled alive into the glowing furnaces of steam locomotives. Chiang put a price of $80,000 on Zhou's head. The Communist command had set up headquarters in the Oriental Library of the cavernous Commercial Press publishing plant on Baoshan Road. Gu Shunzhang, the trade union leader, escaped a minute or two before the doors were battered down.[3]

For many years published accounts described Zhou as having been arrested by Kuomintang forces and escaping, possibly disguised as a woman. A variant of this story found its way into André Malraux's novel of the Shanghai tragedy, *Man's Fate,* but as long ago as 1936 Zhou told Edgar Snow: "Things happened quite differently."[4]

What happened was this: On the day after the massacre, Zhou, accompanied by six bodyguards and Gu Shunzhang, went to the Second Division of the Twenty-sixth KMT Army. The Army was commanded by General Bai Chongxi.

The Second Division was charged with "restoring order" and was disarming the workers militia. Zhou knew that there were Communists and Communist sympathizers among the officers of the division, and he and Gu went there to protest what was going on. Immediately they and the bodyguards were disarmed and put under detention.

The chief of the division, Zhao Shu—a KMT political commissar who was sympathetic to the Communists and whose daughter was a Party member—was not there. Zhou was received by Deputy Commander Si Lie, who was thought to be friendly. His younger brother was an underground Party member and had been assistant to Zhou at the Whampoa Academy.

But Si Lie was hostile. The argument grew heated and it was plain he had no intention of letting Zhou go. Finally, Zhao Shu, the political commissar, arrived and drew Si Lie into an adjoining room. Heated words could be heard. Presently the pair emerged, apologized to Zhou Enlai, restored the arms and let everyone go. Zhou reported to Party headquarters what had happened, then slipped away to Wuhan. But for the intervention of the political commissar, Zhou's career, like that of so many of his fellow Communists, probably would have come to a bloody end.[5]

It was against this background that the thin young man in a gray suit, black briefcase in hand, checked into Room 25 of the Grand Hotel in Nanchang in the last week of July 1927. Under what name Zhou Enlai registered is not known. The Grand Hotel was Nanchang's best.[6] Built in 1923, it stood and in 1984 still stood in the city's bustling commercial heart, surrounded by shops, offices, restaurants, banks, at an intersection then crammed with rickshaws that brought bankers to their counting rooms and well-to-do ladies to the discreet fitting rooms of elegant shops.

The Grand was a monument to provincial chinoiserie, with a central court flanked by luxurious rooms at either side and a splendid banquet hall at the rear, courteous soft-slippered servants, a talented chef, exquisite dishes, and an atmosphere of wealth, quiet, and tradition.

Zhou Enlai was not the only unlikely guest at the Grand Hotel that week. In fact, the hotel had been taken over, top to bottom, rented in the name of the local military command for special use. In Room 20 was He Long, commander of the Nationalist Twentieth Army, a somewhat idiosyncratic sympathizer but not yet a Communist Party member. In Room 24 was Ye Ting, a full Communist Party member and a general in the regional Second Front Army; in Room 9 was Liu Bocheng (called the one-eyed dragon because he had lost an eye), later to become a famous Communist commander. There was no separate room for Lin Biao, who later would play a spectacular role in Chinese military and political affairs. Lin Biao was too junior, only a platoon commander. Nor was there a reservation for Zhu De. He was staying at his own headquarters. Zhu had become a Communist Party member, signed up by Zhou Enlai in Germany, but this fact was kept secret. At this moment he was Nationalist chief of public security in Nanchang and commandant of the KMT officers training corps. This was one reason the Party

Central Committee had picked Nanchang for the revolt and sent Zhou Enlai down to lead it.

The odds for success of the Nanchang undertaking seemed good. Zhou organized twenty thousand troops to back the coup against ten thousand men loyal to the government.

But nothing goes easily for revolutionaries. A new representative of Moscow's Comintern had just arrived in China. His name was V. V. (Besso) Lominadze, twenty-nine years old, a fellow Georgian who had caught Stalin's fancy. Lominadze knew nothing of China, but Stalin thought he could be relied on to carry out orders, and indeed he brought an order, a personal message from Stalin categorically directing that preparations for Nanchang be halted. Lominadze announced that if the uprising was carried out, the Comintern would not permit its advisers (there were a few still tucked away in China) to participate nor let its funds be used in the undertaking.[7]

This edict was delivered to Zhou Enlai twenty-four hours before the deadline for the operation. He defied it and the coup went ahead.

The uprising was carried out with scarcely a hitch. The weather was fine. Great goldfish bowls were emptied and filled with boiled water for the thirsty troops. It is hot in Nanchang in August. There was no rain and the soldiers slept outside in the courtyards. Nanchang then was not the sprawling metropolis of more than one million it had become by 1984. It was a provincial center of about 120,000.

Before daylight the city had been taken. Nationalist casualties were about eight hundred, Communist losses trivial. Whether Zhou had originally intended to hold Nanchang is not clear, but in fact it could not be held because General Zhang Fakui, commander of the Second Front Army, immediately began to move on the city. The rebels had counted on his neutrality if not support.

Within three days the Communists began to move south, and by August 6 Nanchang was back in Nationalist hands. Zhu De consoled his troops: "This is like Russia in 1905," he said, referring to the unsuccessful Russian uprising of 1905, which Lenin called the "dress rehearsal" for 1917.

Regardless of its military outcome, Nanchang was to take on great importance in the Chinese Revolution. It brought together the brilliant group of men who would, as time went on, play leading roles—Zhou Enlai, Zhu De, Chen Yi, He Long, Liu Bocheng, Ye Ting, Lin Biao, Xiao Ke, Nie Rongzhen—many of the famous "ten marshals" named after the People's Republic came to power on October 1, 1949. In recognition of Nanchang, August 1 is celebrated in China as the founding date of the Red Army.[8]

No province in China was to see more of the Communists than remote Jiangxi with its mountain ranges and the great river Gan flowing from the south to Jiangxi's northern perimeter, there to lose itself in Poyang Lake, through which its waters reach the Yangtze.

This remoteness, the poverty of so much of southern Jiangxi, the difficulty that authorities had in imposing their will on the jagged terrain—roadless (as was most of China into the 1930s), traversed only by mountain footpaths employed by people carrying bundles on their backs, horse-and-mule caravans, single file, too narrow even for carts—made Jiangxi a haven for rebellion. The Gan was the grand highway of Jiangxi, the only artery of commerce. No railroads. Everywhere flourished illiteracy, disease, poverty, ignorance, among the province's population. (It was 13,761,000 in 1943 rising to 33,100,000 by 1980.)

Mao Zedong played no part in Nanchang because at the orders of the Central Committee he was busy preparing his own operation, the Autumn Harvest Uprising, a rural revolt aimed at Changsha. Mao had been born to a prosperous middle-peasant family at Shaoshan, not far from Changsha, and much of his early revolutionary career was centered there. He knew the countryside well. It was there that Mao had hammered out his own revolutionary philosophy, a philosophy steeped in knowledge of the Chinese peasant and the countryside. This often put him at odds with the more conventional Communist leadership, particularly the didacts sent to China by the Comintern in Moscow and the Russian-trained and Russian-indoctrinated young Chinese, many of whom were products of Moscow's Sun Yat-sen University, first under the influence of Karl Radek and Nikolai Bukharin and later under that of a very young and very opinionated Russian, Pavel Mif, who at the age of twenty-six became Stalin's chief agent on Chinese affairs, knowing not a word of the language and fresh from a career of Party work in the Ukraine.[9]

Mao's Autumn Harvest Uprising was launched September 8, 1927, under a new flag which he created himself, a hammer and sickle within a red star. The uprising sputtered out and by September 19 Mao was leading a band of perhaps a thousand men, all he had left, toward the village of Wenjiashi, on the road to the Jinggang Mountains. At Wenjiashi, speaking from an improvised platform on the muddy playing grounds of the Li Ren School, Mao called to his men: "Do we dare to carry on the Revolution or not?" The men responded: "We dare!"[10]

Jinggangshan is a spiny-backed outcropping, rising four to five thousand feet, which separates Mao's home province of Hunan from Jiangxi. There are few more remote places in China. Positioned along the border, spilling over the edge of each province, roadless, heavily wooded, Jinggangshan had for centuries been a preserve of outlaws. No authority exerted much effort to find out what was going on at Jinggangshan.

Mao knew something of Jinggang and it fitted his needs at the moment—a refuge in which to build up strength, a place to test out his emerging theory of the use of military force to carry forward the Revolution, a place where peasants could be educated in the practice of Communism.

As they say in Hunan, Mao was a man who "knew heaven and earth" —that is, he was well informed about the area around Changsha. The name Jinggangshan was not new to him. It was well beyond reach of government and dominated by two bandit groups, the band of Wang and the band of Yuan. Yuan's gang, called the Broad Swords, operated out of a town called Maoping, at the base of the mountains. Wang was based up higher.

Of late, Mao had been told, the bandits had shown some signs of political consciousness. In the early part of 1927, they had permitted a Communist force to traverse their territory in order to join the northern expedition on Shanghai. In January 1927, they had joined in an attack on the county seat of Yongxin and helped free Communists confined in the Yongxin jail. If Mao could win the bandits to his side, they could be a considerable asset. If they opposed him, they could make his position on the mountain untenable.

Jinggangshan was a gamble—no roads, poor mountain farms, no industry, no schools in the mountaintops, few landlords to expropriate to sustain Mao's men. The mountain was dark with superstition. People believed in ghosts and the Chinese magic known as *feng-shui* to foretell whether couples should marry, cause women to bring forth sons, locate house sites and wells, heal the sick, cast spells on enemies or rivals. Few people ventured into Jinggangshan. Few left. Ignorance was so pervasive, one Nationalist unit offered a reward for capture of the Communist leader Su Wei-ai. Su Wei-ai is the Chinese word for "soviet."

In the county towns, two or three doctors practiced traditional Chinese medicine with its potions and herbs. No newspapers, no bookstores. Every evil—slavery, oppression, prostitution, syphilis, usury— every backwardness from which China suffered, could be found on

Jinggang. The hills were raddled with feuds, many so ancient their origins had been lost.

Later the Russian-trained Marxists would criticize Mao for Jinggang-shan. They would contend that he had gone against Marxian doctrine; he was not basing his movement on the proletariat, that is, the urban working class; he should be attacking great cities instead of molding an army from what they called déclassé elements—bandits, beggars, prostitutes, society's forlorn and forgotten. They said Mao was little better than a bandit chief, that he wielded a gun and not the text of *Das Kapital.*

In fact, before Mao reached Jinggang he had already been criticized and disciplined, as he had been in the past (and would be in the future). This was for the failure of the Autumn Uprising: He hadn't captured Changsha! He had been expelled from the Central Committee's Polit-buro and removed from his Hunan provincial posts. But it would be months before this news penetrated the wastes of Jinggangshan and it is not likely that it would have influenced Mao's decision to climb these mountaintops that so resembled the guerrilla lairs of which he read in *Outlaws of the Marshes,* that Chinese classic which he pored over with fascination all his life.

Mao's task would not be easy. But hardship and danger were no strangers. Just weeks before, he had been captured by local *mintuan* troops while rallying recruits for the Autumn Uprising. The soldiers had taken away his shoes (as booty; also so his ghost could not chase them) and were marching him to headquarters to be shot. He recalled later that he "borrowed several tens of dollars" from a fellow prisoner and tried to bribe his way out. When that failed he broke away into the underbrush, hid until dark, and next day used his money to buy new shoes, an umbrella, and food, then made his way to safety. Even as he began to climb Jinggangshan, Han Suyin was told, some of his own officers plotted to kill him.[11]

Jinggangshan was not a precipitous mountain. Mao didn't climb (as I had long thought) to the top of a jagged peak and set up camp like one of Sir Walter Scott's highland chieftains. The area embraced about 1,200 square miles, a population of possibly 900,000. It was more than sixty miles long and twenty miles wide and took in all of parts of six counties. There were five fair-sized towns and about a dozen small villages. At the peak, a height which resembled the Sierra Madre of Ernest Hemingway's *For Whom the Bell Tolls,* Mao set up a fortress, guarded by five strongpoints. Each possessed stone embrasures and stone barricades, behind which Mao mounted a few heavy machine guns and his three mortars, only one of which was in working order. There were three steep mountain paths which led to the fastness, small stone barracks for guards. This pinnacle was almost impossible to assault.

Mao was most interested in the towns at the base of the plateau. Here he had his headquarters and here he and his men busied themselves organizing local soviets, preaching Communism, recruiting new men for the Army, and expanding the base.

But first Mao had to come to terms with the bandits. The Yuan and Wang gangs dated back at least to 1921, and there had been bandits as long as anyone could remember. Each gang had two hundred or three hundred men and fifty or sixty rifles. Mao started by tackling Yuan, who in theory was already a Communist. Yuan was wary about Mao. Like everyone in this remote area, he was suspicious of strangers. The population had run away at first word of Mao, but curiosity and good behavior of the men began to bring them back. Mao, looking more like a Mohawk than a Chinese, his hair long and tangled, engaged the people in folksy conversation. He was good with peasants. "What's your name, Cousin?" he would ask, walking up to a man. "How are you called, Sister?" he would say to a woman. Fear was dispersed. But Yuan was cautious. Perhaps Mao planned to wipe him out and take over his gang.

Mao met Yuan on October 6, 1927, at the village of Dacangcun near Maoping. Mao explained that he was a Communist, that his troops were not there to interfere with Yuan but to work with the people, to better their fate. His army was not the KMT. It did not oppress people. Finally Yuan agreed to support Mao—at a price. Mao gave him one hundred rifles. Yuan paid Mao some silver dollars and agreed to set up a small hospital in the former Banlong school building in Maoping, where Mao established his headquarters.

Maoping was a pleasant little foothill town. It had a population of "more than a hundred families," probably about seven hundred people. Mao found a beautiful old courtyard house, the ancestral hall of the Xie family (almost everyone in Maoping belonged to the Xie family), and took it as his residence. It was topped by an unusual octagon cupola which he used as a study, and here as months went by he was to write two pamphlets: *Why Red Political Power Can Exist in China* and *The Struggle in Jinggangshan,* his first effort to explain his theories of using military power and the setting up of revolutionary base areas.

Wang proved difficult. Mao halted at Zhushan (Golden Bamboo Hill) October 23 and met some of Wang's people. Wang agreed to meet Mao the next day at Dajing—Big Well village—near the top of the mountain. Jinggangshan took its name from the five *jing,* or "wells," five villages spread out like a ticktacktoe cross. They were called Big Well, Small Well, Middle Well, Upper Well, and Lower Well, and each was surrounded by sheer cliffs. Some imaginative Chinese thought they appeared to be wells when looked down upon from above.

Wang was skittish and finally Mao sent a reliable man, He Changgong, to work with him and try to bring him around.[12] He found that Wang had a problem—a rival bandit chief named Yin Daoyi, who controlled three counties around Ganzhou. Wang suggested that if the Communists helped rid him of Yin he would lend his strength to them. In February 1928, He Changgong led two Army units and some Wang men on an ambush and captured Yin and some of his men at Nashan. As a contemporary historian told the story: "Wang's men were so happy they chopped Yin's head off and that very evening brought it back to Wang." Wang was happy too. This act convinced him of the good faith and capability of the Communists and he came over to their side, joining the Party in April 1928.

Jinggangshan was a great deal more than bandits and executions. Here on May 4, 1928, at Ninggang, Zhu De brought his forces to Mao's side and the two proclaimed the formation of the Fourth Workers and Peasants Army. Chen Yi came with Zhu as Party representative. Mao and Zhu met in an open square beside the Dragon (Long) River. Then they went to the rooftop floor of a nearby courtyard house with a view from open sides over the gray fluted-tile roofs with their bird-wing eaves, sat down, and began the collaboration that created the Zhu-Mao army and the military power that was to become a central factor in the Chinese Communist revolution.

Zhu brought in nearly 1,000 troops. Mao had, 1,200 or 1,300. Zhu-Mao broadened their base and laid the framework for an independent Communist region which would constitute Mao's original contribution to China's revolution. It would be elaborated in the Central Soviet Area in south Jiangxi and refined in Yan'an in north Shaanxi and, in time, serve as the matrix for China's revolutionary state.

The early period of Jinggangshan had been almost peaceful. Local warlords were squabbling, too busy to heed what was going on in this wilderness. But pressure began to build. Li Zongren, the Guangxi warlord, and Tang Shengzhi of Hunan had made up and were bringing their troops back to fight the "Red bandits." And another problem was emerging. The Zhu-Mao army had grown too big for its base. It now comprised the Fourth Army, with 4,100 to 4,200 men, and the Fifth, with 800. There wasn't enough food on the massif to support so large a force. It had to find another home.

On January 14, 1929, the Zhu-Mao army moved out, leaving Peng Dehuai (who was to become one of the Red Army's finest commanders) and Teng Daiyuan in charge with the Fifth Army.[13] Their orders were to defend the base as long as they could, then rejoin their comrades. That phase was swiftly over. Under heavy attack, the Fifth Army broke up and the fledgling soviet was overrun. By March 1929, of some two thousand persons who lived in the Red villages at the peak of the mountain, one thousand had been executed. In some villages every house was burned. The perpetrators were Wu Shang and his Hunan troops.

There was one footnote. After the Red Army moved out, as Mao told Edgar Snow, the gang leaders Yuan and Wang "returned to their bandit habits" and were killed by the peasants. The recidivism came in less than a year. A special underground Committee of the Hunan-Jiangxi Border Area decided that the pair must be killed after they went on a looting and burning spree, killing villagers and peasants. The decision was made in mid-January 1930, and in late February, possibly February 25, the pair was invited to a meeting of the Yongxin county special committee. They appeared with a group of followers and went to bed in the local hotel. At midnight the execution squads surrounded the place, burst in, and killed Yuan. Wang jumped from a rear window, leaped on a horse, rode off in the darkness, plunged into a river, and was drowned—or so it was said.

The local bands were then dispersed and some joined the Communist forces. But not all. Some went back to the mountain under the leadership of Wang Yunlung, Wang's brother, and bandits again ruled Jinggangshan. From that time forward, no Communist, no Red Army man, could step foot on this shrine of revolution—not for twenty years, not until the People's Liberation Army had triumphed. Only then could Communists return to the mountaintop where Mao had established the first rural soviet in China and begun the long struggle to lay his mark on China's history.[14]

By 1949, Wang's brother was long since dead, but his son ruled on in Jinggangshan until the Red Army caught and executed him. There is still controversy about Yuan and Wang, and particularly about their ending. Mao's remark to Snow suggested a casual killing of the two by aroused peasants. The version presented by contemporary officials in Jinggangshan carries a more formal air—meetings of a special committee, official edicts for execution, etc. During the Cultural Revolution another version gained currency. Wall posters went up denouncing Peng Dehuai for the "murder" of Yuan and Wang, as noted by Han Suyin, who does not believe the Red Guard allegations.[15]

3

ON THE EVE

THE news that Zhou Enlai brought to Chen Yi in his hospital room was not pleasant. Zhou told him that the Central Committee (a euphemism for Li De and Bo Gu) had decided that the main force of the Red Army would pull out in a few days, break through Chiang Kai-shek's encirclement, and move west to set up a new base.

Chen Yi had made the trek south from Jinggangshan with Mao and Zhu De in the bitter cold of the winter of 1929. He had fought beside them to set up the Central Soviet Area in south Jiangxi and neighboring Fujian province. He had seen the area expand until it embraced thirty-five counties, a territory the size of Israel and Lebanon combined, with a population of three million. He had watched Ruijin become the "Red capital" and the base transformed in November 1932 into the "Soviet Republic of China."

Now all this was ending and no cheery words, no phrase-making, could cover up what had happened. Chen Yi had seen it—a year and more of terrible losses, one disastrous battle after another throughout Chiang's Fifth Campaign. Chen Yi was realistic. He did not try to disguise cabbage soup by calling it a heavenly broth. What the Red Army faced was defeat, raw and harsh, and a perilous retreat.

Zhou had a further message. The Central Committee had decided that Chen Yi was not going to go with the main army. He would stay behind and direct military operations in the Communist zone. He would handle the military side and Xiang Ying, a veteran political comrade, would have overall charge. The two would work together. Xiang Ying was, as Chen Yi well knew, close to Bo Gu and Li De, a supporter of the "Russian" line.

Chen Yi would have an army of 25,000 to 30,000 of whom at least 10,000 were wounded, many of them as badly as himself—unfit for combat. How many effectives he would have was difficult to estimate then and is more difficult today. The figures run as high as 16,000, but not more than 6,000 or 7,000 were trained regulars. The rest were militia, many of whom had never held a rifle in their hands. Against them Chiang Kai-shek could deploy 200,000 men—more if he brought in nearby armies. Chen Yi didn't ask what arms and ammunition he would have. He knew it would not be enough. It never was.[1]

Zhou Enlai was too sensitive not to understand that the orders he was giving were not likely to stir Chen Yi's enthusiasm. Zhou stressed the importance of Chen Yi's role, his tested battle capability, his intimate knowledge of the countryside. He had fought over it for years. There was not a mountain pass, not a zigzag river course, he did not know better than his own name. And, as Zhou pointed out, Chen Yi was wounded. The long march would be very difficult.

"How is your wound?" he asked. Zhou knew a lot about Chen Yi's condition because he had been with him on a tour of the front in Xingguo county August 24, 1934, when Chen Yi was wounded at Gaoxingxu.[2]

Chen Yi said the wound was not healing. The doctors hadn't got all the bone splinters out. He had been asking for an X-ray and they hadn't given him one. Zhou Enlai acted immediately. The X-ray machine and the plates had already been packed for moving. They were unpacked. There was no electricity. Zhou had the gasoline generator usually reserved for the wireless transmitter brought to the hospital. New pictures were taken.

Orders were orders. Chen Yi was a good soldier and a good general. He accepted his assignment but he was not comfortable with it. Nor was his comfort increased when he discovered that his colleague Xiang Ying had a totally different concept than he about what to do. Xiang wanted to stand and fight. Chen Yi wanted to head for the mountains and carry on guerrilla warfare, a war of duck-and-dodge. It was, he thought, the only chance of survival. He was overruled.[3]

Chen Yi felt deeply about his assignment. He did not publicly say that he believed that politics, anti-Mao politics, had entered into it, although many of his friends took that view. He accepted the fact that there were legitimate reasons for assigning him: he knew the territory better than any other commander; he was an experienced leader; his appointment would raise the morale of those who had to stay behind. It would make them feel the Red Army was not abandoning the Central Soviet Area. But Chen Yi felt so strongly that more than twenty years later, in 1957, he set forth in careful but clear words his view that it was wrong to place upon an officer such a responsible task without consulting him in advance.[4]

It was not an enthusiastic company that set off from Yudu in those pleasant mid-October days. Chen Yi was not the only one whom Zhou Enlai told of the decisions. He had summoned Mao from Yudu to headquarters at Meikeng to tell him what the Central Committee had decided. There is no record of Mao's response, but he had grown increasingly disturbed about the military course. Twice he had made proposals which were rejected by Li De–Bo Gu. Each was a recommendation that the Red Army break away from its positional defense, get behind the Nationalist lines, beyond the blockhouses, and raid the enemy rear. Once he suggested a thrust toward Hankou and on to Nanjing, and later he proposed a drive into Hunan. It was like talking to the wind. No one listened. "We have a saying that once a strategy has begun it must be played to the end," said Wang Yanjian, the Long March specialist in Beijing.

The new plan, as detailed by Zhou, was that the Red Army strike west, penetrate the four blockhouse lines that Chiang Kai-shek had erected under the guidance of General von Seeckt, and then head for a base area which He Long had established to the northwest on the Hunan-Hubei border.[5] Zhou passed the word to Lin Biao and Nie Rongzhen, commander and political commissar of the First Army Group, and to the commanders and political commissars of the other army groups—the Third, the Fifth, the Eighth, and the Ninth. No one below this level was advised, according to Nie Rongzhen.[6] Except for these top officers, the roughly 80,000 men (the "real figure," as Interpreter Wu Xiuquan said. "We called it 100,000 for propaganda purposes") had no idea of what they had embarked upon.[7]

The actual figure on the strength of the Red Army as of October 8, 1934, taken from the muster rolls and presented here for the first time, was 86,859, broken down as follows:

First Army Group 19,880, Third Army Group 17,805, Fifth Army Group 12,168, Eighth Army Group 10,922 and Ninth Army Group 11,538. There were two independent columns: the Military Commission column 4,695 and the central column, sometimes called the Second Military Commission column, 9,853. The totals did not include paid bearers, sometimes hired for only a day or so.[8]

The eighty thousand were a diverse lot. Among them was the Woman Wei. At seventy-four she is a little butternut of a woman: brown cheeks, crinkly nose, a kind of Mao cap tucked over gray hair; gray jacket, gray trousers, white shirtwaist; black Chinese slippers, very small to fit her very small feet. Wei Xiuying spent half a lifetime in the Red Army, was one of the thirty women who made the Long March with the First Front Army. She starts the conversation by telling how she was sold by her parents at the age of five, or maybe it was six, as a child bride. She never found out how much her family got for her.

The Woman Wei still remembers what happened when her father told her she was being sold. She gathered a heap of stones and hid them behind the door and she got a scythe and put it there. The next morning when a man came to take her away she threw stones at him and attacked him with the scythe. But he was too strong. He overpowered her and tried to carry her away. She kicked and clawed and bit his ears until they bled. He gave up. Then they brought her father's brother, her favorite uncle. She couldn't bite him. He carried her away and finally she fell asleep and woke up at Ruijin, where the family that bought her ran a small store.

As she grew up she worked in the fields and carried hundred-pound loads on her shoulders. She was working in Xingguo, as a slave, when the Red Army came to town. She was often beaten and had little food. She cared for a water buffalo and gathered wood. It didn't take much to attract the Woman Wei to the Red Army. She cut off her long hair, hid her head under a scarf so the family would not see (and beat her), and went to Red Army headquarters to join up. They sent her back home. But she persisted. Finally her owners found out what she was up to. A friend warned that they would have her killed. When she told this to the Red Army they accepted her. She remembers her first battle, at Ji'an. She spent the night in a hut. There was a naked electric bulb burning. She had never seen one and didn't know how to put it out. Finally she took her rifle, reached up, and broke the bulb with her bayonet. The bayoneted gun was a couple of feet longer than she was.[9]

The Woman Wei was one of tens of thousands who joined the Red Army from the "model county" of the Red zone. A division was formed of recruits from Xingguo. Its population was 240,000, and 80,000 impoverished peasants like the Woman Wei joined the Party and the Red Army. No county in China gave more lives to the Revolution—42,399.

The toll for Jiangxi province was 230,000—90 percent of those who died in the Revolution.[10]

Recruiting, recruiting, recruiting. This was the call during the last year the Red Army occupied south Jiangxi. This was what tiny Liu Ying was engaged in at Yudu when Mao Zedong ordered her back to Ruijin. This was what Zeng Xianhui was also engaged in. At seventy-four, Zeng looks a bit like an elderly Khrushchev, his cap perched back on his head, a broad (Chinese) Ukrainian face, squinty eyes, and a smart-aleck country manner. His parents were poor peasants in Yudu. His sister was sold as a child bride. When the Red Army came, Zeng joined the Communists immediately. By May 1934, he was Yudu Party secretary and spending all his time on recruiting. The casualties had been heavy at Guangchang and they needed every man they could get. After he had signed up one thousand recruits he himself joined, became a member of one of the new divisions, the Fifteenth or Young Communist International Division of the First Army Group, of which Xiao Hua, then eighteen, was political commissar. The average age in this division was eighteen. The oldest man was twenty-three; he was the commander.

Zeng's march started at 6 P.M., October 16, 1934. He carried five pounds of rice in his food bag, one hundred bullets, two hand grenades, a rifle, an issue of padded clothes (the weather was still too warm to wear it)—in all, about sixty-five pounds of gear. So far as he knew, they were shifting their base. He knew nothing about a long march, but he would stay with it until it ended at Wuqizhen on October 19, 1935.[11]

The recruits came pouring in. The new Eighth Army was formed, the Thirty-fourth Division, the depleted ranks of the Third Army were brought up to combat strength. The counties were denuded of their male populations. At Changgang, of 407 youths in 1933, 320 joined the Red Army; nothing but women and old men were left. In Ruijin county, nearly 50,000 joined the Red Army from the time Mao first came until October 1934. Some 20,000 or more joined in 1933–34. In the month of May, 1934, 2,000 joined. Most of the 1933–34 recruits went on the Long March.[12] The county numbered its losses in the Revolution at 17,600, not counting possibly 50,000 lives lost in Nationalist reprisals. Professor Hu Hua, a Long March specialist, estimated that about half of those who started the March were new recruits. Casualties had been heavy in officers up to the battalion level.

Every appeal was made to bring young men into the Army. Families who had someone in uniform got a 5 percent cash discount at the stores.

Taxes sometimes were remitted. Families who had given a son to the
Red Army were promised help in tilling their land; if the son was killed,
they would get benefits in cash and free labor. Plaques and testimonials
were presented, as was red paper to decorate the doors of houses. There
were gifts of salt, that rarest of commodities, of firewood and rice. Mass
meetings were conducted and families with men at the front were
brought to the platform, praised, and asked to speak. They were made
to feel that a special bond linked them to the Red Army.[13]

The gifts of salt, fuel, cotton goods, and matches were priceless. The
Communists did everything to encourage smuggling and trade. The
traders were ingenious. They were used to paying bribes. It was profitable to trade with the Communists and so trade went on, greased by
silver dollars. High prices encouraged blockade running. There was
always traffic on the river Gan, and under false bottoms kerosene and
salt (at a dollar a jin—thirteen times the price outside) went in. There
were tungsten mines in the Communist zone and concentrate ship-
ments never ceased despite the blockade. Mao's brother Zemin was
stationed at Yudu to oversee the traffic.[14]

The Communists didn't let Marxian principles stand in the way of
survival. Peddlers disguised as night soil coolies, smuggled in flashlights
and batteries, under their noisome burdens. Blacksmiths, grain dealers,
rice merchants, and even moneylenders were permitted to stay in
business, but a close watch was kept on them. The Communists built a
good reputation for the decent conduct of their troops. True, they
expropriated the rich, but many middle dealers came to prefer the
Communists to Chiang's troops.[15]

There was good reason for the extraordinary support that the peasants gave the Red Army. Landlords charged 50–60 percent interest on
land, 30 percent on money loans, 50 percent on grain, 75 percent on
oxen, 20–200 percent on oil, and 150 percent on salt. There was no way
in which a poor peasant could emerge from debt. Each year he sank
deeper and deeper. In October and November 1930, Mao toured Xingguo county and six others where rural soviets were being set up. He
found that rich peasants and landlords constituted 6 percent of the
population and held 80 percent of the land; poor peasants constituted
80 percent of the total and held 20 percent of the land. He ordered the
holdings of the rich turned over to the poor. His program provided for
remission of usurious peasant debts, distribution of the land, free additional tracts in the unfarmed higher mountains. He called for an end
to gambling, an end to opium use, an end to robbery. The Communists,

he said, were establishing an order in which no one need lock his door. Even the crippled and the blind would get land. It would be tilled for them by the able.[16]

Wu Xing came out of the poverty of Jiangxi, the province that provided the Red Army with so much of its strength. He came from the village of Wu, the same village in Huichang county as Mao's bodyguard Wu Jiqing. "According to my family lineage I should address Wu as 'grandfather,'" he explained as the two were being interviewed in Nanchang. Everyone—almost everyone—in the village of Wu bore the name of Wu. That was true in 1930, when Soldier Wu joined the Red Army at the age of fourteen. It was still true in 1984. Soldier Wu spent his life in the Red Army. He never went to school. His family had no money for that. "I spent my life at the front," he observed. He was, he thought, a typical Red Army man. He had risen to the rank of platoon commander by the time the Long March was over, then went to school in Yan'an and became a division commander. As a youth he had been trained as a bamboo weaver yet earned very little. He considered joining the Nationalist Army but they were, he thought, a bunch of robbers. If you had a decent umbrella they would steal it. When Zhu De and his army came along he heard that they were fair, honest men. Someone from the ranks shouted: "Come along, brother. Join us." He joined and was a Red Army man from that day on.

"I thought of all this," he recalled fifty years later, "when we got to the Snowy Mountains. We came to them and crossed them, one after the other. I thought we would never cross them all, never make it. But if we didn't and suffered defeat—well, so the next generation would succeed and carry on where we left off."

Soldier Wu was not alone in these thoughts. Many a comrade was frightened and lonely when he got away from home. But the others carried on with the kind of faith which possessed Soldier Wu.[17]

It was not easy for the Red Army men to leave the zone that had been their base for years. The majority came from Jiangxi and the majority of that majority came from the Central Soviet Area—the model county of Xingguo, the Ruijin area, Yudu county, Ningdu, and the adjoining parts of Fujian. To leave their native land was a wrenching experience.

"The Soviet area was so pleasant," wrote Yang Chengwu, political commissar of the Fourth Regiment of the Second Division of the First

Army Group. "The people were so dear. To give up all this, to go to someplace strange and far away—how can we think of leaving these hills and brooks we have known for years and the people we have been living and working with every day from morning until night?"

Yang came from west Fujian, just across the border from Jiangxi, part of the Communist base. When word spread that the Red Army was nearby, the villagers came to visit the soldiers. They came from Yang's native county, Changting. They made popcorn, collected eggs, brought sacks of dried sweet potatoes, knitted pairs of socks, prepared straw sandals. They selected a dozen delegates, including Yang's father and the wife of Yang's cousin Yang Nengmei, who was treasurer of the regiment. The delegation walked one hundred li, about forty miles, over the mountains and rivers to spend three days with the soldiers before they left. When they got ready to return home, Yang and his comrades put together all the money they had (not much; Yang had only five ten-fen pieces) to help on the trip back. Yang's cousin Nengmei was away and his wife was about to leave without seeing him, when at the last minute he appeared. They had a few moments together, then Nengmei had to leave. It would be fifteen years—until 1949—before she saw her husband again.[18]

The Woman Wei remembered marching out of Ruijin in the Cadres Battalion of the General Health Department of the First Front Army on a beautiful moonlit night. They put bunches of leaves on their heads as camouflage and halted at daybreak. In the first days there was no bombing. The enemy had not sighted them. Then late one afternoon just at dusk, as they assembled on a mountain slope for a meeting, a Nationalist plane appeared and dropped a bomb. It landed about twenty feet away. Dong Biwu, considered elderly at forty-eight, an amiable veteran of the 1911 Revolution, was speaking. Dong looked at the spot where the bomb had landed, spattering earth over those nearby. He glanced up at the heavens, then back at the marchers, and said: "Comrade Marx is confounding the enemy. The bomb didn't explode." And resumed his talk.[19]

4

THE MAN IN BLEAK HOUSE

THE man who drafted the orders for the Red Army to move out of the Central Soviet Area was one of the last to take to the road. A pack horse was loaded with his supplies, including a precious stock of coffee and a few packs of cigarettes; his fine white cavalry horse stood ready for the saddle; but Li De tarried. He had business to attend to before he finally galloped away as the mists of dawn were rising over the Yudu River.

Li De spent the hours from midnight until nearly sunrise in a final talk with Xiang Ying, who was being left behind in charge of the soviet area. Li De was emphasizing what he must have known was not true —that the soviet area was not being abandoned, that the Red Army would return soon, that its departure for the west would pull Chiang Kai-shek's troops along with it, thus relieving the pressure on the beleaguered Communist lines. Xiang, with the assistance of his military commander, Chen Yi, would be able to hold out.

Xiang's last words, as Li De was to recall, were a warning about Mao Zedong. Mao, Xiang said, was quiescent for the moment, but Li De should not be deceived. Mao would utilize the first opportunity to seize control of the Party and the Army, aided by his supporters among the military. Li De shared this fear, but, as he recalled, when he conveyed the warning a few days later to Bo Gu, his partner was more confident that things would go well. Li De's talk with Xiang lasted so long he did not catch up with the command column until the next day.[1]

Li De was a formidable figure, standing well over six feet and towering above his Chinese colleagues. He possessed a stiff Prussian bearing and was described by Helen Snow as "a pure Aryan, blue-eyed blonde." He had a hot temper. When he was being smuggled into the soviet area, he held a handkerchief over his face to conceal his long nose. A close associate called him a "typical German, rigid and pedantic." He told the Chinese his real name was Otto Braun, that German was his native tongue. When he finally went into retirement, he settled in East Berlin, where he died in 1974.[2] Whether he actually was German or Austrian cannot now be established. The Chinese did not know even in 1984 whether Otto Braun was his real name, and the Comintern's records on secret agents are never likely to be made public.

The evidence that Li De or Otto Braun offered in China is contradictory. Among the names he is known to have used are: Otto Braun (on his passport); Karl Wagner; Li De, his usual Chinese name (Braun thought it meant "Li the German"); and Hua Fu, normally signed to his articles in Chinese publications (Braun thought it meant "China man"). He certainly had other noms de guerre. For many years his existence was not known outside a very small circle.

He told varying stories about his past. The official version, published in his memoirs, described him as a German named Otto Braun, born in 1900, who fought in the German army in World War I and joined revolutionary forces in Bavaria; engaged in street battles in April 1919 at Munich; was arrested in 1920 as a German Communist Party functionary and sent to prison where he made a spectacular escape after eight years, in 1928, slipping into the Soviet Union. The Russians sent him to the Frunze Military Academy where he was trained in tactics and strategy and turned over to the Comintern for assignment to China.

Gossip suggested that Braun was picked for China because of his knowledge of languages (German, Russian, and English) and his experience in street fighting during the German revolution. Sometimes it was said that he fought in Munich, sometimes in Berlin.

Street fighting was said to be the key. The Comintern expected the Chinese Revolution to be a replay of the Russian. True, the Communists and workers had been massacred by Chiang Kai-shek in Shanghai in 1927. But if 1927 was, in the words of Zhu De, the 1905 of China's Revolution, then there lay ahead Petrograd: 1917. No doubt, Moscow imagined, Shanghai's turn would come again and "Otto Braun," the street fighter from Germany, would be on hand to do a better job than Zhou Enlai had in Shanghai in 1927.

That such reasoning lay behind the dispatch of this authoritarian, dictatorial, and often overbearing man to China cannot be totally validated. But this was the impression of the so-called "Russian" faction of the Chinese movement—the clique opposed to Mao Zedong.

Braun left Moscow in 1932 and went east via the Trans-Siberian Railroad to Manchuria Station, where he crossed the border to Manchouli carrying what he later described as a "clean passport, an Austrian one, in the name of Braun."[3]

As he told the story in his memoirs, Braun arrived in Harbin in the spring of 1932, made some "investigatory trips" (he doesn't say where), then went by train to Dairen and by steamer to Shanghai, where in the autumn of 1932 he checked into the old Astor House, a favorite of English colonials. After a few weeks he moved to "an American apartment house." He did not speak a word of Chinese, nor did he possess a bit of background in China. Like most Russian agents, he was a blank page where China was concerned. But he was totally reliable in carrying out orders. That was what counted in Moscow. Moscow did not then and was never to gain much understanding of China, but it placed a considerable stake on the Chinese Revolution. It had put a lot of money into the Chinese Communist Party and was still sending liberal sums through a Berlin bank to what was called the International Red Help Society in Shanghai.[4]

Braun worked hard at his task. He made a trip to Beijing, armed with a letter of introduction from Agnes Smedley, the ardent but anarchistic American who had first cast her lot with the Russian Revolution, then the Indian, and now the Chinese. Smedley's letter brought Braun to Edgar and Helen Snow. Edgar Snow was teaching at Yenching University and Helen Snow was taking courses. Both were sympathizers with revolution and reform. The Snows didn't trust the thirty-two-year-old German. He didn't trust them. Braun seems to have thought that the Snows and Smedley might be American spies. Helen Snow never conquered her distaste for Braun, whom she considered a womanizer (as did many Chinese).[5]

By the time of Braun's arrival, the ramshackle Communist underground in Shanghai was falling apart under the blows of Chiang Kai-shek's secret police. The first catastrophes had occurred before Braun arrived—many upper-echelon Communists had been betrayed by informers, arrested, and executed.

There was no safe place in China for a Communist. The least dangerous was the Zhu-Mao Central Soviet Area in south Jiangxi. In the spring of 1933, Party leaders began to move from Shanghai to Jiangxi and the Red capital of Ruijin. Braun was to follow as fast as he could. First he had to await the arrival of a new chief military adviser, who would be his superior. Finally, in late spring, Braun bumped into his new chief on a Shanghai street. He was Manfred Stern, known under the *klichka* —Russian alias—of Fred. Later, during the Spanish Civil War, he became famous as "General Kleber" of the Loyalists. Fred had traveled halfway around the world—across Europe, the United States, the Pacific, and Japan—but when he got to Shanghai he could not find his contacts.

Shanghai was a hub of Soviet underground activity. Many Soviet agents were of German or American origin. Americans were preferred because, as Steve Nelson, a prominent American Communist who served there, put it, they had "golden passports"—that is, U.S. passports —and were not likely to be arrested. When Braun arrived, the chief Comintern agent was Arthur Ewald or Ewart, whom Braun had known in Germany.[6] Earl Browder, later to head the U.S. Communist Party, was a Comintern agent in Shanghai before Braun arrived. Just after Braun left, Eugene Dennis, later to head the American Party, came in. Harry Gannes, later an editor of the *Daily Worker,* the Communist paper in New York, served there for a while.[7]

Richard Sorge arrived in Shanghai in January 1930 to set up his remarkable Soviet military espionage ring. He had been in the Comintern and no doubt knew Braun. Despite strict conspiratorial compartmentalization, German and Austrian agents were constantly stumbling over each other. Sorge had his own wireless link with Moscow and also with Harbin, another Soviet underground base, but his military line was not available to the Comintern.[8]

Steve Nelson and his wife, acting as Comintern couriers in 1933, brought instructions to the Shanghai bureau from Wang Ming, the Chinese representative in Moscow, and funds for operations. He brought the instructions, she the money. Ewart was chief of the Bureau. As Nelson recalls, the question of leaving Jiangxi was already being debated in 1933 and the instruction from Wang Ming was that the decision was theirs to make. Ewart favored staying, the Chinese representatives said they had to get out.[9]

"Fred," under the name of Kleber, played a prominent role in the Spanish Civil War. He, like Braun, served in the Austro-Hungarian army in World War I, was captured by the Russians, joined the Bolsheviks, fought in the Russian Civil War, then went to Frunze.[10]

Braun and Stern, according to Braun, were quarreling soon, but Stern's presence enabled Braun to move on to the "Red capital" in early October 1933, smuggled up the river Gan in the between-decks cranny of a freight junk. He was welcomed in the soviet area by Deng Fa, chief of the Communist security forces, who was accompanied by bodyguards carrying scimitars decorated with red tassels. Deng Fa was smiling broadly. He and Braun were to become, as Braun thought, firm friends.[11]

Braun already knew he was supporting the Chinese faction headed by Bo Gu, the group called the "28 Bolsheviks," young Chinese who had studied in Moscow and firmly backed the Soviet line. Their leader was Wang Ming, more or less permanently stationed in Moscow. The "villain" whom all opposed was Mao.

Braun possessed enormous prestige and authority. He was an eloquent and persuasive speaker on military matters. He drew on examples from Caesar, Tacitus, Napoleon, Frederick the Great, Clausewitz, and von Moltke. He never showed any doubts.

His own story, as it came out, bit by bit, in conversations with Interpreter Wu Xiuquan and others, differed in many ways from the legend of the "street fighter."

Interpreter Wu recollected that Braun said he was a native of Austria, conscripted into the Austro-Hungarian army at the start of World War I and sent to the eastern front.[12]

In 1916 Braun had been captured and interned in Siberia, where many Austrian prisoners of war—Czechs, Hungarians, Ruthenians, Slovaks—were held.

When the 1917 Revolution broke out in Russia, Braun said, he joined the Red Army. (Almost all the Austrian prisoners of war sided *against* the Russian Revolution.)

Braun told of rising to the rank of chief of staff or commander of a cavalry regiment or brigade (the rank and unit differed in the recollections of witnesses). He fought for three years in the Civil War in the Ukraine and Byelorussia. Then, because of his excellent military record, he was sent to the Frunze Military Academy, where he studied for three or four years.

He was picked for China because of his knowledge and background. He had a particular assignment: to train the Chinese Communists in cavalry, which they lacked at this point (and had little need of, considering the rugged mountain terrain, narrow paths, and difficulty of movement for mounted detachments).[13]

It never occurred to Wu or to any of the Chinese to question Braun's statements. Braun told Wu the Comintern had given him the Austrian passport because, being Austrian, he could defend his cover more easily if it was challenged. His battle expertise seemed too professional to be disputed by Bo Gu and his fellow "Bolsheviks," none of whom had much military knowledge.

The first time Braun and Mao met, in Interpreter Wu's recollection, Braun airily dismissed Mao's ideas. "The golden age of guerrilla warfare has passed," Braun said. Now was the time for the Red Army to stand firm, to engage in conventional warfare. Not an inch of territory was to be yielded. Braun was under the influence of German military theory, which was dominant in the Frunze Academy. He presented almost a mirror image of Chiang Kai-shek's adviser von Seeckt. Braun held that the Red Army must combat von Seeckt's blockhouses with Red blockhouses.

It was not true, as some Chinese commanders said later, that Braun knew only trench warfare; that he consistently favored positional warfare. But it was true that Braun stubbornly resisted any effort by Mao or the Red Army commanders to continue with or return to their free-wheeling system of operations. Braun limited his offensive tactics to what he called "sharp, short blows," jabs into the Nationalist forces, which seldom produced the destruction of KMT units on which Zhu-Mao had depended to acquire arms, ammunition, supplies, and men. Mao had a plain peasant way of contrasting the Red Army and Chiang Kai-shek's army. The Red Army, Mao said, was a beggar and the KMT was not just a king but a dragon king. The Red Army supplied its needs with what it could grab from the table of the dragon king.[14]

Party discipline was tight. Braun had the Comintern behind him and the total support of the "Bolsheviks," and the Bolsheviks ruled the Chinese Party. They had run for their lives from Shanghai, but they now controlled the "Soviet Republic of China." Now, as autumn 1933 gave way to winter 1934, Chiang Kai-shek's Fifth Campaign chewed into Communist territory. The Soviet Republic contracted and then contracted again. By autumn of 1934, the Communists had lost 58 percent of their territory and were down to six counties.[15]

The controversy among the Communists, of course, was not just over military doctrine. It went to the core of the differences between Mao and Moscow's Comintern. Braun's Bleak House in the rice paddies was small—just a bedroom for Braun, a larger room for meetings, and a third room for interpreters and guards. There wasn't much that the sharp-eared young Interpreter Wu did not overhear. Behind Mao's back, Braun and Bo Gu (he had become secretary of the Chinese Party in 1932 at the age of twenty-five) were unsparing in rude jibes at Mao.[16] He was just an "ignorant peasant." He knew nothing about Marxism. His emphasis on the peasantry was superficial. "Marxism can't come out of country hills," Bo Gu would say: "Backward counties cannot emerge as Marxist society."[17] These views reflected those in Moscow. Pavel Mif, Stalin's youthful Chinese expert, and Wang Ming, the equally young Chinese "Bolshevik," who headed the Russian faction of the Chinese Party, took the view that neither Mao nor Zhu De knew much about Marxism. Mif and Wang argued that Zhu-Mao were glorified bandit chiefs in the ancient Chinese tradition of the classic *Outlaws of the Marshes.*[18]

It was in this atmosphere that the stratagems to deprive Mao of power, to restrict his influence, to ship him to Moscow or expel him from the Communist Party, flourished. Almost certainly they would have succeeded had it not been for the rapid changes that affected the international situation. Moscow was always more sensitive to the world power balance than to the reality of China.

Japanese aggression in the Far East and the danger of Hitler in Europe caused Moscow to reassess China. It felt a need for Mao's prestige to strengthen the Red Army and the Chinese Communists. Accordingly, Mao was restored to full membership in the Politburo at the Fifth plenary of the Sixth Party Congress in January 1934 (but did not attend the Congress). The Comintern put a lid on criticism of Mao and published a much edited and revised version of his speech at the Second Congress of the Central Soviet Area held in late January 1934.[19]

This had not the slightest effect on Braun's total control of Chinese military policy. Decisions were made by the troika of Braun, Bo Gu, and Zhou Enlai.

Although Braun contended to the end of his days that he was sent to China only as an adviser; and although contemporary analysts in China agree that technically he was right, the fact is that the Chinese abdicated their authority to him.

In his memoirs Braun writes: "Although I reminded the [Chinese] cadres repeatedly that my position was merely that of an adviser, as time went by it was as if I had supreme power."

Interpreter Wu Xiuquan agreed with this assessment: "I believe that Braun's position was not achieved by seizure but was given him by Bo Gu, and that responsibility for the failure rests with the Chinese."

Wu believed that Braun's arrival was, in the Chinese expression, like "giving wings to the tiger."

"We called him," Wu recalled, "Tai Shang Huang, that is, the God of War. Bo Gu never once rejected his advice."

For this situation, Wu conceded, Zhou Enlai bore responsibility as well. Whether Zhou agreed with Braun or not—and the evidence indicates he came to distrust and disagree with Braun—he did not or could not oppose him effectively.[20]

None of this would have been decisive if Braun's proposals had brought the Red Army success. They did not. They cost the Red Army loss after loss and no advantages; no booty; no gains in manpower; and steadily shrinking territory.

At first Braun had enjoyed broad support from the military commanders. Even Zhu De came almost every day to Bleak House to consult him. The attitude of other generals was the same. Braun had the full backing of the influential Luo Fu (once a San Francisco Chinatown newspaper editor and librarian at the University of California at Berkeley) and Wang Jiaxiang, the wounded military commander.

There were Army commanders, particularly the outspoken Peng Dehuai, chief of the Third Army Group, who took issue with Braun very early. Nie Rongzhen, political commissar of the First Army Group, was much like Peng Dehuai. The leader of the First Army Group, Lin Biao, was equivocal. He consulted Braun, took him seriously, and, so it was charged later, sometimes seemed to be a sycophant.[21]

There is no doubt of the attitude of commanders like Liu Bocheng, the one-eyed dragon. He openly disputed Braun. Sometimes it was something small, such as when Braun punched one of Liu's men on the battlefield and deprived him of his rank.

Sometimes it was more serious, as when Braun one day excoriated Liu Bocheng for poor battlefield direction. Liu, like Braun, had studied in Moscow at the Frunze Academy. He was a tough but scholarly general. "How could you have studied at Frunze?" Braun demanded. "You seem to me just an ordinary staff officer. You have wasted your time in the Soviet Union." Interpreter Wu Xiuquan didn't translate all that. He felt it his duty to try to smooth out relations. But Liu Bocheng understood well enough; his command of Russian was excellent.

Commanders complained about the escalation of casualties. Every battle seemed to cost two to three thousand men. One county after another was falling into enemy hands. This was not the way things had gone under Mao. During the Fifth Campaign, as Zhou Enlai told Edgar Snow, the Red Army suffered a loss of sixty thousand men. Nothing like this had happened before. Worst of all was the battle of Guangchang, April 11–28, 1934—four thousand killed and twenty thousand wounded, the blackest blow the Red Army had ever suffered. It left the way open, sooner or later, for Chiang Kai-shek to capture Ruijin, only fifty miles distant. In fact, during the battle, field headquarters of the Red Army had been moved all the way back to Ruijin.[22]

The brunt of the battle was carried by Peng Dehuai's Third Army Group. Peng was very angry over the conduct of the battle. Otto Braun and Bo Gu came to the front to observe and direct operations. Peng bitterly reported that in the first day he lost more than a thousand men, including every man in a battalion assigned to defend a "permanent" line of pillboxes built at Braun's orders. They were flattened by KMT plane and artillery bombardment. The Red Army had neither planes nor artillery.

There was a blazing row that evening. Braun said Peng should have counterattacked. Peng asked how he could counterattack when his troops had no bullets. He shouted that Braun's orders had been wrong from the beginning; since the end of the Fourth Campaign, the Red Army had not had a single good battle (that is, in the time of Braun's direction).

"You dogmatists," Peng yelled, "are tactical experts only on maps and paper."

If it had not been for the high motivation of the Red Army soldiers, Peng said, "the First and Third Army Groups would have been totally lost."[23] "Your plan has produced heavy sacrifices," Peng shouted. "Do you feel no guilt in your conscience? Do you feel no pain in your heart?"[24] Peng compared Braun to a son who sells off the land of his father without qualms. Interpreter Wu Xiuquan translated Peng's diatribe but did not understand the story about the son. General Yang Shangkun explained that this was a Hunanese way of criticizing Braun for careless sacrifice of Red Army troops.

Peng was surprised that Braun did not get mad, then realized that Interpreter Wu Xiuquan had softened his remarks. He asked General Yang to translate. This had the effect Peng hoped for. Braun began to curse and called him "feudal-headed." Peng replied in kind and then packed a knapsack, expecting to be summoned to return to Ruijin, to be removed from command, to be tried, to be sentenced, to lose his Party membership and be shot. "I was ready," he recalled. "I cared for nothing." To his amazement, nothing happened.[25]

Peng Dehuai and Liu Bocheng were outspoken, frank men. Many

commanders were reluctant to come forward for fear charges might be brought against them. Braun was quick to punish what he saw as failure or mistakes. Xiao Jingguang, later to become head of the Chinese Navy, was a senior officer. He had first gone to the Soviet Union in 1921, long before the "28 Bolsheviks." He had returned there in 1927 and studied in the Lenin Military and Political Academy. His battlefield record was excellent and he commanded the Seventh Army during the Fifth Campaign. Many of his troops were raw, untrained, new. Attacked by an overwhelming Nationalist force, two or three divisions, they fell back in confusion. Braun ordered Xiao to trial, had him convicted and given a five-year term. Several senior commanders, Mao Zedong among them, protested. Wang Jiaxiang, one of the pro-Russian clique, refused to sign the order, and instead of prison Xiao was given a teaching assignment. Braun tried to override the military by appealing to Bo Gu, but Bo Gu would not intervene.[26]

It was not unusual for severe punishments to be meted out by the Communists. Zhang Qilong, chairman of the Hunan-Jiangxi Soviet Border Zone, was charged with being an anti-revolutionary and a rightist. He was made a porter. His superior, Provincial Party Secretary Wang Shoudao, was removed from his post but made a quick comeback.[27]

Deng Xiaoping, then a young Red Army man, was treated not much better, according to one account. He came under attack by the "Russian" faction as a supporter of Luo Ming, Party secretary of Fujian province. Luo Ming was being used in the intraparty conflict as a stand-in target for Mao, whom the pro-Russians did not dare attack openly. Deng Xiaoping, Mao's brother Mao Zetan, Yie Weijun, Gu Bo, and some others were criticized as members of the "Luo Ming faction." Deng lost his posts and started the Long March as a common soldier or, in some accounts, as a bearer in the column of thousands of porters. Several contemporary Chinese historians deny Deng was made to be a bearer, but there is no doubt he suffered in this affair.[28]

Red Army officers, in general, were wary of being accused of Trotskyism or any deviation from the Party line. Such charges were not infrequent. The memory of purges was present in their minds—the campaigns against the AB's (supposed anti-Bolshevik agents infiltrated into Red Army ranks by the Nationalists, as in the Futian Incident, in which, it was said, several thousand men under Mao's command were purged in 1930–31); against Trotskyites (particularly among young students returning from Russia, where they were said to have fallen under the influence of Trotsky's agents); and against all manner of rightists, capitalists, capitulationists, and other deviationists. Some of these struggles represent internal political quarrels. Some were by-products of that paranoia which afflicts conspiratorial, secretive organizations.

Self-confident as Braun outwardly appeared, it is not likely that he rattled across the wooden planks of the Yudu River pontoons on the morning of October 17 in high spirits.

He faced a potentially disastrous retreat across unknown country open to attack by an enemy possessing hundreds of thousands of men and a complex political imbroglio within the Party which could blast him out of control (and even out of existence).

There was another problem, of which no one spoke and about which nothing could be done.

This was Braun's Shanghai connection; in fact, his Moscow connection. Communications had been shaky enough when Braun slipped away from the Chinese metropolis a year earlier. They had steadily grown worse. Braun's link to Moscow went through Shanghai. The Red Army had wireless apparatus, but it was not powerful enough to span the thousands of miles between the Red capital of Ruijin and the Red capital of Moscow. All messages had to be relayed via Shanghai and the clandestine apparatus belonging to the Shanghai Party Bureau.

By spring 1934, Fred Manfred, Braun's superior in Shanghai, had been called back to Moscow, soon to be sent to Spain. He was not replaced. The wireless relay was in the hands of the underground bureau of the Chinese Central Committee, which in effect meant that it was in the hands of two Chinese, both of whom had served in Moscow. One was named Li Zhusheng and in Moscow had acquired the *klichka* of Slavin. (Every Chinese who went to Moscow got a Russian underground name: Interpreter Wu Xiuquan's was Pyatakov.) The other Chinese was Sheng Zhongliang, or Zheng Yue. His underground name was Mitskevich. Chiang's secret police arrested Li in June and threatened him with death; he gave away the location of the wireless transmitter and the identity of Sheng. The transmitter and Sheng were seized and that was the end of the Shanghai bureau and of communications between Moscow and the Chinese Communists. The last message from Moscow known to have been received by the Central Soviet Area was transmitted September 16, 1934. It was an advice that Mao's January report on "the Chinese Soviet Republic" had been published.[29]

Braun was on his own. So was Bo Gu. No more consulting Moscow. No more invoking the authority of the Comintern. It would be nearly two years before the line was put back into place. Now it was every man for himself. It was, as Braun was to note almost forty years later, "most convenient for Mao Zedong."[30]

5

FIRST MOVES

BODYGUARD Wu was a runaway. He ran away from the village of Wu to join the Red Army at the same time his kinsman Wu Xing joined up. The year was 1930 and the bodyguard-to-be, Wu Jiqing, had been working for a landlord as a cowherd. He had no schooling. He could neither read nor write—no barrier to joining the Red Army, where most soldiers were illiterate.

At seventy-four, Bodyguard Wu is a distinguished man of military bearing: Roman head held high, broad brow, strong jaw, straight shoulders. He bears a remarkable resemblance to the late William L. White of Kansas, but lacks White's impish humor. Gu Bo was the man who persuaded Wu to come into the Red Army, and perhaps because of Wu's strong physique he was soon serving in a guards company. Within the year he became one of Mao Zedong's personal bodyguards. Another bodyguard, named Wang Yatang, was picked at the same time. They were chosen by Deng Fa, the Communist security chief, who put them through a thorough check. The principal qualification was the fact that both were poor enough and bitter enough against the ruling system to pass with flying colors. Bodyguard Wu was to work with Chairman Mao for nearly seven years.

Sometimes Bodyguard Wu got other assignments. Once he and Wang were put to work with Mao's brother Zemin, president of the State Bank. This happened in 1932. Zemin, then thirty-six or thirty-seven, was in charge of the Communist treasury—a stock of gold, silver ingots, silver dollars, jewelry, and valuables amassed by the Red Army through expropriations, wealth confiscated from landlords, merchants, the well-to-do. The Army struck silver dollars in its own small mint. Silver dollars were the standard coin of China. The Army had molds for pouring gold buckles, buttons, hairpins, and shoehorns. Gold was usually carried in these forms rather than coins because knickknacks were easier to conceal.

There was, in Bodyguard Wu's recollection, a great bulk of treasure and it had been decided to hide it high in the mountains near Ruijin. The bodyguards had been assigned to help Mao Zemin in this task. Hired porters carried the treasure up the steep, winding footpaths. It was not easy. Silver and gold are heavy. A silver dollar weighed about an ounce and was worth about fifty American cents. Each bearer carried about one thousand silver dollars. There were one hundred or more bearers. When they got near the top, the bearers deposited their burdens and were paid off and sent away. Only the two bodyguards and Zemin remained. They carried the treasure to a secret cave—no simple exercise. There were more than one million silver dollars, as Bodyguard Wu recollected. Zemin sealed the cave and the three came down the mountain. No one else in the Red area knew where the money was hidden.

No specie circulated within the soviet area. Paper bills of the Communist government and the Nationalist government passed interchangeably. Silver or Nationalist banknotes were needed for trade outside the zone and for paying smugglers. The Red Army obtained bank notes and silver by raiding the safe chests of landlords and digging up the earthen pots in which they hid their money. Some peasant's bright eyes had usually marked the hiding of the money.

The Red treasure stayed in the cave until the spring of 1934, when the operation was repeated in reverse. Again Bodyguard Wu was assigned to Zemin, again porters were hired, the cave unsealed, the valuables brought back to Ruijin. There the money was guarded until the Long March, when gold, silver, and bank notes were divided among the armies so each would have funds to make purchases once they left the soviet area. The Army had the strictest rule—ordinary people and peasants must be paid for every chicken, every bag of rice, every peach taken from an orchard. No looting or plundering—except of landlords.[1]

Why was the treasure brought down from the mountain in the spring of 1934? The answer seems clear. By this time the tight troika —Li De, Bo Gu, and Zhou Enlai—that was making the decisions was facing up to the eroding military situation. It was beginning to prepare to leave the Central Soviet Area.

In the years ahead, violent polemics would rage over when it was decided to abandon the soviet area and when the Long March was first contemplated. In the arguments between Mao Zedong and the pro-Russian group, Mao's supporters contended that the Long March was a hasty, ill-prepared venture, done on the fly, the product of panic, not planned.

The weight of evidence lies on the other side. The movement of the "100,000" troops was not a last-minute affair. Arrangements had been made weeks and months in advance. Whether the Long March would be ordered or not, its details had to be worked out long ahead or it would become a rout. The decision to move the national treasure down from the mountaintop fits the pattern of long-range planning.

In the opinion of Interpreter Wu Xiuquan, "preparations started half a year before the Long March." The first act was to begin to expand the Red Army and augment its manpower. The disassembling and packing of heavy equipment took nearly half a year.

Wu's recollections are in line with those of Braun, who claimed that the preparations began as early as May 1934, coincident with the Guangchang defeat.

"I agree with him," said Interpreter Wu, "even though we do not agree on many other things." It was Wu's recollection that the planning was confined to the most narrow circle—Bo Gu, Li De, Zhou Enlai, Luo Fu, and Wang Jiaxiang.[2]

The extraordinary recruiting drive of spring and summer 1934 was an integral part of this plan, to build back the Red Army's strength, to mobilize all available manpower in the Jiangxi area. A parallel campaign was launched to collect foodstuffs: heavier requisitions were ordered; the peasants were appealed to for contributions. There was a drive for loans. More silver dollars were struck. Winter clothing was made. Workshops began repairing guns and weapons. New grenades were turned out. Old battlefields were scoured for spent cartridges. The brass cases were refilled with powder and lead. When lead ran out, wooden heads were whittled. Li De took a hand in overseeing the preparations. Interpreter Wu remembered going with him one day to inspect the firing of the new grenades. Not all of them exploded.

It was obvious that something big was in the works. A propaganda drive was launched to get peasant women to make straw sandals for the soldiers. Sandals wore out rapidly. Soldiers tried to start a march with a couple of pair in their knapsacks. The women were told to make the new sandals of extra thickness, a certain hint of a long march.

So far, Chinese historians have not been able to discover specific directives, memoranda, or orders as to what was being prepared. Often discussions seem to have been confined to Bo Gu and Li De. Not even Zhou Enlai was privy to all these talks. Later it was said that this was due to security, fear that Chiang Kai-shek's agents would learn the Red Army's plans. No signs of a leak can be found in the closest examination of the Nationalist press, nor have KMT officers come forward with claims they uncovered the secret of the Long March. Nationalist commentary reveals an appalling ignorance about the Red Army. For years after Mao had lost out to Bo Gu and Li De, the Nationalists still credited him with command of armies; they seem never to have understood the Communist order of battle.

One of the most careful Chinese Communist historians confessed: "When and where the decision to start the Long March was made we can't find out."[3]

In the summer of 1934, moves got under way that later would be described as preparations for the Long March—breakout, or diversionary action by several Red armies. The first was by the Seventh Army, which pushed out of Jiangxi into Fujian in July and joined the Tenth Army under Fang Zhimin, an able commander and an old associate of Mao Zedong who led the Yiheng Uprising in January 1928. The Seventh Army was led by another experienced commander, Su Yu, who survived until late in 1983.

They had a force estimated by some as ten thousand men but probably much smaller. They moved into Jiangxi. The force was christened the Anti-Japanese Vanguard Column and it had a propaganda task as well as a military one. It was to try to win Nationalist troops over to a joint stand against Japan. This didn't work. The Nationalists smashed the column. Fang was captured, placed in a bamboo cage, carted around the countryside on exhibition, and finally beheaded in Nanchang early in 1935. Su Yu and a small band survived as guerrillas and eventually joined the New Fourth Army in 1938.[4]

Another breakout soon followed. This time it was the Sixth Army Group headed by Xiao Ke. The Sixth was based in the Hunan-Guangdong border area. Xiao Ke got his marching orders July 25 and left, as he recalled, August 7. His instructions were to cut through Hunan and join He Long's Second Army, which had established itself in the remote Guizhou-Hunan-Hubei-Sichuan corner. Xiao had a well-trained force of about nine thousand men. He was low on arms and ammunition, and fifty years later declared that his instructions to bring along his full baggage train, including a weighty printing press, handicapped his movements.

As it turned out, much of his route was roughly along the path that would be followed soon by the main Red Army. Perhaps the most serious problem, as Xiao Ke recalled, was the illiteracy of the population. Many were living like animals, besotted with opium, half naked, with no knowledge of the geography of the countryside.

Xiao Ke, a thoughtful, scholarly man (his force was regarded as one of the toughest in the Red Army; the Nationalists feared, hated, and respected him) who half a century later was heading the Academy of Military Science in Beijing, was still appalled as he spoke of the conditions he encountered in Guizhou. The Sixth Army had no maps except for a general map of China, torn from a school geography. It was about ten by twelve inches and showed only provincial capitals, very important county towns, big mountain ranges, and rivers. It was of little use. Local peasants could not even tell him where they were in the labyrinth of mountains, let alone how to get to the next town.

By October 22, the Sixth Army Group was united with He Long's Second Army Group. Its strength was down to four thousand, but, as Xiao Ke recalled, they had fought some good battles. There is no evidence that they drew any enemy strength off the soviet area [5]

What, in reality, were these troop movements about? This is difficult to perceive today. How could troop movements in midsummer help a massive shift by the Red Army toward the end of October? The timing made no sense. There was no articulation between them.

General Qin Xinghan of the Red Army's Revolutionary Museum in Beijing would later say: "It is a bewildering question."

It was Qin's belief that the preparation of supplies and new recruits had begun early so that the Red Army would be ready for any emergency. If it had to leave the base area, it could do so. But the timing of the breakouts by the Seventh and Sixth armies was another question. There seemed no relationship between them and the mid-October Long March. Even if they had drawn off large Nationalist forces—which they did not—there was no evidence that in midsummer Bo Gu and Li De contemplated giving up the area.

Interpreter Wu Xiuquan, a knowledgeable military officer who was probably better informed about the command decisions of 1934 than any other survivor, having listened to the discussions between Li De and Bo Gu (and Zhou Enlai, as well), could cast no light on the questions. "I find myself in difficulty," he said, "in giving an appropriate answer. This question must be answered by you."

The movements of the Seventh and Sixth armies, he believed, were designed to distract the attention of the Nationalists at a moment when the Red Army was replacing losses by heavy recruitment. But when I asked how diversions in July–August could help the March in mid-October, he responded: "Your skepticism is well founded."

Wang Yanjian, the Long March specialist, called the preliminary moves "the overture to the symphony." But the overture did not seem to be scored in the same key as the symphony.

Even more puzzling is the shift of the Twenty-fifth Army. The Twenty-fifth was a remnant force left behind in the remote Hubei-Henan-Anhui border area. It had been part of the Fourth Front Army, which had pulled out to northern Sichuan. The Twenty-fifth originally had around 7,000 men, but by autumn 1934 was down to 2,900.

In May of 1934, as he recalled fifty years later, Cheng Zihua, a Red Army political commissar, was called in by Zhou Enlai for a talk. At seventy-four, Cheng Zihua carries deep scars of his Red Army career. He was badly wounded in both hands and arms, leaving his right hand more a claw than a fist. He writes with his left hand, also mangled by a bullet and never properly treated.

If Cheng Zihua's memory is accurate, his interview with Zhou supports the theory of a long preparation period in advance of the Long March. Zhou Enlai told him, in Cheng Zihua's recollection, that the Red Army was in a difficult position (it was just after the disastrous Guangchang battle; also about the time the treasure was removed from the mountaintop). The Nationalists, Zhou Enlai said, were infinitely stronger than the Red Army. The Communist base was being whittled down. This was decreasing the potential for manpower and resources. The Red Army faced a "present danger": if it could not supply itself, the base would be lost. What is the solution? Zhou asked, and replying to his question said that the Red Army was prepared to start a prodigious journey to create a new base area where it could get supplies and manpower and begin to grow.

Should the Red Army pursue this course, said Zhou Enlai, the Nationalists would pull out their blockade forces and this would radically affect the situation that he wanted to discuss with Cheng Zihua—the plight of the Twenty-fifth Army. The army was under pressure, it had no professional leadership, the regional Party had asked for help. Zhou was sending Cheng Zihua to take over and shift the Twenty-fifth to a new base. The impending move of the main Red Army should make his task easier.

Cheng Zihua left Ruijin in a hurry, but it was difficult to reach the Twenty-fifth Army. He went to the southern part of the soviet area, slipped over the border into Guangdong "white" territory, and on to the port of Swatow, where he took a steamer for Shanghai. From Shanghai he went up the Yangtze to Hankou and finally arrived at the border region in September, not long before the Long March; but of this he would know nothing for months. Cheng Zihua and the local leaders decided to transfer the Twenty-fifth to the even more remote mountains of northern Hubei, to Tongbai and Funiu, in west Henan. The army was renamed the Second Vanguard Column of the Anti-Japanese Force. The first column had been the doomed Seventh and Tenth armies. On November 16, 1934, with 2,900 men under his command, Cheng Zihua started out.[6]

To relate the movement of the Twenty-fifth Army to any circumstance other than local is difficult. To presume that as early as May 1934 Zhou Enlai had fully formed plans for the great transfer of the Red Army seems equally unlikely.

This period was one of contradictions. There was a baffling failure in the case of the Nineteenth Route Army, the Nationalist Army based in Fujian, next door to the Communists. The Nineteenth was known all over the world for its heroic resistance in Shanghai to the Japanese. It was independent, highly patriotic, and had been banished by Chiang Kai-shek to Fujian because Chiang was fearful of its anti-Japanese patriotism and its challenge to his policies. In November 1933, its commander rebelled and set up an independent regime. The situation was made to order for the Communists, a chance to join with a powerful military force and rally China to fight Japan—the main theme of Communist propaganda. It was the kind of opportunity that Mao Zedong and his associates had shown skill in exploiting, as in December 1931.

When, in December 1931, the Twenty-sixth Route Army based at Ningdu rose against Chiang, the rebellion was calibrated with the Communists. It was even put off a day to December 14 so a shipment of winter clothing and supplies needed by the Communists could be received. On the evening of December 14, Zhao Boshang, chief of staff, invited his officers to a dinner in his headquarters, the pillared Lutheran mission on the banks of the river Mei at Ningdu. The officers ate on the second floor, their bodyguards below. As dinner was served, Liu Bojian surrounded the building with trusted troops and announced the rebellion. Two officers plunged from the second-floor balcony and tried to escape, but the rest joined the coup. In the end, nine of the eleven regiments, seventeen thousand men in all, came over to the Communist cause. The regiments became the Communist Fifth Army Group, one of the most reliable and best-disciplined, serving as the rear guard and again and again saving the main column from disaster.[7]

At Ningdu, the Communists were surefooted and self-confident, but with the Nineteenth Route Army they seemed all thumbs. The first contacts went well. Peng Dehuai's Third Army Group was operating in west Fujian in early August when he received a visit from a "Mr. Chen," who represented Cai Tingkai, commander of the Nineteenth. Peng invited Mr. Chen to dinner, which he served in a big tin washbasin— a concoction of pork and eggs "confiscated from a local despot," as Peng was later to write. The evening was a success; there was much talk of joining forces to fight the Japanese first and worry about Communism later. Mr. Chen went on to Ruijin and had talks there, but signals got crossed and the Central Committee decided to have nothing to do with him. They reprimanded Peng Dehuai—not for talking to Mr. Chen but for lack of etiquette in serving up a banquet in a washbasin.[8]

There matters rested for a while, then two men were sent to negotiate with Cai Tingkai again. They were Wu Liangping, later economics minister of the People's Republic (and sometime interpreter for Otto Braun), and Pan Hannian. They were dispatched by Mao himself, as chairman of the soviet government, and Luo Fu, whose position was equivalent to that of premier. The negotiations, it was said, were successful. The pair returned and reported to Mao, Luo Fu, and Zhou Enlai, who said he was happy that they would all be fighting together against Chiang Kai-shek. The report was delivered at Shazhouba at a time when Luo Fu and Mao were living in the same building.

The decision on the Nineteenth Route Army was of great importance. It would have enabled the Communists to break Chiang's hedgehog of blockhouses. It would have given their cause a national or even international boost, bringing the Red Army out of obscurity. Most people in China (and the few people outside China who knew of the Red Army) thought of it as a tiny band of rebels in remote mountains.

Even more was involved. The Guangdong warlord was hostile to Chiang Kai-shek. Had the Communists made an alliance with the Nineteenth Army, there was a chance Guangdong would have thrown its lot with the new combination. With the support of Guangdong, other warlords might have joined in. Fujian possessed the ocean port of Fuzhou. It was possible—although realistically not too likely—that the Soviet Union might have set up a supply line through Fuzhou. The opportunity was lost because of squabbling among the Communists. Manfred Stern, top Comintern adviser, was still in Shanghai. He violently opposed collaboration with the Nineteenth Route Army, which he called "just a warlord army." Braun seems to have been halfhearted and felt precluded from acting except in accord with Fred's instructions. Later he was to claim that Bo Gu and Zhou Enlai favored collaboration but that the others, including Mao, were opposed. Contemporary Chinese historians find no basis for Braun's assertion. The most violent opponents, Braun said, were the "Shanghai Central Committee Bureau," whatever he meant by that. By this time the "Bureau" was a shambles run by a handful of underlings soon to be swept up by Chiang Kai-shek's secret police.[9]

While the Communists were arguing, Chiang wiped out the Nineteenth Route Army.

The Communist leadership in 1934 was giving every sign of internal disarray—gone was the resolute and daring strategy of Zhu-Mao. Decisions were being made by men with little or no battle experience and even less in dealing with the people (the masses, they would have said). Moscow and Shanghai at a remove of thousands of miles were trying to run things. Braun had been little more than a year in China. He still did not know the country, he did not know the Chinese, did not know their language and wasn't even studying it, did not know the topography, had no understanding of the geography nor of the profound differences between a man of Jiangxi and a man of Guizhou. He did not know the psychology that came into play when a man of Jiangxi found himself in Sichuan, or vice versa, unable to speak to the people around him because of the local dialect, hundreds of li from home with no idea of how to get back or whether he ever would.

He could not have understood the soldiers who came rushing up to Political Commissar Yang Chengwu two days after the Long March had started. The column was moving along a narrow and curving mountain pass. No one was speaking. The soldiers were pushing forward silently, heads down. Two men from Jiangxi hurried up to Yang, breathing heavily.

"Political Commissar!" one cried. "Two days we have been traveling already. Where on earth are we heading? How many more days will we go on like this?"

The two soldiers—in fact, the whole detachment—were in a state of anxiety. Where were they going? Would they ever see their homes and families again? . . . What could Yang answer? He did not know himself. All he could say was that they were marching to the northwest; they would break through the enemy blockade, strike a severe blow at the Nationalists, and defend the soviet base.[10]

It never occurred to Braun that the Red Army men had to have an idea of what they were doing if they were to fight well. They were not automatons, trained in the Prussian army or, perhaps, the Russian army to obey orders never questioning, never thinking.

Braun was a man of such discipline. He was a European, a European military man. He had his own values and concepts. They had little in common with those of the men whom he was, because of a casual edict of some foreigners in Moscow, commanding. As long as he remained in China, Braun never was able to conceive of what it was like to be Chinese. He always drank coffee and smoked cigars (if he could get them). He ate bread rather than rice, even if he had to bake it himself. The Chinese of the "Russian" clique knew, by and large, only a bit more about their country than did Braun. They were intellectuals who had acquired a veneer of Moscow Marxism, and it acted to insulate them from the real China. The big thing they had learned in Moscow was skill in bureaucratic infighting. Mao and his pragmatists—most of them men who had the stain of battle ingrained in their bodies; most of whom had traveled the back paths and lived with the peasants; many of them of peasant background, as was Mao—knew China even if they did not always quote the appropriate passage of dialectic from Marx or Lenin. They were outsiders for the present, unable to affect the course of events. Mao had been an outsider during much of his career as a revolutionary and a Communist. Now he was beginning to sense that his hour was nearing.

6

STRATAGEMS

At first it was nothing but night marching. By day the men stretched out and slept in the shade of the camphor trees or huddled under clumps of alders. They were taking small paths. There were no motor roads in south Jiangxi or neighboring Guangdong, and if there had been they would have avoided them. The Red Army was tiptoeing out of its base and there was no sign that the "great maneuver," as the political commissars called it later in talking to the men, had been detected.

Night marching was not unpleasant. As an officer told Agnes Smedley: "it is wonderful if there is a moon and a gentle wind blows. Where no enemy troops are near whole companies would sing and others would answer." In the early days there was no substantial enemy around and the moon shone and the wind blew softly.

When clouds obscured the moon the troops made torches, sometimes of pine boughs or of hollow bamboo filled with kerosene, but most often of split bamboo tied together. It was a beautiful sight at the foot of a mountain looking up at the snaking line of fire, or looking down from a cliff on the torches flickering below.[1] But it was not always easy or beautiful. In the darkness men sometimes tied white kerchiefs to their backs so comrades could see and follow them. Sometimes they marched with each man's hands on the shoulders of the man ahead so as not to lose the narrow path. Often it was slippery. If one man fell, a whole following squad tumbled down, sometimes to be lost over two-hundred-foot cliffs.

Ordinarily the Red Army men were highly motivated. Propaganda workers fired their spirits. They were told what they were going to do, how it would be done, and why they were doing it. This was a missing ingredient at the start of the March. Zhang Shengji joined the Red Army from the model county of Xingguo in Jiangxi. It was 1931 and he was fifteen. He fought all the way through the March. He remembered that in September 1934, his outfit was still in Xingguo and he watched two Nationalist planes collide in midair and fall flaming to the ground. It was a great thrill. A week later they were ordered to leave—as they thought, for Hunan to set up a new base. "We didn't know things had been going badly for the Red Army," he recalled fifty years later, a fine-looking man of sixty-eight. "We were in high spirits. We didn't know we were going to have to walk so long. You had to be in good spirits if you were going to march fifty miles in a night and take three county seats."[2] Peng Haiqing, another native of Jiangxi, a tiny man of seventy-five with a wispy beard, half-crippled by arthritis, agreed that the troops were neither told that the Red Army had been suffering defeats nor that it was embarking on the Long March. He had been through all the Chiang Kai-shek encirclement campaigns, and had fought with the Third Army Group at Guangchang, the fiercest battle of his career, but he didn't know it was a losing battle. As for the Long March, "it was kept in the dark."[3]

There would be harsh repercussions about the failure of the command troika of Li De, Bo Gu, and Zhou Enlai to carry on the motivational propaganda that had served the Red Army so well in previous campaigns.

The Army moved out in a strange formation. Liu Bocheng, the one-eyed dragon, compared it to an emperor's sedan chair. There were two main columns, one headed by the First Army Group, the other by the Third. It was a long box formation and in the center were the headquarters columns and the five thousand carriers, loaded with every kind of burden.

The command structure was elaborate. Under the Central Military Commission troika of Otto Braun, Bo Gu, and Zhou Enlai came commander in chief Zhu De, vice-commander and general political commissar Zhou Enlai, vice-commander and director of the General Political Department Wang Jiaxiang, and chief of staff Liu Bocheng.

The two columns marching in the center of the box were the First Military Commission, commanded by Ye Jianying, later to head the Red Army and serve for many years as defense minister, and the Second Central Column, headed by Lo Man (Li Weihan). His deputy was Deng Fa, the Communist security chief.

Before the Long March started, every outfit got a code name. The

First Military Column was called Hongan; the Second, Hongzhang. The First Army Group was called Nanchang; the Third, Fuzhou.[4]

The Military Commission column was divided into four echelons. In the first marched Bo Gu, Otto Braun, Zhou Enlai, Zhu De, Liu Bocheng —the top command. It was led by Deng Yuefeng. The second echelon was largely logistics; the third included the engineers battalion, the artillery unit, and a hospital corps. The fourth was the cadres regiment, headed by Chen Geng, with Hong Renqun as his deputy. The Central Column was also divided into four echelons. The first was a training division, headed by Zhang Jingwu; the second comprised supply, shops, communications, training, and the bearers; the third was a hospital unit headed by He Cheng; and the fourth was made up of government and Party bureaucrats and a security regiment. This was commanded by Yao Xie, head of the security bureau, with Zhang Nansheng as political commissar.

The Central Column, the part Liu Bocheng regarded as the cab of the "sedan chair," could not move as rapidly as the combat columns. It was bogged down by the thousands of porters and their loads, as well as the elderly, the ill, and the wounded. As time wore on, it proved a drag anchor on the faster military columns and, inevitably, heavier burdens (the porters were even lugging office furniture and files) began to be dumped.

The Central Column was well protected. It was rare for any casualties to be suffered and they were likely to be from bombing or accidents —a horse shying off the path and carrying a rider down a cliff—not from combat.

In this column, of course, were to be found Li De, Bo Gu, Zhou Enlai, directing operations, and others like Mao and Wang Jiaxiang, suffering from his year-old stomach wound. Here, too, were the thirty women cadres, most of them wives of senior commanders or cadres and many of them themselves senior cadres.

Moving like a lumbering elephant train, the Red Army made its way to the southwest corner of the soviet zone and slipped over the border into "white" territory.

By October 21, it had brushed through the first of Chiang's blockhouse lines with nothing more than token opposition. This line was at the extreme southwest corner of Jiangxi at the river Tao, a tributary of the Gan. They moved into Guangdong province, still heading slightly south of west. To some this seemed a curious course because their stated object was to move to the north and west to join the Second and Sixth Army Groups.

The March started with the best of omens—a victory at the first blockhouse line—and the troops pushed rapidly forward to the second line, and passed it with equal speed and no major difficulty on November 3. A little momentum had been lost, but by November 10 they were over the not-yet-completed right-of-way of the Wuhan-Canton railroad.

It had been a whirlwind campaign, executed with skill, although Otto Braun reported quarreling among the Army commanders over details, particularly lost time by the First Army because lack of maps got them bogged down.

This early success was not an accident. Zhou Enlai had negotiated a secret deal with the Guangdong warlord, Chen Jitang. Clandestine contacts between opposing commanders were not to be uncommon during the Long March.

There were many reasons for this. It was in the Chinese military tradition. The Chinese, eminently sensible people, have never believed in shedding blood in warfare if suitable arrangements can be worked out. Ideology did not entirely disrupt this custom. Many of the men fighting on either side had had long and intimate contact, particularly in the early period of the revolutionary movement when they fought together under the banner of Dr. Sun Yat-sen. There had been years of Communist-Nationalist collaboration.

In the complex game of Chinese politics, Chiang Kai-shek was not all-powerful. He faced an ever-shifting field of regional warlords and power brokers. Combinations kept changing. Alliances were made and broken. The warlords feared that if Chiang grew too powerful their fiefdoms (and revenues) might be lost. They did not wish to see either Chiang Kai-shek or the Communists get too strong. They had no reluctance to a deal with the Communists if it gave them an advantage. Some welcomed the Communist patriotic appeal for a united front against Japan.

These were the factors that motivated Chen Jitang when he sent a secret message to Zhou Enlai in September 1934 proposing private talks. Otto Braun thought Chen Jitang might be afraid lest the Nationalists break through the Communist defenses and march up to the frontiers of Guangdong, which was in a sense shielded by the Communist presence. Whatever the motive, the warlord sent a secret envoy to

Zhou. Zhou reacted immediately and positively. "We can make use of General Chen's anti-Chiang Kai-shek attitude," he said. "We must learn the lesson of our failure in the case of the Nineteenth Route Army."

Zhou dispatched two responsible comrades, He Changgong (who had persuaded bandit Wang to join the Communists in Jinggangshan) and Pan Hannian (later to handle important secret missions to Moscow), to a village in northern Guangdong, where an agreement was worked out which provided that neither side would attack the other. They would exchange intelligence and the Guangdong governor would provide the Red Army with communications equipment and medical supplies. The Red Army walked through Guangdong and the adjacent territory almost like tourists on a stroll. The Guangdong troops looked the other way. The Red Army got excellent intelligence. It knew what to expect and where the enemy would be.[5]

It is possible that the neutrality pact had an effect on the timing for the start of the Long March, although by September preparations were so far advanced that not much change was possible. But it may have confirmed the Communist command in its choice of the Guangdong corner for the breakout. There is also evidence of some understanding with the Guangxi warlords to yield a "corridor" in northeast Guangxi to help speed the Communists out of the vicinity.

The arrangement by which the Guangdong warlord provided the Red Army with communications equipment was not an isolated example. When the Fourth Front Army of Zhang Guotao set up its Sichuan border base, it possessed a rather powerful wireless group. This was strengthened by equipment provided clandestinely by General Yang Hucheng, chief of staff and division commander of the provincial army. General Yang was a Communist sympathizer, one of the many sprinkled through Chiang Kai-shek's army. However, he did not survive to see the victory of the People's Liberation Army. He was involved in the Xi'an Incident (the kidnapping of Chiang Kai-shek) in 1936, was arrested by the KMT and held until just before the Communists came to power, then executed.[6]

With or without the intelligence that the Guangdong warlord promised, the Red Army possessed an extraordinary secret asset. It could read and transcribe the Nationalist Army's communications. It had the same advantage over Chiang Kai-shek that the Allies had over the Nazis in World War II through their ability to read German communications with Ultra Secret. For this capability Zhou Enlai was largely responsible.[7] Beginning in 1930, when Zhou was in charge of Party security and on close terms with Moscow, he arranged for Chinese specialists to be trained in electronics and cryptology, in coding and decoding, in the Soviet Union. In a tour de force, he even arranged for Party members to be instructed in the tricks of the magician Harry Houdini, so that if arrested they could free themselves from handcuffs and leg irons. Where they got that training is not recorded.

In the early days in Jiangxi, the Red Army did not possess wireless transmitters powerful enough to reach Shanghai. In May 1931 they captured two 100-watt transmitters from Chiang Kai-shek's troops. Soon Liu Ding, the first important wireless decoding expert to be trained in Russia, arrived from Shanghai. He had memorized the entire codebook and from this time forward Mao Zedong was able to communicate with Shanghai by wireless and via Shanghai with Moscow.

Liu Ding began a program of interception and interpretation of Nationalist wireless exchanges. The KMT seems never to have suspected what was going on.

The Nationalists used simple codes or no codes at all in this early period. In the First Campaign they transmitted in the clear. In the Second and Third, the codes were so simple no special expertise was needed. By this time the Red Army was well along in its interception program. Wang Zheng, later to be head of the Ministry of Electronics (originally the Fourth Ministry of Machine Building), was a leader in this. He could decipher all the Nationalist front-line exchanges. There was seldom a moment when the Red Army did not know the disposition of Chiang's forces and what their orders were, often intercepting Nationalist messages faster than the Nationalists themselves.[8]

The Fourth Front Army under Zhang Guotao was busy at the same task. After the Long March started, Zhang fed to the First Army a flow of Nationalist intercepts. In his memoirs Zhang writes of sitting up night after night monitoring the traffic and passing on to the First Front Army vital information—often not knowing if his transmissions were being received because for long periods he did not know where the First Army was. The transmitters of the First Army were sometimes not powerful enough to communicate with the Fourth.[9]

So assiduous were the Communists in intercepting enemy traffic that when Otto Braun was still in Shanghai, he was better informed about the Nationalists and their order of battle than he was about the Red Army, because almost every day he received readouts of the latest Nationalist intercepts.

There was a chronic shortage of wireless operators and equipment, and the Red Army made every effort to capture both. (They also had a special program to capture doctors and their medicine chests.) Captured operators were offered incentives to work with the Red Army—extra pay, good rations. Some operators knew the Nationalist codes; this was a bonus.

Because of the shortage of equipment, radio was used in the Long March only for communicating between armies. Contact with lower echelons was by field telephone or courier. Huge coils of telephone wire were lugged by the signal companies, who moved ahead of headquarters, stringing the line between sites picked by the scouting parties. It was cumbersome and ineffective, and it often caused casualties among the signalmen.

So far as was known to the Red Army, the Nationalists never intercepted their wireless traffic.

One thing was apparent as the Red Army moved forward on its long journey. Communications would dictate the pattern of life for the high command. All day the armies were marching and/or fighting. There was no time for reports except urgent battlefield messages. Only with nightfall and the establishment of campsites did the wireless begin to chatter, the couriers to hurry back. Only then could the command get a picture of the combat situation.

Many top Red Army commanders had become accustomed to night work as revolutionary conspirators. Now battlefield conditions compelled them to work all night, night after night. Soldiers spoke repeatedly of Mao and Zhou working long after midnight. How could they get rest? The Army departed each morning at 6 A.M. Soldiers and officers rose an hour earlier to break camp, eat their rice porridge, drink a cup of tea or hot water. The leaders rose at 8 or 9 A.M. Their cooks or bodyguards had already been gone for three hours, having marched ahead to set up fires and cook the leaders' breakfast three hours down the road. It was normal for men at the top to be carried on a litter for the first three hours until they reached the breakfast site. They slept like babes in a cradle, swung along by stout bearers.

"They knew there were no pursuers," commented Li Yimang, chairman of the Association for International Understanding in 1984, who made the Long March in the Cadres Battalion and often saw Mao and Zhou. "They suffered no harmful effects from sleeping in the litters except that they all developed the habit of taking sleeping pills."[10]

Not until the end of October did the Nationalists begin to get an inkling that the Red Army was on the move. But it would be a month before they figured out what was going on.

This was reflected in the Nationalist newspapers. The Nanchang paper published a congratulatory story October 18 about the fall on the fourteenth of the "so-called model district" of Xingguo, which was said to have been surrounded since July. Chiang Kai-shek was at Xi'an and then on October 23 arrived in Chengdu. On the twenty-seventh, the paper reported that the "Red bandits" were trying to break through and escape to the south. They had attacked Xinfeng and Anyuan and were beaten off with huge losses estimated at ten thousand. Mao and Zhu De were said to be in command. The article reported that the Red forces had retreated back toward Ruijin. The next day more incorrect details were published, and on the twenty-eighth the fall of Ningdu was announced. On October 31, the newspaper said that the "base of the Red bandits" had been shattered and its capital shifted away from Ruijin.[11]

Another Nationalist paper reported November 8 that the Communists had suffered defeats but were "proving exceptionally stubborn. It might take some months before they were completely wiped out."

None of these dispatches provided a clue to what was going on. True the Reds were said to be trying to escape, but the focus was on battles for cities, in which, of course, the Red Army had no interest. A month later, December 1, a leading editorial in the Nanchang paper was headlined: "Sorting Out in Former Red Areas." It reported almost ten thousand casualties among the Communists and four thousand prisoners taken. A mass rally was held in Nanchang to celebrate the great victory and offer praise for Chiang Kai-shek.

In reality the Nationalists had suffered a disastrous intelligence fiasco. This may have been due to the absence of Chiang from Nanchang or because of the extreme caution of von Seeckt, who held back Nationalist troops from hot pursuit for fear the Communists might zap them in an ambush. The Nationalists first built blockhouses, then timorously inched forward. Not until October 30, at the earliest, in the opinion of General Qin Xinghan, did they begin to realize a major Communist move was under way.

The Red Army encountered no aerial bombardment and little reconnaissance until November and the impending assault on the fourth blockhouse line. Not until November 28, when the Red Army reached the Xiang River, did the KMT commit a major part of its air squadrons. This was a fighter-bomber force of about two hundred planes, which ordinarily attacked in groups of three. The KMT was still bombing Ruijin long after the Red Army moved out.

The intelligence failure of Chiang Kai-shek was remarkable but not more remarkable than that of the world at large.[12] Not one item of China news, not a mention of Chiang Kai-shek, not a word about the Red Army, not a peep about silver purchases or even railroad accidents, appeared in *The New York Times* during the month of October 1934.

The big news in the *Times* that October was the World Series and Dizzy Dean, Adolf Hitler, the rising crisis in Spain, and, day after day, the Lindbergh kidnapping case. Nothing was happening in China worthy of report in the newspaper of record.

On November 9, the *Times* reported that forty thousand Communists were on the march from Jiangxi and Fujian, where they had been blockaded for many months. Now they were moving westward, looting a territory one hundred miles long and twelve miles wide, along the Hunan border astride the Canton-Hankou railroad. It was a four-paragraph item printed on page 6. That was the first hint in the Western world that the Long March was under way.

Three weeks later, the *Times* reassured its readers. The Communists had been defeated by the Nationalists in Jiangxi.

7

THE CONSPIRACY OF THE LITTERS

ONCE across the Yudu River, Mao Zedong began the Long March on a litter. It was not that Mao was unaccustomed to walking over the countryside. Probably no leader of the Red Army had covered more backcountry li in China's mountains and valleys than he. As a boy he walked everywhere he went. There was no other means of transportation for a peasant lad. In his college days he and his friend Xiao Yu spent six weeks on a walking trip through six counties of southern Hunan. The walk was a begging trip; the idea was Xiao's. The two carried no money, dressed in old clothes, carried worn umbrellas and small bundles for their notebooks and a change of linen. They lived off the countryside, the charity of peasants and, occasionally, of townsfolk. The trip was an adventure and an exploration. They found they could live by their wits and on the generosity of the people, and for the first time Mao began to study the countryside with an analytic eye.

The trip with Xiao was, in a sense, a forerunner of one that Mao took in January and February of 1927. Then, as the Chinese Revolution was beginning to gain momentum, with Communists and Nationalists marching north under the uncertain banner of Chiang Kai-shek, Mao retreated to the countryside and set out on a five-week trip which took him through five districts of Hunan. It was on the basis of this trip that he wrote his famous *Report on an Investigation of the Peasant Movement in Hunan,* which he submitted to a skeptical and antagonistic Communist Party Central Committee.

He predicted: "In a very short time . . . several hundred million peasants will rise like a mighty storm, like a hurricane, a force so swift and violent that no power, however great, will be able to hold it back."

The peasant, he wrote, will sweep all the imperialists, warlords, corrupt officials, local tyrants, and evil gentry to their graves. "There are three alternatives: to march at their head and lead them; to trail behind them, gesticulating and criticizing; or to stand in the way and oppose them."

No doubt existed in his mind. Only the first course was acceptable. "Every revolutionary," he said, "should know that the national revolution requires a great change in the countryside." No need to worry about excesses. "A revolution is not a dinner party or writing an essay or painting a picture or doing embroidery; it cannot be so refined, so leisurely and gentle, so temperate, kind, courteous, restrained and magnanimous. A revolution is an act of violence, an insurrection."

It was on the basis of these findings that Mao nailed his banner to the peasant cause and later was to tell Edgar Snow: "Whoever wins the peasant will win China; whoever solves the land problem will win the peasant."[1]

The trip with Xiao and the five-week walk on the peasant inquiry were warm-ups for what the Long March would provide Mao. Beginning with the Autumn Harvest Uprising, Mao had been living in the countryside, sometimes riding a horse, sometimes going by shanks' mare. His muscles grew hard and strong. But now his body was weak from his long bout of malaria. Dr. Nelson Fu possessed the best quinine and had managed to quell the attack, but he had less success in rebuilding Mao's strength.[2] Dr. Fu had been trying to encourage Mao to eat more. One evening he brought his patient a boiled chicken, but Mao called that special treatment and made Dr. Fu eat half the chicken.

Now and for some time to come Mao would travel on a litter. It consisted of two long hollow bamboo poles, strong and flexible, and a cross-part made of woven fiber. It was light and buoyant, swaying from side to side and up and down like a sailor's hammock. Mao's body—he was very thin and a full six feet tall—sank deep in the litter, so there was no danger of pitching out while asleep, no need to be strapped in. Two sturdy young soldiers carried the litter, resting the poles on their shoulders, the poles long enough so they could see their feet—very important on the narrow footpaths.[3]

Some litters had oilcloth or oilpaper covers, helpful in the drizzly mountains to protect the occupants. Mao could sleep through the rain and he often did.

A census of the litters was almost a Who's Who of the high Communist leadership. Zhou Enlai's wife, Deng Yingchao, ill with tuberculosis and spitting blood, spent most of the Long March on a litter.[4]

Hu Yaobang, in 1984 general secretary of the Chinese Communist Party, and in 1934 leader of the youth league, came down with malaria three days after the start of the Long March and did not recover for more than a month. He credited his survival to the litter and to excellent medical attention.[5]

The litters became the scene of political discussions that prepared the way for bringing Mao Zedong back into power, enabling him to take command of the March and save it from disaster.

These talks revolved around Mao and Luo Fu, the ex–San Francisco editor, and the wounded Wang Jiaxiang, Politburo member and key "Bolshevik." Wang was to be carried on a litter during the whole March. In the early stages he traveled side-by-side with Mao. At night they camped together, talking, talking, talking. Wounded Wang was a rather silent man who liked very much to read. Like Mao he had come from a well-to-do peasant background and his father wanted him to take over the family business. Instead he insisted on an education, went to Shanghai, entered the progressive Shanghai University, joined the radical youth movement and went to Moscow in 1925. He was not quite one of the "28 Bolsheviks" but he did support their line.

Wounded Wang was a thin, thin man. He was thin before he was wounded, thin after that, thin all his life. His face was slightly square, so his wife, Zhu Zhongli thought, his forehead broad, a good speaker, not earthy like Mao but with a humorous touch. His favorite book was the Chinese classic, *Dream of the Red Chamber*, but he read anything. After coming back from Russia he particularly liked Gorky and Tolstoy.

The litters and the campfire rendezvous gave Mao and Wounded Wang a chance to get to know each other, to analyze what had happened in Jiangxi and what was happening on the March. Mao talked about the tactical mistakes, particularly in the Guangchang debacle. Mao's arguments powerfully impressed Wang. Within a month he had swung over to Mao's side. In years to come Mao credited him with the most significant role in his victory over Li De and Bo Gu.[6]

Luo Fu had been moving toward Mao for several months. Their talks at Cloud Stone Mountain during the summer had convinced him of Mao's case. After the April defeat at Guangchang Luo Fu criticized Bo Gu savagely. The casualties were too high, fighting blockhouses with blockhouses made no sense. The Red Army could not win on that track.

Li De was not able to follow the interchange because of his lack of Chinese, but he surmised its gist and tried to reconcile the men. "Both of you returned from the Soviet Union," he said. "You must work together. The Chinese Revolution demands that you work together."

Li De's plea did not succeed. Luo Fu became more and more alienated. He published an article saying that they must not only fight Chiang but struggle against "left opportunism" and a one-sided approach to defending the Soviet Union. This was a shaft directed at Bo Gu and Li De.[7]

It did not take long for Mao, Luo Fu, and Wang Jiaxiang to agree that at the first convenient moment they would demand a meeting to resolve the problem of military leadership. When they got to that point, Li De and Bo Gu were doomed.[8]

Li De knew nothing of the "conspiracy of the litters," but he knew that Mao was talking and that this could do his cause no good. In his memoirs he complained that Mao was moving around, talking now with this commander, now with that, and out of these talks flowed more and more criticism directed against Bo Gu and himself.

The trio, Mao, Luo, and Wounded Wang, came to be known as the "Central Team,"[9] or in Braun's words, "the Central Triad."[10] Whatever the title, the three men were moving to take command of the Long March.

The Mao Zedong who argued from his swaying litter was no country bumpkin, as he was so often depicted by the Russians and the Chinese "Bolsheviks." This was a measure of their ignorance. The Bolsheviks, most of them still in their twenties, had been stuffed in Moscow like Peking ducks with Marxist gibberish mouthed by the equally youthful Pavel Mif and his cohorts at Sun Yat-sen University, now rechristened University of the Toilers of the East.

Only with Mao's death on September 9, 1976, the arrest and destruction of the Gang of Four, and the rise of a new and more realistic scholarship under Deng Xiaoping is it becoming possible to disentangle the real Mao from the caricature created by the hagiographers.

Mao was a generation older than the Bolsheviks. Wounded Wang, director of the Red Army's General Political Department, and a member of the Politburo with three or four years of Moscow training, was twenty-seven in 1934. Bo Gu was twenty-six at the start of the Long March. He had spent four years in Moscow between the ages of eighteen and twenty-two. Wang Ming, the resident "Bolshevik" in Moscow who directed Bo Gu, was twenty-eight. Luo Fu was a bit older, thirty-four.

Mao had not been educated abroad. He did not go to Europe during the Chinese student exodus at the end of World War I, as did Zhou Enlai and Zhu De. Nor had he bowed before the altars of Moscow.

Mao had been born and raised in a peasant household in the village of Shaoshan, less than forty miles from Hunan's capital of Changsha. That forty miles was so great a distance Mao did not cover it until he was nearly twenty. Most of the two thousand residents of Shaoshan bore the name Mao. It was a clan village like most villages of China. Mao's father was a tough, upwardly mobile peasant of the breed that in Russia was called kulaks (fists)—hard, ambitious, greedy, a money grubber. Mao's grandfather had lost the family farm to moneylenders. Mao's father got it back and managed to accumulate four acres with an annual rice production of seven tons—not a bad living for those times.[11]

Mao's father was determined that his firstborn be educated, partly in self-interest—he was rapidly expanding into grain dealing and moneylending and, illiterate himself, needed a son to write and read and keep the books—and also because of his burning ambition to lift up the name of Mao in the world.

Mao went to school at the age of seven. He had already been working in the fields like all peasant children since the age of four. It was a village school, but in five years he learned such classics as the *Analects* of Confucius, Mencius and *Zuozhuan*, the commentary by Zuo Qiuming on the *Spring and Autumn Annals.*

Many years later Mao deprecated his study of the Chinese classics. He told Robert Payne: "I hated Confucius from the age of eight,"[12] but the truth was he absorbed the Five Classics into his system and illuminated his writings with quotations from Confucius and Mencius. In his last decade he was invariably photographed receiving distinguished visitors in his study, stacked floor to ceiling with ancient Chinese texts. Chinese classical thought became embedded in his mind and in the complex personal philosophy he was to evolve. He was, as he said, "making the past serve the present."[13]

Study of Mao's classroom notes at Changsha Normal School No. 1, one of China's finest teaching institutions, reveals the manner in which he integrated Confucian and Mencian thought into his own philosophy. Confucius and Mencius advocated changing reality instead of trying to escape from it, and this was to hold a central place in Mao's thinking.

In his notebook Mao copied out Mencius' observation: "If it is Heaven's will to establish peace and order throughout the land today, who is there but me to achieve it?"

Mao attached to that quotation another, from the statesman Fan Zhangyan of the Song dynasty (989–1050), who declared: "Ponder this problem before everything."

These principles would underlie Mao's political life.[14]

Mao plunged into the reading of China's remarkable picaresque novels—*The Romance of the Three Kingdoms, Outlaws of the Marshes* (sometimes called *Water Margin*),[15] and *Travels in the West,* also known as *Monkey.*

Mao committed to memory the tales of *Three Kingdoms* and *Outlaws* and to his final days read and reread these collections of slightly fictionalized episodes from China's history. He commented on them repeatedly and used them as textbooks for guerrilla warfare. When his enemies accused him of fighting in Jinggangshan or on the Long March in accordance with what he had learned from *Outlaws,* they were right and were paying him a practical compliment.

Mao read Sun Wu Zi's *The Art of War,* written 2,400 years ago, the classic of Chinese military strategy, and the commentaries of Zeng Guofan and Hu Linyi of the late Qing dynasty. These men worked so closely together they were known as Zeng-Hu, just as Mao Zedong and Zhu De were called Zhu-Mao.

Upon this solid Chinese foundation Mao based his broader exploration of the world. He discovered the late-nineteenth-century reformers and critics of the decaying Qing empire, notably Zheng Guanying's *Alarmist Talks in a Prosperous Age.* Zheng called upon China to move toward capitalism and a modern Western system. Mao was enormously impressed. His studies went forward in an atmosphere of tension. His father wanted him to concentrate on math and bookkeeping; he had no use for philosophical inquiries.

It was Mao's mother who was the strong influence of his early years. He worshiped her and again and again uttered words of devotion. She was a hard-working, kind, thoughtful woman ready to help others in need. She sometimes gave rice to starving peasants—but never when her flinty husband was around. She was a devout Buddhist and through her Mao became a believer. When his mother was ill he prayed to Buddha for her recovery, and at fifteen made a pilgrimage to the great temple at Hengshan Mountain, more than one hundred miles from Shaoshan, one of ancient China's five sacred mountains. Like all Buddhist pilgrims, he prostrated himself repeatedly on the way to the temple.

On his mother's death in 1919 Mao wrote in his farewell ode:

> In reasoning and judgment her mind was clear and accurate
> Everything she did was done with planning and with care . . .

When we were sick she held our hands, her heart full of sorrow
Yet she admonished us saying: "You should strive to be good."

Mao soon threw off his belief in Buddha, but Buddhism left powerful traces in his thought. Li Rui, a scholar and a man who served Mao as private secretary until Mao sent him to exile and prison for twenty years, believes that Buddhism gave Mao his conviction that social change calls first for destruction and then for rebuilding.

"The extermination of the world," Mao wrote in his normal school notebook, "is by no means the final extermination. Doom will surely be followed by success. This is beyond doubt. We are eagerly looking forward to the doom of the old world. Its destruction will eventually lead to the establishment of a new one."[16]

Mao did not take his next step up the educational ladder without a row with his father, who wanted him to work for a grain dealer in nearby Xiangtan in preparation for becoming a partner in the growing Mao family business. By this time the Mao household was an imposing one, separate rooms for Mao and his two brothers and adopted sister, a chamber for the parents, a summer and a winter kitchen, an ample living room. The house had a second wing, probably owned by Mao, which was occupied by relatives named Zou. It was, as any visitor today can see, no poverty-stricken peasant hut. There was a fine pond for carp and geese and ducks, ample storehouses for grain, no finer house in the vicinity.

Mao won his argument and early in 1910 entered the Dongshan higher primary school, where he studied science and English and the Chinese classics. He would never master a foreign language, but almost to the end of his days he slogged away at English, trying to ram into his head its harsh syllables. Mao displayed great talent for writing and speaking and made two good friends, the Xiao brothers, Xiao San (sometimes known as Emi Xiao) and Xiao Yu.

Mao's world again burst its boundaries. Xiao San lent him a book called *Biographies of the World's Heroes*. Here for the first time Mao read about George Washington, Abraham Lincoln, Napoleon, Jean-Jacques Rousseau, Peter the Great, Montesquieu. He was fascinated by Washington. Years later he told Edgar Snow: "I first heard of America in an article which told of the American Revolution and contained a sentence like 'After eight years of difficult war Washington won a victory and built up a nation.'" At the time, Mao told Xiao: "China should have such great men as Washington." It is not too much to believe that in those years he began to think of following in Washington's footsteps.[17]

It was now that Mao was introduced to two leaders of the China reform movement that gathered momentum after the defeat by Japan in 1894 and the Boxer Rebellion of 1900. The reformers were Kang Youwei and Liang Qichao, both on the wane of influence before Mao discovered them. There was a lag in penetration of ideas to rural Hunan. News of the death of the Dowager Empress and the puppet Emperor did not reach Mao for two years.

But Mao's pace was quickening. After a period of reading and reflection he arrived in Changsha almost coincident with China's 1911 revolution, the one backed by Dr. Sun Yat-sen. Mao cut off his pigtail, the symbolic act of revolt against the old, and flung himself into the turmoil, writing an essay that revealed the confused mixture brewing within his mind. He called for a new government, headed by Dr. Sun Yat-sen as president, with Kang Youwei as premier and Liang Qichao as foreign minister—a little like a government headed by Ronald Reagan with Walter Mondale as premier and George McGovern as foreign minister. Then he borrowed a pair of rubber boots, intending to rush off to Wuchang, where he heard it was very rainy, and there join the revolution. Before he could put on his boots the revolution came to Changsha and he signed up in the New Revolutionary—but not very revolutionary—Army.

After six months, in the belief the revolution was over, he quit the army, shopped around for a school (he considered a police school, a law school, a commercial school, and even one that taught soap-making), and then decided to study on his own in the provincial library. There he devoured Adam Smith's *The Wealth of Nations,* Darwin's *Origin of Species,* John Stuart Mill, Rousseau, Spencer's *Logic,* Montesquieu's *De l'Esprit des lois,* works on history and geography of the United States and Europe. He read Chinese poetry and Greek classics in Chinese translation, gobbling up books like bowls of noodles, steadily moving from the Chinese tradition through eighteenth- and nineteenth-century European philosophers toward contemporary social criticism. Many of the European works were translated by Yan Fu, a Chinese reformer. Mao read every work that Yan Fu translated.

Bulwarked by this rich confection of Chinese and Western thought, Mao entered Changsha Normal School No. 1. The year was 1913. Of

Mao's entrance essay, the headmaster wrote: "How many among my colleagues can write such a good essay?"

Changsha Normal No. 1 was the forcing bed of Mao's mature philosophy. He spent five and a half years there. The greatest single influence upon him was Yang Changji, professor of ethics, a man who had spent ten years of study in Japan and England, known for his learning as the "Confucius of Changsha." Here, too, Mao met the "Venerable Xu," Xu Teli, who was to accompany him on the Long March, Professor Fang Weixia, and a pleiad of students who were to move with him into the Communist movement—Cai Hesen, He Shuheng, Chen Chang, Luo Xuezan, and Zhang Kundi, all to lose their lives in the Revolution.[18]

Li Rui, after examining Mao's notebooks of the period, found it difficult to distinguish between Mao's own ideas and those of Professor Yang. The two seemed to meld into one. Mao was beginning to blend the diverse ideas to which he had been exposed into a more or less coherent doctrine. This was clearly evidenced in some twelve thousand Chinese characters of notes which he inked into his copy of Friedrich Paulsen's *System of Ethics.*

Mao wrote: "There are people in the world and material objects in the world simply because I exist. If I close my eyes they exist no longer." Later he formalized this as the principle: "Knowledge is obtained by experience."

Over the outer gate of Changsha Normal School, cut into the stone, was the legend: "Seek Truth from Facts." It was put there by the "Venerable Xu." Mao was to make this aphorism the base of his political philosophy.

Mao soaked up knowledge like a sponge. He had never read a newspaper before. In fact, he had never *seen* a newspaper before. Now he read every printed page he could lay his hands on.

Paulsen was a follower of Kant, and Mao began to discover the Germans. In June of 1918 Mao graduated from Changsha No. 1, the third student in his class. His fellow students voted him first in character, first in courage, and first in intellect.[19] Some professors thought he was too independent, too challenging, too apt to break the rules.

"How," he declared one night at the house of Cai Hesen, his classmate and future fellow founder of the Communist Party, "can China come to have a great philosopher and ethical revolutionary like Russia's Tolstoy who will develop new thoughts by washing away all old?"[20]

Mao was twenty-five years old when he graduated. He knew Confucius, Mencius, and China's great literature. He knew Buddhism and

Western philosophy. He had educated himself in the political geography of the United States and Europe. He had absorbed China's military wisdom and the reformist ideals of Dr. Sun Yat-sen. He had become an eloquent speaker, a poet, a patriot, a young but rapidly maturing philosopher. He knew China's heritage and he had lived close enough to China's soil to know her people, her peasants, her problems, her idiosyncratic heritage, her political diseases. He knew that China must change and he was preparing himself to lead that change.

Mao had made himself aware of the outer world. He had followed the progress of World War I. He knew the names of Von Hindenburg, Kaiser Wilhelm II, Woodrow Wilson, Clemenceau, and Foch. He had read about the Russian Revolution and he had found a personal role model in George Washington.[21]

But so far as any evidence exists, he had not in June 1918 read a line of Marx or Lenin. He knew that Lenin and Trotsky played a role in Russia's 1917 revolutions, but the word "Communist" had not appeared in any notebook he had kept, nor were any of his friends, teachers, or acquaintances ever afterward able to recollect that he knew or had heard at that time of the *Communist Manifesto* or *Das Kapital.*

But Mao was at the brink of radical change. On graduation from Changsha Normal No. 1 he set out for Beijing, walking a good bit of the way. Within weeks he had plunged into his first exposure to Marxism through the writings and conversation of Li Dazhao, whose journal, *New Youth,* he was already reading. He could not have studied the *Manifesto* until 1919; it was only in that year that it was translated into Chinese. But his mind had already been fixed on the Russian Revolution. As he would later say: "Three books especially deeply carved my mind and built up in me a faith in Marxism." These three works were the *Manifesto,* a work by Karl Kautsky (Lenin's great opponent, the founder of Social Democracy in Germany), the name of which he could no longer remember, and a potboiler by a man named Thomas Kirkup, called *A History of Socialism.* Mao did not know much about Marxism, but he knew it was what he believed in. He was not unlike some young radical Americans of the 1960s who proclaimed themselves "Maoists" without having read a line Mao had written.

Mao began to call himself a Marxist, but this did not explain his philosophy. He still believed in the Monroe Doctrine, he had not lost his image of George Washington as role model and his belief in the progressive nature of the United States and the American Revolution.

He was powerfully drawn toward anarchism and Kropotkin, as were many young Chinese.

Mao at the age of twenty-five and twenty-six—as on his litter on the Long March at forty—was a man who possessed an extraordinarily rich and panoramic intellectual scope. The words of Marx and Lenin fell on no blank page but upon the fertile soil of an encyclopedic and penetrating mind.

Not one of Mao's colleagues on the Long March possessed the diversity and breadth of his intellect. The "Bolsheviks," in particular, came almost exclusively from the Chinese middle-class intelligentsia. They knew little about social conditions in China, nothing about the life of the villages where 80 percent of the people lived. They had gulped down the self-serving dialectic which was ladled out in the hothouses in which Stalin was training post-Lenin political robots. Stalin and his Comintern had no interest in young Chinese with minds of their own. They wanted human tools who put Russia and her interests first.

Mao's intellectual power, the synthesis he had compounded of Marxism, Chinese philosophy, common sense, and the exceptionalism of China's backward peasant state, proved almost irresistible when concentrated, whether his target was a twenty-six-year-old Bolshevik, a fortyish general like Zhu De, or an ambitious youth like Lin Biao.

To anyone who understood what manner of man was Mao, the outcome of the "litter conspiracy" could not be a surprise.

8

THE WOMEN

MAO'S wife, He Zizhen, did not march beside her husband on the Long March. Togetherness was not the rule, and the rules were strict about husbands and wives. There were only thirty women cadres on the Long March in the main Army and a sprinkling of nurses and orderlies. This was not true of all the armies. The Fourth Front Army included two thousand women and mustered a special women's combat regiment which fought some fierce and deadly battles.

There was one exception to the rule about husbands and wives. This was for Zhu De and his twenty-three-year-old wife, Kang Keqing. They were hardly separated a day of the March, but there was a special reason for this. She was a combat soldier, a markswoman, carrying two pistols and a Mauser. She sometimes lugged three or four rifles on her shoulders to help out tired soldiers and present an example.

Kang Keqing was a robust peasant woman, daughter of a fisherman. She had married Zhu De on Jinggangshan in January 1929, just before Zhu-Mao came down from the mountain. She was only seventeen, he was forty-three, and his wife, Wu Ruolin, a revolutionary, had been executed by the Nationalists in 1928. Kang Keqing had been fighting on the mountain since she was fifteen.

Like most of the women, she was assigned a horse, but she seldom rode it. She marched along with her extra guns and, as she told Helen Snow when it was all over, she didn't think the marching was such a big deal. "It was just like going out for a stroll every day," she said.[1]

"Yes," said Madame Kang Keqing, nearly fifty years later, "I did say that to Helen Snow."

By 1984, Kang Keqing was a forceful, confident leader of the Communist Party of China. For many years she had been one of the heads of its women's activities. She was a public speaker, a policymaker, a stateswoman who had devoted her life not to military affairs, as she had expected during the Long March, but to matters of social and political importance.

She had not changed her feelings about the Long March.

"I am a good walker and a good rider," she said. "I was walking a few dozen meters ahead of a group that included Cai Chang [another woman Party leader] and quite a few other Party people who had studied abroad. They talked all day of their experiences, of their studies abroad, of the good food they had eaten, the places they had visited.

"Every day they talked, laughing and joking. Their presence encouraged us. They laughed and joked. Sometimes they sang the 'Marseillaise.' Yes, I did tell Helen Snow it was like a walk in the country. With all those wonderful people, what else could I say?"[2]

But it isn't likely that too many of her companions, male or female, shared the feelings of Kang Keqing. The March was a tough, dangerous operation and that was true from beginning to end.

Because of her pregnancy He Zizhen spent her time in the convalescent unit to which she and most women had been assigned. She saw Mao only on weekends or those occasions, rare in the early days, when they were camped for a few days' rest. They may have seen each other a bit more than other couples but not much.[3] The "Saturday Night" rule had been in force since Jinggangshan. Exceptions might be made in cases of illness when wives looked after husbands but the rule would not change throughout the March.

Surviving commanders and medical officers insist that there were no major sex problems on the March, that the troops rarely had relations with women along the line of March and, of course, in the main force few women were included. However, Zhu De told Helen Snow in 1936 that rape had been something of a problem in the early days of the March but was brought under control as discipline improved. Rapists were shot after summary trial. It was no problem after the force reached Yan'an. But syphilis was rife among townfolk in north Shaanxi.

There was a strong strain of puritanism in the Red Army although the leaders, in principle, had broken with what they called feudal ideas about the sexes. Soldiers and officers were not permitted to marry without official approval. Even after the March ordinary soldiers were not permitted to marry. Permission was given to cadres and officers, but not lightly.

Many years later, when the question of a divorce arose between Mao and He Zizhen, the Party had to consider and rule on whether to permit it. The Red Army to an extraordinary extent was made up of adolescer t and very young adults. Some 54 percent of the soldiers were under twenty-four. Dr. Nelson Fu calculated that 90 percent had had no sexual experience.[4] The Woman Wei Xiuying, the butternut of a woman who had been sold as a child bride, remembered a young soldier's alarm when she and he were fording a river. Her black skirt billowed up around her hips and the boy cried, "Are you wounded?" She realized he had seen the blood of her menstrual flow. He didn't know that women menstruated. It was an ignorance he shared with many comrades.[5]

Not only ignorance and rules conditioned relations of men and women. There was a comradeship of spirit and shared hardships. Petite Liu Ying, not yet married to Luo Fu, said that men and women worked together with total absence of sexual feeling.

"Sometimes," Liu Ying said, "we lived together and slept together on the same beds for almost a year. We didn't take off our clothes. The enemy was so close and we were so tired. We could not find doors to take off to sleep on. We just sank exhausted on the straw and fell asleep."[6]

This was why there was such great discomfort among the top cadres, both men and women, about Otto Braun's sexual demands. When he arrived in October 1933, he seemed to think that the Red Army was like some other armies. He expected to find female camp followers who would sleep with him. But there were no prostitutes within the soviet enclave. An effort was made to find sexual partners for Braun, but this didn't work out either.[7] The Chinese women quickly rejected him, saying he was big and brutal and hurt them physically.[8]

Braun's Bleak House was located only a short stroll from the residence of the Young Communist League. One of the leaders of the Young Communists had a very pretty wife. Braun was much taken with this young woman and wanted her for his bedmate. He offered her presents. (One of the complaints the Chinese had against Braun was that he had better food and supplies than anyone else.) Braun was hardly tactful in his approaches and the husband quickly became aware of what was going on. Some comrades, possibly including Interpreter Wu, moved to save the situation by finding a solidly built young peasant woman, Xiao Yuehua, who was working at the time for Hu Yaobang, now general secretary of the Party, then a Young Communist League leader.

Xiao Yuehua was not good-looking but she was amenable and strong and she became Braun's "campaign wife." They lived together as long as the Red Army held the soviet zone, but when the March started Xiao Yuehua, like most women, was sent to the convalescent unit. This led to trouble. Neither Xiao Yuehua nor Braun cared much for the situation. They quarreled and Xiao Yuehua quarreled with her women comrades. Some, like Deng Yingchao, the wife of Zhou Enlai, and Kang Keqing, devoted endless time trying to smooth the situation over, to no avail.[9]

"How could they ever get along?" Kang Keqing asked fifty years later. "How could they communicate? He didn't speak any Chinese. She didn't speak anything but Chinese. What were they going to do— get General Wu Xiuquan to interpret for them? I have no way of knowing Xiao Yuehua's inner thoughts—but how *could* they have gotten on? I think that as a wife she recognized Li De [Braun] as a representative of the Comintern and the Revolution. They had no common language.

"Still she managed to get on with her husband somehow. We have an old saying: If you marry a dog—go with a dog; if you marry a chicken —go with a chicken."[10]

Ding Ling, China's famous writer, dismissed Xiao Yuehua. "She was just a country yokel," she said. "She worked for Dr. Nelson Fu as an orderly. She didn't have much skill." The Red Army, said Ding Ling, had a responsibility to see that Braun was properly cared for. He needed a woman and the Red Army provided him with one. "He was treated very well," she said.[11]

Xiao Yuehua came to Yan'an with Braun. She even learned under his tutelage to bake bread and she bore him a baby boy. The child was very dark and Mao made fun of it—saying it didn't do much to support Teutonic theories of racial superiority. Finally, as Helen Snow reported, Xiao Yuehua brought suit against Braun for divorce. It was a scandal-ridden procedure. She demanded 600 Chinese dollars monthly alimony. The divorce was granted—whether she got her alimony is not recorded. She went to Changsha and worked there for many years, dying only in 1983. When she died Hu Yaobang personally saw that her wish that her coffin be covered with the red flag of China and the flag of the Communist Party was fulfilled.[12]

Most of the wives were not domestic. Kang Keqing proclaimed that she never looked after Zhu De. He had bodyguards to cook his meals and sew on his buttons. They cooked for her as well. Kang Keqing did not have a domestic background. Her fisherman father was so poor that the family disposed of every girl baby, each in turn given to another poor peasant—they didn't even sell them. The girl children became servants, farmhands, or kitchen slaves. Kang Keqing had been given away at the age of one month and worked as a slave until she was fifteen, when she ran away to join the Red Army. Zhu De came from an identical background. Five babies in his family were drowned because there was no way of feeding them. He was given away to a childless relative and put into a school for landlords' sons. Had he been a girl, he would have been drowned at birth. Perhaps it was identity of pasts that drew Zhu De and Kang Keqing so close. She was a common soldier until she married Zhu and then she was supposed to do political work. Just before the Long March, she happened to be with a battalion of eight hundred men. The commander was killed during an attack and the men put her in charge. They routed the enemy. Red Army men called her "the girl commander." She had no intention of settling down and having children, and when the Long March was over she plunged into studies, hoping to become a ranking military officer.[13]

He Zizhen was different. She liked to look after Mao and did so when she could. A good cook, she made him the spicy Hunan dishes he loved. Mao was very fond of hot peppers and especially of He Zizhen's hot pepper soup.* You couldn't be a good revolutionary unless you liked red-hot peppers, Mao liked to say to Otto Braun, whose taste ran to sauerbraten and sauerkraut. Braun hated Mao for saying that.[14]

He Zizhen was a woman of beauty, possessed of a temper, a passionate revolutionary. She was twenty-four years old at the start of the Long March and only seventeen or eighteen when she and Mao met on Jinggangshan.[15]

He Zizhen was not Mao's first wife. He had been forced by his father to marry, at the age of fifteen, a chosen bride four or five years older than himself. He went through the ceremony with ritual politeness, but refused to touch the young woman. Her name has never been revealed (because of the scandal of an unconsummated marriage).[16]

Nor was He Zizhen Mao's first love. His first love and first real wife was the daughter of his mentor, Professor Yang Changji, whom Mao followed to Beijing. There almost simultaneously Mao embraced Marxism and Yang Kaihui, a willowy, brilliant woman, eight years younger, dedicated to the cause of a new China. The two saw eye to

---

*Mao's eating habits were curious. His favorite breakfast—when he could get it—was American oatmeal with condensed milk, two eggs beaten up in the oatmeal.

eye on the Revolution and worked hand in hand.

Young people like Mao and Kaihui flouted China's social customs. They poked fun at traditional marriage. Mao's best friend and fellow revolutionary, Cai Hesen, and Xiang Jingyu, a young Hunan woman whom many came to regard as the spirit of the revolution, fell in love on shipboard going to France in 1919. They got married—in their own fashion. They had a wedding gathering in Paris and took a wedding picture showing the young couple with a volume of Karl Marx's *Das Kapital* in the foreground and the Chinese characters "Xiang" and "Cai" written below—a magnificent pun. The characters of their names could be translated "Upward Alliance." Everyone noted in surprise and approval that the bride's character preceded that of the groom.[17] No one in the Revolution came to more tragic ends than this couple. Xiang was arrested in the French concession in Hankou and turned over to the KMT, who executed her at 4 A.M. on the morning of May 1, 1928. Cai was arrested in Hongkong in 1931 and turned over to the KMT. They spread-eagled him, nailed him against a wall, bludgeoned him to death, and cut his chest and stomach to pieces.[18]

Mao and Kaihui's gesture against traditional marriage rites was more subdued than that of their friends. They simply announced they were having a "trial marriage." It was to last for many years. Kaihui bore three sons: Mao Anying, born in 1922, was a handsome, talented man, who was killed by a U.S. bomb in Korea in 1950; Mao Anqing, born in 1923, still lived in Beijing in 1984, married to a woman named Shao Hua. A third son, Mao Anlang, was born in Wuhan in 1927.[19]

Mao left Yang Kaihui in Changsha when he embarked on the Autumn Harvest Uprising in 1927, and they never saw each other again. Kaihui was seized by KMT troops in late October 1930. She was arrested at a house where she was staying in the eastern suburbs of Changsha. Her son Anying was arrested with her and both were taken to prison. She was asked to denounce Mao. She refused and was put to torture. This may have been in Anying's presence. She was executed by a firing squad on November 14, 1930, outside the Liuyan Gate of Changsha. A nurse, Chen Yuting, brought the boy home. Mao's stepsister (actually his cousin), Mao Zejian, working in the underground, had been arrested earlier, and executed August 20, 1929, at Hengshan. There was no connection between the two deaths except for their relationship to Mao. However, the death of Kaihui was directly connected with an abortive attack on Changsha carried out by Mao under the instructions of the Comintern in September 1930. After Mao's forces were driven out, the KMT governor rounded up many Communists and Communist suspects in Changsha and shot them, Yang Kaihui among them.[20]

Mao's sons passed into the care of an aunt, according to a wall poster put up during the Cultural Revolution. For a time they were in the care of a Christian clergyman. The children were taken to Shanghai and entered in a school under the secret guardianship of the Communist Party. But the school was exposed and the police drove the children into the streets. The Mao boys lived on the sidewalks, supporting themselves by begging and selling newspapers. They slept in doorways and an old temple, where they posted a sign saying: "We tell stories—one penny." The youngsters were finally rescued and taken to Yan'an.

Mao had seen little of Kaihui in the years before their separation— they often worked in different places—but her memory burned deeper and deeper in Mao's consciousness as the years passed. In 1957 he published a haunting poem called "The Immortals," dedicated to Kaihui: "I lost my proud poplar . . . tears fly down from the great upturned bowl of rain."[21]

Mao and He Zizhen met at Jinggangshan in 1927. She was a vivid revolutionary, just out of Fuyin missionary high school (*fuyin* means "good news")—slim, energetic, a fine student, throwing her life into the Revolution. She had already fought in a local harvest uprising before she joined Mao on the mountain.

Not only was He Zizhen a revolutionary (she joined the Communist Party in 1926 at the age of sixteen);[22] her whole family was engaged in the cause, impelled by her father, a small businessman, owner of a teahouse, a patriot and an advocate of change. When the Communists abandoned Jiangxi and headed off on the Long March, He Zizhen's father was among the first to be slaughtered in the Nationalist reprisals. The He family lived in Huangzhuling, Yongxin county, north of Jinggangshan and within the zone of Red Army operations. He Zizhen's mother, an intelligent, capable person, managed the household. From 1927 onward the rest of the family plunged into revolutionary work. He Zizhen's four brothers took a role in the Revolution. One was killed while acting as an underground courier. A younger sister, He Yi, joined the Party in 1927 and married Mao's younger brother, Zetan. She was killed in an automobile accident in 1950 while searching in Fujian for Xiao Mao, son of Mao and He Zizhen, born in Ruijin in 1930 and left behind with He Yi and Zetan. After Zetan's death He Yi placed the boy with a peasant family in Fujian. The child was never found.

The parents of He Zizhen gave her the delicate and poetic name of Guiyan which is associated with the Autumn Festival, the season of her birth. Its literal meaning is dragon's eye, a kind of fruit similar to lichi. As she grew to adolescence she felt that dragon's eye was "too soft" a name and changed it to Zizhen, meaning "precious child." She became a beautiful young woman, fair skin, clear eyes, vivacious, well grounded in the classics and ancient Chinese poets. She was one of the earliest women in school to embrace revolutionary causes and led her classmates in cutting off their long braids and in toppling the figure of Buddha from a temple shrine. With a rich strong voice, she was unmatched in oratory throughout the county. She was one of the first in Yongxin to be put on the wanted list by the KMT. She took a leading role in the January 27, 1927, uprising of three counties, in which twenty-eight Communists held in jail, including her elder brother, were rescued from certain execution. He Zizhen's comrades possessed only a few old rifles, but they made so much noise they carried the day. (Wang's gang of Jinggangshan bandits participated in this operation.)

He Zizhen was in the Jinggangshan area and followed Mao up the mountain. Soon she was engaged in dangerous missions behind the lines, once saving herself from arrest by pretending to be a dying patient in a peasant's house. Another time she saved Mao and Zhu De from an ambush while on a reconnaissance mission. She leaped on a horse, pistol in each hand, and galloped off for a dozen miles, diverting the enemy's attention and giving Mao and Zhu a chance to escape.

Exploits like this brought her renown in guerrilla ranks. He Zizhen fought shoulder to shoulder with her male comrades in many of the early engagements on Jinggangshan.[23]

Mao and He Zizhen began living together on Jinggangshan shortly after their meeting in 1927, but there would be no formal marriage until after the death of Yang Kaihui in 1930. Their first child, a daughter, was born in Fujian, across the border from Jiangxi province, where Mao was confined on a mountaintop from July to October of 1929 with an attack of malaria. The exact date and place of the birth are not known. It may have been Gutian in Longyan county.

Mao's base in south Jiangxi and southwest Fujian was not yet well established, and once he recovered from malaria he was quickly on the move. The child was given to peasants to be cared for. In 1932 Mao looked for the girl but was unable to find her. This was at the time of the battle of Zhangzhou High School, south of the area where the child had been left. Another child was born in Ruijin in 1932, the boy Xiao Mao, left behind on the Long March. In 1933 He Zizhen had a premature boy, delivered by Dr. Nelson Fu. The child did not live. Now He Zizhen was moving westward, pregnant again. Mao did his best to protect her under the hardships of the March. After the Red Army had forced its way through the first and second of Chiang Kaishek's blockade lines, Mao sent his number one bodyguards, Wu Jiqing and Wang Yatang, to look after He Zizhen. Mao was unable to join his wife, although they were located not far apart in the column, she in the convalescent unit, he with the cadres.[24]

Mao was a devout supporter of women's rights and women's equality from his earliest days as a student radical. One of his first important articles was devoted to this question. He coined the expression "Women hold up half the heavens." But he was not in charge of the Long March, and the life of the thirty women cadres of the main force started out like a trip into some minor Hades. Whoever was in charge made a mess of things. Everything went wrong. There was quarreling among the women and quarreling between men and women. Many early problems concerned basic questions—allotment and transport of food, who would carry the rice and who would cook it and how much. The women were young, but not many were strong peasants like Kang Keqing. Walking all day or all night up and down stony mountain trails, up three thousand feet, down two thousand, up another three thousand, across a rough three-mile pass, and then doing it all over again—well, they just did not have the muscles.

Bo Gu's wife thought her experience was typical. She was twenty-seven when the March started, a working-class woman whose grandfather collected human excrement and sold it to peasant farmers. She had been sold as a child to an engineer who wanted a wife for his son. She was eleven. At fourteen, she ran away and got a factory job, six days a week and sixteen hours a day. She joined the Communist Party before the 1927 Shanghai massacre, was sent to Russia, spent four years there, married Bo Gu, and had been working in the Central Soviet Area for a year.

She had two children, a boy born in Moscow and a girl born in Shanghai, and was pregnant with a third when a piece of shrapnel hit her in the head during an air raid a month before the March. She miscarried and was more or less recovered by October 14, 1934, when she walked with the others out of Ruijin.

There was nothing beautiful about the early stages, as she remembered in talking about it three or four years later.

"Marching was very difficult," she said. "My feet were so sore I had to wash them in hot water every day."

Because of bad organization, the women didn't get enough food. They were hungry all the time. Men claimed the women got better treatment than they did and didn't carry their fair share of the rice bags. "So there was a quarrel between the sexes," Bo Gu's wife commented.

A reorganization was tried out. The women were placed in a separate unit, with Bo Gu's wife as captain and Li Bozhao, wife of General Yang Shangkun, in charge of the commissary. Strict discipline was imposed, no lagging. Things worked much better.[25] But as minute Wei Xiuying concluded: "It was much harder for women. Every day we were in difficulties. Every day we had a hard time."

Little Liu Ying, brought back from Yudu by Mao Zedong, found herself assigned to Echelon Three of the Central Column (the convalescent unit, where most of the women marched, was Echelon Two).

Echelon Three was logistics. Here were five thousand men carrying the heavy loads of printing presses, money-making equipment, stamping machines, the tools for making guns and bullets. The men in Echelon Three, for the most part, were new recruits or nonrecruits. Some of those carrying the burdens were in the Army, some were not. Their tasks were impossible. Even when the presses and machine tools were taken apart, it took six men to carry a gear, a casing, or a drill. The paths were seldom wide enough for more than two people. Much of the marching was at night. Rain fell. The footing was like grease. Torches could not be lighted because enemy troops were close. Again and again, bearers and their burdens plunged off the thousand-foot cliffs and were lost.

Within a day or two of the start, the bearers began to slip away, going back home. Their morale was low. They saw themselves marching deeper and deeper into strange and dangerous mountains. They would never find their way back to Jiangxi. When darkness fell they silently vanished. It was a hemorrhage which the tiny Liu Ying and the others somehow had to halt. The truth was they couldn't.

Fifty years later, Liu Ying conceded with a wry smile that "it was a very tough job."[26]

The loads were so heavy and the paths so twisting and difficult that in a night of marching the bearers might cover little more than a mile and a half or two miles. The supply column lagged farther and farther behind. Combat troops, including the Fourth Shock Regiment, the assault team that was to become famous for its impossible exploits, had to protect the lumbering baggage train from Chiang Kai-shek's troops. It was like a scene from a bad Western movie. The Indians were coming closer and closer and there was no Seventh Cavalry to ride to the rescue.

Liu Ying marched with the bearers and during their rest periods tried to encourage them and raise their morale. She was supposed to implant revolutionary fervor in the exhausted, homesick, half-fed, and often bewildered men.

"It was hard to recruit transporters," she recalled. "They were hard to hire and hard to recruit. Many of them injured their backs and shoulders, became weak and ill. They were afraid that if they went on with us there would be reprisals on them or their families."

Not even the spun-steel spirit of Liu Ying could counterbalance the weary agony of the transport men. Heavy loads began to be jettisoned. There weren't enough strong backs to carry it all. Something would have to be done.[27]

None of the thirty women cadres died on the Long March, but it is hard to share the opinion expressed by Li Yimang that they did little on the March. The evaluation of Li Bozhao, herself a participant and a survivor, seems closer to the mark. At the age of seventy-three, she spoke reverently of her women comrades, the heroines and martyrs of the Revolution.

She talked of Cai Chang. Cai Chang was the daughter of a distinguished Chinese family. She descended from the famous military commander Zeng Guofan, who broke the force of the Taiping Rebellion on June 1, 1864, slaughtering 100,000 Taipings in Nanjing. Cai's mother was a woman of remarkable personal and political resolution. At the age of fifty she divorced her husband, a well-to-do merchant, and entered primary school to complete her education. She strongly influenced her children to become Communists. Cai Chang carried a worn snapshot of her mother every step of the Long March.[28]

There was no more revolutionary family in China than that of Cai Chang. She attended the famous Zhounan women's normal school, funded by Zhu Jianfan, a very rich landlord. "Today he would be called a 'democratic personality,' " Li Rui observed. He was quite radical and turned over many houses and gardens for the school's use. His daughter, Zhu Zhongli, would later marry the wounded Wang Jiaxiang, and another daughter would marry Xiao Jingguang, first commander of the Red Navy. Another student was Xiang Jingyu, who married Cai Chang's brother Hesen.

Cai Chang and her brother went to Paris in March 1919 in the first work-study program sponsored by Cai Hesen and Mao. Their program was to "furiously read and furiously translate." Their mother went too. She had raised six hundred dollars from a relative to cover the costs. Cai Hesen may have been the first Chinese student to opt for Communism, strongly influenced by the emerging French Communist movement. He and Zhou Enlai founded the European branch of the Chinese Communist Party. Cai Chang joined in 1923. Her brother wielded great influence on Mao Zedong. They were fellow Hunanese and classmates. Cai Hesen and Mao carried on an intensive correspondence while Cai was in Europe and Mao remained in China. Cai Chang, Cai Hesen, and Mao were close, close friends. They once swore a triple oath not to marry; none of the three kept it.[29]

When Helen Snow met Cai Chang in Yan'an in 1937, three of her family had been executed by Chiang Kai-shek and two were in prison. She was engaged in underground missions into Nationalist territory, where exposure meant certain death. She was then as she would be throughout her life an exquisite woman with a lively face, and a slightly lisping accent as she spoke French. Only when you looked deep into her brown eyes did you see the sadness.[30]

There were no complaints from Cai Chang on the Long March. She had, as Li Bozhao said, a strong will. She rarely rode the horse that had been provided for her. She gave it to others, whom she judged more in need, the wounded and the ill. She was twenty-four years old and of slight build, but she climbed up and down the Five Ridges with no complaint. She and Liu Ying traveled together and she, like Liu Ying, tried to raise the spirit of the men on the winding paths of the *Chang Zheng,* the March of 25,000 li. Kang Keqing called Cai Chang's stories and jokes "spiritual food."

"Why do I speak of Cai Chang?" asked Li Bozhao. "Because she commanded the respect and love of the women—and of us all."

In 1984 Cai Chang was living in Beijing at the age of eighty-four. Her health was poor and she had lost her sight. But she carried on her work as best she could. If the Long March possessed a saint, it was she.

9

THE FIRST BIG BATTLE

T HE Red Army won the first three battles of the Long March without difficulty. It penetrated the three lines of fortifications that Chiang Kai-shek had erected to prevent their escape from the "red corner" of Jiangxi. But as General Qin Xinghan of the National Military Museum pointed out fifty years later, the Long March was not just guns and bullets; it was three battles all in one—the battle with Chiang and his regional warlords, the battle against nature and the elements, and, key of keys, the battle within the Communist Party, the battle of leader against leader and policy against policy.

It is not always easy to discover which element has been decisive in victory or defeat, particularly in this case, where as General Qin mused, "Even today many things are not clear."

In the Long March there would never be a moment when the mountains, the cliffs, the turbulent streams, treacherous blizzards, icy rain, snow, fog, scorching deserts, bottomless bogs, hunger, endless marches, would not confront the soldiers with perils beyond those of Chiang's bullets. And behind this *sturm und drang,* invisible to most fighting men, went on a deadly struggle within the high command over policy, power, personality.

The commanders of the Red Army were men of skill and tempering. They had spent years in guerrilla warfare. They had fought together in campaign after campaign. They knew the land and they knew the people. They knew the enemy. They knew their own strengths and weaknesses. Lin Biao's First Army Group was superlative at surprise attack and ambushes. No one surpassed Peng Dehuai and his Third Army Group at frontal assaults, hand-to-hand combat. They had all learned the deceptions and stratagems by which they could outwit a superior foe. They moved with speed, appearing on the scene when the enemy thought them far distant. They traveled light and lived off the land. They were very young, of sturdy peasant stock, strong muscles, resilient. They climbed up and ran down the Five Ridges like mountain goats. They could walk all day and half the night and after a few hours' sleep—or even no sleep at all—fight and win a battle.

The Red Army men were extraordinarily motivated. They fought for a cause to which they gave full dedication. They subjected themselves to every peril. But the new recruits who had been brought into the Army in the recruiting drive of spring and summer 1934 were different. They had been signed up so rapidly that they had little military preparation or indoctrination. They had not been told where they were going or what they were going to do—in part, perhaps, because the high command was not certain itself.

Whatever the reason, a price was paid. Unmotivated men began to drop behind from the beginning. Some were stragglers who could not keep up the pace. More were voting with their feet, as was said of the peasant soldiers who drifted back home from the Russian army on the eve of the 1917 Revolution. The Chinese simply started to walk home before they got so far they couldn't hope to find the way back.

By its standards, the Red Army started the Long March quite well armed. It had 33,243 rifles, carbines, pistols, submachine guns, light machine guns, and heavy machine guns. Of that total, 651 weapons were light and heavy machine guns. It possessed 38 mortars and a few artillery pieces, basically mountain guns. The artillery was discarded very early. They brought along a store of 1,801,640 cartridges, 2,523 mortar shells, and 76,526 hand grenades.[1]

This was a formidable force, but it was opposed by one many times larger. The Red Army commanders calculated that Chiang Kai-shek had mustered about 100 regiments, between 300,000 and 400,000 men, against them. Liu Bocheng, the one-eyed dragon, put the number at 400,000. Mo Wenhua of the Eighth Army gave the number as 300,000 to 400,000, "at a rough estimate." Hu Yaobang, general secretary of the Communist Party in 1984, an eighteen-year-old Red Army youth leader in 1934, estimated the KMT's top force at 300,000.[2]

As soon as Chiang Kai-shek realized the scope of the Red Army's movement, he began to organize a force to contain it. He ordered two of his reliable Central Army generals, Xue Yue and Zhou Hunyuan, on October 30 to bring forward four divisions and attack the Red Army in coordination with a southern column from Guangdong and a western column led by the Hunan warlord He Jian.

Two weeks later he refined his plans. He gave He Jian the title of commander in chief and proposed that he, in collaboration with Xue Yue and Zhou Hunyuan, entrap and wipe out the Red Army at the Xiang River, which flows south to north across Guangxi into Hunan. These generals had, among them, fifteen divisions, or about seventy regiments. Chiang called on the warlords of Guangxi and Guangdong, who had another thirty-odd regiments, to assist in boxing in the Red Army in a triangle in front of the Xiang River, about eighty by thirty miles in dimension, based on the towns of Quanzhou, Xingan, and Guanyang.

This was one of Chiang's better schemes—if it would work. The regional warlords, in engaging the Red Army in costly combat, would be weakened, giving Chiang a better chance to take them over.

The Red Army had no way of concealing its objective. It had to plow ahead and cross the Xiang River. And soon after it crossed the Xiang, it had to veer north to join He Long and the Second Front Army in western Hunan. One look at the map told Chiang Kai-shek the Red Army's course. It was following the path taken two months earlier by the Sixth Army, when it passed this way to join He Long.

As Yu Qiuli—the PLA political director in 1984 and in 1934 a twenty-year-old peasant soldier in the Sixth Army—recalled, the Sixth circled around to Dao Xian and then marched straight west to cross the river near Xingan. "There was very little trouble," Yu Qiuli remembered. "We occupied a hilltop after some fighting. We crossed the hill and got to the river. There was a pontoon bridge. We crossed on that and were over the river by dusk. I remember the soldiers had very high morale."[3]

Had a quiet word been dropped to the warlords of Guangdong and Guangxi? There is no hard evidence, but the Sixth Army drew not the ghost of a response from the Guangxi side. It was just as if someone had said: "We just want to borrow your roads for a bit." (And perhaps someone had said just that.)

The fourth blockhouse line, at the Xiang River, lay within the territory controlled by Bai Chongxi, the fiercely anti-Communist warlord of Guangxi. Fierce as was Bai Chongxi's hatred of the Communists, his number one priority was self-defense. He was not going to be lured into a position in which Chiang would be able to undermine and throw him out.

Was there another quiet "arrangement" to ease the way of the Red

Army across the Xiang River and up into the forbidding Five Ridges of the Guangxi-Hunan border just ahead?

No one has come forward with a tale as specific as that of Zhou's secret dealings with the Guangdong dictator, Chen Jitang, but the evidence suggests that an understanding existed with the Guangxi warlords, Bai Chongxi and Li Zongren. Xu Mengqiu, the first Red Army historian, stated this in 1938. He said the Guangxi leaders had "promised to leave an area open," a thirteen-mile-wide corridor between Jieshou and Quanzhou on the Xiang River, some sixty to seventy miles west of Dao Xian. "The theory of the corridor does hold water," Hu Hua, the leading Party historian in Beijing, has concluded. He believes the existence of this "corridor" is vital to understanding the battle at the Xiang River. The Red Army held the crossings for a week. It could not have done so if Guangxi had put the heat on. Yan Jingtang, defense ministry researcher, and his chief, General Qin Xinghan, do not use the word "corridor," but concede that an "area" was left vacant by the unusual movements of the Guangxi troops which facilitated the Red Army's crossing of the river.[4]

He Jian took overall command of Chiang Kai-shek's forces on November 14, 1934. Xue Yue, the principal KMT general, moved along the right or northern flank of the Communists, paralleling them as they went west and blocking them from the north. Behind the Communists came Zhou Hunyuan, harrying them along.[5]

The Red Army hustled toward the Xiang River in its familiar box formation. The First Army Group, led by Lin Biao, and the Third Army Group, led by Peng Dehuai, pushed ahead on an almost direct course. The Ninth Army was just ahead of the lumbering Central Column, now a bit lightened. Bearers had deserted. Burdens had been discarded, including theatrical costumes and scenery.

The Eighth Army, in which many new summer recruits were concentrated, marched to the left of the Central Military Commission column, where were to be found most of the leading military figures— Bo Gu, Otto Braun, Zhou Enlai, Zhe De, Luo Fu, Mao Zedong.

Behind the command group came the bedraggled porters, some of them Red Army men assigned for disciplinary reasons, including a few degraded officers and possibly some military prisoners.

Bringing up last was the faithful, durable Fifth Army, the rear guard, whose duty, in the words of Interpreter Wu Xiuquan, was to fend off the "courtyard curs" of the KMT, the jackals who harassed the slow supply column.

"The enemy was pressing, circling, blocking, and harassing," Wu Xiuquan recalled.[6]

Three or four of Chiang's divisions were racing the Red Army for the Xiang River city of Quanzhou at the north end of the "corridor," an old walled city on the boundary of Guangxi and Hunan. When Red Army scouts neared its walls, they saw that the Nationalists (He Jian's troops) had already occupied it.

This provoked a squabble in the high command: Should they attack Quanzhou or shift south and cross the Xiang River at another spot?[7]

The Red Army was converging on the Xiang River within the iron triangle that—although they did not know this—had been set aside by Chiang Kai-shek as their killing grounds. It began in the south just above Guilin, that strange land of conical stone and mist so beloved by China's painters, shrine of beauty-lovers and poets.

The landscape was dominated by a forest of stone morels, great blind rocks reaching up through the clouds and ascending to heaven. The valley of the Xiang always had been the major pass from Guangxi to Hunan. Its geological formation was limestone in which wind and water had carved deep rivers and magical hills.

The stone ghosts of Guilin march along the course of the Xiang to Lingchuan, just south of Xingan, the southern marker of the Red Army's corridor. Then the riverbanks turn to hard granite and the gnomes' cones vanish except that here and there they suddenly intrude into the stately granite landscape like wandering spirits in search of a resting place.

This is historic ground. Here is to be found the canal named Ling, built two hundred years before Christ under China's first emperor to connect the rivers Xiang and Li and thus, remarkably, provide a continuous inland water path from Shanghai on the Yangtze to Canton on the Pearl River. In 1984 it was still busily carrying traffic.

In this valley of the moon the first great battle of the Long March took shape.

Almost certainly the Red Army would have slashed across the Xiang and through Chiang Kai-shek's fourth and last blockhouse line had it not been for the unwieldy, unwise, unnecessary baggage train stretching fifty miles behind. Despite losing the race to Quanzhou, the Red vanguard got across the Xiang south of Quanzhou on November 25. Units of the First and Third armies were across by November 26. Just at that time the Guangxi warlord, Bai Chongxi, moved his troops south from Xingan, ostensibly to protect Guilin but actually leaving the corridor open for the Red Army from Xingan to Quanzhou. On the evening of November 27, advance units of the Third and First Army Groups were crossing the Xiang with not much opposition, side by side. Following them, the Ninth came behind the First and the Eighth behind the Third. The central column was between and behind. The major crossing points were Jieshou and Juezhanpu. The river was so shallow that most men just waded over.

The whole force should have been over the river in two or three days, with nominal losses. But the sluggish behemoths of the supply train and the awkwardness of new, untrained troops changed the picture.

All went well in the preliminary stages, as the young political commissar of the Fourth Regiment of the Second Division of Lin Biao's First Army Group could attest. Yang Chengwu was a youngster when the Long March began. He had been fighting, much of the time with guerrillas, since he left his peasant home in Fujian province at seventeen to join the Red Army. The Red Army would become his education, his career, his life.

At seventy, Yang was in 1984 younger-looking than his age, a few streaks of gray in his black hair, wearing dark-blue jacket and trousers of military cut, precise and easy in his recollections. No groping for words; a moonlike face vaguely resembling that of the late Chairman Mao. He began by saying: "I was twenty when I started the Long March and twenty-one when we reached the end. For me it lasted exactly one year and two days."

The first big battle for the Fourth Regiment was at Xiang River. During a pause at a small town called Decitang, about fifty miles east of Dao Xian, a county seat just west of the Xiao River, Yang's regiment got an urgent message to advance as fast as possible, seize Dao Xian and the river crossing ahead of the KMT. The town controlled a mountain pass, critical to the approaches to the Xiang. It had to be secured by the next morning.

"Time was oppressively short," Yang recalled. "Even as we gave the orders the troops started moving." On the way they met a group of peasants, who said there was a pontoon bridge across the Xiao at Dao Xian, made of fishing boats lashed together. If it was drawn up on the far side, the Fourth Regiment could send swimmers across and bring it back.

Five miles from Dao Xian, three KMT planes appeared. The men dove under cover so rapidly the planes did not spot them. By dusk they had reached the outskirts of Dao Xian. A high wall and deep moat protected the town. At midnight a platoon of swimmers was sent over the river. They seized the boats and by daybreak the vanguard had entered the city and captured the Catholic church.

Commissar Yang Chengwu walked down the main street, now filling with people, and heard two old men talking. One with a beard asked a beardless companion: "How did they win the battle? They have so few bullets." The other replied: "They can walk 1,000 li by day and 800 at night. Their bodies are bulletproof. They don't need any bullets to fight with."

Yang went on to the city temple, a Daoist shrine. Red Army propagandists were preparing for a mass meeting. There would be speeches. Food and clothing seized from the wealthy would be handed out to the poor. Ordinary people, Yang observed, had helped the Red Army. Without them, the city could not have been captured.[8]

Before dawn the next morning Yang Chengwu and his shock regiment were racing forward to the Xiang River. They crossed it with no trouble.

But now a dichotomy began to emerge. Reports of Yang Chengwu and many like him spoke of an easy crossing, few casualties.

But a bloody battle was building up for laggard elements. This was the battle as seen by Mo Wenhua, director of propaganda in the Political Department of the Eighth Army Group, advancing beyond Dao Xian to the Xiang twenty-four hours behind the fast-moving shock elements. To Mo Wenhua, the situation quickly became critical. The enemy was closing in, KMT planes bombing the columns and showering down leaflets proclaiming: "Communist bandits! The high command ordered that we wait for you. We are waiting. Hurry up! We beg you. We beg you. We have fixed up a dandy little trap for you."

Mo knew what that meant—another bitter battle. The Eighth was under orders to make a forced march to the Xiang River from Dao Xian. They were not to halt, just bull their way through. The Xiang was about seventy miles distant. A KMT column was racing parallel to them only eight miles to the north. The KMT poured down "a leaden rain," but the Eighth surged ahead.

Just after nightfall, moving into the mountains, the Eighth paused at the town of Shuiche, an oasis of Guilin mountain landscapes, known in all south China. Before dawn the troops had left. "Regrettably," wrote Mo Wenhua, "we had neither the time nor the possibility to do our duty by these sights."

The Eighth plowed ahead in the wake of the Ninth Army and was followed by the Thirty-fourth Division, which got deeper and deeper into trouble. The forward units were breaking through the last of the KMT blockhouses, constructed according to German engineering, of concrete and reinforced steel, impervious to machine gun fire. Red Army blockhouses were built of wood, reinforced with mud and vulnerable to almost anything, including a heavy rain. They had one advantage. They were surrounded with moats and staggered rows of sharpened bamboo sticks, to pierce the feet of ill-shod soldiers. (The same weapon was used by the North Vietnamese against the Americans.)

To neutralize a blockhouse, the Red Army men had to sneak up to the walls and lob grenades through the portholes. The task of the Red Army was to knock out these fortifications and then pass over the Xiang. The river was not a great obstacle. At the fords, of which there were several, the river was about three hundred feet wide but not more than waist-deep. The water was cold and swift, but it could be forded by resolute soldiers.

As the Eighth Army advanced, the men could hear the crossfire of the Thirty-fourth Division behind it, defending Shuiche. From ahead came the sounds of battle, where the main force was crossing the Xiang. A few hours later they again heard the sounds of battle from the Thirty-fourth Division. It was the last time they would hear them. The division perished in this battle, except for the commander and a few stragglers.

For a time the Eighth pushed forward in startling silence. The silence was broken by the chatter of machine guns. Mo Wenhua was marching at the head of the column. The commander fell dead at the first burst. The enemy was in deep forest on hills on either side. The Ninth Army had passed just ahead without encountering enemy fire. Obviously, the Guangxi troops had arrived within the hour's interval. It was three o'clock in the afternoon. A flight of KMT planes appeared not a thousand feet above the column. The troops pushed on. The planes leveled their machine guns, but the soldiers did not halt. The planes flew so low the men could see that the bomb racks were empty. Dusk was falling. The exhausted men stumbled on, asleep on their feet. It was almost dawn when Mo Wenhua saw twinkling lights—a bivouac of Red Army rear troops at a dike along the river.

So it appeared. But Mo saw no pickets, no guard posts, heard no challenges. It was a phantom detachment of a few scouts. The campfires were to persuade the enemy that a large force was protecting the crossing. Mo heard a horse neigh. It was his own. His orderly had waited there for his arrival.

As the sun rose, Mo looked about. Scattered in all directions were books and papers—military manuals, maps, books on strategy, the agrarian question, problems of the Chinese revolution, works on political economy, on Marxism, Leninism, pamphlets, books in English, French, and German. The library under which Red Army bearers had staggered all the way from Ruijin lay here, pages torn, books muddy, bindings crushed. "All our ideological armory, all our military literature," Mo recalled, "had been tossed aside."

If Mo Wenhua had looked carefully, he might have found the reading copies of the plays that Li Bozhao, wife of General Yang Shangkun, discarded as she lightened her burdens at the Xiang River. Everything went. From then on, any plays that the Red Army presented would be brand-new. Li Bozhao, a tiny woman, had trouble crossing the Xiang. She was not tall enough to wade. The water came over her head. Liu Bocheng, the one-eyed dragon, had a mule. He let Li Bozhao hang on to its tail and paddle across.[9]

Without sleep and without food, the men moved on. Planes appeared at 8 A.M. The KMT had moved its base forward to Hengyang, only one hundred miles away, and kept the Communists under almost constant attack. The columns advanced under strafing fire. There was no alternative. If they halted they could not make the crossing in time —they would be killed or captured. They could be killed now or killed later. So they went ahead. "There is nothing more difficult than to advance under the fire of aircraft," Mo observed. "But we could no longer think about ourselves or our lives. We saw our comrades falling under the enemy fire. The planes could kill and wound some of us; they could make our progress more difficult; they could take some of our lives; but they could not win the battle."

Onward they went. But when they reached the Xiang, they were not permitted to cross the river. The Red Army had fallen into peril, and a new battle—one for survival—was under way.[10]

In later years, Nie Rongzhen, political commissar of the First Front Army, would look back on November 30 and December 1, 1934, as the most dangerous days of the Long March. The first-class units of the First and Third Army Groups had gotten successfully across the Xiang River. But time had run out. The slow-moving command column, the sick, the wounded, the women, and the baggage train had not yet crossed.

The timely withdrawal of Bai Chongxi had left the Xiang River fords open to the Red Army. Now it was all changing. He Jian had gotten four divisions up to attack the Red Army's northern flank.

And—most alarming—Bai Chongxi had joined in the fray to prove to Chiang Kai-shek that he was doing his duty.

This found the Red Army in the classic position of military peril—its forces divided, one half on either side of the river. He Jian's attacks began November 28. The fighting in the next three days was as heavy as the Red Army would see in the whole Long March.[11]

Yang Chengwu's Fourth Regiment and the Fifth Regiment were ordered to face north and protect the Central columns from He Jian's Hunan forces commanded by Liu Jianxu. The KMT was attacking south along the Hunan-Guizhou road. Yang Chengwu placed one battalion on either side of the road. At the height of the battle he was wounded in the right knee. Several soldiers were wounded trying to rescue him. Finally, he managed to crawl over the highway and his bodyguard "Little Bai" carried him to safety and, after some argument and threatening to shoot a stretcher team, got him to safety.

There was no more able, reliable, responsible commander in the Red Army than Nie Rongzhen. In 1934 he was thirty-five years old, an "old man," a senior of the Red Army who had come from a rich peasant family near Chongqing to join a work-study group in France in 1920. He worked at the Schneider munitions plant in Belgium and studied Marxism with Mao's good friend Li Fuchun. Nie Rongzhen had spent time at Moscow's Red Military Academy and at the Whampoa Academy in Canton. He was not a man to panic. He came up to the Xiang River with the First Army Group, went across November 26 after the vanguard had moved to the west side, watched the dangerous straddling of the river and understood the implications when he got orders to protect the crossing sites and hold off the KMT until the two central columns and the bulk of Red Army forces had gotten across.

All day long on November 30 the battle raged. The whole army group was involved and gradually it was forced back to its second line of defenses. It was at this time that Commissar Yang Chengwu of the vanguard Fourth Regiment was wounded. Fortunately, he was back in service after ten days.

Nie Rongzhen was not able to sleep that night. He could think of nothing but the peril to the main Red Army forces. He, Lin Biao, and the other commanders spent hours going over the situation. Sometime before midnight November 30, they telegraphed the Central Military Commission:

> Chairman Zhu [De]:
> . . . If the enemy attacks tomorrow with their superior position we cannot guarantee that we can hold out with our available equipment and existing level of troop capability. The Central Military Commission must move all troops on the east side over the Xiang River today. The first and second divisions will continue to resist the enemy tomorrow.

An answer was returned at 3:30 A.M. December 1. It was sent in the name of the entire high military apparatus. The instruction was explicit: The First Army Group must hold on.

> The battle of December 1 will affect our whole army. To be able to move westward will open the path to future development. Any delay will cause our army to be cut up by the enemy. The leaders and commanders of the First and Third armies must go to the companies for pre-battle mobilization. Make all soldiers and officers understand the significance of today's battle: either we win or we lose. . . .

The First Army clung to its positions during even heavier fighting on December 1. About noon it received news that the main forces and the central columns had finally crossed the Xiang.

Never in the history of the First Army had it been so endangered. For the first time in many, many years, First Army headquarters came under assault. Headquarters had been set up on a mountain slope. A bodyguard named Qiu Wenxi rushed in to report that the enemy was approaching.

Nie Rongzhen didn't believe it. The bodyguard must have made a mistake. He took a quick look. The guard was not mistaken. A KMT detachment with fixed bayonets was climbing the slope. Nie Rongzhen ordered the radio operators to disassemble their equipment and get away. He gathered the headquarters staff to repel the KMT assault team and ordered Liu Huishan, later to become head of the Central Committee Guards Regiment, to advise Liu Yalou (later air marshal), positioned farther down the slope, of the attack. As Liu Huishan ran down the mountainside, his straw sandals flapping, a bullet went through a sandal sole without touching Liu's foot.

"It was the strangest sight I've ever seen," Nie Rongzhen recalled fifty years later.

The First Army Group, Nie said, had to provide cover for the slow-moving central columns and also for the newly formed army groups, the Eighth and the Ninth in particular.

"We had to carry out tasks of our own and protect them," he said.[12]

This was a problem shared by many units. When the Eighth Army command (of which Mo Wenhua was propaganda chief) was halted on the east side of the Xiang River, it had to take over the rear-guard responsibility originally assigned to the Thirty-fourth Division, which, as Mo put it, "had taken a different route." In fact, the route to destruction. The Eighth Army vanguard had to wait beside the Xiang River until all the others had crossed. Then it splashed into the waist-deep icy water and crossed over. By that time it had suffered terrible losses.[13]

Late in the afternoon of December 1, an Eighth Army commander appealed to Nie Rongzhen for urgent assistance to help part of the Eighth, which had been cut off and left behind on the east side of the river. Nie Rongzhen had to tell him that nothing could be done now. Darkness was falling.

On December 2, Nie Rongzhen learned that the Young Communist International Division, commanded by Peng Shaohui and Political Commissar Xiao Hua had also been stranded on the east bank. The First Army command sent a rescue force back over the river. It failed.

"We were too slow and the enemy was too quick," Nie Rongzhen concluded. The Young Communist International Division was lost, the Thirty-fourth Division was lost, the Eighteenth Regiment of the Third Army Group was lost, and so were important elements of the Eighth Army. The losses in the First Army Group were severe. The First Division had a strength of 2,800 men at the start of the March. After Xiang it was down to 1,400.[14]

The battle of the Xiang was fought for a week—November 25 to December 3. By most accounts it was a disaster. "Although [the Red Army] finally crossed the Xiang River," wrote Liu Bocheng, "the price was dreadfully high. More than half the troops were lost." General Qin said the precise losses at each fortified line were not known. "Most serious were the losses at the Xiang River line," he said. "By the time the Red Army reached Zunyi (about a month later), there were little more than 30,000 left."

General Xiao Hua was political commissar of the Young Communist International Division, destroyed at the Xiang River. At sixty-eight, he was in 1984 a stocky, lively man with a shaven head which gave him a vague and unwelcome resemblance to Chiang Kai-shek. He wore a finely tailored uniform-cut jacket and trousers, but apologized, "I'm not wearing my uniform"—the dress in which he was most comfortable.

The Young Communist International Division was assigned as rearguard with Peng Dehuai's Third Army and lost well over half its strength of ten thousand young soldiers. Ultimately, the survivors were merged into the vanguard Fourth Regiment.[15]

The fragmentary and often conflicting accounts make clear that a great deal of equipment was tossed into the Xiang River—the X-ray machine and the plates that had been used to photograph Chen Yi's wound, most of the remaining heavier guns, possibly the heavier wireless transmitters and the generator.

The baggage train was enormously lightened, the number of porters reduced; mobility of the Army improved.

Peng Dehuai, in his memoirs, contrasts the "hard fighting" and "many difficulties" his Third Army encountered from the Guangxi forces as compared with the First Army, "on the right wing," which "fared better" with the Hunan troops.[16] There are many contradictions in the accounts. Chinese specialists contend the First and Third Armies were always on the left and right flank respectively. Actually, at the crossing site the Red Army forces were closely pressed together and normal orders of march became entangled.

There is disagreement among contemporary Chinese Party historians over how many troops were lost at the Xiang River and how many dropped out. No one is prepared to offer exact figures. If the Red Army lost forty to fifty thousand men in the first ten weeks of the March—and this is the average of the estimates—it seems reasonable to suppose that battle casualties must have been at least fifteen thousand, most of them at the Xiang.

The heaviest losses were registered in the new segments of the Army. Interpreter Wu Xiuquan estimated that fifty thousand men were added in the months just before leaving the Central Soviet Area.

Otto Braun calculated that one-half of the new recruits were lost by the time the Red Army crossed the Guizhou border, and 75 percent of the "reserves"—by which he meant the bearers whom it had been hoped to incorporate into the Army as they were relieved of porter duties. He said that the Twenty-first and Twenty-third Divisions of the Eighth Army and the Twenty-second of the Ninth Army were wiped out. In the veteran divisions, he claimed, losses were modest.[17]

After Xiang, Braun's absolute control of the military weakened. Zhou Enlai took matters more into hand. But Braun did not relinquish his prerogatives lightly. Zhou Zikun, commander of the Thirty-fourth Division, escaped from enemy encirclement and reported at headquarters. Braun summoned him and fired off a volley of curses: How had Zhou Zikun escaped while his men were lost? why had he not carried out his orders? why was his wife still with him when his division had perished?

Braun said Zhou Zikun should be court-martialed and shot. He ordered the bodyguards to bind him and haul him to the military court. The guards refused.

Bo Gu was present in the room. He sat silent. Mao was also there. When Braun burst out in wild rage, Mao stepped forward and, leading Zhou Zikun from the room, said: "I'll handle this."[18]

Otto Braun's memoirs devote little attention to the Xiang battle. He suggests that despite its losses the Red Army was strengthened by the battle, its fighting quality raised. He puts the principal blame on Zhou Enlai, who, he asserts, prepared the evacuation plan, which called for the removal from the Central Soviet Area of the extraordinary mass of heavy equipment that so burdened the army and slowed its pace. He does not concede that with his dominance over Bo Gu, Braun held veto power over all organizational and battle plans of the Long March.[19]

The battle-hard commanders of the Red Army emerged from the Xiang catastrophe with indignation and anger, which crystallized into powerful sentiment for change.

It would be said in the near future that the end of the rule of Otto Braun and Bo Gu was sounded by the last wavering shots as the Thirty-fourth Division was extinguished by the KMT, and in the wreckage of the great baggage train that littered the Red Army's path for one hundred miles.

10

THE RED ARMY CHANGES COURSE

WHEN the Red Army crossed over into Guizhou province, Scout Kong was in trouble. Each day he had to move far in advance of the Red Army, spy out the land, learn the enemy dispositions, size up the difficult mountains and rivers. Sometimes Scout Kong wore his uniform, more often he wore civilian clothes and tried to blur into the background. Kong Xianquan was born and brought up in Hunan. The moment he opened his mouth in next-door Guizhou, everyone knew he was a "foreigner." In Hunan he carried his bundles on a carrying pole like everyone else. Now he had to learn to wear a woven back basket as the Guizhou people did. If he gave himself away he would be shot.

It had been hard enough getting across the river Xiang. That had gone badly for the Red Army. One reason, as Scout Kong thought, was the use of pontoons. The horses and mules didn't like pontoons. They got frightened. Many had been lost. Movement had been snarled and the KMT bombed heavily while half the Red Army was on one side of the river and half was on the other.[1]

And it had been no picnic climbing Laoshan, the Old Mountain (*lao* means "old" and *shan* means "mountain"), as the natives called it, possibly five thousand feet high, a long steep climb up and a short steep climb down. The path was so narrow the soldiers had to climb in a single file. It was, they were told, 30 li up and 15 li down—nearly eight miles up and three and a half down. By now they understood the "flexible li." The Chinese li is the only unit of measurement that varies in accordance with its difficulty. An uphill li is only half as long as a downhill li. However the li was calculated, the Old Mountain proved a harsh climb. Darkness fell as the men were a quarter of the way up, Lu Dingyi recalled. They were hungry. They had no more dry rations. There was no way of cooking food. In the blackness something caused the column to halt. Time passed. Men fell asleep on their feet. Finally word came that ahead there was a perilous cliff. Some men and animals had plunged off. They would have to wait for daylight. Lu Dingyi's unit was just behind the Red Star Brigade, in which marched so many elderly and important cadres. After a night of fitful sleep, movement resumed. There had been no supper and there was to be no breakfast.

The number of wounded had vastly increased because of the Xiang River fighting. Many, many were being carried on litters. But when the men arrived at the cliff, the wounded, no matter how badly hurt, had to be taken from their stretchers and helped up narrow stone steps a foot wide cut in the cliffside called Leigong Yai, Thunder God Rock, which rose up at a ninety-degree angle. It was much too steep for bearers. Horses with broken legs lay in groaning heaps at the foot of the cliff. Slowly and painfully, the men were helped up the stone wall, one at a time; some were pushed, some were dragged by a rope. Not all made it. Leading horses up the mountain face was even more difficult. Some were lost and with them their hostlers. No one was more brave than the women of the Red Star Brigade, Lu Dingyi thought. Without their sturdy shoulders, many wounded would have been lost.[2]

Zeng Xianhui had never seen anything like it—the poverty of these mountains. Zeng was a poor peasant from Jiangxi, but as the Red Army began to move into the approaches to Guizhou, it entered regions no longer inhabited by Han—that is, Chinese people like the soldiers. They had come to the land of the Miao, a minority race that antedated the Hans and had been driven into these remote stony hills, there to live lives so poor that women could not emerge from their huts—they had no clothes. They sat huddled in nakedness beside straw cooking fires, with the smoke issuing from a hole in the roof. Girls of seventeen and eighteen worked naked in the fields. Many families had only one pair of trousers to share among three or four adult males. The Miao people were frightened by the Red Army, ran from their huts and hid in the mist of the mountains. To them an army meant robbery, rape, murder, the burning of houses, the theft of rice and millet.

This was opium country. Here, as Peasant Zeng observed, almost everyone of the age of fifteen and above smoked opium. They sat outside their huts puffing their pipes with glazed eyes, men, women, and teenagers. The men and teenagers often wore nothing but loincloths, the women not even that. The opium was piled up in brown stacks in the sheds like cow dung put to dry.[3] This was not the country of the placid water buffalo patiently plowing the rice paddies. Here the peasants pulled the wooden plows themselves or depended on bony "yellow cows"—*huangniu* as they were called—listless mongrels, sometimes ridden by young girls as they fitfully hauled the plow through gummy mud. Here the poor peasants—and all of them were poor—lived in houses made of mud and lath, with thatched roofs. Better houses were built of dark wood, with gray tile roofs and bird's-wing eaves. Here the *cao dui*, the haystacks, were cone-shaped like the hats of gnomes, and the camphor trees of Jiangxi gave way to parasol or tung oil trees.

Nothing was so bad as the opium. Guizhou was saturated with it. It deadened, drugged, and immobilized the naked poor and it drenched the local armies. The warlord troops of Guizhou were known as "two-gun men"—one was a rifle, the other an opium pipe.

In the arguments about where the Red Army should go, where its next move should be, opium played a persuasive role. The quality of most regional armies was low, but opium depressed the quality of the Guizhou armies to the depths.

Of Guizhou it was said that there were no three li without a mountain, no three days without rain, no man who possessed three silver dollars. This was almost true. The peasants were not slaves in the legal sense, but in many ways they were worse off than slaves. They owned no land. They were in debt to the landlord from birth to death. There was no escape. They sold their children if anyone would buy them. They smothered or drowned baby girls. That was routine. The boys were killed too, if there was no market for them. The price for children fluctuated. In 1983 an overseas Chinese who had been born in Guizhou came back to his native place. He had been sold as a seven-year-old to a middleman for five silver dollars, a very good price. The middleman exported him to Hongkong, where he was resold for four times as much. Eventually he escaped and made his way to the United States; he returned to Guiyang at the age of seventy-five.

The infant mortality rate in Guizhou in 1934 was about 50 percent. It was so high that a child's birth was not celebrated until it was at least a month old. Life expectancy was about thirty years. Poverty was so intense there was little difference between a landlord and a peasant, at least among the minority people like the Miao and the Dong. Illiteracy was total.[4]

Zhu De kept a notebook in which he jotted down impressions of the countryside. Of Guizhou he noted:

"Corn with bits of cabbage, chief food of people. Peasants too poor

to eat rice. . . . Peasants call selves 'dry men'—sucked dry of everything.
. . . Three kinds of salt: white for the rich; brown for the middle classes;
black salt residue for the masses. . . . Poor hovels with black rotting
thatch roofs everywhere. Small doors of cornstalks and bamboo. . . .
Have seen no quilts except in landlord houses in city. . . . People digging
rotten rice from ground under landlord's old granary. Monks call this
'holy rice'—gifts from Heaven to the poor."[5]

The poverty of the Guizhou countryside made problems for Peasant
Zeng Xianhui. Among his jobs as a cadre was to oversee the expropria-
tion of rich landlords and wealthy peasants. He didn't find many in
eastern Guizhou and the Red Army had strict regulations about minority people. They were to be handled with kid gloves because they had
been subjected to such exploitation by Han landlords. Peasant Zeng's
mind in 1984 still held images of people huddled half-naked in rags
along the roads and of passing out clothing he had confiscated from the
few landlords. As for opium, Peasant Zeng remembered opening up the
barns where the opium balls were kept and inviting the people to come
and take it. The Army had no need of opium, Zeng said. Zeng's recollection may not be entirely precise. Opium in this backward land was
wealth. Other Red Army men recalled using opium as currency to buy
supplies. It commonly circulated in Guizhou as a substitute for money.
Peasant Zeng was firm in his memory that the Red Army did not
destroy opium. "We opened the landlords' warehouses and invited the
peasants to take it on the grounds that it was produced by their sweat
and their labor and belonged to them," he said.[6]

From the moment the Long March started at the Yudu River, a slow
and subtle shift had been manifest in the Red Army's command. The
debate among commanders grew hotter with the disastrous battle of
the Xiang River. The consultations of Mao Zedong with Wang Jiaxiang
and Luo Fu intensified, and some of the generals began to talk quietly
with Mao. More and more commanders at lower levels were speaking
with concern and even alarm. It was obvious that there would have to
be a reorganization; the losses had been too heavy.
Zhou Enlai was an extraordinarily disciplined, even-tempered, and
conscientious Communist, and had never been known to challenge an
agreed Party decision, but now, for the first time—so far as is known—
he seemed to be losing patience with Otto Braun, and Braun, normally
totally insensitive, began to take note of this change.[7]

Once across the Xiang and up into the mountains, the Red Army was relieved of military pressure. The Guangdong and Guangxi armies had turned back, having made certain the Communists were not coming their way. The Nationalist forces under Xue Yue continued to move parallel to the Red Army, but were wary of offering battle. The Hunan troops seemed content to snap and snarl at the rear guard.

A curious incident occurred one night at Longpingzhen, a Miao county town in the Five Ridges. At about midnight, Wei Guolu, Zhou Enlai's bodyguard, was awakened by shouts of "Fire!" He heard the crackle of flames and dashed from his bed, to find the house occupied by Zhou afire. The bodyguard assisted Zhou out of the blazing building. People filled the street. Other leaders appeared, including state security director Deng Fa. There seemed no doubt that the fire was incendiary. Three men were arrested and executed on the spot, but night after night mysterious fires broke out in the Miao towns and villages where the Red Army encamped.[8] Whether the fires were set by KMT agents was never established. Both sides made propaganda over the fires, each charging the other with responsibility.

The perils of the enemy's guns had been replaced by the physical obstacles of the Hunan-Guizhou plateau, dangerous mountains and perilous rivers, exhaustion of the troops, scarcity of food, hostility of the minorities. The Red Army's wireless intercepts revealed that if the columns turned north to join He Long and Xiao Ke, they would have to fight their way through 250,000 or more KMT troops, of whom 100,000 were already in place in Hunan. They knew, even though they had not taken a complete roll call, that their own force was down perilously close to the 30,000 mark, not more than 35,000, including noncombatants.[9]

There was no time for an organized discussion, but when the forces reached the county town of Tongdao, nestled near the Guizhou border, a hasty, informal meeting was called of the major military and political figures.

The date of the Tongdao meeting is usually given as December 11. It was held outside the town, somewhere in the nearby countryside in a wing of a peasant house in which a wedding was in progress, in the recollection of Zhou Enlai.[10] Braun describes it as an emergency meeting of the Military Commission, the Party body that directed the Army. Mao had been removed from the commission more than two years earlier. Now he was invited to join the session and immediately took the dominant role.

The question was whether the Red Army should continue its agreed course and strike north to join He Long. There are no written records of the Tongdao meeting—or none that have thus far been found. Much of the written record of the Red Army march was lost as it lightened its burden by burning or tossing into rivers valuable documents and equipment. Thus the memories of participants, even though the events occurred half a century earlier, become more and more valuable.

Xu Mengqiu, son of an aristocratic scholar, who headed the secretariat of the Red Army Political Department during the Long March, was instructed in Yan'an by Mao Zedong to prepare a history. Xu Mengqiu told Helen Snow in 1936 that he had collected seven hundred documents, but that almost all the rest had been lost. He published the first collection of personal accounts of the March in Shanghai in 1938. Xu Mengqiu crossed the Snowy Mountains without harm, but after he reached northern Shaanxi he froze both legs and they had to be amputated. After a trip to the Soviet Union in 1938 for treatment, he gradually became alienated and after 1945 threw his lot with the Nationalists. He was captured in Nanjing by the Red Army in 1949, was imprisoned, and died there.[11]

Absence of recorded data, changing political situations, and shifting attitudes toward Chinese Communist political and military personalities have hindered until now factual determination of many details of the March.

Although not even a single piece of paper survives about Tongdao (the very existence of the meeting only gradually became known in recent years), there is no question of the importance of its decisions. Speaking for the first time in a military council since 1932, Mao proposed that the Red Army abandon its attempt to join He Long, shift course from northwest Hunan, and move west and north into Guizhou. Here there were much brighter prospects. The Guizhou forces were relatively weak, the chances of being caught in the kind of pincers that developed in the Guangxi corridor were minimal, there should be a chance for a breathing space for reorganizing the shattered armies, for considering the future. If they persisted in the original course, they would head into certain disaster when they encountered the powerful armies that Chiang Kai-shek had positioned to interdict their meeting with He Long.

There was little or no argument. Zhu De and the other military commanders accepted Mao's suggestions immediately. The remainder joined in—Zhou Enlai, Wang Jiaxiang, Otto Braun, and, after Braun had made clear his agreement, Bo Gu. It had been a long time since the Red Army chiefs had agreed on a single question, let alone on a proposal of Mao's. But, as Mao told them, the alternative was almost certain obliteration.

By morning of December 12, the Red Army was on its way again, headed for Liping, a regional center within Guizhou, about two days distant. It had made a vital decision, and the fruits of the "litter conspiracy" had become apparent. The Chinese were rallying to Mao and forming ranks against their German Comintern adviser. Braun noted that he had difficulty in following the discussions, which were informal and rapid-fire. The next day when he asked Zhou Enlai for details, Zhou displayed irritation and said the Red Army was tired and needed a rest and probably would get it in Guizhou. He had never talked to Braun so sharply.[12]

Liping is a fairly prosperous county seat, just over the border from Hunan, in southeastern Guizhou. The county had a population of about 200,000 (in 1984 it was 370,000) when the Red Army captured it with hardly a fight in mid-December 1934. The attack was led by the Sixth and Third Regiments of the Second Division of the First Army Group. The main forces and the Central Military Commission arrived December 15 and 16. Mao, Wounded Wang Jiaxiang, and Luo Fu had previously agreed that at the first "suitable occasion" there would be a meeting to consider military plans and direction. This decision had been tacitly affirmed at the hurried Tongdao discussion. The military pressure was off for the time being. The worst of the mountains and rivers had been crossed (that is, the worst in this particular corner of China; far worse lay ahead). There were enough supplies in Liping so that everyone could have a square meal.

On the evening of December 18, an enlarged session of the Politburo was held.[13] It was held at the Red Army military headquarters that had been set up in a rather handsome shop and house belonging to a merchant named Xu in the heart of Liping, next door to a German Lutheran church.[14] Xu had left town when he heard the Red Army was coming. It was a tense meeting and voices were raised. Zhou Enlai presided and Bo Gu, Wang Jiaxiang, Luo Fu, Mao Zedong, Zhu De, and Lin Biao attended. Probably Otto Braun and other military took part. Zhou spoke several times, openly critical of Braun. Mao expanded on his remarks at Tongdao. He formally proposed that the plan to go north and join He Long be abandoned. In its place he suggested that the Red

Army move west into Guizhou; that it head for Zunyi, Guizhou's second-largest city, and that it form a new soviet base area in that region. Mao noted that they were no longer being attacked by the Hunan troops and emphasized the weakness of Guizhou's opium-sodden soldiers. He suggested that a formal meeting be conducted at Zunyi. Braun, it is said, again raised the idea of leaving the option open for going to the north if the KMT forces could be maneuvered out of position. Braun claims that he was ill and did not attend the Liping meeting. Instead, he writes, he outlined his position to Zhou Enlai, suggesting that the Red Army stay clear of Guiyang, where intelligence reported "six to seven partially motorized" KMT divisions were congregating. He urged that the Red Army head across the river Wu, using Zunyi as a temporary base from which to engage Chiang's forces in battle. There wasn't much difference between Braun's scheme (as recalled thirty years later) and that of Mao. After some argument by Bo Gu, the Mao formula was adopted. The Red Army would head for the Wu River, cross it, advance to Zunyi, and set up a new base area.[15]

At least two military reorganizations were implemented at Liping. The remains of the Eighth Army Group were incorporated into the rear-guard Fifth Army Group, and the "special army group," reserves and support services, largely attached to the central column, was liquidated and the men sent to reinforce badly decimated units, including the Third Army.[16]

Wireless messages went out December 19 to the Second, Sixth, and Fourth armies, advising them of the two resolutions (to change direction to Guizhou and to meet in Zunyi). The armies were ordered to coordinate their actions accordingly. The Second and Sixth were to drive toward south Hunan in order to divert Hunan forces. The Fourth Front Army was to attack in Sichuan to pull Sichuan troops north and away from the projected operations in northwest Guizhou. An advisory was sent to Chen Yi, operating in his rapidly vanishing base near Ruijin.[17]

The Red Army got under way with their new directives at 6 A.M. on the nineteenth, and by the twentieth all the troops had left the Liping region, moving easily and with scant opposition toward the river Wu, their chief obstacle on the way to Zunyi.

The Liping meeting had been completed; its terse decisions were being implemented. There is no sign that Otto Braun realized his days of directing the revolutionary forces of China had come to an end, unless his illness gave a psychological clue to what he feared was happening. It is doubtful that Mao Zedong realized that he now was winning command of the Chinese Revolution and that it would remain in his grip until his last days. Certainly no one else could have imagined this. In fact, no one outside of the tight inner Communist circle would know for many years that the Liping meeting had ever been held.

11

ZUNYI

THE distance from Liping to Zunyi is close to two hundred miles, but there are no big mountains or big rivers until you reach the river Wu, about forty miles southeast of Zunyi. As you make your way west, the countryside becomes more prosperous, the houses more and more are not thatched huts but a half-timbered style reminiscent of old England. The farms are better; conical haystacks give place to haycocks with the trunk of a tree as center pole, the hay circling the tree like a giant hula-hula skirt. It becomes Han country; the minorities are left behind in the mountains.

The wind was bone cold in December of 1934 when the Red Army neared the river Wu, the largest in Guizhou, slate-bottomed, carved through dark-gray basalt, few ferry points, fewer bridges, no fords, the water deep and boiling swift. The Red Army marched ahead at a merciless pace, virtually free of opposition. At the county seats there were small garrisons of *mintuan*, local militia, which often fled without firing a shot.

On New Year's Eve (Western style), the Communist forces reached the busy market town of Houchang, about thirty miles short of the river Wu. Houchang means "monkey town." There were monkeys in the forests approaching Houchang and in medieval times there had been many more. On New Year's Eve the Politburo met, with Mao in attendance, a protracted meeting, going on so long that Mao's bodyguards (he now had four in addition to the two waiting on He Zizhen) began to worry about the New Year's feast they had prepared. The Politburo was once again arguing, possibly about a new notion advanced by Braun. Intelligence had reported that three enemy divisions were approaching. Braun suggested that the Red Army halt and give battle. Mao rebuffed Braun and insisted on pressing ahead for Zunyi at full speed. The order of the day to the troops declared: "Proceed to north Guizhou.

Take Zunyi and Tongzi by surprise, and arouse the masses."[1]

Mao had been assigned to what bodyguard Chen Changfeng considered the finest house he had occupied on the Long March, finer than those of the Central Soviet Area (and those houses, I can testify, were superb, many of them old family ancestral halls). The new quarters were a symbol of Mao's remarkable rise in status. The house had a large central courtyard with rooms on all sides. Someone had made two imposing snowmen and placed them at the entrance, and the courtyard bricks were clean enough to eat from. Three rooms, facing south, had been put at Mao's disposal. A kerosene lamp swung in the center of the middle room. Against one wall was an antique Chinese table and on the wall hung a painting of a laughing monk, hands clasped over his jolly belly. The guards had gotten provisions for a feast, expecting the generals and leaders to join the Chairman.

It was snowing when the Politburo meeting finally broke up, and as the guards escorted Mao back to his quarters they rattled off their plans. Mao growled that there could be no feast. They had to race for the river Wu before those three enemy divisions arrived. He hurried back to his house, telling the disconsolate guards that he had already eaten at the Politburo meeting. When he got to his elegant rooms he glanced at the preparations and said: "It really is like New Year's." Then he turned to his desk and his papers. One guard could not restrain himself: "But we've got your favorite—some sweet fermented rice." Mao relented a bit. He sat down with the guards and had a snack. Then back to work. At 4 A.M. he got word that the first elements of the vanguard had reached the river Wu. Mao and headquarters packed up and set off for the river. All hoped for success at the river Wu, as a good omen for the new year.

As usual it was the Fourth Regiment of the Second Division of the First Army Group, Lin Biao's army, that was assigned the task of forcing the river Wu. Liu Yalou, political commissar of the Second Division, got his orders directly from Lin Biao and Political Commissar Nie Rongzhen. Zunyi was the headquarters of Bai Huizhang, the local warlord. He was a pawn of Wang Jialie, Guizhou's warlord, and had responsibility for what might be called the "Northwest Kingdom," Guizhou's region of wealth founded on opium production, opium distribution, and opium smuggling, chiefly to Sichuan; on liquor production (centered around Maotai); on slaves and serfs—a jewel in the crown of Guizhou's primitive fiefdom.

In the early hours of New Year's Day, the vanguard Fourth Regiment headed by Geng Biao and Commissar Yang Chengwu (now recovered), reached the river Wu. The commanders found the river about 250 yards wide. It was flowing at five to six feet a second. The path down to the river was steep and rocky and about two miles long. On the opposite side, the path was much the same. Both banks rose sheer from the water. A ferry plied back and forth. The Fourth Regiment made a try at seizing the ferry, but it was not successful.

It took more than forty-eight hours of hard fighting to secure the crossing. A detachment headed by Company Commander Mao reached the north bank, but was trapped under an overhang of the cliff. They waited thirty-six hours for the main assault, then opened up on the enemy at close range. It was touch and go until the First Battalion slipped a squad or two over the river and up a very steep cliff to come on the defenders from the flank.

While the skirmishing went forward, an engineers company built a floating bridge of bamboo in about a hundred sections and put it together, like a child's Meccano toy. The strong current made it difficult to manage. Enemy fire wounded a number of engineers but did not damage the light bamboo framework. At one point a three-hundred-foot segment was almost rammed by a smaller section, which broke adrift. The bridge was saved by a Red Army man named Shi Changjie, at the cost of his life.

By January 3 or early on the fourth, the Red Army units had begun to move across the floating bridge. The rest was easy. The Sixth Regiment of the Second Division was ordered by Liu Yalou to take Zunyi immediately. Under Commander Zhu Shuiqiu and Commissar Wang Jicheng, the Sixth raced ahead in heavy rain. About ten miles from Zunyi, they captured a local battalion to the last man. With a combination of guile and practicality, they persuaded their prisoners to lend a hand. They gave the men pep talks, a few threats, and three silver dollars each. After midnight they arrived at the gates of Zunyi. The Communists and their new allies shouted and chanted, blew their bugles, made a great fuss, and proclaimed they were the remnants of a defense battalion being pursued by the Red Army. Within half an hour they were inside the city walls. By daybreak January 7, Zunyi was being taken over. By the next day, occupation was complete and on January 9, general headquarters, Mao, and the leadership echelon arrived. It was a ceremonial entry. It had been raining and the troops were covered with mud. They halted outside Zunyi, cleaned up their uniforms, washed their faces and hands, and came in singing a marching song: "The Three Main Rules of Discipline and the Eight Points for Attention." These were the Zhu-Mao rules for soldiers' conduct set to music:

> The rules:
>> Obey orders in all your actions.
>> Don't take a needle or a piece of thread from the people.
>> Turn in everything you capture.
> The points of attention:
>> Speak politely.
>> Pay fairly for what you buy.
>> Return everything you borrow.
>> Pay for any damage.
>> Don't strike or swear at people.
>> Don't damage the crops.
>> Don't take liberties with women.
>> Don't mistreat captives.

Propaganda workers had put up red banners and slogans. People lined the streets. By this time the Fourth and Sixth regiments were already hurrying on to capture Tongzi.[2]

In the early 1930s, a year or so before the arrival of the Red Army, Bai Huizhang, a freewheeling Guizhou merchant and banker with a hand in all the profitable (and often illegal) enterprises that centered around Zunyi, then a city of about 50,000 (300,000 in 1984), built for himself an imposing residence in the heart of town. Bai Huizhang was one of several brothers who joined in promotion of the family business. Bai's new residence marked his rise in the world: He had been named by Guizhou's chief, Wang Jialie, to be regional warlord and commander of the Second Division of Wang's Twenty-fifth Army.

The house that Bai built was *à la mode* for a 1930s Chinese warlord. It was a two-story colonnaded structure of gray brick, with a lightly overhanging roof and wraparound second-story balcony, a style that might be called warlord *moderne,* a blend of Chinese traditional and paper-thin Westernism. It was, of course, protected by outer walls and a fine gatehouse entered from one of Zunyi's main streets. It had a paved brick outer court and beside the house was planted a locust tree, which still stood in 1984.

Within this place of provincial elegance all was dark wood, heavy furniture in traditional Chinese style, Chinese screens, scrolls, and rather small and dark rooms. There was, surprisingly, no inner court-yard.

Bai's house, naturally, was the finest in Zunyi and it was promptly occupied as Red Army headquarters. Here the Central Military Com-mission and the First Front Army had offices and here Zhou Enlai and his wife, Deng Yingchao, had a pleasant room off the second-floor bal-cony from which Deng Yingchao remembered plucking the leaves of the locust tree. She was still ill, still suffering from tuberculosis, still coughing blood, but Zunyi gave her a rare respite of shared moments with her husband. Zhu De and his wife, Kang Keqing, lived in the Bai house. So did Liu Bocheng and operational chiefs like Zhang Yunyi and Peng Xuefeng. Peng Dehuai, Liu Shaoqi, and Li Zhuoran stayed in the house for shorter periods.

Mao Zedong did not live in the grand Bai residence but in another warlord residence, that of one of Bai's brigade commanders, named Yi Huaizhi. It was also built of brick, with a second-floor wraparound balcony. Here stayed Wang Jiaxiang and Luo Fu, the "Central Team."

Mao's wife, He Zizhen, lived with the other women of the convales-cent unit at Zunyi Middle School No. 3, a famous school in those times, among whose graduates were Yong Wentao, later to be forestry minis-ter, and Han Nianlong, a deputy foreign minister.

In these arrangements there was a notable absence of quarters for Bo Gu and Otto Braun. They were housed across town in a beautiful old Chinese courtyard house opposite the big Roman Catholic church, which was requisitioned as a hospital and used for public meetings. Here Zhu De delivered a speech on January 15 at a memorial for the martyred German Communists, Karl Liebknecht and Rosa Luxem-burg.[3]

The geography of the arrangements told the story. Bo Gu and Otto Braun were out, living in isolation from the rest; Mao and the Central Team were in.

It was decided that an expanded session of the Politburo would be convened on January 15. It would meet at the house of Bai Huizhang for the purpose of assessing the results of the Fifth Encirclement Cam-paign and the failure, thus far, of the Long March, and to take appropri-ate military action.

There was plenty of politicking on both sides. Bo Gu's chief lieuten-ant in trying to line up support was He Kequan (Kai Feng), the Young Communist League head. He talked to Nie Rongzhen several times, half a day at a time, trying to win his support for Bo Gu and Braun—without success.[4]

Not all the time was spent in political discussion. The first days were devoted to securing the military position. The First and Third armies fanned out to protect the area and an intensive effort was launched to prepare for the setting up of a new soviet district.

A Zunyi Revolutionary Committee was formed and a start was made at establishing revolutionary committees in Tongzi and Meitan counties. The Army newspaper, *Red Star,* edited by Deng Xiaoping, published an editorial calling for stepping up of revolutionary propaganda.[5]

Reality, however, rapidly undercut the cheery optimism of the Liping decisions. Red Army intelligence as they left Liping reported Guizhou was defended by only four weak, opium-saturated divisions of Wang Jialie. The Red Army held them in low esteem. But the day Mao entered Zunyi, two top KMT commanders, Zhou Hunyuan and Wu Qiwei, with excellently disciplined troops, moved into Guizhou and quickly took over the capital, Guiyang. This stimulated the Guizhou commander, Wang Jialie, into action. He advanced his Third Division, consisting of seven regiments, to attack Peng Dehuai's Sixth Division.

The Red Army's intercept service was excellently informed of these movements. They knew that Chiang Kai-shek was now directing operations from Chongqing and that he had activated four Hunan divisions, a couple of brigades in southern Sichuan, and three brigades of Yunnan forces. Chiang had 150 regiments, numbering possibly 400,000 men, that might be brought against the 30,000 remaining Red Army men.

The rosy prospects of Liping for setting up a new base area disintegrated. There were other unpleasant discoveries. The Zunyi region was economically backward. It produced a lot of opium but not much food. It would be hard to supply a growing Red Army.

Geographically there were disadvantages. The region was bounded by three important rivers—the river Wu, the Chishui or Red River, which formed a zigzag western boundary, and to the north the mighty Yangtze. If the Red Army settled in, it could be encircled and crushed. So far as can be discovered, the idea simply died in the face of reality.[6]

After supper on January 15, at seven o'clock, twenty men gathered at the Bai mansion, in a rectangular room with plain plaster walls and dark mahogany-stained floor and doors. The room was bare except for a kerosene lantern swinging overhead, a rather battered heavy table in the center, possibly twenty-five chairs of different shapes and sizes in a rough semicircle, a small iron stove (the temperature was January-raw), a few strategically located white-and-pink enamel spittoons, and some ashtrays. Occasionally, bodyguards brought in hot water and tea.

The twenty men had gathered, in a sense, to ceremonialize a profound change in the command and direction of the Long March and beyond that of the Communist revolutionary movement in China. Many would say in the future that it was the single most significant event in the whole Chinese Revolution.

Three men sat in the center of the hall and held their places throughout what became a three-day meeting. One was Bo Gu, twenty-six, secretary and nominal leader of the Communist Party of China, who chaired the meeting. He wore heavy glasses that would earn him the nickname "Golliwog": intellectual, studious, fluent in Russian from four years in Moscow at Sun Yat-sen University, competent in English from earlier years spent in a Communist-sponsored university in Shanghai; a thin, thin man, a man who had fallen under the domination of the Russian leadership of the Chinese section of the Comintern, the closest associate of the German military adviser, Otto Braun, and Braun's unswerving supporter. The second was Mao Zedong, and the third, Zhou Enlai. Other participants moved from chair to chair, sitting where convenient at each session. The chairs were not placed in any order. There were always more chairs than participants.

Next to the door sat Otto Braun. He sat with his interpreter, Wu Xiuquan, on the awkwardly placed chair, "in the position of a defendant." Wu's position was not comfortable either. He was upset and grew more and more angry as the meetings went on. As he admitted fifty years later, he didn't translate as well as he usually did.

Two men attended on litters. One was Wang Jiaxiang, carried on a litter since he had been wounded in April 1933 in Gugong village, Le'an county, during the Fourth Encirclement. He was struck by a KMT bomb as he was leading Zhou Enlai, Xiao Hua, and several others to a shelter. A fragment cut through his hip into his intestines and did deadly damage. A surgeon operated for eight hours without anesthesia and was unable to close the wound. A rubber hose had to be inserted and he ran a constant high fever. The pain was relieved only by morphine, to which he became addicted, until he was sent to Moscow for treatment in 1936. He broke the habit "cold turkey."

Everyone knew that Wang Jiaxiang was going to support Mao.

"Wang has married Mao," was the word that spread from mouth to mouth.

There was not much that these men did not know about each other —right down to their bowel movements. Everyone knew that when time permitted Zhou Enlai retreated to the toilet with a batch of papers and often spent an hour reading them over. Everyone knew that Mao Zedong had chronic spastic bowel problems. His bowels often did not move but once a week. Later on in Yan'an a cheer would go up when word would spread that "the Chairman's bowels have moved." He once told Edgar Snow that his bowels moved best when he was in battle. Never had they moved so well as during his early attack on Changsha.

Until the spring of 1984 there was uncertainty about some details of the Zunyi meeting—the dates, the identity of participants. There had never been any doubt about its results. On March 4, 1984, Central Party historians revealed that an ancient memorandum had turned up in the files which provided much missing data.

The participants, it was now stated, were:

Ten members of the Politburo—Mao Zedong, Zhu De, Chen Yun (whose long-lost memo provided many missing details), Zhou Enlai, Luo Fu (Zhang Wentian), Bo Gu (Qin Bangxian), and alternate members Wang Jiaxiang, Deng Fa (the security chief), Liu Shaoqi (years later to become the principal victim of the Cultural Revolution), and He Kequan (also known as Kai Feng), leader of the Young Communist League.

Seven Red Army men—Liu Bocheng, Li Fuchun (acting director of the Red Army Political Department in place of the wounded Wang Jiaxiang, and a long-term associate of Mao), Lin Biao, Nie Rongzhen (Lin's political commissar and a staunch Mao adherent), Peng Dehuai (tough, anti-Braun, Third Army Group commander), Yang Shangkun (political commissar of the Third Army Group), and Li Zhuoran, political commissar of the Fifth Army Group.

Deng Xiaoping, editor of *Red Star*, and newly named secretary to the Central Committee, was present. So were Otto Braun and Interpreter Wu Xiuquan. Their status was that of observers. Twenty men in all, twenty men on whose decisions the future of China would depend.[7]

Bo Gu spoke first.

He spoke of Chiang's Fifth Encirclement Campaign and blamed the Communist failure on the overwhelming numerical superiority of the Nationalists and poor coordination of movements by Communist armies outside the Central Soviet Area. Bo Gu spoke extemporaneously, no written text, and his remarks concentrated on the objective side of the situation. In the opinion of Interpreter Wu, he assessed the current military position objectively enough and criticized himself for mistakes in the military line, but tried to defend and explain away his mistakes.[8]

No secretaries were permitted to be present at the meeting and participants, with the possible exception of Deng Xiaoping, did not take notes. Most of the speeches were impromptu, and even today not all of their contents has been made public or can be reconstructed from the memories of the few survivors.

Bo Gu apparently did not win his audience. His comrades said he was trying to shirk responsibility. Otto Braun, hardly an objective observer, took a different view. He thought Bo Gu did well. He had emphasized that Chiang was getting loans, weapons, and military advisers from the "imperialist powers." (Apparently Bo Gu did not name von Seeckt specifically.) Bo Gu took the line, Braun recalled, that the Communist strategy was correct but that there had been errors in carrying it out.

Zhou Enlai was the second speaker. He accepted blame for incorrect policies—in particular, for fighting fortifications with fortifications. This, he said, was the cause of the failure of the Red Army in the Fifth Encirclement. He was frank in criticizing himself and did not try to shift the blame. His willingness to accept responsibility went well with his comrades.[9]

Braun was disturbed by Zhou's speech. Zhou, he thought, emphasized subjective factors and subtly distanced himself from Bo Gu and Braun, opening the way for Mao to draw a line between them.

Now Mao took the floor, breaking his habit of waiting until all others had spoken first. He delivered a long address, lasting more than an hour, far longer than any of the others. He criticized Braun and Bo Gu, naming names, charging that they had not given heed to the traditional Red Army policy of a war of movement. The "short, sharp jabs" of Braun had been substituted for the Zhu-Mao tactic of entrapping and wiping out whole KMT units. Mao rejected Bo Gu's thesis that the failures were caused by inferiority in numbers. The Red Army had been up against equally large KMT armies in the First, Second, Third, and Fourth Encirclement campaigns and had defeated them. It was not numbers; it was tactics. The military direction was wrong, he insisted, as recalled by Wu Xiuquan. The Bo Gu–Braun policy had been based on "conservatism in defense," "adventurism in attack," and "flightism in retreat."

Mao declared that the most important task was to solve the problem of military policy. Bo Gu and Braun did not pay heed to the fact that soldiers are human beings and must walk on their feet, eat meals, and get some sleep. If a commander knows only how to lay out positions and set times for action on the basis of a map, without understanding the actual terrain and geography, his strategy "is bound to lose."[10]

Mao strongly attacked the failure to join forces with the Nineteenth Route Army. That, he said, had cost the Red Army an excellent chance to get behind the Nationalist lines and attack from the rear. Zhou Enlai, Luo Fu, and he had all wanted to join forces with the Nineteenth.[11]

Mao got an ovation. He was saying what most of the commanders had long believed.

Braun was badly stung by Mao's remarks. Thirty years later, he was extremely critical of the failure of the Zunyi conference to discuss political as well as military questions—the Soviet Union and world politics were not even mentioned—but the Chinese had decided beforehand to confine their discussion to the military because they knew that if they got into political questions the meeting would probably blow up.[12]

Braun was in a difficult spot and understood that he was. Sitting on the edge of the room, at the door, he was deliberately excluded from the council of the Chinese. He could comprehend what they were saying only through the translations of Interpreter Wu Xiuquan, and Wu became increasingly disturbed and weary as the evening wore on. His translations became shorter and sometimes halted entirely. Braun's mien was ordinarily stolid. He had a square frame and he usually sat like a rock until ready to speak. Now he showed his anger in the changing color of his face. It grew red as he listened to Bo Gu and turned white when Mao began to attack him. At no point did he lose physical control, but he smoked cigarette after cigarette, digging deep into the stock he had gotten from the newly confiscated stores of Zunyi. He looked more and more depressed and gloomy.[13]

The speaker after Mao was Wang Jiaxiang. He had already told Nie Rongzhen: "Let's throw them out of the meeting. Drive Li De [Braun] off the stage!" Wang's support of Mao and Mao's position was no surprise to anyone who had watched the progress of the discussions on the litters. Bo Gu–Braun must go, he said, and Mao must be placed in command of the Red Army.[14]

Braun claims in his memoirs that he made no statement at Zunyi because he had incomplete knowledge of what was being said and decided to wait until he had examined the minutes or at least the summary resolution. There seem to have been no minutes and not until 1948 was the resolution made public. In Snow's long discussions with Mao and the Communist leaders at Bao'an in 1936, the word Zunyi did not cross anyone's lips.

Braun's recollection of nonparticipation is in conflict with the memory of others. Interpreter Wu recalls Braun speaking in his own defense, insisting (entirely correctly) that he was in China only as an adviser sent by the Comintern. He defended the general line of operations, but stated that any blame lay with the Chinese leadership: It was they who made a mess of things; the culprits were Chinese, the Central Committee and others. He did not admit to any mistake. Wu thought Braun had a guilty conscience, but no reader of his memoirs is likely to draw that conclusion. He seemed as firm thirty years after the event as he had been at Zunyi.

Braun repeatedly said he was a mere agent. It was true that he had advanced various proposals, but "as to their acceptance or disapproval —that is your problem."[15] Basing himself on the Chinese archives, Professor Hu Hua stated that Braun made a categorical denial of all criticisms.

The barrage of criticism continued for three days. The sessions were held in the evening, usually starting at seven and lasting four or five hours. The rhetoric grew sharp and Interpreter Wu felt under increasing strain.

Daylight hours were occupied with military matters. A major reorganization was under way. The Central Column and its burdensome congregation of porters was disbanded. The remaining heavy equipment was destroyed or buried for possible recovery later. What had to be brought along was divided among the military units. The young men of the Central Column and the remaining porters, where possible, were incorporated into combat detachments. Little Liu Ying was in charge of much of this work, filling in for Li Linkai, the political commissar of Echelon Three, who was ill.[16]

Recruitment was actively carried on; four thousand men were added. An inventory of manpower confirmed that the Red Army now had a count of barely thirty thousand.

As the meetings wore on, more and more speakers lined up with Mao. Many commanders raised the question of lack of ideological preparation. They contended that heavy losses, particularly by desertion, had arisen because the new recruits were not properly prepared. Contrary to tradition, they did not know where they were going, what they were fighting for, and why sacrifices were necessary. Security, the commanders felt, had been excessive. Even many of the leaders were ignorant of what was going on. Fighting spirit was thereby impaired and the morale of soldiers and officers weakened.

Luo Fu and Zhu De pledged their support to Mao. Zhou Enlai spoke again, acknowledging the correctness of Mao's criticism of the "leftist" line of Bo Gu and Braun,[17] and proposing that Mao be named commander of the Red Army.

Interpreter Wu was impressed by the remarks of Li Fuchun, Mao's old associate from Hunan, who was married to the brilliant Cai Chang, herself one of Mao's oldest friends. Wu was also moved by Nie Rongzhen, who expressed anger at the way Braun had conducted himself. Wu could sympathize with this criticism. He had suffered repeatedly because of Braun's rudeness and had once told a department head: "Li De [Braun] is an imperialist. If I had a choice I would never be his interpreter. As I am assigned to him as interpreter, I must do it."[18]

Nie Rongzhen, speaking from his stretcher (not yet recovered from a wound in the foot which he received after crossing the Xiang River), talked with some anger. Whenever he saw Braun he got mad, being reminded of Braun's method of command, his minute instructions just where each cannon should be emplaced and where duty guards were to be stationed—details that not even army group commanders would bother with.[19] Wu well remembered the cutting edge of Nie Rongzhen's criticism. The First Army Group, of which Nie was political commissar, had not always adhered to Braun's injunction that only frontal engagements with the enemy were permissible. It had on occasion lured the Nationalists into ambush in the old Zhu–Mao tradition and scored some successes.[20]

Peng Dehuai gave a strong speech supporting Mao and criticizing Bo Gu and Braun. So did Liu Bocheng. Surprisingly, Braun felt the remarks of Zhu De, Peng Dehuai, and Liu Bocheng were "moderate" in tone, in contrast to those of the others.[21]

Lin Biao does not seem to have played much of a part at Zunyi, although memories may be distorted by his conduct in the Cultural Revolution and his attempted coup d'état. Most of the military men with whom I talked had been his victims. Wu asserts that Lin Biao did not speak a word, having been a supporter of Bo Gu and Braun and having come under criticism for this. Nie Rongzhen agrees with Wu.[22]

Others, however, remember Lin Biao as supporting Mao's call for removal of Bo Gu and Braun. Lin Biao was said to have become openly critical of the pair after the Xiang River battle and the losses of the First Army Group. Now he became very vocal, very hostile.[23]

Of all the company, only He Kequan, who had studied in Moscow and was a certified "Bolshevik," was almost all-out in support of Bo Gu and Braun. He conceded that they had made mistakes but opposed their removal. He Kequan, Nie Rongzhen felt, was "quite arrogant." He Kequan said to Mao: "You know nothing about Marxism-Leninism. All you have read is Sun Wu Zi's *Art of War.*" He Kequan clung to his opinions despite the actions of the Zunyi meeting and not until later reluctantly acknowledged that he was wrong.[24]

Both Nie Rongzhen and Liu Bocheng proposed that the Red Army shift its course, fight its way across the Yangtze, and in northwest Sichuan set up a new base. They felt conditions there were far superior to those in Guizhou—the province was richer; the transportation (highway system) was very deficient, which gave an edge to the fast-moving, foot-propelled Red Army; the local warlords tended to be antagonistic to Chiang Kai-shek; and there was a larger local population on which to draw for recruits.[25]

Finally Zhou Enlai proposed that the three-man military leadership of Bo Gu, Braun, and himself be suspended. This was approved by consensus. No vote, it is said; no formal votes throughout the meeting. Military direction was now vested in a duo, Zhu De and Zhou Enlai. No mention of Mao in this connection, but another resolution elected Mao a member of the Standing Committee of the Politburo, the inner circle of leadership. Whatever it said on paper, everyone knew who was in charge. Another resolution contained Luo Fu's condensation of Mao's criticism and a final resolution specified that division of work and responsibility within the Standing Committee would be decided upon later.

Already Peng Dehuai had left Zunyi to confront the threat to his Sixth Division by the KMT General Wu Qiwei.[26] Boxes and bags were being packed. Camp was struck. On the nineteenth of January, Mao and the headquarters staff left Zunyi, but not before a meeting, at the Roman Catholic cathedral, of military commanders, which was addressed by Bo Gu (a political report), Zhou Enlai, and Mao. The texts of the speeches have unfortunately not been preserved.

Zunyi was over. The Long March continued. Mao was in charge. China's course had been set for at least half a century to come.[27]

12

MAO TAKES CHARGE

O<small>N</small> the morning of January 19, 1935, the Red Army under the de facto command of Mao Zedong moved out of Zunyi, little more than a remnant of the force that had splashed across the Yudu River three months earlier.

It had lost almost two-thirds of its number and all its heavy guns. It no longer possessed any artillery, give or take a few old mortars and two mountain guns. It counted only sixteen combat and one cadre regiment, in what were still propagandistically called four "armies"—the First, the Third, the Fifth, and the Ninth. Even with frantic recruiting, the force numbered less than 35,000. The great supply train was gone.

The Red Army was further than ever from its goals. It was deeper in the remote interior. It had captured Zunyi, the second city of Guizhou, but few in China could have pinpointed its location and the army was now headed into the endless mountains and wastelands of China's distant frontiers. It possessed few maps, and much of this territory had never been put on maps.

True, it had escaped from Chiang Kai-shek's trap in the Red corner of Jiangxi. It had survived the crossing of the Xiang River. But it had not escaped Chiang and his armies. Not by any means. Chiang was busy at Chongqing, just to the north, rounding up more troops, moving relentlessly to encircle the "Red bandits." He had 400,000 men positioned to block the Red Army, whichever way it turned. If Chiang had missed the kill in Jiangxi and at the Xiang River, he did not intend to miss in Guizhou. The Guizhou army had proved as dissolute and opium-sated as the Communists expected, but now Chiang had mustered the troops of Sichuan, of Yunnan, of Hunan, and his own Nationalist forces to block off the Red Army the moment it approached the perimeter of Guizhou—particularly if it made a move north toward the mighty Yangtze.

Twice the Red Army had been forced to change its direction—first to give up the plan to join He Long and Xiao Ke, the Second and Sixth armies, in Hunan-Hubei-Guizhou, then to abandon the idea of a base around Zunyi. On the day after leaving Zunyi—January 20—in the dreary village of Sidu on the way to Tongzi, a Politburo meeting confirmed the latest change of course—this time to join the Fourth Front Army of Zhang Guotao.[1] Exactly what the situation of the Fourth Army was, they did not know. They were heading for what would prove a blind rendezvous. Mao thought the Fourth Army had a thriving base in northwest Sichuan and a force of 100,000 men or more. He did not know that the Fourth Army would soon pull up stakes and move to China's "Wild West," where Sichuan and Tibetan country overlapped. There had been little communication between the First and Fourth armies. Otto Braun thought that Mao sent out couriers to the Fourth and other armies after Zunyi, but there is no evidence any messengers penetrated to Fourth Army headquarters.[2]

The picture wasn't all black. Because of the heavy manpower losses, the Red Army now had almost enough rifles and machine guns to go around. They had picked up more Mausers in Zunyi. The Red Army used any kind of gun, but Mausers were the standard because they were made in the government arsenals, and of course the Nationalist Army was the Communists' chief source of supply. The surviving troops were battle hardened and lean. By junking the supply column, the Red Army had regained the speed and mobility that was its most valued asset. They could outpace any force Chiang brought against them. They covered extraordinary distances on foot, forty and fifty miles a day. Sometimes they held that pace for several days running. And this up and down mountains and across rivers. The Five Ridges were long put behind, but Guizhou, Yunnan and Sichuan presented one fold of mountains after another, with a river between each fold. There had been no roads in southern Jiangxi. There were few here, with one exception— a genuine if unpaved highway suitable for carts and motor vehicles, which ran north from Guiyang through Zunyi and the Loushan Pass to the Red (Chishui) River on the Guizhou-Sichuan boundary.

For the rest, the Red Army, as always, traveled by footpaths seldom wider than two abreast up and down mountains; none of today's black-top roads with their lazy S-curves and switchbacks. The paths ran straight and true, taking no account of steepness. In 1984 they were still used by peasants because they turned a ten-mile hike into a two-mile climb. Today's telephone and power lines follow the old footpaths. They say in northern Guizhou that any *lao taipo*, old woman, can beat an automobile to the market town because she uses the footpaths and travels twice as fast.[3]

With Mao in command, the troops felt at ease. At last the political commissars could tell them why they were marching and where. Spirit was high. There was no force in China and none in the whole world capable of covering these mountains as fast as the Red Army. Town after town was startled at the appearance of the Communists. They hadn't known they were anywhere near. The Red Army men, for the most part, were small in stature but possessed sinews of steel. They left Zunyi in better shape than since the start of the great retreat. Most had had ten days of rest. They had eaten well. When the Army got to Zunyi, each soldier had been given a silver dollar or two. There was a great Sichuan restaurant in Zunyi where you could get a feast for a dollar. Within a day or two the Red Army had eaten up most of Zunyi's delicacies. Many feasted on Mao Zedong's favorite dish—a concoction called the Moon and Four Stars—alternate layers of lamb, fish, chicken, vegetables, especially taro root (called *tian ma*), dredged in rice flour, steamed overnight. The broth is believed to be a cure for dizziness and headaches.[4] Some bought a rare herb, *tiana (gastrodaelata)*, a local legendary remedy for physical weakness.

The men had new straw sandals. Some had leather-soled sandals, warmer clothing, rain capes made of plaited bamboo, and new straw rain hats. Their rice bags were filled, the medical teams had replenished stocks of iodine and chloroform from the Zunyi pharmacies, as well as herbal medicines. There were even new flashlights and batteries, a stock of kerosene, and stores of sugar and salt.

Mao had some reason for optimism. The Red Army was going forward again under the banner of the Zhu-Mao credo—the sixteen Chinese characters written in the form of a poem which guided it in the years of success before the advent of the 28 Bolsheviks and Otto Braun:

> The enemy approaches, we retreat.
> The enemy halts, we move in.
> The enemy tires, we attack.
> The enemy retreats, we pursue.

This was the essence of guerrilla war and it had enabled the Zhu-Mao army to grow strong. Now it must save it from extermination.

Nothing would be the same after Zunyi. This was the watershed—not just Mao Zedong firmly in command but a declaration of the independence of the Chinese Communist movement, independence from the overlordship of Moscow, which the world would not realize for a quarter of a century but which Stalin long associated with the name of Mao.

It signaled the formation of a great political partnership, that of Mao Zedong and Zhou Enlai, which would last throughout their lives or at least until the final year or two.

On the eve of Zunyi, Zhou was Mao's rival. It was Zhou who had come to the Central Soviet Area in December 1931 and taken over the position of secretary of the Party Bureau, which Mao had filled until he was removed in November. Then in October 1932, at the time of the Ningdu conference, Zhou replaced Mao as political commissar of the First Front Army.

It is true that Zhou had protested Mao's removal and had urged that he be retained, but Zhou went along with the decision and in May 1933 became general political commissar of the whole Red Army. He was in fact a member of the ruling troika together with Bo Gu and Otto Braun. It was also true that since the Ningdu meeting, Mao had no role in Red Army affairs. He had been ill at the time of Ningdu and had been instructed to "take a rest," but he never came back to the Army.[5]

Zhou had stood with the others in the troika, blocking Mao's strategy and overriding Mao's suggestions. There was no collaboration, and if there is no evidence that Zhou supported Bo Gu and Braun in their machinations to get rid of Mao, neither is there evidence that Zhou took a hand in opposing such stratagems.

Years later Zhou sadly confessed that from the time of the Ningdu meeting in October 1932 to the start of the Long March in October 1934, he had not on a single occasion consulted with Mao.[6]

The reason for this may be found in Zhou's almost exaggerated notions of discipline and propriety. He had made it clear at Ningdu that he believed Mao should continue to take a hand in military affairs, but when the leadership decided against Mao he did not challenge the decision. He did show respect for Mao, riding part of the way with him when Mao left Ningdu and expressing hope that he would recover his health and come back to the Red Army. For a time Zhou called himself "Acting Political Commissar," implying that Mao might return. Occasionally he sent papers over for Mao to read "if it is convenient."[7] Zhou's wife, Deng Yingchao, shared her husband's meticulous attitude to Party discipline. She did not raise her voice when the pro-Zhou demonstration in Tiananmen Square in the spring of 1976 was denounced by the Gang of Four and only spoke when Hua Guofeng and the Party revised the official stand after Mao's death and the arrest of the Gang. When she was asked by General Yang Shangkun to help throw light on her husband's attitudes, she said crisply: "He never told me anything that he thought I was not entitled to hear."[8]

Zhou was unlike Mao with respect to Party decisions. Mao did not let a decision stand unchallenged. He tried to see that his view prevailed, as in the period before and after the start of the Long March. Zhou objected occasionally. He proposed breakouts from the Central Soviet Area in the summer of 1934, but yielded to the majority against him in the troika, Bo Gu and Otto Braun.[9]

Before and after he came to power, Mao not infrequently found himself at odds with Stalin. Sometimes he bowed to Stalin because of circumstances or necessity—particularly in the 1930s, when he and other Chinese Communists felt they must place Soviet priorities ahead of their own in order to preserve the Soviet Union as a citadel of world revolution.

That changed when the balance of power changed. Stalin had strongly opposed Mao's post–World War II war against Chiang Kai-shek. He had urged Mao to accept a coalition government. Mao rejected the idea. Late in 1948, when Mao had reached Pingshan county in Hebei province, and was preparing to take Beijing and move on south, Anastas Mikoyan was sent bearing a special message from Stalin: Don't go south of the Yangtze. Let Chiang Kai-shek survive. Mao refused. He presented such powerful arguments to Mikoyan that, Mao thought, he convinced Stalin's emissary of the correctness of his course. He sent Mikoyan back to Moscow. On January 1, 1949, he published an editorial: "Carry Out the Revolution to the End," a personal answer to Stalin: "Those who advise the people to take pity on the enemy and preserve the forces of reaction are . . . friends of the enemy."[10]

Zhou, like most in the leadership group, was a "foreigner." He had spent long years in France and Germany and he had spent more time in Moscow than most people realized. He was a cosmopolitan man, perhaps more culturally at home in Paris than in any other place. He did not grow up with cow dung between the toes of his bare feet, as did Mao. He did not possess Mao's easy use of barnyard idiom, nor Mao's instinct for the Chinese peasant. Zhou and his wife were intellectual companions, bound by common experience in Europe and in the great cities of China. Zhou Enlai and Deng Yingchao were closer to each other than to anyone else in the world.

Zhou was renowned for statesmanship, diplomatic tact, and brilliant intellect. He had a good military background, having served as director of the political department of the Whampoa Academy. He studied military science in Moscow and practiced it in the bloody days of Shanghai and the bold Nanchang Uprising. Now for more than three years he had been fighting in south China. He was in every way a remarkable figure, a man possessed of the talent and background that entitled him to think of himself as a leader in his own right.

Now Zhou threw his full support to Mao. Never to the end of their lives, in the fateful year of 1976, would Zhou challenge Mao's leadership. The complex factors that underlay Zhou's decision cannot be fully explored. Not enough is known of his inner feelings. But from Zunyi forward, whatever his title, he would, in fact, act as chief of staff for Mao Zedong. It was a partnership that had little precedent in Chinese politics.

It is plain enough that there was and always would be differences in political outlook and style between Zhou and Mao. Mao was very much a "native" (the phrase is that of Ambassador Wang Bingnan), a man of the countryside who had gone down to the quay in Shanghai on March 19, 1919, and waved goodbye as his best friends sailed for France and the work-study program in which he had been so deeply involved. He did not join them.

Scholars have long speculated over Mao's act. Some believe he turned back for lack of money; or because of difficulty in learning French; or because he felt ill at ease in the company of those better dressed and richer than himself.

None of these explanations seems valid. Li Rui, the Chinese historian who has devoted much of his life to studying Mao, believes Mao never intended to go abroad. He believed that his friends should partake of Western culture; bring back elements useful to China. This was most important. But Mao's place was China. Had he gone abroad, the core group in China would have disintegrated.

Li Rui believed that Mao had concluded that China must be reformed and rebuilt and that he was the man to do it; that he must be the leader, and so felt a responsibility to remain in China. Mao did not display quite that interest in the West that he should have. It was, Li Rui felt, a shortcoming.[11]

This circumstance played a role throughout Mao's career. Conflict and tension between émigrés and "natives" is inevitable. Some believe that Mao was always jealous of Zhou's finesse and, in later years, his world reputation. Be that as it may, the alliance of these dissimilar persons proved unbreakable. The two were complementary, Mao being the philosopher, the poet, the man who dreamed the impossible dream, the man of incandescent spirit who was prepared for any sacrifice, any strategy that would bring his vision to reality, inflexible in goals but flexible in how they might be achieved, and (until his last years) a genius at utilizing human material, again and again fashioning his enemies and rivals into useful allies; Zhou being the pragmatist, the diplomat, the humanist, the man who minded the store.

Many years later, when Zhou Enlai and Mao had long reached supreme power in China, at a moment when Zhou had survived the madness of the Cultural Revolution by nimble mind, dazzling tongue, and dauntless courage (with Mao lifting not a finger to save him), Zhou was able to say of Mao: "We are all his students, but we cannot do as well as he." He spoke the words, I believe, with total sincerity. I thought then as I heard them, as I think a dozen years later, that Zhou meant what he said explicitly and without qualification. But how he resolved within his mind that *luan,* that great turmoil of Mao's last years which came close to sweeping him and all of China away, I cannot imagine.

It has often been said by foreigners and by some Chinese that Zhou was the perfect courtier, the trusted and obedient executor of policy, the pragmatic administrator who kept the ship of state on course despite Mao's anarchistic flights—for example, the Great Leap Forward and the Cultural Revolution. Zhou was all this and much more, as anyone knows who has heard from Chinese the stories of his small and large kindnesses: of the wounded soldier on the Long March whom he placed on a litter with his own hands, fearful that other hands would not be so gentle; his hard anger when he found his old friend Anna Louise Strong dying in a hospital with no relative to sit at her bedside; the stories of the evenings in his last turbulent years when, worn and worried, he would slip into the kitchen of the Beijing Hotel for a simple bowl of noodles before one more formal banquet at the Great Hall of the People. No wonder a personality cult of Zhou has grown up in late years.

With Zunyi, many pieces of the Long March fell into place. When the Red Army arrived February 5 at the three-border corner of Guizhou-Yunnan-Sichuan, a small town called Jimingsansheng,* Bo Gu was

*Jimingsansheng means "the cock's crow can be heard in three provinces."

quietly replaced as responsible Central Committee secretary in charge of day-to-day affairs and Luo Fu took the job. Mao was formally designated to "assist" Zhou Enlai in military decisions. On March 11, Mao was named to the Military Commission along with Zhou Enlai and Wang Jiaxiang. Of course, Mao's was the decisive presence.

One of Mao's first moves was to try to get in touch with Moscow and tell them about Zunyi. There was no way to communicate except by courier. The first courier sent was Pan Hannian, who had been entrusted with many secret missions to regional warlords. Pan Hannian reached Shanghai but found no Communist apparatus there. It had been wiped out by Chiang's secret police.[12]

In May 1935 a second secret emissary, Chen Yun, author of the newly discovered Zunyi memo, was sent off. He disguised himself as a merchant and left after the Red Army had crossed the Dadu River. In Shanghai, he got in touch with Soong Chingling, who arranged passage by steamer to Vladivostok. On August 5, 1935, a group including Chen Yun; He Shichu, daughter of Mao's Changsha friend and co-founder of the Communist Party, He Shuheng, who had been left behind in the Central Soviet Area, and wife of Chen Gang, a Sichuan official now dead; Pan Hannian; Yang Zhihua, widow of former Party leader Qu Qiubai; and Chen Tanqiu sailed for Vladivostok. Qu Qiubai had been executed by the KMT with much publicity only six weeks earlier. The widow Yang Zhihua was associated with International Red Help, a Comintern subsidiary which assisted arrested Communists and underground workers. Chen Tanqiu was a party founder in 1921 along with Mao and He Shuheng.

Chen Tanqiu was a "left-behind" in Fujian. He had been Luo Ming's successor as Party Secretary there and had himself been criticized, which is probably why he had not been taken on the Long March. Luckier than some, he managed to get out and join the party to Moscow (only to lose his life in 1943, along with Mao's brother Zemin, executed by the Xinjiang warlord Sheng Shicai, who shifted his alliance away from Russia and the Communists to Chiang Kai-shek).

There were, Chen Yun said later, seven or eight in his party. It was quite a high-level group and it may be that its nominal purpose was to represent the Chinese Party at the Seventh Congress of the Comintern, then in progress in Moscow. The Comintern had in 1934 sent an invitation to the Chinese to send a delegation of sixty members to this meeting, originally planned for 1934 but postponed until the summer of 1935.[13]

The delegation didn't get there in time. They arrived on August 20, 1935, the last day of the meeting, too late to report on Zunyi or anything else. The Seventh Congress could have used a little information. In its absence, the Comintern heard a speech by Wang Ming about the rising tide of revolution in China. Finally, in February 1936, the *Comintern Journal* published an article called "The Heroic Western March," by Chen Yun (under the assumed name Shi Ping, which meant nothing to anyone; the article was totally ignored). It did not mention Zunyi. Zunyi was top secret.

Chen Yun's article said nothing of the change in military and political leadership. The move from the Central Soviet Area was mentioned, but Chiang Kai-shek's Fifth Encirclement was called a failure. The "great maneuver" was moving ahead with success (the Red Army had long since reached northern Shaanxi, but this was not noted). The Red Army was preserving its strength and its goal was to expand to one million men. The only negative was that when they left the Central Soviet Area the troops had been burdened with very heavy baggage.[14]

Behind the scenes the Comintern took immediate steps to reestablish communications with China. Pan Hannian was sent back, arriving in Shanghai in November or December 1935, bringing codebooks so that secret message exchanges could resume. It is not clear whether he brought wireless apparatus. Probably not. However, arrangements were made, it is said, for use of a transmitter located in Soong Chingling's house in the French concession, the one where she and Dr. Sun Yat-sen had lived, on Rue Molière.

The question of whether a Communist transmitter operated from Madame Soong's house has been a matter of controversy for years. Many of her close friends, including Rewi Alley, have fiercely denied this, asking how it could be possible with KMT guards outside the house day and night. However, two major Chinese Party historians, Hu Hua and Xiang Qing, declared it did operate there.

Pan Hannian was installed as formal liaison between the Party and the Comintern and Madame Soong, under the cover of being her secretary. Pan, a man of sophistication and education, became one of Madame Soong's closest associates until his arrest in 1953 on charges of being a Japanese spy. He died after twenty years in prison, but following the death of Mao and the fall of the Gang of Four, he was fully rehabilitated.[15]

13

A NEEDLE WRAPPED IN COTTON

Deng Xiaoping started the Long March under a dark cloud. He had been removed from his army and political posts, had been harshly "struggled against," had been held under armed guard and publicly denounced, and his wife had divorced him. It was not the lowest point in his career, but it was a low spot. Some of the stories told about this period are certainly not true. There seems no evidence that he was actually sent—as some claim—to do forced labor. He began the Long March as a worker in the Army Political Department, carrying his own gear like thousands of other Red Army men. He was not—as some have claimed—one of the five thousand human haulers who packed the Red Army's machinery on their shoulders. But these are typical of the legends that have grown up around Deng Xiaoping's early days.

Zunyi changed Deng's lowly status. As was to happen again and again through his career, Deng rose up from political depths to join Mao in the higher echelons.

Not all the details of Deng's fall and India-rubber bounce back are clear in the memories of those who went on the Long March. But of his upward bound there is no doubt. Deng was thirty years old when the March started, son of a petty official of Guangan county, Sichuan, about sixty miles north of Chongqing.

As a supporter of Mao he had suffered for his fiery temperament and plain speaking. The Sichuanese are renowned pepper pots, and Deng fit the mold. He came from a traditional Chinese family. His father, one of the Hakka or "guest people" so common in Guangdong, had moved north to Sichuan.

Deng's father served as chief of a local defense corps organized by the gentry of Guangan county. He was in charge of a contingent of about a hundred men. Deng left home at an early age. He attended secondary school and then took a special course at Chongqing in preparation for going to France on a work-study program. At sixteen he joined a group of ninety-two Chinese students and sailed for France.[1]

In Paris, Deng worked first at the Renault factory and then as a locomotive fireman. He had little money and not much to eat. "I used to be very happy when I could afford to buy a croissant and a glass of milk," Deng told General Yang Shangkun. Deng believed that his diminutive stature (he is only a little more than five feet tall) might be due to his scant diet. His Paris days left him with a lifelong love of French food and particularly for croissants. When in 1974 he was sent to New York to represent China at the United Nations Economic Conference, he was given some pocket money—thirty yuan, about sixteen dollars. He decided to spend it on croissants. Huang Hua, permanent representative to the UN, suggested that Deng wait until he passed through Paris on the way home—the croissants would arrive fresher. Deng took the advice; he bought one hundred and gave them to Zhou Enlai and others who had formed a taste for croissants in their Paris days. Prince Sihanouk, who spent much time in Beijing after he lost out in Cambodia, sometimes cooked a French dinner and sent it to Deng with his compliments. Deng learned to cook in France, making meals for himself and for other Chinese students who lived together in an old house.[2]

As Deng told Edgar Snow in 1936, he spent most of his time abroad working, not studying. He learned Marxism from his fellow French workers, joining the French Communist Party before he joined the European branch of the Chinese Party founded by Zhou Enlai and other young Chinese.[3] In this he followed the path of a fellow Asian revolutionary who was a bit older, Ho Chi Minh, also working in France. The two met in Paris and their paths were to cross not infrequently as years went by. Deng got to know Zhou Enlai well in these days. He was active in the Young Socialist League started by Zhou. He distributed leaflets and cut stencils for the duplicating machine.

Deng came back to China in 1926 via Mongolia and Ningxia after some months in Moscow, where he studied at Sun Yat-sen University. Another student was Chiang Kai-shek's son, Jiang Jingguo. In later years Deng recalled Jiang Jingguo as "getting on pretty well" in the university, which then catered to KMT as well as Communist Chinese. In China, Deng worked awhile with Feng Yuxiang, the "Christian General," close to the Communists. Deng set up a military training school for him near Xi'an. After Chiang Kai-shek's reign of terror in Shanghai, Deng was sent to Wuhan and then into the Shanghai underground where for a time he served as Secretary-General of the Central Committee, an administrative post.

His first big Party assignment came in 1929, when he was sent into south Guangxi to organize what came to be a major guerrilla operation centered around the so-called Seventh and Eighth armies. He was named political commissar.[4]

Deng had a younger brother, Deng Ken, who in later years served as mayor of Wuhan. By 1984 he had retired. A younger sister was still working in 1984 in a scientific institute in Beijing. Deng's mother died when the children were small and they were brought up by a stepmother.

The Seventh and Eighth armies were not real armies—they numbered a few thousand men at best. Deng had great difficulty in carrying out his assignment because the Eighth Army had its base at Longzhou, on the border of Guangxi and Indochina. To reach it, Deng had to go by ship from Hongkong to Haiphong and make his way up through Indochina and cross over to Longzhou. He was aided in this by the Indochinese underground, which was carrying on an uprising in the border area across from Longzhou. Whether Ho Chi Minh was personally active in this operation is not clear.[5] The Indochinese Communist Party was founded only in May 1929 at a meeting held during a soccer game at the Shanghai racetrack. Ho worked closely with the Chinese, in underground Shanghai, Hongkong, and Canton.

Deng's career with the Seventh Army was quickly affected by struggles at the top of the Chinese Communist Party. He was removed as secretary of the Front Committee and replaced by a man named Deng Gang—sometimes confused with him. Deng Xiaoping's real name was Deng Bin. (In France he was known as Deng Xixian.)[6] By the time the Seventh Army was instructed to move out of Guangxi to Hunan, Deng Xiaoping had his job back, but the Seventh Army was little more than a shadow. It boasted three "divisions": The skeleton Twenty-first Division was left behind, in command of Wei Baqun. Deng took the Nineteenth and Chen Haoren the Twentieth, now more realistically called the Fifty-fifth and Fifty-eighth regiments. Soon Deng was sent off to Shanghai to report to the underground Party leadership on what had happened in Guangxi. He arrived there in February 1931.[7]

Deng went up and down at least twice with the Seventh Army. Years later, when, after Mao's death, Deng had finally become China's leader, a knowledgeable Chinese was asked how the people felt about him in view of the frankness and stubbornness that plunged him into one Party dispute after another. "That's why we trust him," the Chinese said.

When Deng came back to the Central Soviet Area in August 1931 and took up the post of Party secretary of Ruijin county, he walked into a mess. The county was in the throes of an "anti-reactionary" campaign, one of those periodic purges that rack secretive revolutionary movements. It had its roots in an almost incomprehensible sequence of events.

In 1926 some right-wing Chinese Nationalists in Nanchang formed a pro-KMT organization which was called the AB. Those were the days of Communist-Nationalist collaboration. The AB's were a minor group of no significance and soon petered out. However, many young Chinese patriots had joined.

In 1930, when young Chinese began returning from the Soviet Union to join the Communist movement, they were asked by Party security agents to list organizations to which they had belonged. Not a few said they had belonged to the AB.

A series of paranoid inferences led the security agents to believe that the AB's were operatives whom the KMT was trying to infiltrate into Communist ranks and that the initials stood for "anti-Bolshevik." Before this dangerous nonsense had run its course, some three to four thousand suspected AB's had been arrested in what was called the Futian Incident and many had been shot.[8]

The fear was heightened by rumors spread by the KMT of its nonexistent underground organization. Party security agents extorted hundreds of "confessions" of membership in the phantom AB organization. There are no reliable estimates of how many were awaiting execution in Ruijin prisons when Deng Xiaoping took over, but they probably numbered in the hundreds.

Deng brought the witch hunt to an end. He ordered detailed examinations of all those being held. Most were sent back to their jobs. If they were found guilty of abuses or mistakes they were fired. Zhou En-lai, on arriving in the soviet area a month or two later, supported a similar approach. Deng was assisted in liquidating the madness by Xie Weijun and other Ruijin Party officials. That was it. The killing ended.[9]

Those arrested had been held as "enemies hidden in the ranks of the Party." All this bore an uncanny resemblance on a small scale to what would happen in the Cultural Revolution and the era of the Gang of Four, in which Deng was to be a notable victim thirty or more years

later. As in Ruijin in 1931, so in Beijing in 1977–78, Deng would ultimately end the hysteria and set free the innocent.

Deng Xiaoping did not hold the secretaryship of Ruijin county very
long. On November 7, 1931, the establishment of the "interim" Chinese Soviet Government was proclaimed, with Ruijin as the "Red capital." A few months later—Deng does not now recall the exact date—
he was shifted from Ruijin to the lesser post of secretary of Huichang
county, and soon after that was given Xunwu and Anyuan counties as
well. It sounded more impressive than it was. The counties were all
recently and only partially liberated. The Red Army never got hold of
the three county seats.

By the winter of 1932–33, Deng Xiaoping was getting into hot water
again. He was well known as an articulate supporter of Mao, and now
Bo Gu and his anti-Mao faction began taking over the Central Soviet
Area and campaigning to deprive Mao of his remaining power.

As Deng Xiaoping recollected in 1984, he held the tri-county post
for about half a year. Although Deng has admonished his colleagues of
the necessity of accurate historical writing and research, he himself has
refused to write his memoirs and has rejected proposals for an official
biography, motivated perhaps by his abhorrence of the cult of personality that grew up around Mao.[10]

The campaign against Mao was initiated by an unsigned article in
the internal Party bulletin, probably written by Bo Gu or Luo Fu. The
Bolsheviks didn't dare attack Mao openly, so instead, in the elliptical
fashion of Chinese politics, they criticized Luo Ming, who was Party
secretary of Fujian province and a staunch supporter of Mao. Deng
Xiaoping was not mentioned but it was well known that he shared Luo
Ming's views and supported Mao.

Almost immediately, Luo Ming was removed from office. Deng was
transferred to the Propaganda Department of the Jiangxi Party Committee, as director.

On April 15 the campaign against Deng went public when Luo Fu
published an article in *Red China*. Luo Fu named names, first among
them Deng Xiaoping, labeled a follower of the "Luo Ming line." The
next name was Mao Zetan, followed by Xie Weijun, who had aided
Deng against the "AB" hysteria, and Gu Bo, a long-term Mao supporter.
All four were removed from their posts.[11] Two were to be left behind
and perish when the Red Army started the Long March.

Deng was now sent to the General Political Department of the Red

Army, to be "struggled against." There are conflicting reports of what happened. Struggles were no kid-glove affairs. Physical violence was common. The subject was kept under detention, and it seems clear that Deng was no exception. An article by Lo Man (Li Weihan) in the journal of the Party Central Bureau, *Struggle,* May 6, called for "an attack without mercy and a struggle with brutality" against Deng and the other followers of the "Luo Ming line." Lo Man was secretary of the Party organization bureau. He was fierce in his demands for Deng's punishment. It was at this time that Deng's wife, A Jin (Jin Weiying), divorced him and married Lo Man, a big, handsome, deliberate man. Whether this influenced Lo Man's harshness toward Deng cannot be established. A Jin was a Cantonese and is remembered as a woman of talent. She, like Deng, had been a Party secretary in Ruijin and was known as something of an individualist. A Jin and Lo Man completed the Long March together, but were divorced in Yan'an.[12]

Deng was charged with following a "rich peasant line" because he believed in leaving the middle peasants alone while expropriating the rich and giving their land to the poor. He also believed in maintaining regional armed forces in the counties rather than uniting them under central direction as the Bolsheviks insisted. And Deng supported Mao's strategy of letting the enemy penetrate Communist territory, then ambushing him and wiping him out.[13]

Deng wrote two or three self-criticisms. He confessed he had undervalued the "offensive line," but this did not satisfy his accusers. "I cannot say more," Deng insisted. "What I write is true." Deng had his back up. He would go no further.[14]

One day as Deng was being brought back to his detention cell by his guards, he encountered Tang Yizhen. She was the wife of Lu Dingyi, deputy premier of the soviet area and later the propaganda chief who was to be so badly injured by the Red Guards during the Cultural Revolution.

"I'm so hungry," Deng told her. "I don't get enough to fill my stomach."

She took pity on him and bought two chickens for a silver dollar. After she cooked them, she sent a message to the guards to bring Deng to her house for dinner. Deng came, ate a chicken, and took the other back to his cell to eat later. Tang Yizhen was compelled to remain behind in the soviet area. Her husband made the Long March and survived.[15]

Deng's conduct under "struggle" was consistent with his conduct in later life. He was prepared to admit mistakes, but would not confess to errors of judgment when he believed himself to be correct. He supported Mao's strategy and he could not be budged on that point.

There are half a dozen accounts of what happened next. Some versions say Deng was sent to the countryside to do forced labor.[16] General Yang Shangkun says "he was sent down to the grass roots," but what he did there Yang did not know.[17] The most precise account relates that he was sent to Nancun in Le'an county, far from Ruijin, as an "inspector." What he inspected, no one seems to know. All agreed it was a lowly post. He stayed there only a brief time, possibly not more than ten days. It was an area of guerrilla warfare. Communist and KMT forces roamed a no-man's-land, all "tangled together," as Yan Jingtang, the military researcher, put it. It was thought in Ruijin that "something might happen"—that is, that Deng might defect to the KMT. So he was brought back.[18]

Deng was now transferred to the Red Army as secretary general of the General Political Department, whose director was Wounded Wang Jiaxiang. He held this job for two or three months and then, it is said, at his own request was relieved of duties and became an ordinary political worker. Another account relates that at his own request he became editor of *Red Star,* the Army newspaper. However, as Li Yimang pointed out, it was not possible to publish *Red Star* during the Long March, so Deng had not much to do but walk along side by side with Li Yimang in the General Political Department. Li Yimang later amended that to say that actually they rode, each being provided with a horse.[19]

Whatever the case, this changed at Zunyi or just before. Deng Xiaoping attended the Zunyi sessions as editor of *Red Star.* Shortly before Zunyi, at the time of the Liping meeting, in his recollection, he became secretary-general of the Central Committee or, as Liu Ying described it, of the "Central Team."

This post sounds more impressive than it was. The function of the secretary, insofar as it can be reconstructed in today's memories, consisted in taking notes of meetings, keeping papers straight, filing documents, forwarding and receiving messages, drafting orders. No messages or documents bearing Deng's signature as secretary-general have been uncovered.

Deng's presence at Zunyi has been a matter of rather recent historical inquiry. Deng himself recalled having been there and General Yang

Shangkun undertook a personal inquiry. Yang had been present but could not recall Deng's being there. Yang asked Premier Zhou Enlai about it in the early 1970s. Zhou said Deng indeed had been present. Later Yang recalled seeing Deng sitting in a corner, busily scribbling notes—either for *Red Star* or because he was secretary. In any event, the notes, like almost all written materials about Zunyi, have been lost.

Just before the Red Army reached the Snowy Mountains in April 1935, Mao decreed that all men in the support apparatus must take military posts at the front. Deng Xiaoping went to the First Army Group to direct political propaganda, and diminutive Liu Ying filled his place as secretary-general until the Red Army reached the Grasslands. By the time the Red Army got to northern Shaanxi, Deng was seriously ill with a form of typhoid fever and was not able to resume work for a considerable period of time.[20]

No one bounced Deng Xiaoping up and down more than Mao Zedong. He once growled that Deng deliberately sat in the back of the room when Mao spoke because, being deaf, he would not be able to hear what Mao was saying. But in 1973 Zhou Enlai was fatally ill and Mao brought Deng back from the purgatory of the Cultural Revolution. Mao spoke warmly of him as a "needle wrapped in cotton," by which he meant Deng was sharp but also delicate. "His mind," said Mao, "is round and his actions are square."

No longer was Deng marching in the ranks as the Red Army set out from Zunyi. He had his horse and he had his new assignments from Mao. But as Deng's fortunes went up, those of another went down. Absent from the high command as the Red Army struck out on its new course to the northwest was the tall figure on horseback of Otto Braun. Even before the Zunyi meetings had concluded, Braun had asked and gotten permission to join Lin Biao's First Army Group in order, as he said, "to acquaint myself through direct experience at the front with the Chinese civil warfare so highly extolled by Mao." He loaded up his horse with special supplies from the quartermaster, again drawing some ugly remarks from the Chinese, and hurried off to join Lin Biao. It took him three or four days, and when he finally met Lin Biao, he claimed, he got a surly reception. Nonetheless, he set in to study Mao's style of warfare, putting aside one of his favorite recreations, poker, with which he had whiled away many an evening with Bo Gu and his two interpreters.

When the Red Army passed through Zunyi briefly again, having taken it for a second time, Interpreter Wu Xiuquan dropped by to see Braun. Wu had gotten himself assigned to the front as deputy chief of staff of the Third Army Group. Braun was sitting at a table, methodically cracking walnuts and eating them. Wu sat down and began to crack walnuts too. Braun looked up and said: "The relationship between us is a military relationship and that relationship has nothing to do with cracking walnuts."[21]

For the rest of the Long March, Braun's role would be that of a spectator.

14

MAO SKIRTS DISASTER

For the first time since the Long March began, the Red Army was traveling on a real highway, and for the first time Mao Zedong rode at its head on a big white horse.* Moving north from Zunyi, Mao's old comrade Zhu De rode on his right, and his new comrade Luo Fu on his left. The battle-worn troops made a fine spectacle as they entered Tongzi to the cheers of two thousand excited people. Tongzi had been seized by Lin Biao a couple of weeks earlier.[1]

The Red Army was entering a mystical kingdom, a land of legend, poetry, and tradition. This was a region of great underground caverns, the Faery Cave and Heaven's Gate, vast expanses of limestone chambers endlessly branching out into passages that no one had fully penetrated. Some said Heaven's Gate was the largest cave in China, or perhaps in the world. Tens of thousands of people could be sheltered in its main cavern.

Tongzi was a small town, but it was famous for its generals. More generals had been born in Tongzi county than in any other in all China. This was a habitat of minor warlords, each of whom built himself a warlord's standard house with the inevitable wraparound second-story balcony. Outside most of them a car was parked.[2] Each warlord possessed a store of gold and concubines. Tongzi and its neighbor, Maotai, fifty miles to the southwest, were renowned centers of wealth (opium and liquor). The first thing the Red Army did when it reached Tongzi was to rush detachments to the limestone caves to recover the gold, silver, and treasure hastily hidden by fleeing generals and landlords. For weeks the Red Army would be rich with the silver dollars it expropriated (but short on rice and food; the area didn't produce much but gold and opium).

*Now to be seen stuffed and preserved in the museum at Yan'an.

The wonderland of Faery Cave and Heaven's Gate would come to prominence in World War II when the KMT set up arms factories and subterranean power plants in these remote recesses to escape Japanese bombing. And here the "Young Marshal," Zhang Xueliang, kidnapper of Chiang Kai-shek at Xi'an in 1936, would be brought as a prisoner, walked for endless distances underground until he had lost all sense of direction, then brought back to daylight and installed in a miniature palace beside the pretty lake called Small West Lake in an echo of the famous West Lake at Hangzhou, there to live alone but for a talented, devoted woman secretary named Zhao, the two falling in love and spending their lives together. When Chiang left the mainland for Taiwan he took them along. They married in 1964.[3]

Again in 1949 the Red Army descended on this romantic corner. Again the warlords deposited their treasure in the caverns. Again the Red Army rooted it out. So many KMT commanders and troops fled to the hills that it was years before all were exterminated.[4]

One Long March general, Luo Binghui, told Helen Snow that the whole campaign in Guizhou was "like a monkey playing with a cow in a narrow alley."

I don't believe Mao would have described it like that. His objective was clear—to find a path north across the Yangtze River so he could join the Fourth Front Army led by Zhang Guotao. Chiang Kai-shek had a pretty shrewd idea that Mao wanted to go north, and had positioned first-class troops to bar his way.

Even before he had left Zunyi, Mao sent Lin Biao ahead in hope he could clear a path over the Yangtze, possibly between Luzhou and Yibin, a river stretch 90 to 150 miles southwest of Chongqing, where Chiang sat directing operations aimed at sewing up the Red Army in the Guizhou-Yunnan-Sichuan pocket much as he had tried to do earlier in the Jiangxi "Red corner."

Mao had split his forces. Lin Biao at the head of the redoubtable Second Division and the Fourth Shock Regiment was probing for a crossing of the Red River at Chishui preliminary to tackling the Yangtze. Mao was leading the First Division of the First Army Group and the other top units westward from Tongzi and finding the road a shambles, not to be compared with the highway from Zunyi. Chen Yun, writing under the nom de plume of Dr. Lian Chen, called it the worst road he'd seen on the Long March. He watched Mao climbing a hill, stick in hand. It had been snowing and Mao was up to his knees in mud.

He evidently had slipped and was covered with dirt from head to toe.[5]

Mao was leading his column west toward the Red River, hoping to wheel north and follow in Lin Biao's footsteps as soon as Lin achieved a breakthrough. Peng Dehuai's Third Army Group—all of these "armies" were little more than divisions in size—was moving on a similar westward course a little to Mao's north. The Ninth Army was engaged in reconnaissance and the Fifth, as usual, was on rear-guard duty almost at the heels of the Third. Whether it was wise of Mao to divide his small force into so many columns was argued after the fact, but his aim was to confuse Chiang Kai-shek as to his intention of forcing a crossing of the Yangtze and to make that crossing at some point not yet protected by Chiang's troops. He hoped that the bad relations between Chiang and the Sichuan warlords might work in his favor.

But war often proves to be a summation of miscalculations. Lin Biao, usually clever and surefooted in finding a way around enemies, ran into trouble. He had gotten to Tucheng on the Red River without a hitch. People met him with red flags and the Guizhou troops fled in panic across the river. He then headed for Chishui, another Red River town, a bit farther north, where he anticipated a similar welcome. The workers in a small government arsenal at Chishui had staged a demonstration on January 16 and Lin thought that should help. Lin Biao had four thousand men under his command. They were excited at the prospect of seeing Chishui because it had electric lights, something most of them had never seen. But when Lin arrived at Huangpidong, a village not far from Chishui, he found the enemy had a strong blockhouse on one side of the road and a powerful position atop a small mountain on the other. The enemy forces poured down heavy machine gun fire. Lin's Third Regiment did its best, but could not get through the corridor of fire. Lin sent them around the little mountain, looking for a rear approach. There was none. His men fought all day and got nowhere. They could see the main road about a mile away and clouds of dust as KMT reinforcements rushed toward Chishui. Lin fought until dusk, then pulled back some distance, and reluctantly sent off an overnight message to Mao, reporting his lack of success.[6]

For a couple of days Mao's main column had been dogged by an enemy force. Not much attention was paid to it. There had been Guizhou regiments trailing the column and it was taken for granted that these were Guizhou "two-gun" men. On January 27, Mao was encamped on the outskirts of Tucheng on the Red River. Peng Dehuai's

Third Army was not far away. The Fifth was also close by. It was decided that evening that in the morning Peng's Third Army would turn on the trailing enemy force, thought to number about two regiments, possibly two or three thousand men, and wipe them out. This was the kind of operation for which Zhu-Mao were famous. It would get rid of pursuers and free the Red Army to move swiftly on the heels of Lin Biao as soon as he reported—as they expected momentarily he would—that he had found a path to the Yangtze. They would be free of pursuit and should get north of the Yangtze before Chiang knew what was up. It was a daring scenario but an entirely plausible one.[7]

At dawn on the morning of January 28, the Third Army attacked. Mao set up a command position at a village called Qinggangpo, a couple of miles east of Tucheng. He put his post on a round hilltop just beyond the village, which gave him a fine field of observation—nearly 360 degrees. Everything seemed set for a quick kill. Usually a battle of this kind was over in a couple of hours. The Fifth Army was positioned so that it could quickly deliver a knockout blow.

Sometime fairly early in the morning, Mao received the bad news from Lin Biao of his failure to break through to Chishui. Lin had halted overnight at a point about twenty miles north of Mao, a half day's march away. His fast-moving men normally traveled at what would today be called a jogging pace.

Not long after receiving the message from Lin Biao, Mao began to realize that something was going wrong with his kill-and-destroy attack on the two-gun men. By midmorning it was apparent that the enemy was not fleeing the battlefield in panic. The Red Army was fighting well, but so was the enemy. In fact, he grew stronger and stronger. By noon, Mao and his commanders knew they had a dangerous fight on their hands. The enemy was not a sluggish Guizhou outfit but a topnotch Sichuan army commanded by Guo Xunqi, nicknamed Panda, under the direction of the Sichuan commander in chief, Liu Xiang, at Yibin on the Yangtze. Nor was this, as they thought, a force of only two regiments. It was two brigades—that is, four regiments. Nor was this all. As the battle grew more fierce, more Sichuan regiments appeared, until there were eight in all, at least ten thousand men, well trained, well disciplined, well led. Mao had blundered into as critical a battle as the Red Army would fight in the whole Long March. His intelligence reports could not have been more mistaken.

In numbers the Sichuanese were about equal to the force that Mao had deployed—not the four-to-one advantage he had expected. He was fighting man for man. True there should have been another ten or fifteen thousand Red Army men not too far away, but somehow they never were brought into the fight. Lin Biao with possibly four thousand of the Red Army's men was, like Sheridan, twenty miles away. Every signal was flashing danger and the day was little more than half spent.

Twice, top commanders went down to the battlefield. For both Zhu De and Liu Bocheng to leave GHQ and personally inspect operations was a sign of utmost urgency. When it became apparent that the Sichuan commander had put eight regiments on the field, the outcome hung in the balance.

So critical was the situation that Mao, Zhou Enlai, and Zhu De took personal command of the battle.[8]

The Red Army had two mountain artillery guns left—all the artillery that had survived. Rather late in the battle, Zhu De brought one of the guns into action. There were only two or three shells. These were fired at a Sichuan training brigade which had carried the battle vigorously to the Red Army. When the shells had been fired, Zhu De ordered the gun tossed into the Red River. There was no more use for it.[9]

At 2 P.M. came another sign of tension. Lin Biao—twenty miles away—was ordered at full speed to Qinggangpo to reinforce the heavily engaged Third Army. Since Lin Biao could not arrive until after nightfall, this betrayed concern that the Red Army might be in even more difficulty before morning.

An hour later, at 3 P.M., the battle still raging, losses more and more heavy—at one point Kang Keqing, wife of Zhu De, had fled for her life, escaping a surprise attack in a rain of bullets[10]—an emergency meeting of the Military Commission was called, the only known Red Army emergency meeting in the midst of battle. But this was no ordinary battle. It was now clear that the fate of the Red Army might be at stake. If more enemy brigades appeared, would the Red Army be able to hold them off? No one could say. By midafternoon the reserve of reserves, the elite Cadres Regiment of military cadets, the life guard of the high command, was sent into the struggle (it acquitted itself well). The emergency meeting took extraordinary steps. It ordered the battle broken off at dusk. Bridges across the Red River must be thrown over with no delay. The campaign to the north across the Yangtze was canceled. When if ever the main force would join the Fourth Front Army and Zhang Guotao events would show. Sichuan was postponed. The Red Army would seek refuge in Yunnan. New orders were rushed out to Lin Biao. He must join the evacuation before the enemy closed off the crossing of the Red River. Every effort would be devoted to escape, to preserving the Red Army as a fighting force. Mao had been in command for ten days and now the fate of the Army hung in balance.

Mao got a break. When Lin Biao had arrived at Tucheng a few days earlier, he had captured a floating bridge across the Red River. It was still in place. At 6 P.M. the engineers were ordered to put this bridge in order and build two more. Three times during the night Zhou Enlai came down to the riverside to inspect the work and encourage the engineers to hurry even more. The bridges must be ready before the sun rose.

The weather was benign. The bitter cold of the Five Ridges had moderated. No more snow. The river was broad and shallow and quiet at this season. The engineers did their work well. The pontoons were as wide as a highway. Lin Biao got his troops across in time at Yuanhou, a bit to the north. Before dawn on January 29, the Red Army was moving briskly across the Red River. How many casualties they left behind is not recorded, but both Communist and KMT sources agree that they were heavy on both sides. Some KMT accounts suggest a figure of two thousand or more Communists killed and wounded. No contemporary Communist source would venture an estimate. They would not even specify what the KMT figures were because they were "too high and misleading." When the Red Army got to Zhaxi (now Weixin) in Yunnan, they claimed their total roster was about thirty thousand. If that figure was correct, their casualties must have been heavy enough to wipe out most of the four thousand or so recruits they had picked up in Zunyi and environs.

Once the Red Army moved into Yunnan, the Sichuan and Guizhou forces wheeled away. The Red Army—and Mao—was safe for the moment. It had been a very close call. In his first battle since taking control, Mao had skirted disaster. Qinggangpo was not a battle that would enter the history books. In fact, this is the first account of it to appear in print.[11]

Before daylight the Red Army was streaming over the three pontoons and by 10 A.M. the whole force, including the troops of Lin Biao, was on the other side, the bridges had been pulled up and destroyed, and Mao was headed for Gulin in the projecting finger of Sichuan and then on to Zhaxi, where the Red Army would regroup, recruit, and replan.

At a point most probably just after the crossing of the Red River, tragedy again entered the life of Mao's wife, He Zizhen. Attended by Dr. Nelson Fu, she gave birth at 9 P.M. of an evening, to her fourth child, a girl. The Red Army was on the run. GHQ and Mao were pulling out at 4 A.M. There was no way to make proper arrangements for the care of the infant, nor was it possible to bring it along. A few hours after birth the child was taken from He Zizhen and turned over to a peasant couple. There was no time to think of a name. The baby was wrapped in a fine piece of black cloth, given to the peasants along with sixteen to twenty-four silver dollars. The peasants pledged themselves to care for the girl. Before dawn Mao, his wife, and the Red Army were on the road, the enemy in close pursuit. No trace of the child was ever to be found.

That is the story as told by Wu Jiqing, Mao's bodyguard, in attendance on He Zizhen at the time. He first said the child was born at a place called Baisha, but Baisha is 130 miles from the Red River. Later he said perhaps it was Fengxiangba, north of Zunyi, or possibly Weixin (Zhaxi), over in Yunnan. None of these locations exactly fits a moment when the Red Army was on the run—although, to be certain, the Red Army was always moving under high tension.[12]

He Zizhen's tragedy was that of the women on the Long March. Little Liu Ying, though not married to Luo Fu until the end of the March, well understood the plight of the women.

"He Zizhen was already pregnant when the Long March started," Liu Ying recalled. "She gave birth to her child and had to leave it behind. There was no alternative. The troops were on the move. It was very sad, but under those dangerous circumstances we could not pay attention to personal feelings."

The women of the Long March were in no position to raise children. It might sound brutal, but, Liu Ying said, they simply had to give the children away or abandon them. It made the women feel better. It was just like abandoning equipment.

He Zizhen had not been the only woman on the March to face the terrible dilemma. There was Zhang Qinqiu, later minister of the textile industry, persecuted to death in the Cultural Revolution. She commanded a women's regiment in the Fourth Front Army. Her husband was Chen Changhao, political commissar of the Fourth. She, too, gave birth to a child and left it behind. So did Liao Siguang, wife of the youth leader He Kequan (Kai Feng), who sided with Bo Gu at Zunyi. This child was left with a peasant family. At first the peasants refused to take it, but they finally were persuaded. The beautiful wife of Xiao Ke, commander of the Sixth Army, found herself pregnant in the winter of 1936 while the Sixth Army was en route to join the Fourth Front Army. In early July in the Grasslands, she gave birth to a boy in an open ten-foot-square enclosure built for her by the troops. The walls were about five feet high.

"The birthing was fairly smooth," Xiao Ke recalled, "and after one or two days she went forward on horseback."

She and her baby reached Yan'an safely. The child was known as the "Grasslands baby" and much was made over him in Yan'an. Late in 1936 the boy was taken to his grandmother in Hunan. But there, near Changde, said Xiao Ke, "he became one of the ten thousand or so people who lost their lives under the attack of germs released by the Japanese."[13]

Most of the children left behind with peasants died. A few were found. Some mothers recovered their children; others discovered the children knew nothing of their real parents and left them in the families where they had grown up.

"The woman had to make a choice," said Liu Ying. "Did she love the Revolution or did she love her child? They loved the Revolution more, and that was their hard decision."[14]

It was most difficult to be a woman on the Long March, in the belief of Ding Ling, China's famous writer, a woman who spent a long life at the heart of controversy—a revolutionary, a romantic, a figure of literature, morals, and politics. She did not make the Long March, but she arrived in Yan'an shortly after the Red Army. She knew them all. She had been one of China's most fiery rebels, imprisoned by Chiang Kai-shek, her poet lover executed by Chiang; a champion of women's rights against Mao in a time when she felt he was male-chauvinistic; a victim, naturally, of the Cultural Revolution.

The women of the Long March, she said, were "fine ladies, of course, but a bunch of tough women or they never could have walked for 25,000 li, walking all the way from Jiangxi to northern Shaanxi." True they had horses, but they often did not ride. Many had husbands, but they used to joke that "mules are better than husbands—husbands are expendable, mules are not."

Pregnancy was hard; some women said it was the greatest disaster that could befall them. To walk day after day with an ever-extending abdomen was no joke. It was just as hard riding horseback. And then after the birth to give up their infant . . . They had to go on with their work regardless.[15]

A match for the trials of He Zizhen and the women on the Long March can be found in another epic march—the westward cavalcade of American pioneers across the prairie. Not a few American women faced the same choice: to keep their child and endanger the family or go forward and abandon the child.

Mao led his army swiftly out of the perilous encounter with the Sichuan troops. As happened again and again on the March, once the provincial forces made certain the Red Army had been diverted from their region, the fury of the assault tapered off. Mao began the Chinese New Year, the Year of the Pig, in Zhaxi, northern Yunnan. The vanguard arrived just after February 4, 1935; Mao, about February 6. There was no New Year's feast. There was nothing to celebrate; nor was there food. Some of the troops went for two days on empty bellies. It was cold, raw, miserable weather. Mao sorted out his troops, scaled down their designations. They got one day's rest. Chen Yun noted laconically: "It was very cold. During the night snow fell."[16]

The Red Army had planned to head west, then swerve north for another entry into Sichuan. Mao switched signals. His intelligence reports and wireless intercepts showed that Chiang was moving his troops west, expecting to crush the Red Army when it again approached the Yangtze. Mao decided on an unexpected tactic, one out of the book of Zhu-Mao. On February 11 at Zhaxi, Mao's decision was approved. He would double back on his tracks, reenter Guizhou, and make another pass at Zunyi. More and more his campaign was beginning to look like a chapter from *Outlaws of the Marshes*. There was a difference. As the Red Army moved on, single file, many were losing their illiteracy. Luo Fu had invented what he called "See Man's Back"—on their backs soldiers wore white linen towels on which Chinese ideographs were painted. As they walked they learned to read.

15

HOLDING CHIANG KAI-SHEK
BY THE NOSE

THE Red Army's order of the day for February 16, 1935, could serve as a slogan of the Long March:

> We must be prepared to walk on highways and also on small roads.
> We must be prepared to travel on a straight line or on a zigzag course.
> We must not damage property because we may come that way again.

It was issued by the Military Commission, but it reads like pure Mao. For the next six weeks this slogan would control the life of the Red Army. Never again would it march and countermarch in such bewildering order. It bewildered Chiang Kai-shek and his commanders. Sometimes the KMT reports of the Red Army were nearly a week late in locating the Communist forces.[1] Sometimes Mao's own generals were bewildered, particularly his protégé Lin Biao, who complained that the troops were being moved too rapidly, pushed too hard, needed rest. His objections were overridden.

Chiang Kai-shek had shifted his troops in anticipation of a new thrust by the Red Army across western Guizhou toward the Yangtze. By the time he got his men in place, the Red Army was moving in the opposite direction. It slipped across the Red River for the second time at Taiping and Erlangtan and swiftly retraced its steps, recapturing Tongzi February 24, on the way back to Zunyi. A company of local troops fled as the Red Army approached.

Now there was another huddle of Red commanders. Lin Biao, or so it is recalled in the anti–Lin Biao atmosphere of today, objected to the dizzy zigzags. He wanted to take the pressure off and proposed a leisurely approach to Loushan Pass, key to Zunyi. There were no heavy enemy units at Loushan—so intelligence said—and Lin argued for a day's delay to give the troops a breather. Doughty Peng Dehuai argued that they had better take advantage of the enemy's weakness and attack the next morning, February 26. The Military Commission came down on Peng's side—one of not a few clashes Peng was to win over Lin Biao during the Long March.

The troops pushed ahead at breakneck speed. They were worn by continuous marching, as even Peng Dehuai conceded. At eight or nine o'clock on the morning of the twenty-sixth, Wang Jialie, the Guizhou warlord, set out from Zunyi in an effort to cut off the Red Army before it could reach Loushan Pass. Word was passed to Peng about 11 A.M. Each force was about forty-five li—that is, eleven or twelve miles—from the pass. Peng set his troops marching at the double (they had been at double pace off and on for several days).[2]

It was a race against time. Peng's Third Army Group was under Lin Biao's command for this operation, but Peng led them to success, occupying the steep pass at about 3 P.M. on February 26 with only minutes to spare. As his men reached the crown of the mountain, looking down toward Zunyi, from the north, they saw the enemy forces only two to three hundred yards away. It was a close call. Peng reported that he suffered only one hundred casualties.[3]

Today Loushan Pass seems a wide, rather gentle gradient up which heavy trucks and buses climb the blacktop in unending stream. Fifty years ago, the walls of the pass were jagged, cutting down sharply to a broad unpaved road used for trucks, motorcars, and carts. The Red Army did not take advantage of the highway to put itself on wheels. This was merely a brief excursion away from the small paths of which the order of the day had spoken.[4]

The five-minute advantage by which Peng Dehuai's troops won the Loushan heights gained the Red Army and Mao Zedong the first segment of the biggest victory of the Long March. The pass had been defended by only one regiment, which Peng's troops demolished. Before nightfall the pass was secure, but between the pass and Zunyi stood Wang Jialie with eight regiments and General Wu Qiwei coming up with two divisions.[5]

The Third Army thundered down from Loushan Pass on February 27 and together with the First moved rapidly toward Zunyi, smashing the enemy forces as they advanced. Within the next few days they knocked out two enemy divisions and eight regiments, killing or driving into the mountains some 3,000 Nationalists and taking 2,000 prisoners. They captured 1,000 rifles and 100,000 rounds of ammunition. The Nationalist press admitted "extremely great losses."[6]

But there were Red Army losses as well. Deng Ping, chief of staff of the Third Army, personally directed the assault on Zunyi. He watched through his field glasses from a hillock about four hundred yards away as the Eleventh Regiment tried in vain to scale the city walls. He told its commissar, Zhang Aiping (in 1985, Minister of Defense), to order a new effort.

A scout came up to report that there was an inner city wall which was giving trouble. Enemy gunners, their attention attracted by the scout's movement, showered the observation post with fire. Deng Ping was instantly killed by a bullet.[7]

The gnarled old Scout Kong led his team into the Loushan battle as a shock force. They were armed with heavy and light machine guns and Kong carried his long Mauser pistol. Everyone had been newly outfitted at Zunyi, but there was still not enough to go around. Kong's outfit had only four padded jackets for each dozen men. They took turns wearing them. In Suiyang county, south of Loushan Pass, halfway to Zunyi, a KMT bomb exploded near Kong and fragments shattered his hip. He was brought by stretcher to Zunyi and taken to the Roman Catholic church, where a surgeon operated on him, after giving him "opium water" to deaden the pain.[8]

The old cathedral was filled with wounded that night. KMT air squadrons were trying to halt the Red Army's drive. Hu Yaobang, in 1984 general secretary of the Communist Party, but then an eighteen-year-old Young Communist League leader, was with the Thirteenth Regiment of Peng Dehuai's Third Army Group, a vanguard unit. Hu Yaobang was one of thirty-two members of the Central Committee of the youth league who made the Long March. Only fourteen or fifteen survived to northern Shaanxi. Hu, small, energetic, wiry, had recovered from the typhoid that struck him down at the beginning of the March. He was a member of the Central Work Team of the Army and very proud of his position.[9]

On the afternoon of February 27, Hu Yaobang was waiting with his propaganda team not far from Zunyi. As soon as the troops had broken the main resistance, Hu Yaobang was to enter Zunyi and help establish order. A squadron of low-flying KMT planes roared down and a bomb fragment caught him in the right hip, inflicting a serious wound.

Hu Yaobang was carried into Zunyi on a litter and taken to the church. There he was operated on by Dr. Wang Bin, still alive in 1984 in his eighties, whom Hu Yaobang regarded as the number one surgeon in the Red Army. Later in the March, Wang was one of the doctors who attended Zhou Enlai, deathly ill of a liver infection. Dr. Wang Bin was one of the KMT surgeons captured by the Red Army and won over by good treatment. He held the rank of major. "It was Red Army policy to win over the technical people to our side, particularly wireless operators, medical personnel, men who could operate heavy machine guns," Hu Yaobang recalled.[10]

Hu Yaobang was carried on a litter for several days after the operation, then rode a horse. The jolting was very painful. He rode for eight or nine days, then gave up his horse to someone who needed it more.

"I never had any feeling about death," Hu Yaobang recalled about these times. "There wasn't any alternative. We just fought on. If we didn't fight, we'd be killed anyway."

Hu Yaobang well remembered Scout Kong Xianquan. There were a number of important Red Army men wounded at Zunyi. One was Luo Ming, of the famous "Luo Ming line" and former Party secretary of Fujian province. He, too, was hit by a bomb fragment. So was Zhong Chibing, Political Commissar in the Third Army.

"Kong kept us awake all night," Hu Yaobang recalled. "He kept shouting: *Sha! Sha! Sha!* [Kill! Kill! Kill!] That was what the Red Army men cried as they charged the enemy."

Scout Kong suffered his wound in the small village of Heishenmiao, just south of the Loushan Pass. After being operated on in Zunyi, he was transported on a litter. His hip bone had been splintered and the wound did not heal. He was carried as far as Qianxi county in Bijie prefecture, on the Red River, a journey of a fortnight or more. Then, Scout Kong was left behind. For twenty months he was bedridden.

But Scout Kong's plight was not too bad. A doctor and a medical orderly had been left behind to care for the him. Scout Kong was given more than three hundred silver dollars to maintain himself (the Red Army treasury was flush with warlord dollars). Kong was placed with a local landlord, who was told: You will be held responsible for the safety of this man. If you protect him well we will be grateful. If anything happens you will be held responsible. The doctor and the orderly were supplied with silver dollars to maintain themselves and buy medicines. Kong was given a list of the drugs he would need.[11] This was very special treatment. Red Army regulations of that time provided that officers of regimental or higher rank if wounded or ill must be carried to the end of the Long March on a litter, if necessary. Kong was only of battalion rank. Special provision was made for him because he was so well known for bravery and daring. Ordinary Red Army wounded who were left behind usually were provided with ten or fifteen silver dollars.[12]

The landlord with whom Kong was left was favorably inclined toward the Red Army. He was superstitious and thought the red flag was an omen of good fortune. The men who brought Kong to the landlord told him they had taken his picture and one of his house. "Don't forget," they warned. "We have pictures. We will come back and check up on you."

Shortly after the Xi'an Incident in December 1936, when Chiang Kai-shek was kidnapped and a united front of the KMT and Communists was formed, the local governor called on all Red Army men to come out of hiding, promising amnesty. But Kong's landlord wouldn't let him go. "Suppose," he said, "three or four years from now the Red Army comes and you are not here—how can I prove that I kept you safe from harm?"

Kong finally recovered and went to work as a stonemason, becoming known as the "lame mason." He married in 1940. His wife died, and he remarried in 1950. By 1984 he had seven children, four boys and three girls. "If I did that today," he said, "they would take me to the hospital and castrate me." He got a minor administrative post when the Communists came to power. In 1966 in the Cultural Revolution he was arrested, put in a truck, and carted around the countryside, displayed and bedeviled as a traitor.[13]

Nationalist General Wu Qiwei fled with his battered two divisions east toward the river Wu. The First and Third Army moved in for the kill. The Red troops did not eat all day. They were too busy attacking and slashing to bits the remnants of the divisions. At the river, KMT General Wu found a pontoon bridge and started his troops across it. Before he could get all his men across, the Red Army arrived. He cut the rope that held the bridge fast on the southern bank. The bridge swung about and was crushed by the fast current. More than 1,800 of General Wu's men were marooned on the north bank. They surrendered and handed over their weapons.[14]

The victory at Loushan Pass was exhilarating. It lifted the spirits of the soldiers, worn to the bone by weeks of double-speed marches, lack of food, lack of sleep, battle after battle. It was, as Peng Dehuai said, really two victories, first at Loushan and then before the river Wu. And it brought much-needed reinforcements. The prisoners, officers and men, were assembled, addressed by Communist agitators, and invited to join the Red Army. About 80 percent signed up, forming a new division. Each enlisted man was given three silver dollars, and armed with guns seized from the beaten KMT. Those who did not wish to join were given travel money and told to go wherever they wished—north, south, east, or west. Senior and junior officers were invited to personal interviews with Zhu De, who spoke of the Red Army goals of fighting Japan, of saving the country, and expressed hope that all of China's fighting men would form a united front.[15]

Peng Dehuai had a new chief of his Political Department, Liu Shaoqi, later China's President and principal target of the Cultural Revolution. Liu, tall for a Chinese although not quite as tall as Mao, was thirty-five. He had been born to a fairly well-to-do peasant family only five or six miles from Mao's birthplace of Shaoshan. The Liu family was about one generation behind the Mao family in its rise from ordinary peasantry. Liu's father and uncle had become middle peasants at a time when Mao's father had already become a rich peasant. Liu Shaoqi's brother became a rich peasant and hired peasants as laborers, just as Mao's father did.

Liu Shaoqi went to Changsha Normal No. 1 a bit after Mao and then moved to Beijing, where he and Mao met. Liu had hoped to go to France on the work-study project but there wasn't enough money, so he went to Moscow instead in 1919 and became a Communist in 1921. He and Mao became close after they had worked together organizing the great Anyuan coal strike. Liu was an energetic man, very disciplined, conscientious, a good speaker but quiet in his private life. He loved to play with his children. One of the things he taught them was poker.[16]

Liu started the Long March as Central Committee representative to the Eighth Army, survived the Xiang River disaster, and went on to the Fifth Army. Now he began working with Peng Dehuai. He traveled all the way on the Long March before being dispatched on secret and dangerous work in north China.[17]

Liu Shaoqi attended the Zunyi conference. He and Peng had long talks. Peng told him that his men did not fear forced or night marches —they feared illness that might make them fall behind.[18]

The Red Army raced west again, Mao now formally installed, as of March 11, as a member of the Military Commission along with Zhou Enlai and Wang Jiaxiang. It was to be a time of feints and deceits that would surpass anything the Red Army had executed. But its objective was simple—to escape to the north. Chiang Kai-shek had stationed Zhou Hunyuan with an excellent Nationalist army to the south of Zunyi. The KMT generals were ordered on no account to move unless Chiang gave a direct order. Unless Mao could lure these troops out of their strongholds, they would constitute a deadly threat to any attempt to cross the Yangtze.[19]

But in fact, Mao had given up plans for a direct crossing of the Yangtze. What he wanted to do now was to make the Nationalists *think* this was his intention. Actually, he had decided to cross a western extension of the Yangtze called the River of Golden Sands.

"The Red Army had the initiative," recalled Liu Bocheng, the one-eyed dragon, "and moved powerfully among the perplexed KMT troops. One moment it seemed as if the Red Army was heading east, when actually it was marching to the west. The bewildered enemy thought we were planning to penetrate north by crossing the Yangtze, when actually we aimed to swing around and strike another blow at him."[20] One day Mao drew a line on a map and said: "Victory lies in our success in drawing the Yunnan troops out of Yunnan." Only thus could he cross the River of Golden Sands.

Marching and jogging along good roads lined with mulberry trees, the fields of rape beginning to yellow, the wheat spring-green, heavy sorghum stalks pushing up through the black earth, young rice in the paddies, the Red Army took aim for Maotai. It was a bit early for the pomeloes, those fat, rather shabby fruits looking like large misshapen grapefruit, fuller of seeds than a dragon of teeth; a bit early for harvesting the great fields where already the poppies had begun to show pastel white, pastel azure, vague pink.

Morale was high, despite the grueling pace. The troops had won a great victory and shaken off the gloom that had hung over them like a cloud from the start of the March, on October 16, 1934. Mao was confident once again after the bitter experience of Qinggangpo. He wrote his first poem of the Long March to celebrate Loushan:

Idle boast the strong pass is a wall of iron,
We are crossing its summit,
The rolling hills sea-blue
The dying sun blood-red.[21]

In the villages the troops slogged past small sugar presses. Here and there they grabbed pieces of cane and crushed them between their teeth, letting the sweet sticky juice refresh their throats. Women sat in the warm sunshine in front of their houses, pounding the rice in great red earthen bowls. Half-naked children played in the dust. As the men approached Maotai they came on small grog shops, each with its copper still, gooseneck tubing, and fermenting vats where a colorless fiery liquor was produced.

Maotai was a dirty village of three or four thousand, squeezed up along the sixty-foot bluff of the Red River, with narrow muddy streets, houses of plaster or of mud and wattles, some with roofs of thatch, some with reddish tiles. Over it all hung the pungent smell of fermenting mash, a mixture of sorghum and wheat. That was the business of Maotai, brewing a powerful drink, almost pure alcohol, and shipping it and opium to Sichuan. Maotai was the center for traffic in both. It was a big transshipment point for salt. The salt came by caravan from Sichuan. The dealers dropped their loads and took back liquor and opium. The people of Maotai were poor, but the distillers and merchants were rich. The rich fled when the Red Army suddenly appeared.[22]

Production today of maotai is largely concentrated in a big mile-long series of state owned plants along the banks of the Red River, now, as then, a muddy, sluggish, unpleasant-looking stream.*

Legend has it that the young Red Army soldiers, country boys still in their teens, did not know what maotai was, that they poured into the grog shops along the single street, sloshing maotai on their tired and blistered feet until alcohol ran in rivers out of the shops and into the gutters. This nonsense probably was invented to demonstrate the puritanism of the Red Army. Actually the troops were forbidden to enter the maotai shops, but of course they did, with the inevitable results. (There were three large stills employing thirty to forty people, and many small family stills.) Rumors spread that Otto Braun drank so much maotai that he was unconscious for a week. This was only typical of the nasty stories told about the Red Army's erstwhile director.[23] Almost

---

*The maotai distillery was the only facility to which I was refused admission on the whole route of the Long March. Don't ask me why.

everyone sampled the maotai, and what maotai wasn't drunk was loaded up and carried along by the Red Army.[24]

The town of Maotai was taken with hardly a shot. The crack Second Division of the First Army captured it with only twenty casualties, and on March 16–17 the Red Army crossed the Red River for the third time at the Maotai ferry, moving in the most ostentatious way possible, day and night at a single point as if to invite KMT attention—and indeed, that was Mao's purpose. In no time, the KMT spotted what was going on and sent some planes to harass the troops. One bomb fell near Zhou Enlai, hitting the house next to that where he was working. Efforts were made to persuade him to take shelter. He refused. The bombing was light. Some of the planes dropped big rocks bearing armament numbers painted in white. The KMT may have been temporarily short of ammunition.[25]

It seemed like a strange maneuver. Once the Red Army was across the river, Mao ordered the men to halt, except for one regiment, which was sent racing north about one hundred miles to Gulin, a large, sparsely populated county just across the line in Sichuan. It proceeded to Zhenlongshan, making lots of noise to attract attention. Some KMT newspapers mistakenly reported Guiyang had been captured by the Red Army. The idea was to make Chiang Kai-shek think they were headed for a Yangtze crossing and if possible get him to pull his troops westward in that direction. With attention focused on the column moving toward the Yangtze, Mao quietly moved his main force back to the Red River, and on the night of March 21 and early in the morning of March 22 sent his troops over the river again, using three separate crossing points.

Mao's strategy worked. Chiang Kai-shek had been watching intently from Chongqing. Now he perceived in the erratic maneuvers of the Red Army a military body in its death throes, thrashing about, unable to escape. He flew from Chongqing to Guiyang on March 24, and set up headquarters in a spacious new building with a fine view over a small river. It is now used as the Guizhou Ministry of Hydropower and Forestry. He was accompanied by his Australian adviser, W. H. Donald, and his wife, Soong Meiling. Chiang and his entourage were installed on the second floor, with double sentries at the staircase in addition to his personal bodyguards. He also brought along a dozen generals.

The task, as Chiang defined it, was to draw the circle tight around the desperate Red forces and extinguish them. He had between 500,-

000 and 750,000 men on the chessboard, closely positioned to prevent Mao from escaping north across the Yangtze (which he thought was Mao's intention), westward into Sichuan or Yunnan, south across Guizhou toward Guangdong and Guangxi, or eastward back toward Hunan and Jiangxi. Trapped. Mao was trapped. This time Chiang was certain of it.

There were not, actually, many troops in Guiyang. All of the high-ranking officers of the Twenty-fifth KMT Army were at the front. Wang Tianxi, director of Guiyang public security, was the highest-ranking man in town. Chiang brought him in to report on the local situation and named him garrison commandant, chatting with him amiably.

Wang Tianxi was young and impressionable, as he later was to concede. "I was duped by Chiang's niceness," he said. Chiang invited him to move into headquarters and live there. Chiang was worried about the Red Army's puzzling movements, and when his commander, Xue Yue, was unable to get aerial reconnaissance reports for three days running, Chiang cursed him on the telephone. One of Chiang's bodyguards told Wang Tianxi that when Chiang was really angry he threw the receiver to the floor and stomped around like a small bull, purpling the air with curses.

After a few days, reports came in that the Red Army was moving east through Xifeng and Kaiyang counties and apparently intended to cross the river Wu and attack Guiyang. By March 30 the river was being crossed, not without some hard fighting, and anxiety began to rise in Guiyang. Chiang had dispersed his troops in four or five directions to block the Red Army, but he had only a handful in Guiyang.[26]

According to some accounts, Chiang's wife became so frightened she began to send telegrams around China asking that troops be rushed to Guiyang.[27] Chiang ordered Garrison Chief Wang Tianxi to strengthen the defenses of Guiyang. Wang organized a battalion of military police and two companies of firemen and policemen—four hundred men altogether—and in twenty-four hours had completed a new system of fortifications along the city walls. Chiang was skeptical that the work could be completed so rapidly. He went out in the morning with Soong Meiling and Donald to make an inspection. As they were at the walls, General Gu Zhutong rushed up to report that the Red Army was only seven or eight miles to the northeast. (Actually it was passing through Zhazuo, almost twenty-five miles away.)

Chiang had already given the order—although he was not aware of its consequences—which was to ensure the success of Mao's extraordinarily deceptive strategy. The KMT leader had telegraphed the Yunnan commander, General Sun Du, to hurry to the defense of Guiyang with his three topnotch brigades. This would be sufficient to hold off any attack by Mao. Mao had no intention of attacking Guiyang, although he was most eager that Chiang believe this was his plan. By setting Sun Du on the march for Guiyang, Chiang had, in effect, opened the path for Mao to streak for the River of Golden Sands.

This was not yet clear, of course, to either Mao or Chiang. Sun Du was some distance from Guiyang and Mao's troops might arrive at the city walls within an hour or two.

"How far is it to the airport?" Chiang asked anxiously. Garrison Chief Wang Tianxi began to calculate. Before he could respond, another report came in: Plainclothes detachments of Communists had already been spotted close to the airport. It was too late to think of escaping by plane.

Chiang paced back and forth silently, then turning to Wang Tianxi, he said: "Get me twenty reliable guides, some big strong horses, and two good sedan chairs—as quick as possible." Wang Tianxi rushed off to round up the escape caravan. By midmorning he had the cavalcade assembled and reported back to Chiang. As he was reporting, new word came in: The Red Army was bypassing Guiyang and moving in the direction of Longli, about twenty-five miles to the east.

Chiang reflected, checked the map carefully, red pencil in hand, then said: "I think they are heading back for Hunan and Jiangxi." As he was discussing this possibility Yunnan General Sun Du arrived. He reported that his three brigades were entering the city. Chiang asked Sun Du his opinion of the situation. Sun Du tactfully deferred to Chiang: "I trust your opinion."

"I know you must be very tired," Chiang apologized, "but I have to ask you to do me a great favor and lead your troops in the direction of Longli."

Chiang explained he had directed Xue Yue to advance from Zunyi to the east to intercept the Red Army, and had telephoned He Jian to deploy forces in western Hunan.

"Your officers and men," said Chiang, "must be very tired. I'll send them a few thousand yuan to encourage them."

The next morning there was a new alarm—heavy firing south of the city. It was the Red Army, speeding toward Yunnan.

General Chen Cheng, another KMT general, observed to Garrison

Chief Wang Tianxi: "This enemy of ours is very, very cunning. He makes a sudden turn to the west and now they are on their way toward Yunnan. What can we do about it?"

Wang Tianxi concluded: "This military operation was very skillful. They held Chiang Kai-shek by the nose."[28]

16

MAO'S GREAT DECEPTIONS

Mao's great deception worked. It left Chiang Kai-shek and his generals in confusion. They could not divine where the Red Army was going. It became a Scarlet Pimpernel. They saw it here, they saw it there, they saw it everywhere.

In fact, the Red Army *was* everywhere. Probably never before or afterward had it been so scattered, moving simultaneously in so many directions.

Often the Red Army men themselves did not know what they were doing or why they had been given an assignment. In fact, there were those who began to grumble that Mao did not know where he was going, that he had no plan, that his movements were decided upon on the spur of the moment. There may be some basis for this view. Whatever the cause it kept Chiang Kai-shek off balance. In retrospect, his campaign bears the mark of genius.

The trail of Mao as he crisscrossed Guizhou again and again is not easy to reconstruct nor is it any easier for the reader to follow than it was for Chiang Kai-shek's commanders.

Nothing was more puzzling than the orders which Mao gave to his Ninth Army, which had been moving rapidly eastward across central Guizhou. When it got to the north side of the river Wu, Mao ordered it to halt without crossing the river. He kept it there for days, poised, it would seem, for a thrust north into Hunan.

The commander of the Ninth, an extremely competent commander named Luo Binghui, faithfully carried out his orders even if he could not fathom their purpose. He was an experienced guerrilla from Fujian who had risen to command the Twelfth Army (long since reorganized out of existence).

Now Luo Binghui commanded the Ninth. Mao highly praised him in talking later with Edgar Snow. Luo would lose his life fighting the

166

Japanese. His wife accompanied him on the Long March, the only lily-footed woman on the March (one whose feet had been bound in her infancy). Walking 25,000 li on cruelly misshapen feet was a trial more severe than any faced by the men. She was, moreover, pregnant, and gave birth to a child on the March.

The Ninth Army stayed behind, cut off from the rest of their comrades, not knowing what orders would come next and if it would ever rejoin the main force. Wang Shoudao, later Minister of Communications in the PRC, recalled one of his comrades saying he was certain they would not die a lonely death away from their Commander, Zhu De. His remark reflected a fear that this might happen. The Ninth stayed in the area of the river Wu, carrying out operations against You Guocai, a Guizhou general, with considerable success until April 29, when they were ordered south to cross the Beipan River and move west.[1]

Mao divided his main force, the First and Third Army Groups, and sent them flowing along the roads and paths around Guiyang. Some went far to the east before wheeling south and then southwest. The KMT seemed to regard the eastward push the main threat, probably because Chiang was so certain the Red Army was headed back to its old habitat in Hunan and Jiangxi. Other units broke off near Guiyang and moved swiftly south and then west in the direction of Yunnan.

Xue Yue, one of the ablest of Chiang's commanders, harassed the Red Army along its northern perimeter and continued to do so all the way across Guizhou. The Yunnan troops joined in as soon as Chiang became convinced the Red Army was not threatening Cuiyang.

When the weather was good—and it was steadily improving as spring advanced, despite Guizhou's reputation for rain and fog—Chiang's planes bombed the Communists. Often there was no place to hide. It was difficult to find quarters to bed down for the night. Chen Shiju, commissar of a training battalion of the First Army, was moving south from the Longli area. Nowhere were billets available. The night was almost half over when he arrived at a broken-down building already filled with Red Army soldiers, some asleep, some undressing, some boiling water. All was quiet. The only sound was the tap-tap-tap of a wireless operator's key. In a small hut Chen Shiju found Mao, Zhou Enlai, and Zhu De working on operational plans for the next day, April 10, 1935. They told him to keep on the road until he found a decent place for his men. Bright stars illuminated the way and a soft spring breeze blew. The troops went another couple of miles and found some huts. Chen Shiju put his men into these, they shared two fat pigs, confiscated from a landlord and roasted over an open fire, and fell asleep. It was after 1 A.M. and they had been marching since 6 A.M. the previous morning.

In the morning the battalion gulped down the remains of the pigs and headed for Dingfan (now Huishui), about ten miles away and twenty miles south of Guiyang. It was a beautiful morning. The men marched beside a river, the sound of ancient creaking water wheels mingling with the singing of the soldiers. The fields were wide and bright with green wheat. A light wind came across the river and stirred the quivering leaves of the willows. Chen Shiju felt happy and at peace. He could hardly believe that men were fighting and killing only a few miles away.

The training battalion moved ahead in the sunshine, hardships forgotten, and approached Dingfan, chasing away the mintuan, or local defenders. While the training battalion rested for a day in Dingfan, other units leapfrogged ahead in a southwestern direction.[2]

KMT newspapers present a picture of disorderly, chaotic flight by the Red Army. The reports of KMT commanders like Xue Yue and Long Yun told of hideous Communist losses running a thousand or more a day. By this time the Red Army strength was probably down to not much more than twenty thousand men. At this rate, it should have been wiped out by the first of May. It wasn't.[3]

There was no reflection in Nationalist press accounts that Chiang Kai-shek or his command had an inkling of the Zunyi deliberations and the restoration of Mao Zedong to command. Actually, so far as the evidence goes, there is no sign the KMT ever knew Mao was not in power. The same goes for Zhu De. From beginning to end, Chiang thought that he was fighting the Zhu-Mao Red Army. The Communists kept their political quarrels to themselves, some of them to this day.

The British Reuters news agency correspondent Thomas Chow reported in a dispatch of April 9, 1935, that Zhu De had been killed in battle at Zhutoushan (Pig-Headed Mountain) in an attempt to capture Guiyang. Zhu De's body was described as having been wrapped in red silk and was being carried by his Red Army comrades as they continued their march. The Red Army, the dispatch reported, had shrunk to ten thousand men. Zhu De snorted when Agnes Smedley, his American biographer, asked him about the report several years later. He said he had never been wounded on the March, although the KMT often reported his death. Nearly fifty years later, Zhu De's widow, Kang Ke-qing, confirmed her husband's statement. "He was never wounded in his whole military career," she said. "Neither was I."[4]

It was about this time that Zhu De read in a KMT newspaper of an attack on the home of his second wife at Yuchen, and his son at Nanchi. His wife had been seized and his son had escaped but was being "hunted down." He never heard of either again.[5]

To the north of Guiyang, according to Nationalist press reports, Wang Jialie, the Guizhou warlord, had taken the field again. He claimed to have obliterated the Communists in "ten fierce battles." He reported the Red Army was trying to fight its way north to join He Long and Xiao Ke. There is no evidence that this was true. On the contrary, Red Army veterans (and even some KMT newspaper reports) pictured Wang Jialie in a panic, people swarming out in the towns and villages to demonstrate against him and greet the Red Army. Wang Jialie's troops scuttled away rather than do battle. Zhang Aiping, the future Defense Minister, pictured Wang Jialie as "in deadly fear" of the approach of the Red Army.[6]

There was confusion aplenty. The Red Army units and KMT units crisscrossed each other west, south, and east of Guiyang. But amidst the turmoil the Red Army managed to recruit several thousand men to replace the gaps torn in their ranks by combat and exhaustion.

Wang Jialie could take credit for one thing. On April 19 he correctly reported that the Red Army was headed for Yunnan. This was the first definite KMT report. But it did not save him. As soon as the Guizhou hurly-burly was over, Chiang shipped Wang Jialie off to military school and put in a new warlord, obedient to his will.

The Beipan River cuts across the southwest corner of Guizhou, flowing from northwest to south, eventually joining the great West River, which finds its way to the sea through a multitude of exits in the delta around Canton. The Beipan is sometimes called the "small Yellow River," a considerable exaggeration.

Mao's tactics drove the KMT commanders dizzy. But Mao was acting on the hardest kind of realism. There was no way for the Red Army to get across the Yangtze. It was too heavily defended. The approaches were guarded by powerful KMT formations. Chiang Kai-shek could quickly move his armies from place to place along the broad Yangtze banks.

The only reasonable possibility left to Mao for going north was the

River of Golden Sands. And even here his choice was limited. The River of Golden Sands was one of those surging streams that had their origin in the Himalayas. There were not many crossing points. Unless Mao could seize a crossing in the great bend of the river where it cut down to become the border between Yunnan and Sichuan, he would be driven farther and farther west into the dangerous approaches of Tibet, a region of impassable mountains, sparse and often violently hostile population, little food, not a chance for recruits to make good his heavy losses.

Mao had to take tremendous risks. But he had few alternatives. His ability to reach the River of Golden Sands depended on two circumstances: failure, once again, by Chiang Kai-shek to penetrate his intentions, and speed enough to give Mao time to make an unhindered crossing of a river that was bound to be a formidable obstacle.

Xiao Hua, a twenty-year-old Jiangxi peasant youngster who rose to be commander of the elite Second Division of Lin Biao's First Army Group, wrote an epic poem about the March, much loved, he recalled in 1984, by Mao Zedong and Premier Zhou Enlai. One verse that Zhou Enlai particularly praised described Chairman Mao in the Guizhou campaign "performing magic in making military decisions."* It may often have so seemed to the KMT commanders, but not to Otto Braun. Braun had now left his post with Lin Biao and the First Army and rejoined the central column. He rejected the idea that Mao was guided by a plan or strategy, and asserted that the March "increasingly resembled a retreat and eventually degenerated into outright flight." The troops became so weary they hardly knew where they were, and he told of falling asleep during a night march and not waking until he found himself in an icy stream, drenched from head to foot.[7]

In a sense, the Beipan River would be a dress rehearsal for what was to come at the River of Golden Sands.

Shock forces were sent ahead to secure crossings. One was the Fourth Regiment of the Second Division of the First Army, of which Yang Chengwu was political commissar. The regiment was already famous when he joined it in 1933 as a peasant youngster in Fujian. It had been formed of men who had participated in the Nanchang Uprising of August 1, 1927, and of others who had fought with Mao

---

*As Zhou lay dying of cancer in January 1976, he asked that Xiao Hua's epic (which had been set to music) be played for him. By edict of the Gang of Four, Xiao Hua said, this was refused. (Xiao Hua, personal interview, Beijing, 3/16/84.)

Zedong on Jinggangshan. Commissar Yang Chengwu was to stay with the vanguard unit through all the heavy fighting—the encirclement campaigns, the breakout across the Yudu River, the four blockhouse lines, the Xiang River, the big Guizhou battles, and all those to come. It was, he said, very helpful in writing his book that he had stayed with the same regiment through the whole March. Twice Commissar Yang Chengwu was wounded, but he was never long away from his outfit.[8]

The Fourth Regiment started its drive for the Beipan River with a surprise attack on the market town of Ziyun. The regiment made a hundred-li march, arriving at the town at 4 A.M., and quickly ousted the surprised defenders. It got some unexpected prizes. The local tailors advised them that they had made up two hundred KMT uniforms but the soldiers fled before they could pick them up. The regiment paid the tailors, took the uniforms, and found them very useful in playing tricks on local Nationalist forces. The people put up red welcome banners, opened all their shops, and at nightfall presented the Fourth Regiment with two thousand silver dollars.

The Fourth Regiment encountered a region settled by Yi tribesmen. Here they managed to persuade the Yi, fiercely hostile to Han Chinese, to let them pass through, promising they meant no harm and would not linger. The Yi even brought them food, an almost unprecedented gesture. The regiment reached the Beipan, found large groves of bamboo beside it, cut down trees, fashioned a floating bridge in peace and quiet, and at eventide began to cross over.[9]

The Eleventh Regiment acted as the vanguard for the Third Army under Peng Dehuai and Political Commissar Yang Shangkun. They ordered regimental commander Zhang Aiping to secure a crossing of the Beipan. The regiment had a fifty- or sixty-mile march to the river. They started in unseasonable fog and chill but made the march with little difficulty, aided by the fact that the local troops were eager to negotiate for peaceful crossings of their territory. The leader of the local *mintuan* forces gave the Red Army free passage and a gift of rice and pork. The Eleventh Regiment had no trouble all the way to the river. When they reached it, they found they could walk across. The first battalion then pushed downstream fifteen miles to Baiceng and seized the major river ford for some main units—the command column and the Fifth Army. Here, too, they made a deal with the local defenders. "We only want to cross the river. Nothing else," the Communists said.

The local command agreed not to interfere and gave them boats for the crossing.[10]

There is no record of what Mao Zedong said when he crossed the river at Baiceng, but he must have felt a strong sense of China's past and his own deep identification with it. Here at Baiceng, Mao was only a mile or two from Kongminggang, the region where was entombed Zhuge Liang, a legendary strategist and great popular hero of the period of the Three Kingdoms. Zhuge Liang lived from 181 to 234 A.D. He is immortalized in *The Romance of the Three Kingdoms,* Mao's bible from childhood and, as much as anything, his military text for the Long March. The twisting, dodging, crafty campaign in Guizhou, the strategy of driving south into Yunnan in order to open the way to go north, could have been (and may have been) invented by Zhuge Liang. In fact, many commanders in the Red Army referred to Mao as Zhuge Liang. Did Mao take an hour or two to pay homage at this shrine of his great hero? There is no record that he did, but it is impossible to believe that he did not.[11]

The Nationalist air force was like a cloud of steel mosquitoes around the Red Army. There were casualties every day. The Third Army had hardly crossed the border into Yunnan—headquarters had been set up in flat open country about five miles out of the town of Baishui in Zhanyi county—when a flight of KMT planes came over. The only cover was a small clump of trees. Yang Shangkun, political commissar of the Third Army, was riding with Interpreter Wu Xiuquan. Wu had a large white horse. The others were mounted on sober brown or black horses. The white horse stood out brilliantly against the red soil. The planes spotted it and dropped a stick of bombs. Yang Shangkun was wounded by splinters in the calf of his leg. He had always complained to Wu about the horse. It was small satisfaction that the horse was killed in the bombing. Wu was unscathed. Yang had to be carried in a litter for some days. But the road was so bad that, as he approached the River of Golden Sands, he had to walk for some distance. Of the three bomb splinters he caught, one was still in his leg in 1985.[12]

One Red Army column approached Yunnan to the north of the main crossings. It reached Yangchang in Panxian county, on the Guizhou-Yunnan border, in late afternoon, and the convalescent unit to which He Zizhen had returned after giving birth to her child near the Red

River crossing was resting there on a hillside. Someone was giving a propaganda talk. The wounded and ill were scattered about the green slope, relaxing in the sunshine, when the sound of airplane motors was heard. Many convalescents were unable to move from their litters. "Hurry," cried He Zizhen. "Get the wounded under cover."

Before anyone could act, a plane swooped low, dropping small bombs and strafing the group with machine gun fire. Several bearers were killed and He Zizhen saw a wounded officer trying to rise from his litter. This was Zhong Chibing, the regimental political commissar wounded at Loushan Pass. As the plane returned for a second strike, He Zizhen threw herself over him. A bomb spattered her with shrapnel and she suffered seventeen wounds, including a bad head wound, and lay in a pool of blood. She remained unconscious for several days. When she came to herself she told the nurses not to tell Mao of her wound. "He is busy and I don't want him to worry," she said. She asked the doctors to leave her in a peasant hut to recuperate. They did nothing of the kind. They put her on a stretcher and sometimes carried her on their own backs over the hard places.[13]

Tragedy dogged He Zizhen to the end of her days. She reached Yan'an in poor health and there bore a daughter, Li Min, known affectionately as Jiaojiao. She quarrelled with Mao over his flirtation with a handsome actress from Shanghai named Lily Wu. Lily's Chinese name was Wu Kuangwei. She was fluent in English and acted as an interpreter for Agnes Smedley and Helen Snow. She became acquainted with Mao in the cave shared by Smedley and Snow which he occasionally visited. Mao liked to drink coffee, dunking his crackers in it, play solitaire, or listen to Smedley's portable phonograph as the women conducted interviews. Lily Wu appeared in plays conducted by the Yan'an dramatic society, including Gorky's *Mother*. He Zizhen blamed Smedley for encouraging her husband's flirtation and once, according to Mrs. Snow, threatened to have Smedley killed. Smedley took the threat seriously and changed beds with Snow. In the ensuing scandal Lily Wu was sent away from Yan'an and Smedley's stay was cut short.[14]

In 1937 He Zizhen left Yan'an for Xi'an, hoping to continue to Shanghai for medical treatment, but the Japanese had taken over the city. She received Mao's approval to go to Moscow, where she gave birth to a sixth and last child, a boy. She was joyous. She had been happy on the train trip to Moscow, little Liu Ying recalled. Liu Ying was one of the party, together with the elderly Xu Teli, Mao's Changsha teacher; Xu Mengqiu, the Party historian, who had lost his legs; Zhong Chibing, the commander whose life He Zizhen saved on the Long March; and Cai Shufan, a commander who had lost an arm.[15]

Mao favored the trip. He thought He Zizhen had spent so much time in pregnancy that she never had a real chance to study. Perhaps in Moscow she could get both medical care and education. It didn't work out. Her boy fell ill at the nursery school and died of pneumonia; there was no penicillin. She began to suffer psychological trauma. She stayed on and on in Moscow. Mao sent their daughter Jiaojiao to keep her company. World War II came. She and Mao exchanged a few letters through Jiaojiao. She sent him some presents—fresh mustard leaves, which he liked, a winter bamboo shoot, melons. Mao sent her Chinese fruit.

Not until 1948 did He Zizhen come back to China. Long since, Mao had divorced her (with Party permission) and married Jiang Qing, whose affection for He Zizhen was minimal. There had been no connection between the arrival of Jiang Qing in Yan'an and the leaving of He Zizhen for Moscow—contrary to some Western speculation. "Jiang Qing just took advantage of Mao's vacant bed," in the words of little Liu Ying.

He Zizhen wanted to return to Beijing, but Jiang Qing saw to it that she got no closer than Tianjin. In 1950 He Zizhen met with Mao once in Shanghai and again at Lushan. For a while her health was not bad, but its balance was unstable. Sometimes she suffered hallucinations and paranoid fears. In Shanghai she occupied a small room in an ordinary apartment house. Chen Yi, the old commander, now mayor of Shanghai, learned she was there and came to her aid. When he left Shanghai in 1960, he moved her into the two-story house he had occupied, but she continued to live a hermit's life. The long shadow of Jiang Qing hung over her. For a time Jiang Qing even succeeded in alienating Jiaojiao from her mother. Old comrades were refused permission to visit Zizhen.

When Mao Zedong died in 1976, He Zizhen asked to come to Beijing and was permitted to view Mao in the glass sarcophagus in which he had been placed—Jiang Qing and the Gang of Four were under arrest.* Some of the women who had made the Long March with He Zizhen visited her in the army hospital where she stayed. She received them in a wheelchair. Tears came to her eyes. Not much was said. In

---

*Unconfirmed rumors circulated in Beijing that He Zizhen testified in the investigation of Jiang Qing.

June 1979 she was elected to the National Committee of the People's Political Consultative Conference and her name appeared in the newspapers for the first time.

On April 19, 1984, He Zizhen died in Shanghai. The cause of death was announced as a stroke. She had been half-paralyzed for several years. She was, of course, a casualty of the Long March, as much as if the bomb in western Guizhou had killed her outright in 1935, making her the fifteenth to die of the thirty young women who completed the March with the First Front Army.

"She was," said Liu Ying, "just a simple country girl." "She was," said Mao's bodyguard Wu Jiqing, who cared for her on the March, "a brave and courageous woman."

17

THE GOLDEN SANDS

L E Cercle Sportif Français was housed in a little stucco villa tucked into a narrow lane near the railroad station in the small French quarter of the sleepy provincial capital Yunnanfu, known now as Kunming. Two cement tennis courts had been laid out in front of the house and spectators could sit on a pleasant veranda, sipping a Pernod or a whisky-soda while waiting their turn at play.

Le Cercle was the hub of such foreign life as went on in the capital of Yunnan. It had no bar, but a Chinese attendant knew everyone and brought their cassis or pink gin without a word said. No bourbon. Whisky was Scotch whisky. Wine could be ordered but seldom was.

The foreigners met at Le Cercle in the afternoon. They played tennis, bridge, or mah-jongg, drank, and exchanged the gossip of the day. You could almost number the foreigners on the fingers of your hands—the French consul general and his two vice-consuls, the British and American consuls and their assistants, the American head of the Chinese customs service, the French head of postal services, and the Frenchman in charge of the salt gabelle. There was a newly arrived Japanese consul in 1935, but he spoke neither French nor English and seldom appeared.

A few other foreigners inhabited this obscure southwestern corner of China—a YMCA man named Roger Arnold, an American naturalist and eccentric named Dr. Joseph F. Rock, some French businessmen, four Greek hotel proprietors, and a few American missionaries, many of them connected with small Bible faiths. One missionary family of twelve sustained itself by begging in the streets.[1]

In the early 1930s, Kunming was a city of 150,000. It possessed a thin, very thin, French veneer. A narrow-gauge railroad had been built in 1900–10, linking the city with Hanoi and Haiphong in Tonkin, as northern Vietnam was then called. A few boulevards in the center of town were lined with "French" trees, as the Chinese still say—that is, French plane trees. A French "quarter" had sprung up around the railroad station—a few small hotels, operated by Greeks, and a handful of shops owned by French and Greek-French businessmen up from Hanoi and Saigon. Yunnan was what was then called a French "sphere of influence" in China.

On the evening of April 29, 1935, the young English vice-consul, Cy Carney, was dining with his young American colleague John S. Service and his wife, Caroline Service. For a fortnight they had heard rumors about the Communists. The Red Army had been active next door in Guizhou. Travelers from Guiyang brought reports of the fighting and in recent days foreign missionaries had been picking their way out of Guizhou and coming down to Kunming, terrified of the approaching "Red bandits."

There had been talk of evacuating foreigners, and Caroline Service had packed a trunk of valuables—the baby clothes she had bought from Montgomery Ward (she was expecting her first child in July), her wedding silver, and Jack's gold watch. She hadn't finished packing because the rumors had died down a bit. But on the evening of April 29, Vice-Consul Carney had great trouble getting to the Services' house. All rickshaws had been commandeered by the local military to haul sandbags and ammunition, and patrols of soldiers stopped Carney a dozen times, telling him he must get off the street. They were building barricades and sandbag barriers on the main streets and at Piccadilly Circus, as the foreigners called a central square in the fashionable suburb on the south of the city. Carney decided to stay overnight with the Services rather than try to break through the melee back to his quarters.

At 2 A.M. came a great pounding at the gate of the Services' compound. A messenger brought a note from the American consul, Arthur Ringwalt, warning that three thousand Communists were said to be about eight miles east of the city at a place called Dabangqiao, and another seven thousand a bit more distant. A special train had been laid on by the French to take foreign women and children from Kunming to Tonkin. It would leave the station at 7:44 A.M.

Service and Carney scurried about town in the predawn hours, warning missionaries and the few other foreigners. In the morning Caroline Service boarded the train with her trunk (she never saw Jack's gold watch again) and two Siamese kittens in a wicker basket, which she was determined to send somehow to her mother-in-law in Shanghai.

The train was filled. There was another pregnant wife, all the foreign women and children in Kunming, and Dr. Rock, who had decided that because his health was precarious and his books and relics were priceless, he had better get away with what he could carry. The train chuffed off to Tonkin in a pouring rain.[2]

Kunming's scare over the "Red bandits" was not unlike that at Guiyang, except that Kunming was even more defenseless. There were only five hundred local militia in town. Had the Communists wanted to capture Kunming, they could have done so with no real battle.

But they didn't want the city. All they wanted was for Chiang Kaishek and the warlord of Yunnan, Long Yun, to pull back more troops to defend it, just as Chiang had pulled in the Yunnan troops to protect Guiyang. It was a variation on the trick Mao Zedong had played on Chiang before, and Chiang, like a Pavlovian dog, responded just as Mao wanted him to. He withdrew three regiments from the vicinity of the Golden Sands, leaving the river virtually open, and moved troops toward Kunming.[3]

Chiang did not personally rush to Kunming, as many Chinese and foreign accounts declare. He stayed in Guiyang and summoned a special meeting of his top military chiefs. Contrary to what many have reported, Chiang and his wife, Soong Meiling, did not become frightened to death in Kunming and scuttle down the French railroad to Hanoi. When Chiang did move, it was to Chengdu.[4]

Mao set the stage for his breakout north across the River of Golden Sands with utmost care. The Red Army approached Yunnan from Guizhou in three main groups, in part because Chiang's best general, Xue Yue, with a well-trained Nationalist force, managed to place himself in a blocking position in western Guizhou.

The main Red force, the Central Column, the First, Third, and Fifth Armies crossed into Yunnan along a spread of 120 miles from the Nanpan River in the south to the vicinity of Panxian, where He Zizhen was wounded, in the north.

Once into Yunnan, Mao moved his forces in a fashion calculated to confuse the Nationalists and particularly Long Yun, the warlord, who was in Kunming watching the Red maneuvers with apprehension. He had sent his best troops into Guizhou and there was no way of getting them back fast enough to help in defense of Kunming. He began frantically to call in the county militia or local defense forces, the mintuan, although they were hardly a match for the battle-hardened Red Army.

Mao brought the main body of the First and Third Armies into Yunnan almost due east of Kunming and then began to swing them to the north, moving with customary speed. The headquarters column was advancing toward Malong, about sixty miles east of Kunming, when a squadron of KMT planes flew overhead. They dropped no bombs and disappeared to the east. The Red Army commanders were puzzled until they realized that the KMT had no idea the Red Army had penetrated Yunnan to such depth. A bit later, Zhou Enlai and his bodyguards spotted three trucks coming from the Kunming direction, raising a dust cloud. They drove right up to the Red Army column, and halted in surprise when Zhou ordered his detachment to surround them. The convoy had been sent by Warlord Long Yun to Xue Yue. It was carrying a collection of topographical maps of Yunnan at the Nationalist general's request. Long Yun had planned to send the maps by plane, but the pilot was ill, so he sent them by truck. He filled the trucks with provisions—Yunnan hams, something like Smithfield hams, regarded as the best in China, and medical supplies, a gift to his fellow general.

Mao made good use of the maps in working out details of his crossing of the River of Golden Sands. It was, as his companions pointed out, a leaf out of his favorite pages of the war of the Three Kingdoms. The great hero Liu Bei conquered Yunnan with the aid of a map given him by the Yunnan ruler, Zhang Song.[5]

The Ninth Army, finally released from its "hold order" on the north bank of the river Wu, had moved into a new holding pattern just below the neck of Yunnan and barred any direct approach by the Nationalists to the Golden Sands crossing sites. Like most of the Red Army in Yunnan, the Ninth was experiencing remarkably little difficulty, because of the warmth displayed by local people. The Ninth captured a succession of county seats, first Xuanwei and then Dongchuan (Huile), about 105 miles to the north of Kunming and twenty miles from the River of Golden Sands. The mintuan here, as elsewhere, didn't want a fight with the Red Army, but the town magistrate, Yang Maozhang, wanted to defend the prefectural capital. The residents rose up against him. They welcomed the Red Army. Magistrate Yang and a local "tyrant" were led before a mass meeting of ten thousand, condemned to death, and shot. The Red Army distributed Yunnan hams, wheat, and rice to the poor. It seized sixty thousand silver dollars from landlords and recruited several hundred men.[6] The Ninth Army got so many silver dollars they staggered under the burden. They loaded them on mules, and once they rejoined the First Army, shared their treasure, bought kerosene, flashlights and batteries, cotton cloth, and new weapons. "It was a windfall of profit," Xu Jitao of the Yunnan Provincial Museum remarked.[7]

The main body of the First and Third Army moved north, with the Fifth Army, as usual, in the rear guard. Mao sent the elite Cadres Regiment ahead to secure the first crossing site at the River of Golden Sands in its great bend southward into Yunnan.

The key assignment, however, went to Lin Biao, the young eagle of the Red Army. In that glorious spring of 1935, the Yunnan fields a heaven of pastel—pearly white, dawn pink, lavender—the year's opium crop nodding in the sunshine, there was no brighter star in the Red Army than Lin Biao.

He was given by Mao a task that tested his powers to the fullest. It was to convince Long Yun, Xue Yue, and Chiang Kai-shek that the Red Army's objective was the capture of Kunming. Lin Biao was to drive as close to the city as possible, to make the threat totally realistic. He was given what was called a division of first-class troops, six regiments, almost ten thousand men, according to one estimate.[8]

Lin Biao crossed into Yunnan from Xingyi in Guizhou, moved a bit south, and then advanced on Kunming from the southeast. By the twenty-ninth of April he had reached Dabangqiao, only eight miles east of Kunming. From the high hills his scouts could see Kunming in the bright morning sunshine. This was the approach that set off the panic and sent the foreign wives hurrying down to the safety of Tonkin. Lin Biao paused in that vicinity to deepen Kunming's apprehensions and give his troops a little rest from the breakneck pace. This was the day that Mao's crack Cadres Regiment had reached the Golden Sands River and made a crossing, putting a party over the river, probing for a good landing site. And on that day, April 29, Mao completed his plans for crossing the Golden Sands. Landing places were allotted: The First Army was to cross at Longjie, the southernmost of the crossings; the Third Army at Hongmen, thirty or forty miles downstream to the northeast, and finally Jiaopingdu for the Cadres Regiment, already reconnoitering in that vicinity.[9] By May 1 the Cadres Regiment had secured the Jiaopingdu crossing. That day Lin Biao received a telegram from Mao. It ordered him to break off the feint against Kunming and come with all possible haste to the River of Golden Sands. If he was not able to arrive by May 7, the high command could not guarantee the crossing site would still be held.[10]

Never had Lin Biao's troops moved more rapidly—while still maintaining the appearance of a threat to Kunming. They circled the city to the north and a little west, capturing the county seat of Fumin, twenty miles northwest of Kunming. The panic in Kunming continued. Long Yun continued to pull in reinforcements. The KMT slanted south toward Kunming instead of west toward the Golden Sands.[11]

There were no highways. None of today's blacktops bordered with great eucalyptus trees (imported originally by the British from Australia). Nor did eucalyptus forests yet cover the high mountain slopes. But as the soldiers came over the hills and out to the plateaus, which today in spring are golden with wheat, they saw incredibly beautiful opium poppies as far as their eyes could see. Opium poppies were Yunnan's wealth. The Red Army confiscated enormous quantities of opium. It was the bread-and-butter of the countryside. The Red Army used it as money, trading it for supplies, or simply distributed it with a free hand to the peasants, comforting themselves with the thought that it was, after all, the product of peasant toil and sweat. Later on, after liberation, the People's Republic inherited a fearsome opium problem. The growing of the poppy was forbidden. Every effort was made to rehabilitate addicts. Propaganda, persuasion, medical treatment, and harsh penalties were employed, but it was not wiped out overnight. Nor were the "bandits"—the KMT remnants who survived in the remote hills and mountains into the early 1950s, supporting themselves by the opium trade.[12]

Far outdistancing pursuit, Lin Biao headed straight north, arriving in Yuanmou county, just short of the Golden Sands River, on the evening of May 3, having covered the hundred miles from Dabangqiao in a little more than forty-eight hours. They moved so fast that they lost many stragglers. The men simply could not keep up the pace. They lagged behind and many were captured and shot on the spot by the KMT.[13]

The country grows increasingly rugged near the Golden Sands. Even today there is no road that comes nearer than twenty miles to the great bend of the Golden Sands from the south. Long March veterans or historians who want to revisit the site of the battles must hike by foot or ride a mule.

Lin Biao pushed on to his assigned crossing at Longjie the next day and ran into trouble. There were no boats. The river was wide and swift.

He threw over a floating bridge of bamboo rafts. The current carried it away. On May 6, Lin Biao was ordered by Mao to come to the Jiaopingdu crossing, fifty to sixty miles away along the roadless riverbank, across perilous cliffs and ledges. The May 7 deadline remained.[14]

Jiaopingdu (*du* means "crossing") from ancient times has been a well-known crossing place for caravans entering northern Yunnan with loads of salt or silver or hides and grain from Sichuan and for herbs and secret Tibetan medicines and filigree work from the not-too-distant approaches to Tibet. From the Yunnan side came convoys of opium, gold (from the placer mines along the Golden Sands River, famed from antiquity for gold dust and gold nuggets), rich embroidery of gold and silver threads, and other exotic goods.

On the north (or west—the river makes such a turn that directions are topsy-turvy) bank of the Golden Sands—or Jinsha, to give it its proper Chinese name—there was a caravanserai. Here, as April turned to May, about thirty traders waited with their pack horses and mules. They had brought their goods to the river's edge and were waiting the arrival of a caravan from Yunnan. When they arrived they would be ferried across the river to trade with the men from Sichuan.

The caravanserai was operated by the eldest of the four Zhang brothers from Hongmenchang village. His younger brother Zhang Chaoman was in 1984 a fine strong man of seventy-one with a lithe figure, sinewy muscles, and baldish pate. Sitting on the balcony of a guesthouse that overlooks the Golden Sands from the Sichuan side, he spoke of his experiences fifty years before. He remembers the spring of 1935 in sharp detail.

One day some men came to him. It turned out that they were a propaganda team from the Cadres Regiment and they were in search of boats. "Don't be afraid," one of them said. "We are Red Army men and we are here to kill the landlords and the evil gentry. In ten years we will come back and give the land to you."

Zhang said they weren't going to find any boats. All were hidden. They repeated that they needed boats, and boatmen too. Zhang went to his brother, who said there was no way in which he could get any boats. They found one that was half sunk on the riverbank and the Red Army men tried to make it watertight by stuffing the holes with cloth that they bought from the traders. They found a couple of boats on the other side of the river. One way and another, they got five boats together, two on the Sichuan side, three on the Yunnan side. A capable boatman, Yang Menzhi, agreed to take nine Red Army men over in a raid on the Sichuan side. The men carried Mauser pistols and flashlights and frightened the local soldiers with the lights so that they ran away. They seized five boats that night.

They ferried a couple more loads of Red Army men over to the Sichuan side, where they made a sneak attack on the local toll tax-house. They banged at the door, the boatmen shouting in Sichuanese because the Red Army men didn't speak the dialect. "If you don't open the door we will go along without paying our tax." That got the door open in a twinkle. The Red Army men rushed in. Several men had been playing mah-jongg and smoking opium. They were quickly disarmed. The soldiers found five thousand silver dollars in tax receipts, which they seized and put in what they called the Reserve Fund for Resisting the Japanese. They collared about sixty men, half of them local KMT soldiers. The next day they found two more boats, making seven in all. By this time they had twenty-six boatmen, and would get ten more.

The moment they finished clearing out the customs office, boats began to bring Red Army troops across. The movement was to go on for nine days and nine nights. For every day's work the boatmen got a silver dollar in pay and a silver dollar in bonus. If they preferred, they got their pay in opium, five ounces a day. The larger boats carried sixty men, the smallest twenty. The crossing took three minutes. Each boat was given a number and a captain.

The river walls rise sharply at the crossing site and the approach from the Yunnan side is a long, narrow trail that leads down the cliffside for a couple of miles to a narrow sandy beach. About fifty feet from the river's edge stood (and still stands) a boulder about ten feet high. From the top of this boulder Liu Bocheng, the one-eyed dragon, chief of staff of the First Army, stood throughout the nine days and nine nights, directing the crossing. He was assisted by Ye Jianying, who acted as political commissar of the crossing site.[15]

Twice enemy reconnaissance planes flew over, but the river is too narrow for bombing. Horses were afraid to come aboard the boats, so they were led by their halters, swimming beside the boats. The crossings never stopped. Huge bonfires were lighted at night to allow ferrying to go on without halt. Not a man was lost in the operation. Women and wounded were handled in separate boats. From beginning to end the traffic flowed smoothly.

Mao Zedong, Zhou Enlai, and the top command crossed the Golden Sands in the darkness before dawn of May 1. They had ridden a good sixty miles that day. On the Sichuan side the golden beach of Yunnan was absent. The boats then (and now) ease up to a narrow shelving shale beach that slants upward in a stony scramble to a level about twenty feet higher. There a narrow path leads along the bank to another, higher shelf. There is little space for the deployment of troops and supplies. Along the second shelf are a series of eleven sand caves, cut in the bluff by generations of rivermen. In this cave complex, headquarters was set up. Mao had a cave, there was one for Zhou Enlai, for the other commanders, for the wireless operators, security guards, and the rest of the central apparatus.

Mao mildly reprimanded his bodyguard, Chen Changfeng, for his delay in finding a board to use as a desk. For Mao's bed the bodyguard put down an oilcloth and laid a blanket on top of it. He couldn't make nails stick in the sand walls, so he could not hang up Mao's maps.

The caves still existed in 1984, little changed in fifty years, connected by a hewn-out passageway along the cliff, small, dim, dismal. They provided protection against air attacks, but the command would have found it more pleasant tenting on the ledge where the guesthouse is now located.[16]

The weather was oppressively hot. The Cadres Regiment suffered badly from the heat in its race north to the Golden Sands. Climbing the tortuous paths can be agony in sweltering May weather, as the writer learned over these same trails. The speed of the Red Army men is hardly to be believed. It is reflected in the KMT press reports, which lagged five to seven days behind events. For instance, on May 5, *Ta Kung Pao* of Tianjin belatedly suggested that the goal of the Red Army "appears to be Sichuan." By this time the Red Army had been crossing the Golden Sands River into Sichuan for six days and would complete the operation in another three.

The Third Army had difficulty with its Hongmen (Xincun) crossing, south of Jiaoping. They put a floating bridge over and sent the vanguard Thirteenth Regiment across, but the current washed the bridge away. Zhou Enlai ordered them to use the First Army crossing at Longjie, a decision quickly countermanded because the First Army found it impossible to cross there.

Both the First and the Third armies put their main strength across at Jiaoping, the Third completing its crossing May 7 and the First, May 8. The rear-guard Fifth Army, with three to five thousand men, held off attacks by a KMT division of nearly ten thousand led by Wu Qiwei in Luquan county, just south of Jiaoping, for a week before crossing on May 8 and 9.[17]

The Ninth Army, still operating as a blocking back for the main force, moved up to the Golden Sands at Shujie, about thirty-five miles north (downstream) from Jiaopingdu, May 6 and crossed the river May 9, swiftly rejoining the main force at Lugu, north of Xichang.

The way up from Jiaopingdu had been opened May 1 within a few hours of the crossing by the Cadres Regiment. They had two or three hours' sleep and then were ordered forward, clambering up the not-too-steep elevation behind the landing site. There they confronted a tortuous path that zigzagged straight up three hundred feet. It brought them to a lengthy alluvial plain as wide as a couple of football fields, its floor studded with basalt and granite boulders, some higher than a man's head, some the size of a basketball, some small as a baseball. To the left rose harsh black rock piles, to the right a sharp dropoff toward Jiaopingdu. Not a few men remembered the folk saying that it is easier to climb to the heavens than travel the paths of Sichuan, stone tracks along which it is seldom possible to walk two abreast, looping along the edges of mountain precipices.

It was hard even for hardy young men to keep to their feet, crossing the stony fields. They pushed ahead under a quickly broiling sun four miles and mounted a steep path to another plateau, half covered with stones, half with grass. Here they looked straight up at the jagged features of Lion's Head, a great massif that crops out from the west at an altitude of a thousand feet. It dominates the small plateau and in its crags a KMT defense battalion had positioned itself, firing down the throat of the Cadres Regiment, youngsters of eighteen and nineteen, half-dead from the fatigue of yesterday's sixty-mile march, the crossing of the river, and the hike over the alluvial rubble. Lion's Head was impregnable. It could hold out against ten thousand men.

From its peak heavy boulders crashed down amidst the Red Army attackers. Here a man's legs were crushed, there another lay unconscious after a stone smashed his head. KMT machine gun fire struck sparks off the boulders and ricocheted in all directions.

Slowly the Red Army men inched forward from boulder to boulder. Some found a ravine that provided a bit of protection. Nearer and nearer they advanced. Finally the bugler blasted out the call: Attack! Shouting *"Sha! Sha! Sha!"*—Kill! Kill! Kill!—they closed in and the KMT men, a local battalion, fled in panic toward Tongan.

The vanguard pursued. Their path led upward again, a twisting stone course that clings to sheer walls and skirts seven-hundred-foot dropoffs. Back and forth, up and around, climbing and climbing until their muscles felt like glowing iron and their knees turned to gelatin. To their left rose the Mountain of Fire, the sun blazing against it. Sweat stopped running. They were dehydrated. Still they pushed on seven or eight miles, then down a corkscrew stone path, steep as a mountain cascade, onto a valley floor where the little town of Tongan lay. The enemy had fled. The vanguard waited. There was no follow-up. No reinforcements. Wearily they retraced their steps to Lion's Head, set up a defense perimeter, and waited for orders.[18] Just another day's soldiering for these young Red Army men. To one who followed in their footsteps fifty years later, it seemed a miracle.

Mao stayed at Jiaopingdu until the First Army Corps completed its crossing May 8. Then he moved on with the command column over the mountain trail to Tongan and beyond, where the Red Army already had the district center of Huili under attack.

Liu Bocheng stayed atop his big boulder to the last. He directed that machine guns be set up to protect the rear guard from last-minute attack by the rapidly advancing KMT forces. All of the large boats were brought over to the Red Army side of the river, and were cut adrift and quickly smashed on the rocks by the rapidly moving Golden Sands current. The boatmen who stayed to the end got a bonus of thirty silver dollars. The Red Army didn't compensate boat owners except for one boatman who owned his own boat. He got eighty dollars.

Once the Red Army left, many boatmen were rounded up and persecuted by the KMT. The eldest Zhang brother was arrested, tortured, and fined two hundred eighty dollars. The other three, including Zhang Chaoman, ran away and escaped arrest.[19]

Finally, when all the Red Army men were safely across and all the boats destroyed, Liu Bocheng mounted his horse, and rapidly climbed the mountain trail, ready for the next battle.[20]

The Red Army was across the River of Golden Sands. It had slammed the door on pursuit. Not yet was Mao Zedong wholly free from Chiang Kai-shek. But he was north of the Yangtze. Not since October 16, 1934, had the Army gained such a success in maneuver, such freedom of operation. They had been in the field seven months. The losses had been heavy. They were down to under 25,000 men. But they had survived. Mao's strategy had paid off. The crossing of the Golden Sands would become an epic in Red Army history.

There was another factor not to be overlooked. Almost everywhere in Yunnan the Red Army had found popular support. Local soldiers had not fought hard. The local officials often were sympathetic.

Warlord Long Yun had walked a tightrope. He did not aid the Red Army but he did not expose his military strength to major erosion. He had the example of Wang Jialie, the Guizhou warlord, played out before him. Wang Jialie had been badly beaten by the Red Army. He had suffered disastrous losses and a heavy blow to prestige. Wang was offered a choice by Chiang Kai-shek. He could keep his post as commander or he could keep the post of governor. Not both. Wang Jialie opted to keep his command. Chiang Kai-shek then instigated Wang Jialie's lieutenants to demand more money. The trouble grew so serious that Chiang was able to remove Wang and send him off to military school, putting Chiang's puppet in his place. Warlord Long Yun was not going to let this happen to him.

On April 27, 1935, Long Yun received a telegram from the representative of some influential people in Hongkong. It said: "I have talked with people in Guizhou and Hunan. My impression is that they just want to see the Red Army out of this area and the Red Army wants to go through Yunnan into Sichuan, so better let them do that without having to fight." Long Yun noted on the telegram: "This is a statement based upon the interest of the Southwest."

It is likely that the telegram had something to do with Long Yun's less than all-out opposition to the Red Army.[21]

As in crossing the corners of Guangdong and Guangxi, the contradictions among China's warlords, their fear of Chiang Kai-shek and desire to hold on to their fiefdoms, were giving the Communists a secret edge in the critical battles.

18

THE CHICKEN-BLOOD OATH

THE old Ming dynasty city of Huili, dating to the fifteenth century, lay about thirty-five miles northwest of Jiaopingdu. Toward this provincial center Mao and the Red Army headed once they had crossed the River of Golden Sands. The city had been put under siege while the crossing was still in progress, but was not yet in Communist hands.

Mao wanted a place where the Army could rest for a few days and refit before moving north through the rugged mountains inhabited by an earlier, non-Chinese race, the Yi.

There were not a few political questions that had to be sorted out. Zunyi, and the decisions that had put Mao in charge, was four months in the past. The Red Army's strength was sinking close to twenty thousand and there was little prospect of recruitment in the country of the Yi and that of the Tibetans which lay beyond. Mao had safely brought his fighting band across the upper Yangtze; he had once again foiled Chiang Kai-shek, but there was always one more river to cross, one more mountain to climb.

Chiang thought he had locked up the Communists in the Red corner of Jiangxi. They escaped. He thought he could wipe them out at the Xiang River. They battered their way across. He thought he had trapped them in western Guizhou. But Mao slipped away. Finally he believed he would catch Mao before he got to the River of Golden Sands. He didn't.

The campaign had begun to look like one of Walt Disney's early cartoons in which Mickey Mouse again and again escaped the clutches of the huge, stupid cat.

Mao was, it might seem, on a roll, to use the idiom of today. Everything was going his way. But it did not so appear to all of his colleagues, particularly not to Lin Biao. Lin Biao had performed brilliantly since Mao's return to leadership. He had captured Zunyi with hardly the loss of a man. He had failed to break through to the Yangtze in northwest Guizhou, but that was beyond any commander. His daring sortie against Kunming and the race to the Golden Sands showed a wizard's touch.

But Lin Biao was deeply dissatisfied. Weeks earlier he had been complaining that Mao was exhausting the troops by his erratic war of movement. Evidence is now being presented to suggest that on several occasions during Mao's zigzag campaign Lin Biao balked at his orders (although always carrying them out). Some of these accounts may be exaggerations by Red Army survivors who suffered at Lin Biao's hands during the Cultural Revolution. Not a few of their comrades lost their lives through Lin Biao's intrigues, and many endured years in prison and months of torture.

Mao's hopes of turning Huili into another Zunyi—a breathing space for political discussion, for reorganization, for replenishment of men and materials—were dashed. Huili was an almost medieval city, protected by a broad three-hundred-year-old moat and two high, stout walls, an outer and an inner perimeter. The Red Army tried and failed to take the town by surprise. A thousand men of the KMT Twenty-fourth Division held them off. They slammed the gates, manned the walls, and repelled Peng Dehuai's Tenth, Eleventh, and Twelfth regiments. In the first assault the Eleventh got through the east gate and the Twelfth through the west, but they couldn't scale the second wall.

The area between the walls was filled with houses and huts. The defenders evacuated the residents and set fire to the houses, driving the Red Army back to the first wall.[1] The KMT ordered the city dwellers to make great caldrons of hot rice porridge. They poured the thin gruel over the heads of the Third Army men as they climbed up their bamboo scaling ladders. Many were horribly scalded and fell from the ladders. This second assault was repelled May 10.

The Red Army then resorted to a technique they had not used before. They dug tunnels under the east and west gate towers and blew them up. The Huili residents were terrified, but the Red Army was unable to penetrate the defenses.[2]

That same night, May 12, Mao convened the Huili meeting in a blacksmith's shop outside the city walls.

It was an extended session of the Politburo. Eighteen persons attended: Mao, Zhu De, Zhou Enlai, Chen Yun, Bo Gu, Wang Jiaxiang, Liu Shaoqi, Yang Shangkun, He Kequan (Kai Feng, who had opposed

Mao at Zunyi), Liu Bocheng, Lin Biao, Nie Rongzhen, Luo Fu, Peng Dehuai, Li Zhuoran, Dong Zhentang, Deng Xiaoping, and Deng Fa.[3]

Otto Braun said that he was invited to attend at the last moment. He had no interpreter and depended on Bo Gu for sketchy fill-ins. No military men attended, Braun reported.[4] No one else recorded Braun's presence and several military men provided detailed accounts of what they and others said. Braun is probably mistaken, as he often is, handicapped by lack of notes and writing thirty years after the events.

Lin Biao's views were at the center of the discussion. The twenty-seven-year-old commander had drafted and sent to Mao Zedong a letter calling for him to turn over his active command to Peng Dehuai, the old (he was thirty-seven) leader of the Third Army. Salt and bread of the China soil, a tough Red Army commander who looked a little like a bulldog and fought like one, Peng was a rough-hewn man with strong back and shoulders, from years of early labor. In the words of General Yang Shangkun, close friend and comrade, Peng possessed "a statue-like face set with dark, sparkling eyes imbued with a powerful and unyielding spirit."[5]

There was nothing about the life of the Chinese peasant that Peng had not endured. At the age of seventy, his grandmother had tottered out on her bound feet to the village street in Wushi, Hunan, Peng's three small brothers with her, and begged for rice at the lunar new year's holiday. The smallest brother soon died of starvation. Peng went begging only once. Never again. Instead he hiked up the hills, barefoot in snowy winter, and cut brush for firewood. He tended a water buffalo for five coppers a day and later turned a waterpump in a coal pit for thirty coppers a day, until the owner went bankrupt, owing Peng a year's wages.

Peng got his first revolutionary spark from a great-uncle who fought with the Taipings in the rebellion of the 1850s. Then, said the uncle, the Taipings found food for everyone, the women unbound their feet, and the land was shared among the tillers.

"This," wrote Peng Dehuai in one of the autobiographical sketches he penned for the interrogators who beat and ultimately tortured him to death in the Cultural Revolution, "instilled in me the idea of taking the landlords' riches to the poor."[6]

Until 1916, Peng worked as a day laborer on the dikes of Lake Dongting in Hunan, then he joined a warlord's army at five and a half silver dollars a month. He soldiered for the rest of his life, graduating from the Hunan Military Academy, entering the Red Army in 1928 and ultimately commanding China's forces against the Americans in Korea.

All his life Peng spoke frankly, bluntly, and he wrote in plain, vigorous Chinese, often at great length so that no one might doubt his opinion. He was, as his men often said, "married to the Revolution."[7] In the hands of his torturers he shouted his denials and pounded the table so fiercely the walls of his cell shook. "I fear nothing," he bellowed. "You can shoot me. Your days are numbered."[8]

Lin Biao did not present the bluff, lusty face of Peng Dehuai. He was ten years younger, rather slight, oval-faced, olive-skinned, dark, handsome. Peng talked with his men. Lin kept his distance. To many he seemed shy and reserved. There are no stories reflecting warmth and affection for his men. His fellow Red Army commanders respected Lin but when he spoke it was all business.

Wu Xing who became a division commander in 1948 served under Lin Biao on the Long March as a platoon commander in the headquarters company.

"Lin fought good battles and was a fine military commander," he said. "He was very good to those who worked with him." He agreed that Lin was not talkative. "He liked to be alone," Wu Xing recalled.[9]

When the Red Army got to Yan'an the custom of Saturday night dances at a pleasant courtyard called the Date Garden sprung up. Mao Zedong and Zhu De danced a kind of bear-hug waltz and swung around the floor with a succession of excited young partners. So did Peng Dehuai. Zhou Enlai danced with grace, but Lin Biao shunned the floor despite the persuasion of the young women of Shanghai and Beijing who had come to Yan'an to join the revolutionary cause. (Ultimately, he did marry one of the invading beauties.)[10]

Lin Biao was the darling of Mao as he had been the darling of Chiang Kai-shek and the Soviet marshal-to-be Blyukher at the famous Whampoa Military Academy in Canton before Chiang turned on the Communists at Shanghai in 1927. Lin Biao, son of a tax-ruined factory owner in Hubei, cast his fate with the Communists, joined Zhou Enlai at Nanchang in the August 1, 1927, uprising, and at the age of twenty-four, in 1932, was commanding the First Army. Now he was twenty-seven, and no one had such a reputation for daring and deception. It was said that he never launched a battle unless he was certain he could win it.

The contrast between Mao's top field commanders could hardly have been more sharp, but on the Long March they worked well together, Lin specializing in feints, masked strategy, surprises, ambushes, flank attacks, pounces from the rear, and stratagems. Peng met the enemy head-on in frontal assaults and fought with such fury that again and again he wiped them out. Peng did not believe a battle well fought unless he managed to replenish—and more than replenish—any losses by seizure of enemy guns and converting prisoners of war to new and loyal recruits to the Red Army.

By the time the Red Army paused at Huili, men and commanders suffered from deepening fatigue. They had been run ragged. Questions kept rising: Where are we going? What is the plan? A great many came from Jiangxi or Hunan. Now they were in Sichuan—in the remote reaches of Sichuan. They felt alien and lost. They did not speak the Sichuan dialect. How could they ever find their way back to Jiangxi or Hunan?

Otto Braun, not a wholly trustworthy witness, insisted that the problems were critical and deep-seated. He contended that dissatisfaction with Mao's leadership arose soon after Zunyi. It had been mollified by the victory at Loushan Pass, but did not vanish. He claimed Luo Fu and Lin Biao had charged Mao with "flight before the enemy" and "military bankruptcy." He said Peng Dehuai and General Yang Shangkun "basically agreed" with them. No other source goes so far. It seems certain that Braun's feud with Mao caused him to exaggerate. He claimed Luo Fu hinted to him that he would prefer a new leadership trio—Lin Biao, Peng Dehuai, and Liu Bocheng. Braun said Bo Gu was fearful that the Red Army might be pushed farther toward Tibet or Burma.

To Braun's surprise, Mao called him in one day for a chat. Mao admitted the situation was serious, but expressed confidence that ultimately they would cross the River of Golden Sands. If necessary, he was prepared to lead the Red Army over the Tibetan approaches of Sikang and Qinghai to Xinjiang, where he would request aid from the Soviet Union.[11]

Nonetheless there were questions. Mao had saved the Red Army, but what would they do now? They had not been able to join He Long and Xiao Ke. They had not been able to set up a new soviet base. The Fourth Army Group of Zhang Guotao was somewhere on the move and there had been virtually no communications since Zunyi.

These were the issues that provoked Lin Biao's concern. He had discussed the matter with a group of commanders, notably with his coequal Nie Rongzhen, political commissar of the First Army. Sitting in on the meeting, as well, were Zuo Quan, chief of staff, Luo Ruiqing, security chief, and Zhu Rui, senior staff officer.

Lin Biao proposed that the active command be turned over to Peng Dehuai and that Mao confine himself to overall policy and planning, along with the other members of the Military Commission, Zhou Enlai and Wang Jiaxiang.

Lin complained that Mao was compelling the troops to travel unnecessary distances. He likened the Red Army's route to a strung bow. The troops marched along the bend of the bow rather than the taut string. No shortcuts.

"This," Lin said, "is exhausting our troops. Mao's command style is not going to succeed."

Nie Rongzhen sharply disagreed! "We are in the pocket of the enemy. If we do not move back and forth with great unpredictability, how can we break out?"

Lin proposed that Peng Dehuai be made overall front commander in charge of field operations. Peng, in Nie Rongzhen's recollection, flatly rejected the idea.[12] Peng in his prison memoirs recalls reading Lin's letter while at the Huili meeting. He said he "did not mind, considering it a matter of directing field operations." He pointed out that the First Army, which Lin directed, and his Third Army had not infrequently operated under a single command.[13]

The Red Army was again being reorganized to compensate for its reduced size. The First Army was brought down from three divisions to two and the Third Army was cut back from three divisions to four regiments. In the Fifth and Ninth armies, divisions were abolished.

Mao decided to comb out the Central Column and send all able-bodied men to combat units. One who was so assigned was Deng Xiaoping. He was relieved of his Central Committee secretarial duties and sent as propaganda chief to the First Army. In his place was put diminutive Liu Ying. It proved a turning point in her life. She now became secretary to the "Central Team." She had never done anything like this before and Luo Fu, a member of the "team," helped her out, showing her how to make minutes of meetings, keep track of records, and write up orders. She had known Luo Fu in Moscow when she was a student at Sun Yat-sen University and he was a teacher. When they returned to the Central Soviet Area she saw him occasionally. He headed the educational commission. She had, as she said, no desire to get married or "be tied up with children." Now the two began to draw closer. In 1984, she chuckled as she recalled those days. "Chairman Mao used to make jokes about us," she said. But nothing more happened for a while.[14]

Another document was placed before the Huili meeting, a telegram signed by Liu Shaoqi and General Yang Shangkun, which made suggestions for further operations. The suggestions had originated in informal talks between Peng Dehuai and Liu Shaoqi at the time Liu joined the Third Army after Zunyi. Peng's idea was that the Nationalist forces were getting as tired as the Communists and it might be a good time to revert to the original plan of joining He Long's Second Front Army.[15]

Mao had no difficulty in coping with these challenges to his authority. He ridiculed Lin Biao: "What do you know? You are just a kid. It is necessary for the troops to travel on the curve of a bowl."[16]

Mao said that the proposals of Lin Biao, and the telegram of Liu Shaoqi and Yang Shangkun, showed a "mood of right deviation," in Peng Dehuai's words, by which he apparently meant that they did not show an aggressive spirit. Peng made a small self-criticism. Later on, the affair would acquire sinister and grave overtones for Peng Dehuai, Yang Shangkun, and Liu Shaoqi (but not for Lin Biao). For the moment it seemed to have blown itself out, and as Peng wrote in his memoirs-by-torture: "I figured that time would clear things up."[17] It did not.

The other question before the meeting was what to do next. Mao had already decided that they must move north through the Yi country and cross the Dadu River, which lay beyond. The Dadu was a formidable obstacle. And there was the possibility that Chiang Kai-shek might cut them off. In that case the only alternative was an extraordinary and probably impossible flight through the Tibetan mountains.

Once they crossed the Dadu they could hope, if all went well, to join the Fourth Front Army of Zhang Guotao. There was a little hitch about this. They did not know exactly where the Fourth Front Army had gone. They may not have known it was in motion and had given up its Sichuan-Shaanxi base. Neither army had heard—lately—from the other. Wireless communications seem to have broken off early in 1935, at the time the First Front Army was darting about Guizhou. Each knew the other was in movement; each knew the general area; but neither had a precise fix.[18]

There was no disagreement with Mao's decisions. Otto Braun recalled being asked his opinion. He joined in the general agreement. Unity, all felt, was what was now needed, not recrimination. Ahead there lay perils enough.[19]

In General Qin Xinghan's opinion, the Huili discussions served a valuable purpose. They ventilated the grievances that had built up since Zunyi. No one spoke in opposition to Mao, although others had privately voiced opinions similar to Lin Biao's. Mao had a chance to explain his views and they were then communicated to the officers, cadres, rank-and-file.

Most important was a firm and clear decision on what to do next. Mao's plan to go north through the Yi country and cross the Dadu River was approved. It would not be easy. The Red Army could expect trouble, for wireless intercepts revealed that Chiang was beginning to move troops in the direction of the Dadu. Another race for time was in the making.

The distance from Huili to the Dadu River was, give or take, about a thousand li, half of it shorter uphill li, half of it longer downhill li. As the crow flies it was about three hundred miles. As the Red Army soldier climbed, it was nearer five hundred, along a "road" that for the most part was a narrow stone path like that of the cliff-hanging trail from the Jiaopingdu past Lion's Head to Tongan and Huili.

The order was the usual: Beat Chiang Kai-shek to the river crossing. The Red Army was on the move by the fourteenth or fifteenth of May, staggering the takeoff because the paths were too narrow for large numbers of troops.

The weather was a blessing. Mid-May is the ecstatic height of the Sichuan spring. The mountains burst with color. Azaleas and rhododendrons tumble down the stony slopes for a thousand feet. Iris shows its cobalt flags in blazes of hundreds of feet. The air is soft with the fragrance of oleanders and roses. It is heaven, as anyone who has passed that way, whether in mid-May of 1984 or mid-May of 1935, can certify. Not many Red Army veterans remember the flowers. They do remember they were greeted like a victorious host with cheers and banners and throngs of people, in every village and town as they pushed up the valleys and over the hills. Nowhere in the months of marching had people been so enthusiastic, had their welcome been so hospitable— buckets of candy and sweetmeats, baskets of newly ripened apricots, clusters of tart red cherries. Much of the time the Army moved at night. They seemed to be out of range of Chiang's planes for the moment. Nationalist press reports lagged a week and more behind as to the whereabouts of the "fleeing Red bandits." When they got to Mianning, in south-central Sichuan, at 9 A.M. May 23,[20] they had been traveling for eight nights and had covered 550 li, more than half the distance to

the Dadu. Fireworks were set off. Stands set up in the street offered tea
—with sugar—free to the Red Army. Residents were angered when the
soldiers sought to pay. Street banners proclaimed "Welcome to the Red
Army" and "Support the Communist Party." A band of Army political
workers had arrived beforehand to prepare a proper welcome.[21]

Troops bivouacked on the main streets, relaxing from their march.
Others went to the Catholic church, where they were welcomed by the
Chinese priest. Five foreign missionaries had taken refuge in the
church. Commissar Wen Bin invited them to stay and give a report on
the latest news.[22]

The writ of the Nationalist government ran feebly in these valleys
along the river Anning. At Mianning, people told the soldiers they had
kept the city gates open all night waiting for them. They steamed
pork-filled dumplings to feast the Army. They were not afraid, they
said. The well-to-do had fled. The Red Army opened the jail and freed
the prisoners, including many Yi.[23]

Arrival at Mianning brought the Red Army to the edge of a region
that inspired some fear. It was what many Chinese called Lololand, not
knowing that *lolo* is a pejorative to the ancient Yi people who inhabit
the area. The Yi came long before the Han, somewhere out of the
Burma-Tibetan ethnic pool that lies on China's western reaches. These
people, tall, dark, distinctively un-Chinese, with their own shamanistic
religion, their deep belief in magic and spirits, different in language,
with an imperfectly developed script, feared and hated the Chinese.
The fear went back hundreds if not thousands of years, springing from
the conflict of the superior Han civilization with the primitive Yi. Hans
had driven the Yi into the hills, where they poked out a meager living,
herding sheep, cultivating a patch of corn or millet on the mountainside, living in such poverty that most men wore only a tattered cloak,
women a rag or two, and children nothing. In contemporary times they
had been oppressed by warlords and Nationalist troops. It went without
saying that any soldier was a bandit. Against soldiers anything was fair
—magical spells, rocks rolled down from cliffs, poisoned arrows, or
tommy guns they had seized from cowardly KMT booty patrols.

Not far from Mianning rose a secret mountain spring, known only
to the Yi. From this spring flowed a strange water with deadly effect on
the vocal system. It acted something like laughing gas: People burst into
laughter and could not stop. The Yi paralyzed their enemies with this
water, making them laugh themselves to death.[24]

The Yi were a slave society, dividing themselves into "black bones" (the nobility) and "white bones" (the slaves). The white bones usually were not of Yi origin. They were captives taken in battle—Han Chinese, Miao, Tibetans, other minorities. Caste lines and taboos were fearsome. A black bones woman who had sex with a white bones man was punished by death. A black bones man was severely fined. No man ventured forth without a weapon—a knife or a bow and arrow, an old musket or a new submachine gun. Robbery was regarded as an honorable profession, particularly against Hans. Ceremonies, incantations, oaths and blood rituals made up the fabric of Yi society.[25]

The Red Army practiced an enlightened policy toward minorities. It treated them with great consideration, trying to compensate for past Han savagery and win them over. Mao had briefed his leaders on this at Mianning before they headed into Yi country. They must avoid conflict with the Yis because no delay could be brooked in reaching the Dadu ahead of Chiang Kai-shek.

Mao was splitting his forces. One of them would take the "main" stony trail to Anshunchang, an important Dadu crossing seventy miles due north. A smaller diversionary force would hasten by smaller paths to Yuexi and then on to a more southern crossing at Dashubao, across the Dadu from the town of Fulin, where the KMT was known to have a small garrison.[26]

The main force, led by Liu Bocheng and Nie Rongzhen, would head over the Xiang Mountains to Anshunchang. The vanguard was the First Regiment of the First Division, with a special work team commanded by Xiao Hua. The vanguard was accompanied by an engineering detachment, laden with bridge-building materials, planks, ropes, joists, and tackle it had assembled at Mianning.

On the morning of May 22 at about 9 A.M., the vanguard arrived at the village of Daqiaozhen, on the border between Han and Yi settlements, fifteen kilometers from Mianning.

It was a sunshine-and-showers day. As the men climbed the flinty path to higher elevations, cascades of azaleas, pink and white, draped the cliffs.

At the village of Gumazi, Xiao Hua's detachment was halted by hundreds of Yi armed with sticks, clubs, guns, rocks, spears, bows and arrows. The Yi shouted: "We want money! Give us road money!"

Fifty years after that May morning, the military poet Xiao Hua recalled the details with precision. Xiao Hua was carrying some silver dollars in anticipation of the Yi demand. He passed over two hundred dollars. The Yi vanished but soon came back for more. Money was not the solution. The engineers company had been surrounded and sent back to their starting point, their equipment confiscated.

Xiao Hua asked an interpreter (a local Han merchant) to explain to the Yi that the Red Army only wanted to pass through. "No passing!" shouted the Yi. A tall, middle-aged Yi rode up on a mule. He was an uncle of Xiao Yedan, chief of the tribe. Xiao Hua told him that his chief, Liu Bocheng, wanted to talk to chief Xiao Yedan. He would like to become his blood brother. Xiao Hua presented the uncle with some rifles and a pistol as a token of goodwill.

Soon Xiao Yedan and an escort of a dozen men appeared. Xiao Yedan was a tall, handsome man, a fine rider, mounted on a spirited black horse. Xiao Hua brought up Liu Bocheng, that genial, bespectacled, battle-scarred Red Army officer. Xiao Yedan knelt at Liu Bocheng's feet. The one-eyed dragon lifted him up and swore he wanted to become the blood brother of the Yi. Once the KMT was overthrown, Liu Bocheng would help the Yi regain their rights and privileges.

The party went to the edge of a crystal mountain lake and drew two bowls of clear water. A great cock, all purple and golden and red, was brought, its beak was broken, and the fresh blood sprinkled into the bowls. Liu Bocheng, Xiao Yedan, and the uncle knelt before the bowls. Under the blue sky and bright sun Liu held aloft his bowl and swore: "To Heavens above and Earth below I, Liu Bocheng, pledge my willingness to become a sworn brother of Xiao Yedan." He lifted the bowl and drained it at a draft. Xiao Yedan and the uncle lifted the other bowl and drank it, declaring: "If this oath be violated may we die like chickens." The ceremony was over. The oath was sealed.[27]

The Red Army men withdrew for the night to a Han village. In the morning Xiao Yedan and a Yi escort rode with them through fifty kilometers of Yi country to the first Han village (where the Hans wanted to kill Xiao Yedan, just because he was a Yi). The Communists spent an hour or so trying to smooth relations between the Hans and the Yi. Then they went forward, encountering no more real difficulty except with the rugged terrain and exhaustion from the swift pace.

In the dark hours before morning on May 24, they came to the heights above the Dadu River and saw through the fog a few flickering lights of the village of Anshunchang, a hundred huts on the riverbank.

The story was not so pleasant for some detachments that followed. The Fifth Army, in the rear guard as always, lost a good many men to the Yi. These were stragglers; when they dropped behind, the Yi were on them in a flash. They did not waste bullets. They simply took their guns, if they had guns, robbed them of their food and knapsacks, stripped them of their clothes, and left them in the woods. Few of these naked soldiers managed to save themselves. They froze to death or starved in the mountains.

At seventy-five, Peng Haiqing was a tiny man half-crippled by arthritis, with a wisp of a beard and a shrunken little face, but he well remembered the Yi. When Mao came down from Jinggangshan, Peng had left his poverty-stricken mother, father, and three brothers in his native Ji'an county of Jiangxi, to find his fate in the Red Army. He fought through all the Jiangxi campaigns and served with Lin Biao's First Army Group in the Long March. He had no idea things were going badly in the Central Soviet Area, knew that Guangchang had been a fierce battle, and wasn't told they were going on the Long March. His unit just started walking, and kept on walking and fighting all the way. When he was asked about the Yi, he put his head back and let out an ear-piercing call: Whoo—ooo—ooo—oo—oo. Whoo—oo—oo. It was as startling as General Patrick J. Hurley's Cherokee war whoop when he got off his plane in Yan'an during World War II to meet Mao Zedong.

That was the Yi, Peng said. They came rushing down the mountains shouting: Whoo—oo—oo. He and his comrades had been carefully briefed. Under no circumstance were they to fight the Yi. No shooting. So when a hundred Yi came whoo—oo—ing down the cliff and surrounded Peng and his four Red Army comrades, they didn't fight. "We could easily have gotten away," Peng said. He was carrying a heavy machine gun. All his comrades had rifles. They stopped stock-still. The Yi took their guns and their clothes and dashed away. They took everything but Peng's heavy machine gun. That was too heavy for them. Peng and his group were lucky. They were quickly picked up and went on with their march.[28]

Ding Ganru in 1984 was the retired deputy chief of staff at Chengdu. He was sixty-seven and had joined the Red Army at the age of fifteen in 1932, serving with the Fifth Army all the way on the Long March. He spent fifty-two years in the Army, and retired only after two heart attacks.

"We came after everyone else," he recalled. "Sometimes it was hard."

He thought the chief problem with the Yi was their poverty. Yi women were so poor they wore only a kind of small apron to cover their front and rear. The Yi sniped at the Fifth Army from the hills, "but luckily their aim was not very good," Ding Ganru said. The Fifth Army offered to pay them money for safe passage, but this did not do much good. "They took away their cooking woks and buried them and their rice before fleeing to the hills," Ding said. "We offered to pay one hundred silver dollars for one hundred jin of rice, but they ran away. Sometimes we dug up the rice and left IOU's. After 1949 the Yi brought out the IOU's and we paid them."

Occasionally the Fifth Army had to violate its rules and seize rice from the fields without paying—there was no other way of getting food.[29]

The Red Army's diversionary column—which does not seem to have diverted anything—got to the Dadu May 23, after passing through the Yi town of Yuexi at 2 P.M. May 21. It came out on the Dadu at Dashubao. A small KMT unit retired across the river to a Nationalist garrison at Fulin without fighting.

The Red Army had beaten Chiang Kai-shek to the Dadu. It remained to cross the river.

19

THOSE LEFT BEHIND

THE main Red Army had now moved so far west, Chen Yi no longer knew where it was to be found. Back in the southeast corner of Jiangxi province, the Wuling Mountains were clothed in their spring garb of rain and fog. From the hilltops, Chen Yi's world seemed made of cotton, with here and there a chunky shoulder of granite piercing the white billows. It was not possible to keep the slow, steady drizzle from soaking through plaited bamboo rain capes. Mist softened the tropical spring green of the forests, the red gashes of eroded gullies, and the terraces bright with new rice. Smoke hovered over the winged tiles of the roofs and smothered the peasants in their huts, refusing to rise through the rude smoke holes in the thatched ceilings.

It was a typical spring day in this corner of China. Such days had been trying men's souls for an eternity. Now on this dismal afternoon Chen Yi's small band, the remnants of the force that had been left behind when the Red Army embarked on its Long March, had assembled, beside them their gear, sodden with rain, their remaining guns and bullets shielded under rain capes. They were awaiting the order to pull out.

There had been thirty thousand men, including at least ten thousand wounded, left behind when the Red Army moved across the Yudu River October 16, 1934. Now it was March 4, 1935. Most of that force had been wiped out. The Red capital of Ruijin had fallen November 10, Yudu on the seventeenth, and Huichang on November 23. The Soviet Republic of China was only a memory.

From the beginning, things had gone just as badly as Chen Yi had feared when Zhou Enlai came to his hospital room on that October day and said he must stay behind. There had been a basic disagreement with Political Commissar Xiang Ying, who was a supporter of Bo Gu and Otto Braun and was Chen Yi's superior. Xiang Ying couldn't get it through his head that the small, poorly trained force, the Twenty-fourth Division and a ragtag assortment of ten other regiments of local militia and recuperating wounded, could not possibly match the 100,000 men whom Chiang Kai-shek was moving in on them.[1]

Chiang had ordered his commanders, at a meeting at Nanchang, not to permit the "revival of the revolutionary government from its dying embers." Chen Yi told Commissar Xiang Ying that "defeat is defeat," and that the only way to survive was to go to the mountains. Xiang Ying called that "moody pessimism." There things had stood.

Chen Pixian was only nineteen at that time. In 1984, he was a small, very neat man, a vice-chairman of the Standing Committee of the People's Congress, wearing an olive-drab suit of military cut. He brought three of Chen Yi's four surviving children, each now playing a vigorous individual role in contemporary China, to join us in talking about the man with whom he had been so closely associated for many years.* In 1934, Chen Pixian was a youth leader who had been assigned, somewhat to his surprise, to stay behind in the Central Soviet Area, and he was to fight the next three or four years at Chen Yi's side.

He had thought that Chen Yi was right and Xiang Ying wrong as to what should be done, and he was deeply concerned about the fate of the prominent Party figures who had been left behind. He remembered seeing Qu Qiubai, onetime head of the Party, forty-six years old, tubercular, cooking his New Year's supper of gruel and eggs over a smoky fire of wet wood. How could Qu Qiubai possibly survive guerrilla war?

Commissar Xiang Ying seemed to believe that the Red Army would soon win big victories and they would all join in a new soviet zone. He refused to prepare people for a crisis.[2]

Chen Pixian remembered going to evening performances of the Workers and Peasants Theater Society, the theater with which Li Bo-zhao had worked before leaving on the Long March with her husband, General Yang Shangkun. She had collaborated on the play *To Die Or to Fight—for Whom,* written at Mao Zedong's instruction, and had written another herself, *We Must Win Victory,* in the heyday of the Central Soviet Area.[3] The programs Chen Pixian saw were the same as ever— folk dances, plays, solo performances, group songs like "The Guns of Victory." It was an outdoor stage and of course it rained every night. That didn't keep people from coming, with umbrellas or straw rain gear.

*Chen Haosu, the eldest, known as "little tiger" as a child, is now deputy mayor of Beijing.

Town after town fell to the KMT. The landlords came back, slaughtering as they came. There were special anti-Communist units. Assassination teams. The landlords threw their peasants out in the mud, saying, "See if you can be 'Red' for the rest of your life."[4]

The Red capital, Ruijin, had been only slightly damaged by the small bombs the KMT dropped. Now KMT troops burned buildings that had been used by the Communists. Anyone thought to be a Communist was tortured and executed. At Dabodi they buried 100 people alive. The number slaughtered cannot be calculated precisely, but the population of Ruijin county shrunk from 300,000 in 1934 to 200,000 in 1949. Not all of the missing had joined the Red Army.[5]

At seventy-nine, Zhong Qisong in 1984 was a kind of Popeye the Sailor Man, small as a grasshopper, a chain smoker and a lively storyteller. He was proud of his family—his wife, seventy-two, two daughters, three sons, eight grandchildren, four great-grandchildren—they were nineteen altogether. "This is what Communism has brought to my family," he said.

When the Long March started, he was left behind in Changgang in the model Red county of Xingguo, which provided so many men to the Red Army. People who could not conceal their Party connections fled to the mountains. Some went to Ruijin. They had instructions: Never admit you belonged to the Party. Admit you did chores for the Party. If you admit membership you will be killed.

When the KMT came back and offered amnesty, they gave themselves up. They were supported by the clan system. Everyone admits he did a little for the Communists and the clan backs you up. Every clan member backs every other clan member. If you are out of your own county, use a clan name and the clan will back you anyway. Each one testifies in behalf of the other—no one is punished.

Well, almost no one. Some were turned in by personal enemies. Some had bad luck. Probably two thousand of the nine thousand Red Army and Party people left in the county were killed, some publicly, some secretly by KMT death squads. Popeye Zhong escaped from Xingguo when the collapse came. Ran to the mountains. No one ever knew just what he was doing, so he and his wife were not punished. In 1954 he rejoined the Party.[6]

By December 1934, the losses were so great Chen Yi and Commissar Xiang Ying were forced into guerrilla warfare, like it or not. They formed a command troika with He Chang, an old party member. With the remnants of the Party and the government, they made their way to Renfeng, south of Yudu, to await instructions. Small bands were sent to the mountains. By February, Chen Yi and Commissar Xiang Ying were surrounded. They had about two thousand troops and two thousand wounded. One day, Chen Pixian heard an officer haranguing the troops, saying that they were about to fight "the last great decisive battle between the Soviet Republic of China and the KMT." Chen thought that was nonsense.

The next day, St. Valentine's Day, February 14, 1935, a cadres meeting was called, at which Liu Bojian, director of the Political Department, declared, "We must bring a great change to our work." In other words, guerrilla war in small bands.

Chen Pixian was shown two telegrams from the Central Red Army. The first reported on the Zunyi meeting, the change in leadership, the return of Mao Zedong. The second instructed them to wage guerrilla warfare "in and around the Central Soviet Area."[7]

As small parties slipped out under cover of darkness, Chen Yi moved to cope with the plight of the wounded. The wounded did not want to be left behind, but there was no way in which they could keep up with guerrilla movements. Chen Yi summoned a meeting of local cadres and inhabitants. He spoke with great emotion: "Take these soldiers into your homes. They are our sons. They are very young. They can make good sons and good sons-in-law for you. They can marry your daughters. They can work for you and you will have one more pair of hands in your family. You will have their labor and perhaps someone to take revenge for you." Before Chen Yi had finished, tears had come to the eyes of the peasants and of the wounded. And to those of Chen Yi as well. Within half a day, every wounded man had been placed with a peasant family, dispersed invisibly in the countryside, each equipped with several silver dollars, medicine for treating their wounds, and five jin of salt, a priceless gift in this region of KMT blockade.*

On the morning of March 4, 1935, the remaining troops were assembled. Rain pelted down. In a small hut a wireless operator worked his key, trying to get a message through to the Central Army (now in eastern Guizhou). Commissar Xiang Ying still felt he must get approval of their pullout from the Central Committee.[8] Again and again the wireless key sputtered its call. No response.

Finally, most of the force started off. Rain slushed down. The trails

---

*A jin is a little more than a pound.

were greasy with mud. You could not see a hundred yards. Chen Pixian
went with this detachment—about eighteen hundred men, including
the Party and government apparatus, such as it was, and the Sixth
Independent Regiment. By evening they had gotten safely to Lifan
Bridge, and paused for a meal. Then they pushed forward in total
darkness. No moon. They walked in single file across a valley floor and
had begun climbing a narrow upward trail, when they heard a few
shots. They paused. The firing died away. It was only landlord guards
firing a salute to what they thought was a local militia unit. At 3 A.M.
they reached the Damaling hills, to rest, eat dry rations, and prepare
for the battle they knew they would have to fight at dawn.[9]

Noon came at Renfeng. Still no wireless contact. One P.M. No contact. The rain came down. He Chang decided to wait no longer. He
moved out with two small battalions, a few hundred men. Soon they ran
into a KMT ambush and scattered, but managed to reassemble at Shi-
han village and cross the Huichang River. Quickly surrounded there,
they fought for several hours, unable to break through. He Chang was
badly wounded. KMT soldiers dashed toward him, shouting: "Catch
him alive!" He Chang put his gun to his head. He cried: "Long live the
Revolution," and used his last bullet. He had fought with Chen Yi, Zhou
Enlai, and the others in the Nanchang Uprising of August 1, 1927, had
been a member of the Party Central Standing Committee, and deputy
director of the Red Army Political Department. He was twenty-nine.

At Renfeng the command party waited. The rain had not ceased.
Finally contact was made. A request was sent for approval of the breakout plan. At about 5 P.M. a reply was transmitted, but Chen Yi and
Commissar Xiang Ying could not read it. The code had been changed.
The men stared at the jumble of ciphers and shook their heads. They
burned the message and ordered the wireless operator to bury his
apparatus—the oilcloth to cover it was ready and a pit had been prepared. The unintelligible encoded message was the last signal they
would receive from the Red Army for three years.[10]

From then on, as Chen Yi once told John S. Service, the U.S. diplomat attached to the Dixie Mission in Yan'an, "we lived like animals."

Neither Chen Yi nor Commissar Xiang Ying was in shape for guerrilla war. Chen Yi's hip wound was far from healed. Often he had to be
carried on a litter. Xiang Ying was nearsighted and suffered from night
blindness.

It was early evening on March 4, 1935, before they got down from the mountain. They had a battalion of perhaps three hundred men and were attacked almost immediately. They dispersed their men and when they reassembled had only two hundred. Later in the evening they ran into another firefight. They found leaflets dropped by KMT planes describing Chen Yi and Commissar Xiang Ying and offering fifty thousand yuan a head for their capture. They decided to slip away and try to break through with a few bodyguards. It would relieve pressure on the remnants of their battalion.

As they sought cover in the mountain thickets, they encountered a barefoot man, little more than a skeleton, wearing an ash-covered helmet. He was a Party worker named Zeng Jicai, who had known Chen Yi in 1929. He had been removed from his post as Daiying Party secretary after a "struggle" on grounds that he was a "right opportunist." He had been wandering over the countryside as a beggar, using his helmet as a pot to heat the handfuls of rice he begged. Chen Yi enlisted him as a guide. They hid in the mountains for a day and then walked through Zeng's native village. His family had been slaughtered by the KMT except for his mother-in-law, who fearfully gave them some food.[11]

In 1984, Liu Jianhua looked like a businessman in his mid-sixties. He was deputy chairman of the Jiangxi Provincial Peoples Congress and he spoke a bit like a bureaucrat. Fifty years earlier he had been a youngster in the South Jiangxi guerrillas, a friend of the Woman Wei, and they were still friends and comrades. When the Woman Wei Xiuying was ordered to Yan'an in 1941, she left her pistol with Liu Jianhua and said: "If you are well and alive when we meet again, I want my pistol back." When the Woman Wei came back in 1949, she wrote Liu Jianhua and he wrote back: "You are alive and I am alive but I haven't got your pistol nor have I got my own. They were both taken by traitors, but the fact that you are alive and I am alive proves that the Party has won a historic victory."

In November 1934, Liu Jianhua was a teenager with the youth league. The Central Soviet Area had not yet been overrun and he was sent with about six hundred men commanded by Li Letian to set up a guerrilla base on Youshan Mountain, a forested region that spilled over the Jiangxi-Guangdong border beyond Anyuan. The base was commanded by Yang Shangkui.

Liu remembered the arrival of Chen Yi and Commissar Xiang Ying. They came on March 9, with a single guard, having slipped through swarms of KMT patrols in disguise.[12]

A few days later, at dusk, the remnants of the force arrived. There had been fearsome losses. They came in two groups, one led by the handsome Cai Huiwen, who had led the Party and government detachment, and the other led by Chen Pixian. Each had about eighty men. Chen Yi greeted the weary men with enthusiasm: "The KMT boasted that they would wipe us out at Renfeng, but here we are chatting at Youshan."[13]

One of those lost in the breakout was Liu Bojian, wounded and captured as the detachment led by Cai Huiwen was breaking through. Liu was riding a white horse, which was shot from under him. As he led a group up a valley, he was wounded. Several men tried to rescue him, but they were killed and he was taken prisoner. He was marched to the Dayu prison in southern Jiangxi province and interrogated by Chiang's "Office of Pacification." Then he was paraded in chains through the streets. Before he was shot, on March 21, 1935, at the age of forty, he wrote a poem:

> Chained and shackled, I was paraded through the streets.
> My heart swelled with pride and defiance,
> For I was a prisoner struggling in jail
> For the freeing of workers and peasants all over the world.[14]

Liu Bojian was one of that famous group of young Chinese who went to France in 1919–20 with the work-study group Mao helped to organize. He joined the Communist Party in 1922, studied in the Soviet Union, like Deng Xiaoping was assigned by the Party to work with the "Christian General," Feng Yuxiang, and as a secret underground Communist, worked in the Twenty-sixth Route Army. After the Ningdu Uprising, which brought the Twenty-sixth into Communist ranks, where it became the ever reliable rear-guard Fifth Army, he became head of the Fifth Army political department, and had almost certainly been left behind because of his association with Mao.[15]

In January of 1935, Qu Qiubai, a distinguished writer, a founder of the Communist Party, a onetime general secretary, and a close friend of Mao in the last years; He Shuheng, Mao's old comrade at Changsha Normal No. 1 and fellow founder of the Communist Party; and several others left their hiding places near Ruijin and started for western Fujian province in hope of escaping, via Swatow or Canton, to Shanghai or

Hongkong. Qu Qiubai was thirty-six, an "elderly" by the accounting of the teenage Red Army. He Shuheng was sixty-one.[16]

A group of women comrades started with them. They included the wife of Gu Bo, Mao's veteran supporter; Zhou Yuelin, wife of Liang Botai, deputy director of the Central Soviet Government office; Tang Yizheng, wife of Lu Dingyi, propaganda official who made the Long March (she was the lady who cooked the chicken for Deng Xiaoping); Zhang Liang, probably the wife of Li Liuru and member of the Central Committee Bureau; the wife of Commissar Xiang Ying; and a Party worker named Huang Changjiao.

The fate of these women was tragic. Zhou Yuelin was long accused of having been a traitor and responsible for the death of He Shuheng. Her name was cleared and the charges dropped, presumably after the death of Mao. She was still living in 1985. The fate of Zhang Liang (also accused of being a traitor) is not known. Nor is that of the wife of Commissar Xiang Ying. Tang Yizheng suffered the cruelest fate. She was executed by the Red Army on charges—later proved false—of having betrayed leading Communists to the KMT. Huang Changjiao survived despite many hardships.[17]

For years, the circumstances of He Shuheng's death were not known. It was said that he had been in the breakout party at Renfeng, March 4, in a group that was wiped out en route to Youshan. He was carrying party funds, seals, and documents. He leaped over a cliff rather than be captured. Two KMT soldiers found him badly wounded and shot him.[18]

He Shuheng's old friend and fellow "elderly," Xu Teli, who had known He Shuheng from Changsha days, believed he had been taken captive and shot by his guards while trying to escape. In another version, He Shuheng's guerrilla band was surrounded by the enemy, and rather than flee, he swore that "I will give up my last drop of blood for my country," pulled out his pistol, and shot himself.

None of these stories is correct. Actually He Shuheng and Qu Qiubai, disguised as merchants and traveling with a small escort, were spotted eating breakfast February 24, 1935, at Xiaopeng village in Shuikou township in Changting county, just over the line in Fujian province. The Second Battalion of the Fourteenth KMT Regiment, led by Li Yu, was nearby and surrounded the village. The group decided to disperse. In the skirmish He Shuheng was seriously wounded and fell into a rice paddy, where two KMT men found him. As they leaned over to rifle his pockets, He Shuheng leaped up and grappled with them. One of the soldiers fired two shots and killed him.[19]

Qu Qiubai escaped that encounter, but soon he and most of the others were rounded up. Qu Qiubai was carted off to Changting prison. For four months he was held in a cell while, it would appear, the KMT debated what to do with him. His health was very poor. He was not only a famous Communist (albeit a repudiated Party leader) but an extraordinary literary figure. Indeed, in his autobiographical fragment, *Superfluous Words*, written in prison, he seemed to regard himself more as a man of letters than as a political figure. But this was toying with words. He had spent years in Moscow, translated Russian works into Chinese, and written a classical sketchbook of Russia, *Journey to the Land of Hunger*, but he was a leading Communist.

He sat in his cell, smoking endless cigarettes, drinking, and pondering his life and the future of China. There were charges at one time that *Superfluous Words* was a forgery. Or had been tampered with. That does not seem to be true. He had not turned his back on Communism. He specifically wrote: "To say that I have given up Marxism is not correct."

On the morning of June 18, 1935, he sat writing a poem, to which he attached a brief preface:

On the night of June 17, 1935, I dream I am walking on a mountain path. The setting sun is glorious but is sometimes hidden, and a cold stream murmurs nearby. It was like a fairy land. In the morning as I was reading the T'ang poets I came upon the line "Setting sun, in ragged ridges, now bright, now dim." I made a poem, on the spot, a composite of four lines:

> Setting sun, in ragged ridges, now bright, now dim,
> Falling leaves and cold stream, in two tones sing requiem.
> Ten years solitude was mine to endure,
> Ties all dissolved, my heart clinging to half a hymn.

As he finished the lines a guard came to take him to the execution grounds. Weak as he was, he walked calmly to the spot, lighted a cigarette, drained a glass of whisky, and stood singing the "Internationale" in Russian as the shots rang out.[20]

Zetan, brother of Mao Zedong, was thirty years old when he was left behind at the start of the Long March. In late February or early March 1935, Mao Zetan, leading a group of twenty guerrillas, left the mountain area east of Yudu en route to west Fujian. He was probably heading for Changting.[21]

He stopped overnight in a mud-walled house near Honglin (Red Forest), in the mountains ten miles from Ruijin. Not long before daylight on the morning of April 23, Zetan detailed a soldier to watch for any suspicious signs. The sentry found a patch of grass, lay down, and went to sleep. A passing KMT patrol found him and he revealed that there were a dozen men with rifles, including Mao Zetan, in the house. The KMT surrounded the place. Zetan sent his men out the rear door and covered the front himself, killing the first attacker. Then a KMT soldier mowed him down from the rear.[22]

The KMT made a clamor over the killing of Mao Zetan. The papers carried big stories. His body was brought to Ruijin and displayed. Photographs of the dead man were published. The Twenty-fourth Division commander got a special citation from Chiang Kai-shek.[23] Today the village where Zetan was killed is named for him. No trace of the inattentive (or traitorous) sentry was ever found.

The record of the dead is a Who's Who of the revolutionary movement. More prominent Communists died among those left behind than in any other period of the struggle.

Gu Bo was moving a group of twenty or thirty guerrillas from the Guangdong mountains to southern Hunan when he ran into a KMT patrol and was killed. When Mao learned of the death in 1937, he wrote a notice: "My good friend Gu Bo was a handsome man. He always tried to make progress. Now he has died for the country. I hope the country folk will attain Gu Bo's goal of national liberation." Li Cailian, the Guangdong-Jiangxi border military leader, was killed. No one knows when or how. Fang Weixia, a professor at Changsha No. 1, friend of Professor Yang Changji, Mao's mentor and father-in-law, and friend of Mao was arrested by the KMT in western Jiangxi and executed.[24]

Two of those who suffered with Deng Xiaoping in the "Luo Ming line" affair and were left behind in the Central Soviet Area—Mao Zetan and Gu Bo—died in the guerrilla areas. So did Gu Zuolin, who had been secretary-general of the Central Committee bureau when it moved to the Central Soviet Area. He had been a student in Moscow and died in May 1034 before the Long March started.[25]

On and on the roll goes. The list of the dead and the missing will never be complete.

20

THE LEGION OF DEATH

C HEN YI and Commissar Xiang Ying became the closest of friends and comrades in the unending struggle of Youshan Mountain. They moved and fought by night. By day they concealed themselves in the most dense forests, turning into hunted animals and developing the instincts of animals. A careless footprint, a wisp of smoke against the sky, the sound of a tree being cut, could betray them. Never did the two spend a night under the same shelter. Often they moved more than once between dusk and dawn.

They were fighting blindfolded. They had no notion of what was happening in the world. The Red Army—did it still exist? Had the retreat ended? Had the Red Army won great victories? They did not know. They had no wireless. There were no post offices to plunder for KMT newspapers. Months passed when they saw no papers. The poverty-gnawed mountain peasants were illiterate. They knew nothing beyond the forest, they heard nothing; few cared.

Chen Yi's comrades on the distant Long March heard nothing from those left behind. No messages. No couriers. Except for the publicized cases of Mao Zetan and Qu Qiubai, all was silence. And word of the deaths of Mao Zetan and Qu Qiubai did not trickle through for months. When it came, there was no way to know if it was true or false. After all, the Nationalists had reported again and again that Mao Zedong and Zhu De were dead.

Long after the March was over, after the Red Army was comfortably (comparatively) settled in northern Shaanxi, in the cave town of Bao'an, and Edgar Snow made his way into Red territory and interviewed Mao Zedong, the situation was still murky. Snow asked Mao and Zhou Enlai in the summer of 1936 about those left behind. Mao told Snow he did not know. He had heard nothing. The last wireless message had come in the winter of 1935. Whether they were alive or dead, he had no notion.[1]

Chen Yi was a cultured man. Like so many revolutionaries, he was a product of Sichuan, where his father was a magistrate in the town of Lezhi. He went to school in Chengdu and learned to play basketball at the local YMCA, of which Jack Service's father was the head. Chen Yi was short and stocky. He never would have made today's teams. He told Service in Yan'an in 1944: "All the others will tell you they are sons of poor peasants or proletarians. Not me. I come from a bourgeois family." He went to France on the work-study program, joined the Young Communist League, came back to China, joined the Kuomintang and the Communist Party (not incompatible in those days), and worked as an assistant political instructor at Wuhan Military Academy. He had been through all, or almost all, the Communist military operations—Nanchang, Jinggangshan, the battles of southern Jiangxi. In an army of generals who were poets—some good, some mediocre—he was the best, second to or equal to Mao himself. He never wrote his memoirs, but he captured the drama of his life in poetry. Like so many early Party men, Chen Yi was outspoken, outgoing, and even toward the end of his life, in the terrible days of the Cultural Revolution, he never learned to bridle his tongue.

Now, in the gloom and mist of Youshan Mountain, survival was what counted. "We had six hundred soldiers," Liu Jianhua (age seventeen in 1935) estimated. "They had forty thousand. The principle was to survive. We had no tents. We preferred to live in huts of bamboo. But cutting bamboo made a noise. So we used cedar bark. But if we used too much bark the enemy would notice that trees had been stripped. So we cut grass for thatched huts, but grass only grew on the fringe of the forest. That was too dangerous. We had to live deep in the woods. Finally we got peasants to buy cloth in the villages and made cloth tents which we covered with oilcloth."[2]

"The best thing for huts was cedar bark," Chen Pixian recalled. "In some places we found huts used by mushroom pickers. We disguised them with leaves. But mostly we did not stay under cover. We slept in the open under trees or on the grass. We put up cloth shelters. We had no beds, not even planks to sleep on."[3]

Once some soldiers took shelter from the rain in a cave. In the morning they found they were sharing it with a tiger. The tiger fled at daybreak. They never knew whether they or the tiger had found the cave first.

Here at the Yudu River, October 16, 1934, in southern Jiangxi, the Red Army started its Long March.

Women fighters of the Red Army, veterans of the Long March.

The author's party on a Long March trail, skirting Fire Mountain, en route to the Jiaopingdu crossing of the Golden Sands River.

General Qin Xinghan atop the great boulder from which Liu Bocheng directed the Red Army crossing of the Golden Sands River.

Along the trail to the Golden Sands River, Lion's Head in the background, Charlotte Salisbury riding in the foreground.

Luding chain suspension bridge across the Dadu River, seized by the Red Army in a critical battle.

Luding Bridge as sketched by Huang Zhen, Long Marcher later to become a leading Chinese diplomat. No photographer accompanied the March; Huang's sketches are the only pictorial record.

Zhang Chaoman helped ferry the Red Army across the Golden Sands. Fifty years later at seventy-one he was still a ferryman.

The Red (Chishui) River was crossed four times by the Red Army. Here at Maotai, where the famous fiery Chinese liquor is distilled, is one crossing site.

The Great Snowy Mountains of northern Sichuan took a heavy toll of Red Army lives—men frozen to death, killed in falls, dead of exhaustion, lack of food, and the effects of high altitudes.

For 560 days, until Easter Sunday, April 12, 1936, when this picture was taken, the Reverend Rudolf Alfred Bosshardt of the China Inland Mission accompanied the Long March as a prisoner of General Xiao Ke of the Sixth Army Group.

Li Bozhao, wife of General Yang Shangkun, made the whole Long March as a propaganda worker, writing and putting on plays, teaching soldiers songs. She died April 17, 1985, in Beijing at the age of seventy-four.

Tong Guirong, widow of Long March hero Liu Zhidan, with her daughter Liu Lizhen, in northern Shaanxi, 1936. Five-year-old Lizhen wears a Red Army uniform sewn by her mother.

Liu Zhidan, Red Army hero saved from execution in northern Shaanxi by Mao Zedong. Pictured in early Nationalist uniform after graduating from Whampoa Military Academy.

The whole population of Hadapu in southwest Gansu turned out to welcome us, the first foreigners (they thought) to visit there in the fifty years since the Red Army passed through.

Chatting with Hu Yaobang, general secretary, Chinese Communist Party. Clockwise from left: author, Jack Service, interpreter Zhang Yuanyuan, Hu Yaobang, Charlotte Salisbury, Caroline Service.

General Yang Shangkun, vice-chairman, Central Military Commission; Jack Service; Huang Hua, former foreign minister.

Li Xiannian, President of the People's Republic of China and a Long March commander.

By day, the mountainside belonged to the Nationalists. By night it was guerrilla land. Chen Yi and his men emerged from hiding, went down to villages, bought supplies, spied out the land, occasionally ambushed a few unwary Nationalists. They even held meetings in villages. They never went in groups of more than three to five. It was in these days that Chen Yi wrote the poem "What Shall I Do If I'm Captured and Beheaded."

Commissar Xiang Ying told Edgar Snow in August 1938 that for two years he wore the same cotton uniform. He never took it off at night. He never took off his shoes. He was ready to flee at the slightest notice.[4] Like animals, the guerrillas could *smell* the presence of another human being. They could hear the rustle of feet on leaves, the tiny sound of a crunched twig. They knew by a glance at the grass whether anyone had passed by.

Food was the problem. There was little or none in the mountains. It had to be bought in the peasant villages. Here the guerrillas were saved by the landlords. For the landlords it was self-interest. They gave the guerrillas money and sometimes rice in return for protection. Unless money and food were given, the guerrillas warned, they would destroy the landlord houses and crops. Families too. At night the guerrillas came down to the villages and picked up food. Or the peasants supplied it directly. When KMT patrols were scouring the mountainside, the peasants brought rice bags up the slope and left them for the guerrillas. Landlords seldom told the KMT about the guerrillas. They knew they would face death or flight if the guerrillas found they had been talking.

The landlords even bought ammunition and guns for the guerrillas. Not many. But every gun helped. The guerrillas seldom had a chance to capture weapons. The landlords, of course, bought the guns from the KMT.

Women guerrillas gathered intelligence. They could move more easily in the villages. They dressed as peasants. Liaison depots, where information could be left, were set up every six or seven miles.

It was dangerous work. Commander Li Letian's wife was caught by a KMT patrol in one of the villages. She took refuge in a peasant hut, but the troops found her and shot her.[5] The enemy was not just the KMT. There were, alas, traitors within the Communist ranks.

The case of the Widow Huang is one in point.

Huang Changjiao had been a woman Party worker in Ruijin in October 1934, when, as she put it, "the Central Red Army left the

Central Soviet Area to march north to fight the Japanese." She had been asked to go on the March and work with a rear-echelon hospital unit along with He Zizhen, Mao Zedong's wife and her friend.

The group started off, moving southward, and crossed the Yudu River at Huichang, en route to Anyuan and the border of Guangdong. Then there was a halt and a reorganization. The Widow Huang was pregnant and it was decided that she and five other women would not go on the March. They protested, but were ordered to stay in the soviet area for what was euphemistically called "underground struggle." Who was responsible for this change and what was its motivation are not clear. Certainly the chances for survival would not be high. Among the stay-behinds were the Widow Huang; the wife of Gu Bo, also pregnant; and Zhou Yuelin, the wife of Liang Botai.

It was decided to send the party to western Fujian. The Widow Huang had a horse because of her pregnancy, but one day it ran away. Finally they headed east across the mountains, constantly dodging KMT patrols. They got past the patrols and arrived at Shuikou in Changting township, Fujian. There plans were again changed. Someone—it is not clear who—decided they were to return to the mountains around Ruijin. Gu Bo's wife had delivered a baby boy, but she was compelled to leave it with a peasant family and go with the group.

The Widow Huang returned to Ruijin county and became chief of a small underground organization in the mountains. But a local Party secretary ordered her to go live in disguise as a peasant. She objected. He insisted. She said she did not speak the local dialect, was illiterate, and would be found out. He ruled that she must go. By Party rule she was entitled on being discharged to receive one hundred kilos of rice and twenty silver dollars. The man gave her the rice but, she said, put her twenty dollars in his pocket. A few days later he went over to the KMT.

That left the Widow Huang alone in a wild mountain forest at Jiaohuoshan. She was near her time, starving, and had nowhere to turn. She came down the mountain and took refuge in a small hut. That night she was surprised by a guerrilla band that used the hut for liaison. They had eighteen or nineteen men, one of three bands on the mountain.

"I've lost contact," the Widow Huang told the guerrilla chief, Liu Guoxin. "I am alone. I have no place to go." He let her join the band. They lived on one meal a day, which they ate at midnight when they slipped down to a village. They didn't dare build a fire for fear the KMT would spot it. It was time for her baby. The guerrillas did not think it wise to bring her with them. They persuaded her to stay with a peasant family and become a guerrilla contact. By day she scouted the mountainside and at night reported at an old Buddhist temple. She brought rice to the guerrillas in a hollow bamboo pole. But the guerrillas were betrayed and shot. After that Widow Huang went on living alone on the mountainside as a peasant, saying nothing, head down, alive but cut off from the revolution. In 1949 all changed. She came out in the open, got in touch with the Party, and became a member of the county assembly. She had survived, the only one of the band.[6]

Chen Yi's injured hip gave him constant trouble. It did not heal. By June 1935 he could not walk. The guerrillas had practically no medical supplies, only four kinds of Chinese remedies—Bagundan, Wanjinyou jelly (Tiger Balm ointment), Rendan (Jindan, a Japanese pill for headaches and fevers), and Jiguangshui, a liquid. Chen Yi rubbed his wound with Tiger Balm and put a new bandage on it. Soon it improved.[7]

Chen Yi was able to hobble about during the summer, but by September the pain was excruciating and his leg had begun to swell. He managed to get to a meeting at Nanxiong county, stumbling over the hills with a cane, and decided to deal once and for all with his leg. He ordered his guard to squeeze the pus out of it. Chen Yi went white with pain. The guard halted. Chen Yi ordered him to continue. He said he couldn't; Chen Yi was shaking all over. "All right," Chen Yi said, "get a rope and tie me up so I don't shake." The guard tied Chen Yi's leg to a tree and squeezed until he got the pus and a bone splinter out of the wound. The guard bathed the wound with salt water and bandaged it with a clean cloth coated with Tiger Balm. (According to another version, Chen Yi himself poured liquid Tiger Balm, the famous Hongkong cure-all, into the wound.) He shook like Saint Vitus' dance but soon he gained control, laughed, and said: "After this there will not be a counterattack." There was not. The wound healed and never recurred.[8]

Gong Chu was one of the principal officers left behind, chief of staff of the Central Military Zone and commander of the Seventy-first Regiment of the Twenty-fourth Division, the main military force defending the zone. In May 1935 Gong Chu killed his political commissar, got in touch with the Guangdong warlord, and was assigned the undercover task of wiping out Chen Yi and Commissar Xiang Ying. Gong showed up near Youshan with a band of "guerrillas" and carried out a sham battle with a KMT unit in order to gain credibility. Then he intercepted five of Chen Yi's men, hoping that they would lead him to the Youshan hideout. Four guerrillas fled. The fifth, Wu Xiaohua, was seized. After apologies, Gong said he had some important information for "Mr. Zhou and Mr. Liu" (cover names for Chen Yi and Xiang Ying). Wu Xiaohua led Gong toward the guerrilla hideout. When he got close enough, he shouted to the sentries, "These men are reactionaries," and dove over a cliff. The sentries fired warning shots, and Gong and his men fled.[9]

Chen Yi and Commissar Xiang Ying moved from mountain to mountain. They had to keep in motion to escape the KMT. They were on Dayu Mountain in Jiangxi when Gong Chu tried to entrap them.

Chen Yi had lost touch with the main Red Army. They no longer had any communications. They had tried to smuggle letters out to Lu Xun and Mao Dun, sympathetic prominent writers, in hope they might get in touch with Mao. No luck.

Chen Yi's desperation led him into a dangerous trap in the winter of 1936. An underground courier brought word that Chen Hai, a Communist who had been infiltrated into the KMT forces in Dayu, at the foot of the mountain, had received a message from the Central Committee, which he wanted to pass on.

Chen Yi—over protests from Commissar Xiang Ying—decided to meet Chen Hai himself. At dawn the next morning, he walked down the mountain into Dayu and made directly for Chen Hai's house, where he asked a woman doing the laundry if Chen Hai was at home. "He's gone to *tuanbu* [regimental headquarters]," the woman replied, without looking up. Chen Yi misunderstood. He thought she said *tangpu* [candy store]. He knew the candy store just outside the city gate was an underground drop. When he approached the store he saw it had been closed with a paper seal on the door. An old man told him to get away quickly—that Chen Hai had turned traitor and brought the troops out.

While Chen Yi was in town, Chen Hai had come up the mountain to guerrilla headquarters, hoping to intercept him. He had three hundred men. Chen Pixian and Commander Yang Shangkui barely escaped into high brush at the top of the mountain. After a two-hour search, the troops set fire to the mountain. The flames consumed the guerrilla camp and came closer and closer to the hidden guerrillas. A sudden thunderstorm put out the fire.

Chen Yi had made his escape from Dayu and was returning to the base on Meiling Mountain when he was intercepted by a KMT search party. Chen Yi protested that he was a teacher from town and had come to the countryside to buy tea—for which the region was famous. A KMT officer decided Chen Yi was an educated man, apologized for the rough words of the soldier, and engaged Chen Yi in a literary conversation. Chen Yi was afraid he might be exposed. Spotting a roadside toilet, he ran for it, saying he had a terrible stomachache. The squad waited patiently. When they finally went to look for him, they found he had fled.

Chen Yi climbed back up to headquarters. Night had fallen and the huts had been burned and the area devastated. No one was to be seen. He could not believe the band had been wiped out. He began strolling about, talking in a loud voice: "I am old Liu. Just back from town. The enemy has left. Come on out."

Nothing happened. He tried again. "Listen to my accent. I am old Liu. Can't you understand? Come on out quickly and let's get away from this place."

This time it worked. A guard recognized his voice. Soon the troop had reassembled and was on its way to a safer place. Later on, Chen Yi was to say that the spirit of Marx, in heaven, had brought the thunderstorm that saved them.[10]

Sometimes the KMT organized "search and destroy" missions. In the spring of 1936 they got orders from the high command to rally ten thousand peasants equipped with matches, knives, and food for a seven-day operation. Anyone who resisted was subject to execution.

The search began with the people divided into companies of two to three hundred, each with a KMT company behind. They came up the mountain singing and shouting. One group of peasants was ordered to set fire to the grass on top of hills. They sabotaged the order by tumbling into a river, bringing the soldiers with them. The matches were soaked.

On the third day of the mass mountain movement, the peasants began to complain that their homes and families had been left unprotected. They melted away and the search sagged to an end.

But for a time, the guerrillas could get no food from the villages. They subsisted on wild strawberries, bamboo shoots, a kind of banana-like fruit called bajiao, a partridge-like bird called stone chicken, snakes (considered a delicacy; very easy to catch at night with a light). A great treat was bees, crispy and fragrant when fried. There were many mountain goats, wild boars, leopards, and tigers, but the guerrillas dared not fire their guns for fear of attracting attention.

The guerrilla struggle in the mountains of Youshan, Dayushan, and Meiling went on and on. In December 1936, the Long March of the main Red Army had been over for more than a year. All the other armies had gradually made their way to north Shaanxi. But the guerrillas fought on. The Xi'an Incident of December 1936—the kidnapping of Chiang Kai-shek, which led to a formal truce between the KMT and the Communists, a united front against Japan—came and went.

No change for Chen Yi, Commissar Xiang Ying, and the band of three hundred men and women, the tattered remains of the thousands who had been left behind.

Sometime in the winter of 1937, Chen Yi heard about Xi'an from the KMT newspapers, but not until September 1937 did the KMT begin to relax its pressure.

Finally Chen Yi slipped down the mountain to Dayu and to Ganzhou. He talked to local KMT commanders. They said the talks must occur at a higher level. Commissar Xiang Ying went off to Nanchang. He met with Ye Jianying and Bo Gu at the liaison office of the Eighth Route Army. It was true. There was a united front. But still the fighting went on in the mountains.

One day in early November 1937, a sedan chair, carried by four bearers with an escort of KMT soldiers, arrived at a guerrilla sentry post in the mountains of the Guangdong border. A well-dressed man wearing a wide-brim felt hat of the kind landlords wear in contemporary Beijing plays stepped out. He wore a Red Army blouse, black leather shoes, and dark sunglasses.

He paid off his bearers, dismissed the KMT guard, and walked up the hillside to guerrilla headquarters, where he handed over a letter signed by Commissar Xiang Ying, introducing him as Chen Yi. What, the guerrillas asked, was Chen Yi, if it was Chen Yi, doing with a sedan chair and KMT escort?

Only two months before, a gentleman describing himself as a Party liaison officer had arrived at headquarters, swiftly followed by a KMT assault force.

Was this another? They took no chances. They moved Chen Yi swiftly to another location and doubled the guards. Chen Yi told them of the new united front—the KMT and the Communists joining to fight Japan. The guerrillas decided he was a KMT agent and demanded that he confess. They bound him, put him in the next room, and began to debate. Chen Yi could hear the discussion and he heard them decide to kill him. He shouted: "You can't do that! It would be a great mistake!"

Next day Chen Yi found himself surrounded by people. A public trial was about to begin. His hours seemed numbered. A man came out, smoking a long-stemmed pipe. Chen Yi recognized him as a long-standing guerrilla chief named Tan Yubao.

"Is that you, Comrade Tan?" Chen Yi asked.

"Who are you calling comrade?" Tan snapped. "You have gone over to the KMT. You're a traitor."

Chen Yi tried to explain who he was and that he had been sent by the Party.

"Which party?" demanded Tan. "The KMT? I know who you are. I heard you talk at Jinggang Mountain. You talked about revolution then. But what are you doing now? If you don't confess I'll cut off your head!"

The men started to argue. Chen Yi said they must join to fight the Japanese. Tan was all for fighting the Japanese, but wanted no dealings with the KMT.

Tan got angry. "You intellectuals are just a bunch of opportunists," he shouted. "For three years I haven't heard a peep out of you. What have you been doing?"

Chen suggested he send someone to Nanchang to talk to Commissar Xiang Ying or to Wuhan to talk to Ye Jianying.

Finally, exclaiming, "My God, this traitor is very tough," Tan sent Chen Yi away, still bound. The two men had a private talk and Tan finally agreed not to shoot Chen Yi until he could check out the story.

Four days later the couriers were back with documents attesting that Chen Yi was actually Chen Yi and that the Party line was precisely what he said it was.

Tan broke down: "We have been separated from our comrades for three years. It has been three years since the Red Army left. You don't know how difficult it has been to carry on." He unbound Chen Yi's arms and the two men sat down and talked until dawn about their life in what some would come to call the legion of death. Neither knew that this was only a foretaste of the sacrifice and struggle ahead.

21

LUDING BRIDGE

THE Red Army now was treading on ground hallowed in Chinese literature and history, steeped in the blood of saga and war, a world of legend. This was the ancient kingdom of the Dukes of Shu in the time of the Warring States, two thousand years ago, the tales of which Mao knew so well. Here the army of the State of Shu—five hundred thousand strong—had marched and countermarched across the river Lu (now called the Dadu) and over the River of Golden Sands in endless crusades. No one knew the kingdom of Shu—its heroes, the craggy peaks where sorcerers lurked, the river sheers, the stratagems by which the generals of Shu misled their enemies—as did Mao.

The Red Army could not take a step on this earth without marching into a heroic epic of China's history. Mao found himself walking through the pages of the beloved books of his childhood much like an Englishman suddenly dropped into the time of King Arthur and the Knights of the Round Table.

There had been more recent and more bloody passages in this mountain saddle which girdled the waist of Sichuan. Here was where the last act had been played out in the great drama of the Taiping Rebellion of the mid-nineteenth century. Here the last Taiping leader, Prince Shi Dakai, and his forty thousand warriors had gone to their deaths, the waters of the Dadu running carmine for days, the wives, the generals, the sons of the prince taking their own lives on the banks of the river and the prince himself carted off to Chengdu and the death of the thousand cuts.[1]

Everyone in the Army knew these stories. On the night the First Army vanguard reached the bluffs of the Dadu, Zhu De sat by a campfire and told a tale that he had heard a score of times as a boy in his poor Sichuan home, where each winter an old weaver came by to weave into blankets the coarse cotton thread Zhu De's mother spun.

The old man had been a Taiping warrior and it was of this time he spoke around the smoky hearth, the legend of Shi Dakai, who, he said, had never died. When all was lost, said the old weaver, Shi Dakai's Fourth Daughter—not a real daughter: a ward whose life he had saved and who had wanted to become his concubine (but he refused) and who had married a man who looked exactly like Shi Dakai—had persuaded the prince to escape and let her husband be sacrificed in his place. For years the prince, said the weaver, had wandered the land. He had been seen by many people. One of them was a boatman on the river Min, saved from drowning in an angry storm by the timely appearance of the prince. On dark nights along the Dadu, said the weaver, you could hear the wailing of the spirits of the Taiping warriors. They would wail until they were avenged. The weaver would quote lines from a poem by Prince Shi:

> When Heaven is deaf to all judgment or feeling
> How can I save the people with my bare hands?

Of course, Zhu De told the soldiers, the tale was not true. Shi Dakai was sliced to death in Chengdu and his troops were slaughtered. Zhu De could have quoted a passage from the memoirs of Viceroy Luo Bingzhang of Sichuan, who executed the prince:

> On the 13th he came into camp leading his child, four years of age, by the hand, and gave himself up with his chiefs and followers. Shi Dakai and three others were conveyed to Chengdu on the 25th and put to death by the slicing process; the child was reserved until the age prescribed by regulations for the treatment of such cases.[2]

A Red Army man came up with some pig entrails, a liver, and a pig's stomach. "How do you cook these?" he asked. "Cut it up," Zhu De said, "and I'll fry it. I'm very good at that. Next time you find a stomach get a little vinegar and pepper and I'll help you fry it." The storytelling went on. Dong Biwu told the men that Monkey, in the famous Chinese fairy tale, had passed this way on his journey to India, skirting the Mountain of Fire and singeing his tail. "That's why monkeys have no hair on their behinds." "Why didn't you singe yours?" asked a sassy *hongjui*, a little "Red devil," one of the ten- and twelve-year-olds adopted by the Red Army. Dong changed the subject.[3]

Mao did not encourage such storytelling. The KMT was spreading propaganda that the Red Army would be wiped out just as the Taipings were. They were approaching their last battle. Soon the Dadu would run as red as it had seventy-three years before. Mao said in a flat voice that there would not be another slaughter on the Dadu. Of that he was confident. He did not want his troops worrying about the water devils that lay in wait for drowning men in the depths of the Dadu. "This cannot happen to us," Mao said. "We are revolutionaries. History has changed, we have changed. The past does not return."[4]

The Dadu is a powerful mountain-sourced river rising in the approaches to the Himalayas in a remote northwest province of China called Qinghai, a wilderness of desert, mountains, forests, with few Han Chinese, and in 1935 no roads, only caravan tracks. The river flows with great speed almost due north to south, and then swings east, crashing into the river Min, a great tributary of the Yangtze, south of Chengdu. The Dadu's walls are narrow. Jagged black cliffs in May are snowy with azaleas, rhododendrons, roses, and a profusion of blue and yellow flowers whose names escaped the amateur botanists on our 1984 expedition. It is spectacular in beauty and spectacular in difficulty for an army—hard to cross, hard to climb the footpaths, which cling to treacherous banks. The river is not wide but the speed of flow, the whirlpools, the great rocks, the dizzying alternation of current, bring fear to the eye. It is a dangerous place.

In 1935 bridges did not exist—with one exception, Luding Bridge. An intrepid American woman traveler gave this impression in 1908:

> The Lu Chiao [Luding Bridge] is a famous iron chain structure. It is a suspension bridge swinging across the turbulent Tung [Dadu] river in one span of 370 feet. The bridge dates back to 1701. The thirteen chains provide side supports as well as those for the bridge floor, but when one notes the open spaces, the irregularly laid planking of the flooring, the infrequent palings connecting the side chains, and the general airiness of the whole construction hanging so jauntily over wild and swirling water, one cannot help but feel that the bridge is sketchily built. Travellers from India, Tibet, Nepal and other parts of High Asia have safely crossed the raging Tung by this tenuous cobweb of man's ingenuity. It holds the charm and glamor of mystery, hidden away in this obscure Chinese valley. Most people walk over because of the considerable swaying. Bob and I did so. . . .[5]

Luding Bridge, built in the reign of Emperor Kang Xi by Engineer Lu, links Beijing and Chengdu with Kangding and Lhasa. In the days when Nepal paid tribute to Beijing, their treasure caravans passed this way. The thirteen chains are made of large links, as thick as a rice bowl, the iron hand-smelted over charcoal. Nine chains form the floor of the bridge, with two chains on either side to steady man or cart. Wooden planking was placed on the strand of nine chains so that men and women, carts and animals, could cross with little difficulty. The river is a scant one hundred yards wide at this point and the great chains are anchored in huge stone buttresses at either end with artistic, enamel-painted bridge houses, their pagoda roofs, columns, and tiles colored then (and now) in imperial red. The western bridge house burned a few years ago. It has been lavishly restored.

The Dadu bridge is very handsome. It bows in the middle, but since the suspension is short the bow is not deep and is high over the water even in times of flood. The swaying as you cross is that of a great hammock.

A wonderful assortment of fanciful accounts has grown up over the years of sights and sensations in crossing the bridge. The waves, some said, leaped up like dragons, trying to pull men down into their depths. Some accounts declare the bridge to be "over a mile long."

The reality is more impressive than the imagination. After close to three hundred years, the bridge is still giving good service although closed to cart and animal traffic now. With the construction of many nearby small suspensions and a couple of motor bridges, it is gradually becoming more of a tourist attraction than a public utility.[6]

A few years ago one of the chains snapped while a group of soldiers was crossing. No one was hurt, but steel cables have been stretched under the planking. They can't be seen.

Mao and his men did not start out for Luding Bridge. The plan was to cross at Anshunchang, the customary ferry from west to east. They reached it in the early hours of May 24, 1935. Before dawn they were mounting an attack on this hamlet of one hundred families. It was rainy, the path down to the riverside was slick, but the village was captured without difficulty by Yang Dezhi, commander of the First Regiment of the First Division of the First Army. The First Company of the First Regiment carried out the operation. It proved a serious disappointment. Only one boat was captured. Division Commander Yang sent seventeen volunteers across the river in the single boat.[7] Each had a submachine gun and seven or eight hand grenades. The boat was manned by eight local boatmen; it took a lot of muscle to cope with the swift current. The boatmen were promised that if anything happened to them, their families would be cared for.

As soon as the boat moved into the river, the enemy opened fire. But the First Regiment had an expert gunner, Zhao Chengzhang, who had served in France in World War I. He was a dead shot. He hit the target one hundred times out of a hundred. He had only four shells left for the mortar, but with four shells he put four enemy guns out of action.

The Red Army found two more boats downstream, built bonfires at night, and kept the ferry going around the clock. But it was obvious this would not do the job.[8]

The Red Army had to get across the Dadu *fast*. It could not wait a week or two while it put its men boat by boat over the river. The example of Prince Shi Dakai never left their minds. Delay had been fatal for him. When his wife gave birth to a boy, he halted *everything* for a three-day celebration. By the time he resumed, the river was in flood and the Qing armies had caught up with him.

Mao swore that would not happen to the Red Army. A meeting of Mao, Zhu De, Zhou Enlai, Lin Biao, and Peng Dehuai was called. Plans were changed. Instead of using the normal Anshunchang crossing, Mao would send his shock troops up the near, or right, bank of the river, along an almost non-existent path, seize Luding Bridge, and cross the Dadu from this unexpected point. No one went that way. The traffic on Luding Bridge normally came west from Chengdu, one hundred twenty-five miles to the east, moved up along the east bank of the Dadu, crossed over to the west by Luding Bridge, and then went on west to Tibet and Lhasa. Or it came east from Lhasa and followed the route in reverse.

Once again, as so often in the past, Mao chose the unexpected, almost impossible route. It was decided to send the Fourth Shock Regiment under Commissar (now General) Yang Chengwu to break the trail and carry out the surprise assault.[9]

Everything depended on the ability of the Fourth Regiment to crash its way over the spiny path that threaded the sheer cliffs along the Dadu and make it to Luding before the enemy guessed Mao's intentions. The Dadu flows north to south at this point, crossing the Chengdu-Tibet route like a T.

Because of the high Snowy Mountains, there was no easy way to approach the Dadu from the south, nor to get onto the westerly road from Luding toward Tibet. The mountains were just too high—twenty thousand feet.

The decision to push up the west bank to Luding was one of several routing decisions by Mao that have raised questions. Mao chose to cross the Golden Sands at Jiaopingdu rather than at an easier site used by the Second Front Army. The Second had no difficulty at all. Other debatable decisions lay ahead—those for the crossing of the Snowy Mountains and of the Grasslands. Lack of reliable intelligence may have been a factor. Only Zhu De among the commanders had ever crossed the Luding Bridge—and that was in 1922, when he and some companions made a hazardous escape into Sichuan from Kunming, where they had been fighting in a Sichuan warlord's army. They managed to get across the Golden Sands and Luding Bridge to safety.[10]

Now began a military operation which would become a legend.

Commissar Yang Chengwu of the vanguard Fourth Regiment of the Second Division of the First Army, hero of that legend, was in 1984 a fine-looking man at seventy. He had told the story many times but delighted in it. He waved three long slender fingers to drive home a point and consulted his book, *Memories of the Long March,* for a date or two. He remembered with glee that KMT planes were dropping leaflets warning that the last days of the Reds were at hand. Like Prince Shi Dakai, their blood would redden the Dadu River.

The order came in the hours after midnight of May 27. He was to set out up the west bank of the Dadu from Anshunchang and capture Luding Bridge, about ninety miles to the north. He was to capture it within three days. The regiment started out. The path, as he recalled, wound like "a sheep's gut" around and up and down the mountains. To the right there was a straight fall to the Dadu. About nine miles upstream, they drew enemy fire from across the river, very narrow here, and struck off into the mountains. There were no real paths. Often they had to cut toeholds. The troops had raced two or three hundred li in the past two days. They were tired before they started.[11]

At Yedading, about sixteen miles up the Dadu, the Fourth Regiment routed a defending company of a hundred men. Then it was up a big mountain and down the other side, where the defenders had destroyed a bridge over a small swift stream. The Reds cut trees, made a rude footbridge, and went on. They were coming downhill now and a scout reported that a battalion of the KMT Twenty-fourth Division was positioned on a cliff overlooking a village called Pusagang. The path was narrow, the cliff where the KMT were set up was sharp, and on the other side a drop-off to the Dadu. Commissar Yang Chengwu sent a small party to circle back of the mountain, climb to its heights, and attack the enemy from the rear. An hour later they had driven the KMT out and were advancing again. At nightfall they halted at Shiyueting. They had made forty kilometers—about twenty-five miles—over the tough twisting trail, fought two battles. They spent the night there.[12]

At 4 A.M. on May 28, the regiment was up. By 5 A.M. they had had breakfast and were on their way. No more than a mile or two beyond the village, a courier dashed up. New orders. Yang Chengwu read them:

> The Military Commission sent in a telegram stating that the left route army is given until the 25th to take Luding Bridge. You must march at top speed and take every possible measure to accomplish this glorious mission. We are prepared to congratulate you on your victory.

The telegram was signed by Lin Biao.[13]

The date for fulfillment of the task was set for May 29, of course, not the mistaken May 25 of this copy of the telegram.

May 29! Yang Chengwu could hardly believe his eyes. That was tomorrow. They had done twenty-five miles the first day. They had nearly seventy miles to go, fighting battles as they went. It would have been a difficult assignment to complete in two days. To do it in one . . . !

But, as Commissar Yang Chengwu laconically observed, "orders are orders." There was no time for a big propaganda fest of the kind they used to fire up the troops to heights of enthusiasm. There wasn't time for anything. The troops hurried along, the commissars trying to talk to them as they climbed and slipped along the narrow path. By 6 A.M. of the twenty-ninth they must arrive at Luding Bridge.

Fog closed in on the marchers as they began an ascent of Menghugang, Fierce Tiger Mountain. It was ten miles up and ten miles down. At the top, another KMT battalion had dug in. Under cover of the fog, the Red Army men came up to the redoubt unperceived, hurled in grenades, charged with bayonets, and the battalion fled. They chased them to the village of Moximian, where they arrived at 2 P.M. The bridge was out. It took two hours to repair it in the fog. Four hours more. They arrived at Kuiwu. It was 6 P.M. Thirty-five miles to go. No sign of the enemy. On they went. The fog and drizzle made the path slippery. The men cut bamboo staves as they walked. Darkness fell. They marched in the murk.

On the other side of the Dadu, growing more narrow here, there were KMT troops. They had caught occasional glimpses. Reinforcements headed, like themselves, for the Luding crossing. There was no stopping for supper. The men went without or munched cold rice. The evening wore on. About 11 P.M., at a place called Chumi, Commissar Yang Chengwu spotted lights across the river. It was the KMT battalion. They had lighted torches to make their marching easier. What to do? Commissar Yang braved it out. They had captured the KMT codewords and bugle calls. He had his bugler signal to the KMT on the opposite shore that they were KMT too. They had wiped out a band of Red bandits. The KMT answered in kind. Commissar Yang told his men to light torches. They cut pine boughs and bamboo splits, lighted them, and the two columns marched along side by side for eight or ten miles, divided only by the narrow Dadu. "We fooled them," Yang Chengwu says with glee. Afterward, while the KMT bivouacked for the night, the Fourth Regiment went on.

Yang Chengwu did not know that his comrades of the First Division of the First Army were driving up the left bank not far behind. The left-bank road was a good one, the main caravan trail. It was (and is) a pleasant road at mid-May: pear orchards, blooms now gone; apple orchards, some still in bloom; grape vines; good solid houses, stone below and wattle-and-clay above, red tile roofs; somehow a little flavor of the Basque country.

The First Division men fought a few battles, were held up a bit by heavy rain, but made good progress. The Dadu here forms a sharp vertical V, often narrowing to, say, one hundred yards in width at water's edge. No problem in shouting from cliff to cliff. From the left bank the trail followed by the Fourth Regiment is clearly visible, not quite as high as the soldiers' tales suggested, not more than two or three hundred feet above the river at some places.[14]

The rain began to stop. The clouds passed over and stars came out. The night was quiet, punctured only by the heavy breathing of the men, the occasional crunch of a rock falling off the path. Some fell asleep as they walked. Others tumbled off the path. Some men unrolled their puttees and tied themselves together so they would be pulled along if they started to fall.

During the night the Fourth Regiment abandoned all of its equipment except guns and ammunition. All knapsacks, all food, every bit of weight was left by the wayside. The men jogged along the trail, guns in hand.

At daybreak they arrived at Sangtianba, just two miles short of Luding Bridge. They had made it. How were they to capture it?

Dawn came. It was a scene of beauty. The end of May is the height of the Sichuan season for a kind of small pink semisweet cherry that makes the valley floors blush with color. Loquats are being harvested, and walnuts. Tomatoes are ripe for market, oleanders ablaze, potato fields white with blossoms and swarming with bees. Pink azaleas ruffle the mountain slopes. From his observation post Commissar Yang Chengwu could see the dirty little town of Luding across the bridge, the bright-painted bridge houses and the delicate sway of the bridge. There was only a handful of KMT troops on his side, but across the river there were several hundred—perhaps more, depending on whether the reinforcements whom they had raced by torchlight had gotten up the river.

The Fourth Regiment occupied the few buildings at their end of the bridge and a small Catholic church, where officers and men gathered for a pep talk. Occasionally the enemy would lob a mortar shell across and bits of brick and mortar would scatter.

The Second Company, headed by Liao Dazhu, was picked as the assault team. The Third Company would take the backup position and lay new planks on the bridge. Most of the planks, as Commissar Yang could see through his binoculars, had been removed.

Yang Chengwu believed men fought best on a full stomach—he ordered company cooks to prepare a good meal. Then the men got ready for battle. The assault was set for 4 P.M. He mounted heavy machine guns on an elevation just back of the bridge to lay down covering fire. Riflemen were deployed to add to the firepower. They had no mortars or artillery.

Twenty-two men led by Captain Liao Dazhu made the assault. Each carried a tommy gun or a pistol, a broadsword, and a dozen hand grenades. They had to crawl on the great iron chains, swaying above the river. The enemy had removed the planks two-thirds across. The buglers of the Fourth Regiment sounded "Charge!" The machine guns opened fire. The twenty-two men began to inch their perilous way across. As they advanced, flames sprung up at the opposite end. The KMT had set fire to the bridge house.

It was a fine day. The rain had blown away. The sun was out. It was hot and the men sweated as, link by link, never looking down at the turbulent current, they advanced across the bridge. Link by link. Hand over hand. Commissar Yang watched in agony. The Third Company men, new planks in hand, began their crawl behind the assault men, putting down planks as they crawled. Ahead, the flames leaped up. The KMT had poured kerosene on the wood. But there was no stopping the assault team. On and on they went. At the far end they clambered onto the remaining flooring and charged through the smoke and flame. They fired a burst from their machine guns as they went. As the soot-blackened Red Army men, some with clothes aflame, dashed out onto solid land, the KMT fled.

Eighteen of the twenty-two men survived the suicide attack, came through unscathed, a single act of bravery that ensured that Mao's calvary would be a triumph and not a disaster. Quickly the mopping up began. Within two hours Luding and the bridge were securely in Red Army hands.

One more impregnable position had been abandoned by the KMT. KMT commander Li Quanshan had two battalions at his disposal (one was that which came up along the river parallel to the Fourth Regiment). He used only one to defend the bridgehead. He put the other on the riverbank, where it served no purpose.

"That night was very tense," Commissar Yang Chengwu recalled. He maintained a full alert against counterattack. A patrol he sent down the left bank road toward Anshunchang soon brought back a wounded man from the First Division. It was their first intimation that men who crossed at Anshunchang were near. About midnight Liu Bocheng and Nie Rongzhen arrived, and Yang Chengwu took them to see the bridge. Liu Bocheng stood silent a moment, then said as the bridge swayed silently over the river: "Oh, Luding Bridge! Now we are victorious, but we have sacrificed so much."

They went across the bridge to look at the inscription carved on a granite stone in the time of Lu the bridgebuilder:

> Towering mountains flank Luding Bridge
> Their summits rising a thousand li into the clouds.

In 1935 there still lived in Anshunchang Song Dashun, an old scholar approaching ninety, who had been a young man in the time of Prince Shi Dakai. Li Fuchun, acting head of the Red Army Political Department, called on the old man. He had passed the imperial scholarly examinations at the township level. Why, asked Li Fuchun, had Prince Shi Dakai failed?

Because, said the old man, of the delays. The advance of the prince was blocked by the Dadu, which he could not cross, and he could not move to the left because the Yi had destroyed the bridge over the Songlin River and the Qing troops prevented him from going to the south.

How do you compare the Red Army and the army of the Taipings? Li Fuchun asked. They are all good, but the Red Army is better, the old scholar said.

The Taiping army was composed of what were called "spirit warriors"—that is, they could not be killed. Yet here on the Dadu they had met disaster. Perhaps, recalled Dr. Dai Zhengqi, who made the whole Long March—he was not a doctor in those days, just a seventeen-year-old medical attendant—it was about this time that he began to hear people call the Red Army "supermen." He had never heard that expression before.

A few years ago, an old KMT officer who had fought at Luding was asked why so few Red Army men were killed in taking the bridge. It was, he said, because the KMT guns were so old and their cartridges were moldy. Most of their bullets did not even carry across the river.

How many men did Mao Zedong move across Luding Bridge and the Dadu River? There is no exact compilation. He had started with eighty-six thousand when he crossed the Yudu. The closest estimate of the number who crossed the Dadu is twelve or thirteen thousand.

The heroes of Luding Bridge did not go unrecognized. Each received a new linen tunic, a notebook, a fountain pen, an enamel bowl, an enamel pan, and a pair of chopsticks. "I shared in that award," General Yang Chengwu said shyly.

It was the greatest gift the Red Army soldiers could receive—better, far, than medals of gold.[15]

22

THE GREAT SNOWY MOUNTAINS

Mao Zedong did not rush to Luding Bridge to congratulate Yang Chengwu and the heroes of the Fourth Regiment. It was three days before he appeared, forty-eight hours after Lin Biao had arrived to hail his men.

Mao made a leisurely progress up the west bank of the Dadu, following the thousands of Red Army men who had already traversed the crude path hacked out by the assault team. He walked most if not all the way at a modest pace, out of concern, his bodyguards said, for their physical exertion. Occasional halts were made to let engineers widen the trail or to let Red Army detachments move ahead over the rickety bridges. Mao made early camp before sunset and on the second night stopped over at Moximian, getting to Luding Bridge late on the third day. Both Zhou Enlai and Zhu De got there ahead of him.[1]

Yang Chengwu greeted Zhou and Zhu De and escorted them across the bridge. They were met on the far side by the one-eyed Liu Bocheng and by Nie Rongzhen. Zhou, accompanied by his bodyguard, personally replaced some broken planks on the bridge in anticipation of Mao's appearance. When Mao finally got there, not long before dusk, he walked across the swaying bridge, his admiring bodyguards noted, without fear and heedless of the swirling waters of the Dadu below. Mao joined his high command on the far side and they entered the grubby town of Luding and sat down to a feast of rice, pumpkin, potatoes, and (probably) chicken and pork.[2]

Finally free of fear of pursuit, Mao and his men had to decide what to do next. The Red Army slowed to a walk. Mao and the command spent a long day and night at Luding, then pushed on a short distance and, according to Mao's bodyguard, "rested for a few days" at Hualing-ping.[3] The shock force, headed by Yang Chengwu, took off June 2, 1935, at top speed as usual, on a strike toward the northeast in the direction of Tianquan, about forty-five miles away.[4]

The situation was contradictory. Mao was free of danger of attack by the KMT. There was no enemy to stop him from joining Zhang Guotao and the Fourth Front Army in northwest Sichuan. But there was one snag—Mao didn't know exactly where Zhang was and Zhang didn't know exactly where Mao was. In fact, the two men and their armies were not more than one hundred miles apart as the crow flies, separated by the Great Snowy Mountains.

Chinese historians have been unable to discover documentary evidence that the two armies knew where each other was at the time Mao crossed the Golden Sands River. There is the same blank for the Dadu. Intermittent wireless contact had been maintained in the early stages of the Long March. However, Zhang Guotao recalled that he had no advance warning of the March itself and heard about it only several days after it started. That, of course, was consistent with the extreme secrecy with which the ruling troika of Otto Braun, Bo Gu, and Zhou Enlai guarded their plans. Many of their closest colleagues were as much in the dark as Zhang Guotao. Even after he heard that the First Front Army was on the move, Zhang didn't know what was intended but surmised that the Army was in trouble.[5]

One reason for sparse communication between the armies was that the Fourth Front Army had lost a codebook and feared it might have fallen into the hands of Chiang Kai-shek.[6] Even so, Zhang Guotao claimed that once the First Front Army got into Guizhou, his wireless intercept service began to act as "eyes and ears" of the Long March. He recalled that often he stayed beside the wireless transmitter until early in the morning to be certain that the Fourth Army summaries of intercepts got through to the First.[7]

On January 22, 1935, Zhang received from the Central Committee a report on the decisions of the Zunyi conference.[8] He was instructed to conduct operations to aid the First Front Army in crossing the Yangtze River. Not much came of this. There was little the Fourth Army could do and the First Front Army never really got close to a major Yangtze crossing site. This instruction, in the opinion of General Qin Xinghan, was still in force at the time the First Front Army crossed the Golden Sands. But there is no evidence either army acted on the basis of it.

Communication was difficult. Not only was there fear that the code was not secure, but both armies were on the move. Zhang had decided to take his armies across the Jialing River into the extreme northwest corner of Sichuan close to Tibet. The plain, unadorned fact is that no evidence has turned up of any message or any courier going between the armies after January 22, 1935. Sometimes one side or the other heard something through the "bamboo telegraph," rumors going from person to person or some scrap of information gleaned from a KMT newspaper. It wasn't much, particularly as Mao led his forces around in circles in Guizhou, and Zhang in April put his armies on the move for the remote northwest.

Around the end of May or the first of June, in Zhang's recollection, he got word (from where?) that the First Front Army had crossed the Golden Sands. In fact, if Zhang's memory of dates was accurate, the First Front Army had already completed the crossing of the Dadu.

Small wonder that Mao paused awhile after Luding to try to get a better fix on where he would find the Fourth Front Army.[9]

Li Xiannian in 1984, the robust and durable President of the People's Republic, a senior veteran of seventy-five, recalled that in early June of 1935 he was instructed by Zhang Guotao to send a force to meet the First Front Army, the arrival of which was expected. Neither the date of arrival nor the whereabouts of the First Front Army was made known to him. He sent one of his divisions south and captured a place called Maogong at the northern end of the Snowy Mountains.[10]

The lack of hard evidence on what the First Army knew about the Fourth and vice versa is underscored by contemporary Chinese historians. They insist that the First Army "should have known" by the time it crossed the Golden Sands that Zhang's forces were in northwest Sichuan, and Zhang "should have known" where the First Army was.

The fact is obvious that neither did. Sometime in early June, each made a rough calculation of where the other was.[11]

There is no record of when Mao decided to cross over Jiajin Mountain, a fourteen-thousand-foot pass in what was called the Great Snowy range. Probably this was decided at Tianquan, where the road forks and where most of the Red Army halted for several days.

Mao had three alternatives. He could go to the west of the Snowies on a high but well-used caravan route that would take him to Aba, the capital of the Tibetan country of northwest Sichuan and Qinghai—a bit longer and moving almost entirely through fairly well populated and hostile Tibetans. He could take another road, east of the Snowies, which led ultimately to Songpan—but there was considerable danger of attack by the KMT along this route.

The third alternative was a rough path in the middle over the Snowies, a poor trail but one that was used by local inhabitants, including women and children. Mao's established preference had been well demonstrated: In case of doubt, take the small road, the back trail. That was what he opted for at this juncture. It is possible that he estimated (correctly) that this path would bring him closest to his objective: union with the Fourth Army of Zhang Guotao.

Mao was taking a calculated gamble so far as the record goes. Unless an itinerant peddler, a mountain herdsman, or some random traveler brought word to Mao—and of this there is no record—he made his choice of crossing the Great Snowy Mountains without any assurance that when he came down the other side of the majestic range he would find himself at a rendezvous with Zhang Guotao.

It was a fateful decision. Neither Mao nor any of his troops had had experience in climbing snow-clad mountains. They had little experience with snow. Most came from the hot, moist, subtropical or semitropical areas of south China, where snow was a rarity. The Great Snowies are year-round snow mountains, impressive to the eye, marking the horizon in what seems almost a circle once you have entered them. The snow-clad peaks rise on all sides, jagged and majestic as the Canadian Rockies. They push up far beyond the treeline. Today's modern road moves upward on endless switchbacks. All green is left behind. The mountain turns barren and brown. Soon it is snow country, even in May and June, great fields of snow extending endlessly over the peaks and down the other side.

Snowy mountains in China are objects of awe and superstition. Jiajin was called Faery Mountain by the local inhabitants, who told the Red Army men that only angels could fly over it.[12] If you opened your mouth at the peak of Jiajin, the God of the Mountain would choke you to death.[13] One Long March veteran remembered being told to talk in whispers on the mountain because there was so little oxygen.[14] Jiajin, in a word, was a magic mountain. Birds could not fly over it, and the best thing for humans was to give it a wide berth.

By the time the Red Army reached the foot of Faery Mountain, it had been on the Long March for eight months. Many men had been fighting three or four or more years. Their life had settled into a routine —hard, difficult, but somehow reassuring in its structure. Dr. Dai

Zhengqi at sixty-five was a senior health officer in 1984. He had been fifteen years old and a propaganda worker when he started the Long March in 1934. Soon he became a medical orderly. There was not a detail of Red Army life that he did not know.

He could follow the daily routine with his eyes shut. The ordinary soldier like himself, he said, marched much farther than the 25,000 li that was the map route of the year's journey from Jiangxi to northern Shaanxi. Often they marched 80 to 160 li—20 to 40 miles—without stopping, and they did not go in a straight line. It was up and down and back and forth again and again. Many medical workers wound up crossing the Great Snowies three or four times, caring for the ill and the dying. For many men it was a march of 30,000 to 40,000 li.

Day began when they heard the whistle blow. It might be 6 A.M. Not infrequently it was 5 A.M. or 4 A.M. They had fifteen minutes to get their gear in order, return boards or doors they had borrowed from peasants to sleep on, and give back the straw they had borrowed for bedding. They had another fifteen minutes to wash, brush their teeth (unfortunately, Dr. Dai recollected, not all soldiers brushed their teeth), eat breakfast (half a pound of cooked rice; sometimes sweet potatoes), put another ration of rice in their food bag for lunch, and form up with their unit. Sometimes there wasn't any rice, if the vanguard units had scraped the bottom of the barrel ahead of them.

Dai, as a propaganda worker, carried a sack, a small bag, a pistol, and a bucket of paste to put up posters. When he became a medical attendent he carried a medical box in which he had vaseline, iodine, carbolic acid, aspirin, cotton bandages, and absorbent cotton.

A man's load was about twenty-five pounds. Before the march started each morning, every man was told what the distance would be. There were two short breaks in the day—a ten-minute rest in the morning and twenty minutes later on for lunch. No siesta. Everyone got a rest if enemy planes came over: They huddled on the side of the road and relaxed until the whistle sounded again.[15]

Before starting to climb Jiajin, each soldier was briefed on the perils of high altitude, snow, and cold. They were told to protect their eyes with strips of cloth to prevent snow blindness. They were told to walk steadily without pause, not to halt on the heights, to eat well before starting, to wear heavy clothing (most of them had only their badly patched light cotton uniforms). At starting level the temperature was at sultry summer highs. As they climbed, they quickly became bathed in perspiration.[16]

Propagandists put the medical guidance—as was the Red Army custom—into doggerel for the troops to sing and commit to memory:

> The Jiajin Mountain is very high—
> We must pay attention.
> Wrap your feet and rub them well.
> Don't take any rest at the top.
> You must climb this mountain.
> If the sick can't walk
> We must help them.[17]

Ji Pengfei in 1984 was a gray-haired man of seventy-four, a state councillor, a onetime foreign minister. He was rather tall and as a young man had been very strong and athletic. He crossed the Great Snowies as a member of the Central Medical Commission.

One problem with Jiajin, he said, was that it sloped upward so gently. You could see the snow-covered fields at the top. They did not look far away. You did not sense you were mounting so high because you did not realize that you were already at a high altitude when you started upward. The men were exhausted by months of marching and inadequate food. The climb seemed to go smoothly and then suddenly you entered a world of snow and ice. Your eyes were blinded. There was no path. You slipped on the ice and fell. You tried to get up and you found you had no strength. You had not thought of dying. You did not realize that at the altitude of 14,000 or 15,000 feet there was little oxygen. You tried to get up and sank back dead.

The medics quickly realized that the men could not halt at the peak. A pause could be fatal. They had to get over the crest as rapidly as possible and down to altitudes where there was more oxygen. It was terrible not to rest. Your muscles seemed to have vanished. But you had to keep going. Once you got over the top it was best simply to slide down. Let the ice take you to the bottom. There was no real path anyway. Some bones were broken. Some men were lost—catapulted off the cliffs. But it was the best way.

The worst losses were among the logistic personnel. The carriers. There were still carriers. The cooks, for instance.[18]

The cooks—against orders—were carrying sixty and eighty pounds of burden—their heavy cooking woks loaded with rice and food. Cooks in the Third Army halted on the heights to prepare fresh ginger and hot pepper soup to revive altitude victims. (Mao had advised the body-guards to fortify themselves with ginger and hot peppers before start-ing the climb.)[19] "We won't let one man die in the Snowy Mountains," the cooks insisted. But while they were passing out hot soup, two cooks collapsed and could not be revived. By the time the March had reached northern Shaanxi, the unit had lost nine cooks.[20]

The thin air was especially difficult for the weak and the wounded. It was, Ji Pengfei recalled, almost impossible to care for the ill. The only remedy was to get them off the mountain. No one had the strength for that. Before they could be brought to lower altitudes they were dead. Often they died as the medics tried to lift them out of the snow. "We lost many good people," Ji Pengfei said. "The weather was cold. Men froze to death. Some simply could not breathe."

Details were sent out to pick up stragglers. Often the "stragglers" turned out to be corpses buried in the snow. The altitude was so high you could not boil water at normal heat. Matches didn't burn easily. There was no wood for fires. No villages. No people. It took all day to get over the mountain and when the men got down at the other side they were still at a high altitude.[21]

Water was a problem. There was no way to boil the snow. Soldiers scraped off the top layer and refreshed themselves with snow. There was no way to provide toilets. No means of digging pits in the ice and rock. The men wore their usual straw sandals. Some found rags to put around their feet. More didn't. Many suffered frostbite. Some soldiers crossed the mountains in bare feet. Most had only cotton uniforms. Many suffered snow blindness and had to be led down the mountain-side. After a few days their sight was recovered.[22]

For the Woman Wei, the Snowies and the Grasslands that lay be-yond the mountains were the worst times of the March. "After we crossed the Snowies I lost my menstrual periods," she said. "That was true of all the women."[23]

Ding Ganru, a twenty-year-old, went over the Snowies with the rear-guard Fifth Army Group. They came last. "There was a lot of political work before we crossed," he said. By which he meant the commissars warned the soldiers to loosen their clothing before they started, to make breathing easier; told them to walk slowly but steadily, and never, never to stop walking. "We were like a group of school kids being taken to a park," he said. When they got to the top, the instruc-tion was: "Just sit down and slide." They did that, but some of his comrades slid off the mountain and were never seen again.[24]

Li Yimang, in 1984 active in cultural exchange work but in 1935 a political commissar, idiosyncratic about the Great Snowies as he was about almost everything on the Long March, didn't think it was a difficult experience. The last of the Five Ridges was much worse. "The Snowy Mountains are rather low," he contended. "The road up is very easy. Not steep. It is not steep going down, either." He did concede that it was icy and slippery going down, that it was cold. There were no people. The Tibetan herdsmen had all fled.[25]

There were others for whom the Snowies were not so great a challenge. One was Zhong Ling, a twelve-year-old when he joined the Red Army in 1931 and only sixteen when he crossed the Great Snowies. At sixty-five in 1984, he was a doctor with a youthful face, bone-framed glasses, gray trousers, gray socks, light bluish shirt, very much a professional. He was not old enough when he joined the Red Army in his native Jiangxi to be issued a rifle. He worked in the propaganda section and painted slogans on walls. His family was desperately poor. Four months a year they did not have enough food to feed themselves. They had to borrow from the landlord and they never got out of debt.

Dr. Zhong was a medical orderly on the Long March. "We were Red devils," he said. "We were young, had a lot of vitality. We recovered easily. I didn't think much. I ate, slept, and marched. Never thought that anything was dangerous. We crossed rivers on inflated pigskins. I never fell in."

There were problems on the Snowy Mountains, but they didn't bother him. He should have had warm clothing. He didn't. He just had an undershirt and a plain cotton shirt. It was June, but it was snowing on top of Jiajin. He wore his straw sandals. No leg wrappings. His feet didn't get frozen. He never felt short of breath. He was briefed: No stopping. No resting. Do it all in one swoop. He walked down the far side of the mountain and didn't see anyone die. As far as he could recall, no one he knew in the Third Army medical group died.

"Remember," he said, "I was young. I wasn't affected. I didn't think much."[26]

Party General Secretary Hu Yaobang was only a year or two older than Zhong Ling, but he did not have such buoyant memories of the Snowies. He recalled seeing KMT planes. They could not get up to the altitude of the Red Army's trail. "We shouted to the pilot, 'Come on up.'" The second of the Snowies was the worst, he said. It took two days to cross and they had to camp on the mountainside, wrapped in their blankets and huddled to each other for warmth. "Being young," he said, "we survived it."[27]

To most of the Red Army men the Snowies were the worst experience the Long March had yet presented. Worse than the battle of Xiang River, worse than the Five Ridges, worse than the four crossings of the Red River. Far worse than the Golden Sands or Luding, where the fighting involved only small numbers of troops. Commanders were laid low. Lin Biao, the vigorous young commander of the First Army, lost consciousness several times at the crest of Jiajin. Only with the aid of his bodyguards was he able to get across. The same thing happened to Xu Dinin, intelligence chief of the Red Army.[28] Mao, according to his bodyguards, had great difficulty. The bodyguards helped him, but got into trouble themselves. Mao did not wear a padded jacket, and his cotton trousers and slippers were soon soaked. His party was hit by a hailstorm and took shelter under an oilcloth. Bodyguard Chen Changfeng almost fainted and was helped by Mao. Chen, in turn, got the Chairman going again when he halted to encourage some troops.[29]

Zhou Enlai's guard, Wei Guolu, called the Snowies the hardest part of the March. Men joined hands to keep from falling. Fog and mist alternated with sudden storms. Small avalanches crashed down from the peaks. Bodyguard Wei became dizzy and lost strength. He had to halt every few paces for breath. Progress became slower and slower. The wind rose. Wei saw a man from his hometown collapse. Before he could get to him, the man had stopped breathing. They put the body into a mountain crevasse and buried it in snow. By three in the afternoon they had made it to the peak and started the descent.[30]

By the time they got to the bottom of the mountain, Zhou Enlai was coughing. He had caught cold. It was the first symptom of an illness that would come close to taking his life.[31]

The Fourth Front Army dispatched Li Xiannian to meet the First Front Army. Li, Commissar of the Thirtieth Army, had been stationed at Lixian (Zagunau). He took his Eighty-eighth Division and part of the Twenty-fifth and Twenty-seventh Divisions of the Ninth Army and captured Maogong (now Xiaojin) on June 8 and then Dawei, the exit point of the trail over the Snowy Mountain, on June 9. The commander of the Twenty-fifth Division, Han Dongshan, telegraphed Li Xiannian that he expected the First Front Army to arrive June 10. Li Xiannian was astounded. He had no idea that it was so close and he doubted the report could be correct. He telegraphed his commander to make a new check. The commander wired back: "No, it's true. They're here."[32]

It *was* true. The First Army vanguard got over the mountain June 11 and came down the road to Dawei on the morning of June 12.[33] Dawei is not quite twenty-five miles from the foot of the mountain. There was an exchange of shots when the scouts of the First Front Army sighted the outpost of the Fourth. Neither side knew whether the other was friend or foe. No one was hit in the exchange. Bugles hurriedly were blown. Quickly each side learned who the other was.[34]

First Front Army troops streamed down the mountainside and into Dawei. Li Xiannian hurried up the trail from Maogong and on June 14, Mao, Zhou Enlai (not feeling very well), Zhu De, Peng Dehuai, Ye Jianying, Lin Biao, and all the others came off the mountain. "There was an atmosphere of jubilation," Li Xiannian recalled. "Everyone was very happy. The First Army men looked tired after their long march. We Fourth Army men were stronger and in better shape. I can't begin to describe the atmosphere."[35]

Dawei was just a cluster of houses—about 106 households—with a large lamasery on a hill above the unprepossessing village. This was opium country, deep opium country. At least one-third of the land was devoted to the poppy, and in early autumn each year there was a big opium market at Dawei (and in many other towns in this area).

On a sloping field above the village but below the monastery, a great rally was held on the evening of June 14. Survivors believe that ten thousand persons gathered. Mao spoke of unity and the need to go north to fight the Japanese. There were theatricals, songs, dances, and a feast. The Fourth Front Army provided food and supplies from stocks it had confiscated from landlords.[36]

Li Bozhao danced and sang, and again and again the audience shouted: "Encore! Encore!" She danced a great favorite, the Russian sailor's dance *yablochka,* which she had learned in Moscow. The crowd would not let her stop, and she seemed to have energy to dance all night.[37]

Mao and Li Xiannian had a talk that evening. Mao asked how many men Li had in his army (he had headed the Ninth Army but now he headed the Thirtieth). Li said he had more than twenty thousand. Mao asked how old he was. Li said he was twenty-five or twenty-six. Fifty years later, Li was still apologetic about his preparations to meet the First Front Army. "They got in just after we did," he said. "We hadn't expected them so soon. We did our best. We even gave them about a thousand men to fill out their formations. There was no place for any quarrels between the two armies."

Next day Mao and his top command moved on up the road. There were more mountains to cross, more Snowies, and then he and Zhang Guotao would finally meet—for the first time since 1923, when they had taken different sides at the Third Congress of the Chinese Communist Party at Canton.

23

REUNION

I T was raining. It had been raining for several days. The trails were muddy. Mao and Zhu De and Zhou Enlai had been spending a few days in Maogong, where they arrived on the evening of June 15. There was a Catholic church in Maogong, overlooking the river, where on the evening of June 16 Mao made a speech. He had quarters in a fine building facing the courtyard of the church. Zhou Enlai, Zhu De, Bo Gu, and Luo Fu took a house nearby. Mao almost always stayed in a house separate from his comrades.

Snow lies almost around the year in the high passes coming down to Maogong. There was snow in late May 1984, just as in June of 1935. It mottles the green pastures and clings to the rhododendrons that climb the mountainsides to eleven thousand feet.

Mao and his group rode down the narrow valley of the Maogong River, draped with lilac-hued rhododendrons and their waxy dark-green leaves, the hills splashed with masses of violets—or flowers that look to the amateur eye like violets. The valley is not wide enough for much land to be cultivated, and houses are few. Despite the rain, the journey was in pleasing contrast to the trials of crossing Jiajin.[1]

Mao had only a few of his commanders with him. This was probably not by chance. He had sent Peng Dehuai of the Third Army and Lin Biao of the First off in different directions, with most of his troops. Perhaps he did not distrust Zhang Guotao, but he was taking precautions. The two men had not seen each other for twelve years and had never been close.

Mao arrived at the town of Lianghekou on June 24 and took up quarters (probably) on the lower floor of a rather imposing lamasery. (The lower part of the building has since been demolished and is now used as a lumberyard.)[2]

It was still raining on the morning of June 25. Mao waited until he

242

got word that Zhang Guotao was approaching. Then he and his party made their way to a village called Fubian, about a mile outside town.[3] Great preparations had been made. There were slogans painted on the walls, posters on the village street, and banners of red with greetings painted in white. A field telephone had been strung from village to village so the armies could keep in touch, and a platform had been set up in a meadow for the ceremonies. It was a historic occasion, the two principal Communist forces and their leaders coming together for the first time. Zhang had been in the field with the Fourth Front Army, establishing a series of base areas, for five years. Mao had been at the same task since 1927, except for the period when Bo Gu and Otto Braun set him aside.

The rain pelted down as Mao waited beside the road under an oilcloth shelter. About 5 P.M., Zhang Guotao, riding a fine white horse and with an escort of a dozen mounted men, could be seen spattering along the muddy road. Mao and his men left their dun-colored shelter and stepped forward. In a moment the horsemen clattered up. Zhang Guotao, a tall, full-bodied man, his face light-hued in comparison with the weather-beaten visage of Mao, leaped from his horse. Mao stepped forward and the men embraced.[4]

The troops cheered. The populace, several thousand strong, cheered. The men went to the platform, water dripping from their uniforms. Mao gave a speech of welcome and Zhang replied. Then they traipsed into town, arms around each other's shoulders, and made for the big lamasery, where a banquet was being held.[5] Li Qin, a vigorous sixty-eight in 1984, the tail of his shirt showing under his neat jacket, saw them walking together. He was fifteen then, a little Red devil of the Fourth Front Army, and vastly excited. He recognized Zhang Guotao and someone shouted: "That's Mao Zedong!" He had often seen Zhang Guotao, and thought he was very soft-spoken and kind to his soldiers.[6]

The outward trappings of celebration were present—banners, bunting, great bowls of steaming chicken and pork, mounds of rice, vegetables, pots of soup, wine, and local variations of that remarkable Guizhou invention maotai.

But underneath—and not far underneath—there ran a current of bitterness, hostility, suspicion.

There were questions, back and forth, as to the size of the two forces. At one point Zhang approached Zhou Enlai and said: "How many people do you have?" Zhou, ever the diplomat, responded: "How many do you have?" Zhang said: "We have a hundred thousand." Zhou replied: "We have thirty thousand." Zhou's exaggeration was a good deal broader than Zhang's.[7]

Each side played it close to the vest. Neither was frank and open. But it was obvious that the First Front Army was only a shadow of what it had been at Jiangxi—probably not more than ten thousand men, although Zhang Guotao could not calculate precisely since Mao had dispersed his men to various locations. Zhang was overstating his strength—much as the First Front Army had at the start of the Long March. But it was easy to see that the Fourth was far larger than the First Front Army. Zhang had seventy to eighty thousand combat troops and maybe another seventy thousand noncombatants. He outnumbered Mao nearly ten to one.

Contrast was to be seen in the two leaders—Zhang full-faced, not corpulent but his body fleshy, his face unmarked by hunger or hardship; Mao thin, his features taut and face deeply lined, his manner nervous. Zhang wore a finely cut uniform of gray; Mao wore his old Long March tunic, threadbare and mended.

One Red Army soldier could not restrain himself about how fat the horses of the Fourth Front Army were. Mao reproved him: "Don't envy the horses."[8] There was a good deal of envy that night and later a feeling among the Long Marchers that Zhang was an ambitious, possibly unprincipled man, flaunting his successes, showing condescension toward Mao's forces. Perhaps Mao's men were overly sensitive, but they had been offended at the manner in which Zhang swept up to Mao and his command, waiting on foot in the rain, almost spattering them with mud before dismounting. Their ears were irritated at the way in which the Fourth Fronters called Zhang "Chairman." "Chairman" was a title they reserved for Mao Zedong. The caps of the Fourth Army men were bigger than those of the First. Fourth Army men were called "big heads," First Army men "small heads."

Things didn't go much better at the banquet. Zhang Guotao thought the jollity was just on the surface. Mao went into his routine about hot peppers. If you couldn't down hot food you couldn't be a real revolutionary. Bo Gu, a Jiangxi native by birth, challenged Mao. Jiangxi people, Bo Gu insisted, made great revolutionaries and they did not care for Mao's Hunan hot peppers and chili. Reluctantly but laughingly, Mao had to concede that point. Zhang Guotao thought this was very "dull." He resented the fact that no one seemed interested in having him tell about the achievements of the Fourth Front Army. Nor did anyone tell him the details of Zunyi.[9] For their part, Mao's men claimed Zhang

Guotao wasn't interested in what the First Front Army had done. After dinner, Zhang invited Zhu De to a talk that lasted until three in the morning. Was Zhang trying to win Zhu to his side? Perhaps. Or he may just have been pumping him for information. Zhu De left no record. Zhang's summary was put down long after he had broken with his Communist comrades. He quoted Zhu as saying the main Red Army was only "a skeleton" and "all the muscles are gone." He said Zhu estimated its numbers as ten thousand, not far from reality. All the artillery was gone, there were few machine guns, and the men had only five or six bullets for their guns.

This was quite close to the mark. Less credence, perhaps, should be placed on those parts of Zhang's summary which quoted Zhu De as criticizing Mao and praising Zhang's Fourth Army.

The surviving descriptions of Zhang Guotao by Long March participants stress his softness, his arrogance. Otto Braun called him a "tall stately man of about forty who received us as a host would his guests. He behaved with great self-confidence, fully aware of his military superiority and administrative power."[10] The Red Army men contrasted Zhang's attitudes with the modesty and battle-worn simplicity of their leaders. It is hard to say how much this reflects political differences. Photographs, however, support the descriptions of Zhang. He looks soft in contrast to the lean, bony image of the Long Marchers.

In fact, no one in the Communist Party had better credentials than Zhang Guotao. He was thirty-eight years old in 1935, born into a rich landlord family, a student at Peking University while Mao was an assistant in the library there, got acquainted with Mao at that time. The two were among the twelve founders of China's Communist Party in 1921. From the earliest times Zhang had been a Party leader, a member of its Central Committee, of the Politburo, of the Orgburo. He had played a role—a small one—in the Nanchang Uprising with Zhou Enlai. He had spent three years in Moscow. In 1931 he was sent by the Shanghai bureau to lead the extremely important Eyuwan base area. From that time onward he had been in the field. His record was the equal of Mao's in Jiangxi. He had fought and won important battles against Chiang Kai-shek. He had moved his base twice—first from the Eyuwan area on the Henan-Hubei-Anhui border to the Shaanxi-Sichuan border, and then in the spring of 1935 to northwest Sichuan. His associate in these operations was a fine general, Xu Xiangqian, who became one of China's ten marshals after the establishment of the People's Republic.

Zhang Guotao's style was not that of Mao, but he had been more successful than contemporary Chinese historians acknowledge.

Zhang had demonstrated a flair for independent operations which
had not infrequently gotten him into arguments with the Central Committee (as had Mao). His move from Eyuwan to the Shaanxi-Sichuan
area in 1932 had been criticized because it lacked Central Committee
approval (a bit like Mao at Jinggangshan). But it was successful and the
criticism died away. The move to northwest Sichuan was more severely
criticized, but with the Central Committee on the Long March, communications hardly extant, Zhang could not be too severely censured
(nor was he).

Zhang had made arrangements—or attempted to make arrangements—to live and let live with the warlords of the provinces in which
he operated. When he came to Sichuan in 1932, he sent letters to Yang
Sen, the Sichuan warlord, and Tian Songyao, whose Sichuan area he was
occupying. Tian refused to accept the letter. Yang received his letter
but paid no attention to it—his territory was not affected. A third letter
went to Sun Weiru, number two in Shaanxi to warlord Yang Hucheng.
Sun Weiru came to an agreement with Zhang Guotao. (After liberation,
Sun became vice-governor of Shaanxi.)[11]

When Zhang went into Sichuan he did not carry out land reform or
establish a soviet government. The Central Committee criticized him
for this. About two months later, he corrected his mistakes—probably
after deciding to stay in the region.[12] Zhang had no understanding with
Sichuan warlords in the northwest region he now occupied. He was well
able to handle any military threat they might mount.[13]

Just before the reunion, Zhang had given another display of independence. He controlled a very large geographical area—the counties
of Jinchuan, Xiaojin (formerly Maogong), Songpan, and Heishui. This
covers 89,000 square kilometers today and probably was considerably
larger in 1935. The population in 1984 was three-quarters of a million.
It was 200,000 or 300,000 in the mid-1930s—very lightly inhabited for
China, but a fertile, productive agricultural region. He had 80,000 combat troops and an equal number of noncombatants.

On May 30, 1935, on the eve of the arrival of Mao and the First Front
Army, Zhang announced establishment of what he called the Northwest Confederation. It would not have a formal soviet organization but
would be a mixed regime consistent with the very high minority (a
majority here) population. Zhou Chonquan was installed as chairman,
with a capital in Beichuan. Beichuan was in a mountainous Tibetan

region in the Snowies about 80 miles north and a bit east of Chengdu. One of Zhou Chongquan's first exercises was to teach his men how to eat *tsampa,* the principal Tibetan dish, an unsavory concoction of barley flour and what is euphemistically called "five elements tea." It is a doughy lump, eaten with the fingers.[14]

Zhang Guotao's army differed from Mao's First Front Army. Zhang had many women in his formations, including a fighting women's regiment of two thousand. He maintained excellent relations with the minorities, largely because, being less mobile than the First Front Army, he could demonstrate that his forces were not like the marauding warlord armies. Like other Red armies, he expropriated the rich and distributed their property—grain, opium, cloth, money—to the poor, taking sufficient for his own supplies. At this point his army was well provided and he was able to give a good deal of food and cloth to the impoverished First Front Army.[15]

Zhang did not, so far as can be established, interfere with the production of opium—the big cash crop of the area. But his army did seize opium along with other landlord assets and use it as cash to pay for supplies and provisions.[16]

Zhang's soldiers were not allowed to use opium. But there were exceptions. Jin Jinchuan, a very elderly Chinese doctor, had the opium habit and was given opium to support it.[17]

Internal security was very tough in all the Red armies. As Peng Dehuai wrote in his prison memoirs: "Everybody in the Army worried about his safety" (he was speaking of conditions as early as 1931 and 1932). "There was not much democracy," he added. "The Section for Eliminating Traitors, which had originally been under the Political Department, now became a Security Bureau at the same level as the Political Department."[18] This development did not spare the Fourth Front Army. Li Xiannian, in 1931 a young Fourth Army platoon leader, recalled that a vicious purge was ordered when Zhang came to the Fourth Front Army.

Many arrests and executions were carried out. These took the life of a Fourth Army division commander, Xu Jishen, graduate of Whampoa Academy and a comrade of Xu Xiangqian, who was to be Zhang's longtime associate. Xu Xiangqian was also accused, but managed to clear himself.

Despite these "mistaken ideas," as Li Xiannian characterized them, Zhang Guotao was able to fight some excellent battles.

He did not, however, abandon the practice of arrest and execution of officers whom he mistrusted.

"I could give you a list of forty people killed in purges in the Fourth Front Army," Li Xiannian said. In 1931 almost all the regimental officers were purged, and that, said Li, was how he became a regimental officer. His commander, a former KMT officer, was purged. Later he was returned to duty and was killed in combat. Li thought more men were purged in the Second Army than in the Fourth.[19]

While the feasting went on at the lamasery in Lianghekou, an artist named Liao Chengzhi languished in custody in Zhang's army. Liao had been secretary of the Sailors Union in Shanghai before he was sent in 1933 to join the Fourth Front Army. In 1934, so it was said, it was noted from his Party registration statement that his father had been a KMT representative and his mother was a member of the KMT Central Committee. He was charged with being an undercover KMT agent, bound and compelled to march with his arms tied behind his back.

Few charges could have been more tendentious. No one in China or in Zhang Guotao's intelligence department could have been unaware of Liao's identity. He was the son of revolutionary parents whose names were a byword in China. His father, Liao Zhongkai, was the architect under Sun Yat-sen of Soviet support and cooperation with the Communists and was assassinated in Canton by right-wing plotters (possibly including Chiang Kai-shek) after Dr. Sun's death. Nothing but vicious paranoia could be at the base of the charges against the son. Nonetheless, Liao Chengzhi would have been executed except for one fortuitous chance: his ability to draw and trace maps; his stencils were superb. Liao's mother was, and remained all her life, an extremely close friend of Madame Soong Chingling, Sun Yat-sen's widow.[20] As years passed Liao himself became one of Madame Sun's close confidants and had a major career in the regime of Mao Zedong. During World War II he was kidnapped by the KMT in Chongqing and again saved from death only by Madame Soong's energetic intervention. Later he became vice-chairman of the People's Congress and died only in 1983. He was carried along by Zhang until the Fourth Army finally came to northern Shaanxi, in October 1936. Zhou Enlai immediately intervened and obtained Liao's release. When Liao was given freedom, he took his drawing paper, the waxed paper he used for stencils, his brushes and knives, put them on a table like an altar, bowed to them, and said: "If it were not for you I would have been killed." He was an uncle of Anna Chennault, widow of the founder of the Flying Tigers.[21]

The pro-Moscow clique in the Party was known as the 28 Bolsheviks. Xu Yixin was called the twenty-ninth member of the group (actually there were many more, possibly a hundred). Because Xu Yixin was very small he was designated a "half-Bolshevik," and occasionally the group as a whole was called the 28½ Bolsheviks. Xu Yixin had been assigned to the Fourth Front Army and he represented it in clandestine negotiations with KMT General Yang Hucheng on the Sichuan-Shaanxi border in 1932. Later Zhang Guotao violated the agreement and in February 1934 wiped out one of Yang's regiments. Xu Yixin protested and Zhang Guotao arrested him. Xu, too, was a prisoner at the time of the Lianghekou talks. After the establishment of the People's Republic, Xu Yixin became ambassador to Pakistan.

Another Fourth Front Army prisoner was Luo Shiwen, who had been Party secretary of the independent Sichuan area. He brought a force of three hundred men to join Zhang Guotao in northwest Sichuan. Zhang did not trust him and put him under house arrest. Later he was arrested and killed by the KMT in Chongqing.[22] There were many such cases.

On June 26, the Communist leaders convened at 9 A.M. in the old lamasery. There were, by Zhang's reckoning, six members of the Politburo present: Mao Zedong, Zhang Guotao, Zhu De, Zhou Enlai, Bo Gu, and Luo Fu. Liu Bocheng, the one-eyed, was there too, as was Deng Fa, the Red Army security chief, and possibly Xu Xiangqian, Zhang's principal commander.[23]

A slightly different lineup is given by Wen Xingming of the Maerkang Museum staff. He named the participants as: Mao, Zhou Enlai, Zhu De, Liu Bocheng, Luo Fu, Liu Shaoqi, Kai Feng, Nie Rongzhen, Zhang Guotao, Lin Biao, and Li Fuchun.[24]

Zhou Enlai presided. Mao spoke first. He proposed that the Red Army continue to move north and to the east in the direction of Gansu and Ningxia. He said, according to Zhang Guotao, that the Comintern had suggested a move toward Outer Mongolia, where contact with the Soviet Union was possible. It turned out that this was a "last resort" suggestion wirelessed before the start of the Long March, according to Bo Gu. Bo Gu confirmed that the Red Army had not been in touch with the Comintern since "that time," which he estimated at ten months earlier—that is, the previous August.[25]

Zhang Guotao contended that Mao's speech made a rather favorable impression on him. He said Mao mentioned neither fighting the Japanese (probably, he thought, because none of them knew much about the Japanese at that point) nor going to northern Shaanxi, probably not being informed about the Communist base there.

The current Chinese account of the talks is somewhat different. It has Zhou Enlai giving the opening speech and stressing three main points: strategy in fighting the Japanese, the question of going to the north, and the problems of leadership.[26]

Zhang reports himself as suggesting two alternatives to Mao's Gansu-Ningxia plan. One was to extend his present base area farther in northern Sichuan, Gansu, and Sikang. The other was to push through the Gansu corridor, west to Xinjiang in the far northwest, where there was the possibility of contact with the Soviet Union across the border.[27]

The meetings, according to Professor Hu Hua, probably the best-informed contemporary historian, decided to continue the work of building up the soviet area in northwest Sichuan which Zhang Guotao had founded. It was agreed that Songpan county, key to the best (only) road skirting the terrible morass of the Great Grasslands, would be captured to open the way for movement into Gansu.[28]

There were five points in the resolution approved by the Lianghekou meeting, but the text has never been published.

Some points were critical of Zhang—particularly with regard to the shift of his base to northwest Sichuan. If Zhang is to be believed, Mao was sarcastic about the move, suggesting it increased the difficulties of the Long March. Zhang suggests that there were no formal decisions at Lianghekou and that Mao promised there would be further deliberations. This is probably disingenuous. There was plenty of talk outside the formal meeting and continued probing as to the position of each side. Zhang kept trying to find out more about Zunyi and the Huili conference.

The Lianghekou meeting lasted three hours. After lunch, as Zhang recalled, Zhou Enlai came to him with a proposal for the formation of a "united command" in which Zhang would be vice-chairman of the Military Commission. It provided some integration of forces. Zhang expressed himself as delighted. Later in the afternoon Zhou brought him a directive for the forces to move north. Zhang claimed he argued a bit but accepted this.

The directive, according to Nie Rongzhen, read: "The main force of the Red Army is to move north and eliminate the enemy in the course of mobile warfare, first capturing southern Gansu, to establish a base in the area Sichuan-Shaanxi-Gansu . . . to win a victory of several provinces first and then all of China eventually."[29]

Behind the scenes there was maneuvering. Peng Dehuai in his prison memoirs recalls a visit by Huang Chao, Zhang Guotao's secretary. The secretary brought with him several catties of dried beef and several sheng of rice. He made Peng a present of two or three hundred silver dollars. He asked Peng questions about the Huili meeting, and presented some arguments in favor of going south before going north. Peng said that was like the strategy of Zhuge Liang, the Three Kingdoms military adviser, so well known to Mao Zedong, and his plans for consolidating the Kingdom of Shu.[30]

Nie Rongzhen had a similar story. He was invited to dinner by Zhang on June 27. Zhang kept talking about how tired Nie Rongzhen and the others must be and how energetic they had been. He said he had decided to give two regiments to supplement their troops, which, as Nie said a bit sorrowfully, turned out to be only a thousand men, or about two battalions.

Nie Rongzhen recalls that Peng Dehuai was present at the dinner. As they left, Nie asked Peng: "Why did he invite us to dinner?" Peng smiled: "To give you some men—aren't you going to take them?" "I certainly am," Nie replied. As he walked away in the night, he kept turning over in his mind what it might be that Zhang *really* wanted.[31]

There was, Nie Rongzhen said, plenty of troublemaking. Someone, he said, fed Zhang erroneous information about the Zunyi meetings and this heightened Zhang's suspicions about Mao.[32]

Whatever the relations between Mao and Zhang—"cool" is the adjective contemporary Chinese historians employ—the rank and file of the First and Fourth Front armies, in general, were delighted with each other's company.[33]

Li Bozhao, wife of General Yang Shangkun, wrote a song in collaboration with Lu Dingyi, chief of the Propaganda Department, to commemorate the joining of forces.

In 1984, Li Bozhao, at the age of seventy-three, sang in her delicate, soft voice:

> One was very great in fighting
> And not afraid of hardship.
> The other was very good
> At strategy and tactics.

"The first two lines," she said, "are about the Fourth Army. The second couplet is about the First Front Army."

Li Bozhao had poignant memories of Maogong. There a beautiful, spirited young woman of nineteen, named Jiu Xiang, came to her and pleaded for permission to join the Red Army. Her mother was a Han, her father a Tibetan, a small merchant. He sold scissors, needles, and thread. She had not seen him since she was a little girl. Her mother was dead. She called Li Bozhao "elder sister" and begged to come into the Red Army. The Army had the strictest of rules: no admission of women. But Jiu Xiang would not take no for an answer. She slept on the floor of the propaganda office.

Li Bozhao went to Li Fuchun, husband of Cai Chang. She said the girl had no father, no mother, was very poor, and wanted to join the Red Army no matter what. Li Bozhao got permission for the girl to join. She helped carry the loads, she proved wonderful in finding food where there was no food, she was gay and cheerful, she made flour cakes and other goodies for Li Bozhao and her assistants.

"She died in crossing the Grasslands," Li Bozhao said. "She got lost in the wastes and was never found. She probably died of starvation. I still miss her." A tear came to the corner of Li Bozhao's eyes.

On the morning of June 30, Mao started out again, accompanied by Zhou Enlai and possibly Zhu De. He headed north across more of the Snowy Mountains, the second large mountain in the range, called Mengbi, a peak of over fourteen thousand feet, just two hundred feet lower than Jiajin. It was not so severe a climb as Jiajin. They went up through passes, mostly below the snowline and across pastureland, and did not encounter great perils. It was a long climb and they had to camp overnight on the mountainside. Perhaps they were lucky. Some Red Army men recalled terrible difficulties. There was a good deal of snow on the mountain on a day in late May just fifty years later.

The First Army passed along the same route. Zhang Guotao left the next day, not in very good spirits. He wrote that he felt he had been slandered and badly treated by Mao and the First Front Army. They had deliberately tried to deceive him and he was glad to have them gone.[34] Deep trouble lay ahead.

24

BACK OF BEYOND

THE Red Army was now moving back of the beyond, deeper and deeper into what the English explorer Sir Eric Teichman once called "the least known area of China." The country was unmapped, unexplored, uninhabited, uninhabitable. It was really not China. No Chinese felt at home in this landscape of the moon, snow mountains and barren wastes to the horizon.

Not even the Chinese postal service, operated by British experts, penetrated this territory. There were no post offices beyond Maogong and Songpan, no postal station south of Huili.

When the Red Army struck out for the Golden Sands and headed over the Great Snowies toward the Grasslands, it was moving off the map. There were no points of reference, few dwellings. The only people were Tibetans, who had for four centuries been inching their way into this unknown world.

Now even the Tibetans had fled in fear to wilder reaches, except small bands who laid down volleys of gunfire from the hills or rolled boulders to crush unwary Red Army men. The soldiers were forbidden to fire back, but more and more the rules began to be bent.

To the Chinese this was uncanny country. Never had they seen a place with so few people. It seemed dangerous. No roof for their heads, no one to talk to. From dawn to dusk they met no living creature. Once in a while they saw what looked like a lumbering heap of dirty rags— a yak. No people. No food. Or if they found food it was not rice. The cooks did not know how to prepare these rough upland grains. They came from the south, China's rice bowl. Many soldiers ruptured their bowels ingesting raw, unmilled wheat.

The Red Army men could not comprehend the place. This was not ignorance or superstition. They had broken through a geographic barrier. They had entered the high plateau of the Snowy Mountains, and whether climbing peaks or marching across meadows, they were moving at altitudes of ten or eleven thousand feet and higher. The Snowies were not a well-defined range. The men seemed to be crossing them endlessly, one Snowy Mountain, one high pass, after another. Would it ever end? Would they ever get back to a China where they felt at home?

A couple of days after the meeting at Lianghekou, Mao and his column came down from the Snowies and proceeded from a cluster of houses, now known as Red Army Village, across twelve miles of broken country to Zhuokeji, site of the yamen, the residence and fort of the Tibetan chieftain.

Here they found what many would remember as one of the remarkable sights of the six-thousand-mile hegira—a seven-story tower, a fairy tale of carved wood and hewn stone rising like an Asian pillar of Pisa. It was surrounded by block-solid fortresses of stone, three and four stories high, fitted with cannon embrasures and slits for archers like those in Norman castles.

The yamen was so vast some said it could accommodate five to six thousand persons—almost the whole First Front Army at this point—in its chambers and courtyards. It was sited at the confluence of two small streams, which served as a moat. Its back braced against a craggy outcropping.

For centuries the yamen had stood impregnable. Its master, a staunch KMT supporter, fled at the Red Army's approach. Mao and his high command rested here. In their reminiscences Long Marchers wrote with awe of the seven-story atrium, lined with wooden columns, lacquered in red and black and green, tiers of balconies, carved in wood and decorated with precious stones set into the pediments. Tapestries hung from the walls, living quarters were fitted with silken couches and carved stools, tables and cabinets. Tibetan scrolls filled the walls and there was a library of Tibetan and Chinese classics. One floor was devoted to shrines to Buddha framed in jade and gold and silver. There were sparkling windows of glass.

The ground floor was devoted to kitchens—great stoves, enormous pots and pans and kettles of iron and copper and brass, enough for an army. One wing housed a stable. On the second story was stored food —bins for grain and rice and flour, cupboards of spices, sugar, and salt, racks for carcasses of sheep and yak, earthen Sinbad jars of beans and oil, toolrooms, an armory, and dormitories for guards and troops.

The third floor was inhabited by the chieftain, with reception rooms inlaid with marble and malachite; sleeping quarters (Mao slept here), with a fine teak bed, antique Chinese chairs, chests inlaid with mother-of-pearl, and a red lacquer desk. On the fourth floor was the Buddhist shrine: recessed figures of the Buddha, brass gongs with red silk tassels, Tibetan sculptures, drums, scrolls, and scriptures.[1]

Mao's stay in these opulent quarters was not long, but Red Army units remained behind in Zhuokeji to rest, collect supplies, and carry on propaganda among the Tibetans.

The historic hatred of Tibetans for the Hans had been inflamed by KMT propaganda. Tian Bao, a member of the Party Central Advisory Committee, a Tibetan, a member of Zhang Guotao's Fourth Front Army, remembered being told as a child that the Han people were constantly attacking the Tibetans. When the Red Army approached, the KMT spread word that the Communists had come to kill Tibetans and eat their children. Naturally, the Tibetans feared and hated them. When the Fourth Front Army came in, later to be joined by the First Front Army, they stayed for months and months. They slaughtered cattle and expropriated grain. While they paid for food with silver dollars or IOU's, the Tibetans' impression was that the Red Army stole their property.

"The First Front Army went right through," Tian Bao recalled. "They moved through empty villages; the people had run away. If the troops were to survive, they had to slaughter any cattle they found and dig up the grain that was hidden. It is difficult to say whether it was all paid for. This left a bad impression. On the other hand, the Red Army had to live. It is hard to say who was right and who was wrong."[2]

Nerves were bad. The possibility of ambush by Tibetans was ever present. Red Army men were set upon, robbed, stripped, and killed. Past casualties and sacrifices had left the Red Army with an unbalanced structure—a preponderance of cadres, a paucity of enlisted men; some units were made up largely of cadres. This caused tension.

One day Mao heard his chief bodyguard, Chen Changfeng, shouting at another bodyguard, who was shouting back. Chen had a case of galloping dysentery. He had been unable to restrain his bowels and had spattered the other man. Mao stalked to the scene. "Look at yourselves," he said, like a stern schoolmaster. "How many of us there were when we started and how few of us now. Is it worthwhile to quarrel like this?" The bodyguards were shamed. Chen offered to wash the filth from his companion's trousers. The other bodyguard wouldn't let him. Together the men made themselves presentable and the March went on.[3]

The Red Army advanced toward Maoergai, through Matang (where there were hardly any huts for shelter and Mao spent a rainy night in a hammock), over more mountains, through Maheba, Heishui, along the roaring Heishui River, its waterfalls sounding like the hooves of ten thousand horses, halting along the way, again and again, to harvest wheat or barley standing in fields bereft of peasants. Zhu De took a leading hand. He joked with younger men and women that they could not carry forty to fifty jin of grain as he did. Zhu De's wife, Kang Keqing, as hearty a farm girl as China possessed, still carrying at least one rifle and a knapsack on her strong shoulders, matched her husband with her scythe.[4] The urgency of gathering food was on everyone's mind.

On July 1 the Red Army vanguards reached the area of Maoergai and occupied the large Tibetan settlement about July 10. It numbered nearly four hundred families, many living in two-story stone-and-mortar houses with flat Tibetan roofs, white prayer flags on all sides (these were white rags tied to slender poles to carry prayers to heaven). Fierce spirit guards, witches out of *The Wizard of Oz,* stood (and still stand) at the lanes into the villages to protect against marauders and disease. Maoergai was the center of the wheat country. The grain stood yellow-brown in the fields, ready for the scythe. A year's harvest was said to yield enough to feed the people for three years.

The Red Army settled down for a long stay, a chance to rest, refresh themselves, repair worn clothes and equipment, and fill their food bags. Now there could be talks about the future. All signs pointed to better times ahead.[5]

Or did they? Maoergai lies in Songpan county, about thirty miles west of Songpan and sixty miles short of the Gansu border. The distances sound trivial. They could well have proved fatal. The town stands at the edge of what the Chinese euphemistically call the Great Grasslands, an enormous tundra that lies in deceptive quiet just south of the Yellow River. Here the armies were straddling the continental divide, the rise of land that separates the basin of the Yangtze, which encompasses southeast and central China, from the drainage system of the Yellow River, China's sorrow, that extraordinary watercourse which arises on the roof of the world and flows along the northern quadrant of China, finally doubling around on its course to the sea, carrying such a volume of water that again and again in history it has gouged out new valley courses hundreds of miles from the old.

Here in this high terrain, thousands of feet above sea level, the basins of the river systems adjoin, and the Red Army was crossing from the Yangtze system, into the Yellow River system.

The benignly named Grasslands represented a deadly trap, so water-sodden a whole army could sink in its depths and leave no trace. The only thinkable route ran through Songpan, garrisoned by KMT troops. Its possession was vital. At Lianghekou there had been full agreement that Songpan must be captured and that Zhang Guotao would do it.

Hardly had the Red Army occupied Maoergai than Zhou Enlai drafted a plan of operations against Songpan. He turned it over to Zhang Guotao. Zhang, or so it is charged by contemporary historians, altered the plans. Instead of directing an immediate assault, he sent his Thirtieth Army to make a feint against the town. It put Songpan under siege but it did not move in for the kill. The town was only lightly garrisoned by a KMT commander named Hu Zongnan. In 1943 Hu Zongnan, in a conversation in Chongqing during the period of KMT-Communist cooperation, revealed "at that time I had a very small force. My headquarters were in a courtyard house in the town. I remember thinking that the Red Army had the town surrounded and that if I was captured what should I do?" He recalled that he had an old teacher from Whampoa Military Academy—Zhou Enlai. "He will take care of me," Hu Zongnan thought.

But Hu Zongnan didn't need his old friend. Reinforcements were sent in and the Thirtieth Army was pulled back. Zhang's switch of orders on Songpan is now characterized as deliberate sabotage because, in fact, he did not want to go north. He thought the KMT was too strong and that the Red Army should head west and south.[6]

This was probably the last operational plan to be drafted by Zhou Enlai for many weeks. He had not been well since the Snowy Mountains.[7] He had developed a cough and his bodyguards saw that he was weak, although he did not complain. They tried to get him to take more rest. Zhou habitually worked until two in the morning. Instead of going to bed, he often put his head down on his desk, slept for a while, then awakened and went on working.

"The vice-chairman became thinner and his already by no means short beard grew even longer," his bodyguard Wei Guolu recorded.

Now Zhou fell into a critical illness. He nearly lost his life.[8] His temperature rose to 104 or 105.[9] Mao sent for Dr. Nelson Fu, but he was too distant (actually with the Fourth Front Army) and a doctor known as "the bearded Dai" was summoned from the First Front Army.[10] Zhou's illness involved his liver and is called by the Chinese "hepatic abscess." It sounds like acute hepatitis. The extremely high fever continued for some days. Zhou became delirious. He was treated with snow poultices, relays of Red Army men bringing snow from nearby mountains. His wife, Deng Yingchao, came to his side. She did not, contrary to romantic stories, take on his full care. Her own health was still precarious. Accounts that she roamed fields and forests looking for edible herbs and greens seem dubious. She did make a nourishing broth of white fungus. Zhou was not able to attend the conference of the Politburo, the military command, and Zhang Guotao at Maoergai in late July and early August.[11]

General Yang Shangkun recalled that Zhou was ill for about two months—part of July, August, and early September. "He was suffering from liver inflammation," he said. "We thought he was going to die."

Once the Army began to move, Zhou had to be carried on a litter. Mao called on the Third Army to help out. Peng Dehuai was lugging two of the eight mortars the Red Army now possessed. He decided to junk them. That relieved forty men.

The detail was placed in command of Chen Geng, a top political commissar, a shy, boyish man of thirty-one, red-cheeked and snub-nosed. He had been a cadet at Whampoa under Chiang Kai-shek and became one of the Red Army's most capable commanders.

He had served with Chiang Kai-shek in early battles of Dr. Sun Yat-sen's forces against the Canton warlords and saved Chiang from taking his own life in a moment of despair after his division had been routed. "I must die here," Chiang had cried. "I have no face left." As the enemy advanced and Chiang was about to put a bullet in his head, Chen picked him up, carried him from the field, as he told Edgar Snow, and got him to safety.

Later, when Chen Geng was captured by the KMT, Chiang tried to induce him to return to the Nationalist fold. Chen refused in contempt, but Chiang allowed him to escape, apparently in hope that soft treatment would encourage other Communist commanders to come to his side.[12]

"You saved Chiang's life," Zhou Enlai joked to Chen. "Now you are going to save mine."[13]

Gradually Zhou's health returned, but he played no role in the climactic events with Zhang Guotao.

The surface quiet of these days was deceptive. It was a time of intense political maneuvering between Mao Zedong and Zhang Guotao. The differences between the two camps had emerged sharply. Its cause was the same—policy, personality, and power—that had lain at the heart of the other great conflicts of the Long March.

Zhang had operated independently and successfully for years. He had no personal ties drawing him to Mao. He had no affinity for the "Bolsheviks" although he had spent a good deal of time in Moscow. He talked with all of the political and military figures in the First Front Army but, so far as one can tell, did not recruit any allies. His most sympathetic relationship was with Zhu De. Although Zhu De's role seems equivocal, although he tried to assist a commonality of views between Zhang and Mao, when the chips were down—as soon would be proved—he was a Mao man, not a Zhang man. There is nothing in Otto Braun's memoir to suggest Braun was attracted to Zhang, much as he distrusted and disliked Mao. The same seems true of Bo Gu. The memoirs of Nie Rongzhen and Peng Dehuai do not suggest that Zhang made headway with them.

The reverse is also true. Mao's men sought to win over Zhang's commanders. They did not succeed. The one man whose diplomatic skills might have fashioned a consensus was Zhou Enlai. His illness made that impossible.

The crux, in the opinion of Li Xiannian, then Zhang's brilliant young commander, was that Zhang "had the ambition to replace Mao and the Central Committee."

Zhang said to himself, Li Xiannian suggested, "The First Front Army is small and weak. I have got eighty thousand in my army. Zhang should be making the decisions and replacing Mao and the Central Committee."[14]

Argument went on as the columns made their slow progress toward Maoergai. Zhang and his spokesmen did not cease arguing for a move toward the west, toward Qinghai, deeper into Tibetan and minority territory. Mao and his men contended that the Red Army would be lost in such a remote area, devoid of resources, with not enough food, no possibility of recruits among the minorities, lost below the rim of the horizon. If they went north into Gansu and Ningxia, they would be in Han territory, there would be food and recruits.

The farther west they went, Mao argued, the less weight would the Red Army have on China's political scene. The argument went on at Maoergai and after.[15] The arrangements at Lianghekou for integration of the First and Fourth armies, such as they were, came into force July 8. On July 18 an order provided that Zhou Enlai give up the post of general political commissar to Zhang Guotao. June 29 was the effective date when Zhang Guotao became a vice-chairman of the Military Commission, sharing this post with Zhou Enlai and Wang Jiaxing. Mao remained chairman. A seven-member presidium was formed of Mao, Zhu De, Zhang Guotao, Peng Dehuai, He Long, Zhou Enlai, and Ren Bishi (of the Second Army).[16] Chen Changhao, Zhang's political commissar, became head of the general Political Department.[17]

All of this seemed quiet and peaceful, but a bomb of contention was ticking. The memoirists conflict over the Maoergai meeting—over where it was held, how many meetings there were, who attended—but not so much over what happened. Hu Hua, the best of the Long March historians, places the date as August 6 and the site as a lamasery in Shawo.

Zhang Guotao also describes it as being held in Shawo, a lovely Tibetan village in a wooded valley, "a world of its own," five or six miles from Maoergai. He complains that the First Front Army surrounded the place, controlled all access, refused to allow his political aide, Chen Changhao, to attend, compelled Zhang to pass through a series of checkpoints. He said: "General headquarters need not worry about the safety of the central organs now that they guard themselves so closely."[18] Nie Rongzhen said the meeting was held at the headquarters of Zhang's own Eleventh Division and Hu Hua agrees. Nie said he had heard that Mao reproved Zhang, saying, "the meeting you called for is a meeting under military supervision," a reference to the military forces Zhang had concentrated. It was clearly a case of mirror images.[19]

Both Zhang and Nie Rongzhen agreed that at the Shawo meeting Zhang proposed bringing more members into the discussion. Zhang said he wanted younger members to participate. Nie thought Zhang wanted to add new members to the Politburo and the Central Committee. Both reports may be true. Zhang, despite his vast predominance of force, was the lone representative of "his side" in the Politburo and the Central Committee.

There is no evidence that the participants spent any time talking about Japan, and it has been positively established by contemporary

Chinese historians that there was no talk of a united front with Chiang Kai-shek to fight Japan. This question for years caused controversy, because on August 1, 1935, the Seventh Comintern Congress in Moscow adopted a united front resolution, so worded as to suggest that it originated in China. The fact was the Comintern had no communication with the Red Army and no precise knowledge of where it was. The first Mao knew of this resolution was when Lin Yuying, a Comintern emissary and a relative of Lin Biao, arrived in northern Shaanxi in late November or early December 1935. Lin Yuying had memorized the declaration before leaving Moscow. He was flown to the Mongolia-China border (possibly dropped by parachute) and made his way on foot, dressed as a trader, into northern Shaanxi, accidentally encountering Luo Fu in a small village near Bao'an.[20]

A second meeting was then held in Maoergai, on August 20. Chen Changhao, Zhang's political man, was present. There is no record of any disagreements. The decisions of the Shawo meeting were endorsed.[21]

In early August, a compromise was hammered out. If they couldn't resolve their political disputes, perhaps they could draft a military program. What was agreed was to divide their forces into two columns, left and right, and mix them so that each column included some from the First Front Army, some from the Fourth Front Army. There would be a central command, also mixed, with Zhu De as commander in chief, a reasonable choice since he seemed to have the confidence of both Mao and Zhang.

Zhang was chief political commissar. Liu Bocheng was chief of staff. The high command moved with the Left Column, which was made up largely of Fourth Front Army units. The Fifth and Ninth armies of the First Front Army (down to two or three thousand men each) were included in the Left Column.

The Right Column was the same kind of mixture. It was led by Lin Biao and the First Army and included Peng Dehuai and the Third Army and the Thirtieth and Fourth armies from the Fourth Front Army. The Right Column had a unified command. The Fourth Front Army's commander, Xu Xiangqian, was in charge, with Ye Jianying as chief of staff and Zhang's man, Chen Changhao, as political commissar. In point of fact, the Right Column as well as the Left were under the command of Zhang Guotao. He had probably thirty thousand troops in line, compared with possibly nine thousand of the First Front Army.

Mao, the ill Zhou Enlai and the Wounded Wang Jiaxiang, Luo Fu,

Bo Gu, Otto Braun, and the Central Column formed part of the Right Column.

Almost all of July and a good part of August had been spent in making these arrangements. There was an agreement on a preliminary objective—a thrust into southern Gansu in the direction of Minxian.[22]

At long last the KMT was beginning to bestir itself. There were Nationalist troop movements. The temperature in this high northern elevation was beginning to drop at night. It was time to get moving. About August 23, the two columns got under way. By agreement, the Left Column headed for Aba, the Right Column for Baxi, several days' march distant, at the far edge of the Grasslands.

25

A MAGICAL CARPET

I N the summer, the Tibetan said, his face a fold of wrinkled bronze, his brown wool robe belted with an orange sash, his feet in soft leather boots, and a rakish felt hat on his head, it is a magical carpet of flowers that stretches as far as the eye can see, every color you can imagine: vermilion, violet, blue, yellow, rose, purple, white—all colors under heaven.

He was speaking of the Grasslands, an inland Sargasso Sea which lies on the eleven-thousand-foot plateau between the watersheds of the Yangtze and the Yellow rivers. It looks as innocent as the Cornish downs in spring, but Baudelaire's *Fleurs du mal* were angelic beside its malevolence.

By mid-August the flora have started their swift decline, but in the blaze of noon their colors make your eyes ache and their fragrance sends your heart skipping as you traverse this flat land, broken only by emerald tufts and low hills on the horizon where dawn's dusting of snow still sparkles.

Today those verdant plains, many of them ditched and drained, match those of Montana and Wyoming in fertility, white with sheep, dotted black with yaks, and with clusters of felt yurts where herdsmen camp to watch over their flocks.

Fifty years ago it looked much the same. But when the Red Army came through there were no yurts, no herdsmen, no yaks, no sheep; just the silent flowers, luring men to walk amongst them. So it looked on August 21, 1935, when the vanguard, the extraordinary Fourth Regiment of the First Army Corps, headed as always by Yang Chengwu, set off into this pleasant ocean of beauty. Yang Chengwu had been told of its dangers, first by his commander, Lin Biao, on August 17, when he was assigned the vanguard task. It would not be easy, Lin Biao said, directing him to report to Mao Zedong at Maoergai.

The perils of the Grasslands were no surprise. Mao warned Yang Chengwu that beneath the flowers lurked bogs that could swallow a man in a minute. Somehow Yang Chengwu must find a road through this watery waste, along which the Red Army could move with safety. The enemy was nature, not man. The crossing must be made swiftly. Nationalist forces once again were gathering for the kill. Mao questioned Yang closely on the condition of his men and their clothing. The weather of the Grasslands was more changeable than the mood of a sulky Suchou beauty: sun one moment, hail the next, rain, mist, sleet, fierce winds—a devil's brew.

Fifty years later, in June 1984, it had not changed: hard frost, twenty degrees at night; at dawn a red sun over the meadows; dark by 8 A.M., black clouds, drizzle, fog, downpour, whipping winds, driving sleet, snow in heavy flakes that buried roads, meadows, hills, blotted out vision, drove caravans into cover, and transformed the flocks of yak and sheep into plodding snow mounds. Down came snow for two hours, then a slackening. Wind sweeps the steppes. The sun emerges pale, wan, shaken. More wind, rain. By midafternoon blue skies, melting snow, a touch of spring that vanishes in icy frost as the sun blazes out of sight beyond the Yellow River.

What about guides? Mao asked Yang Chengwu. Yang said he had an old Tibetan, a man in his sixties, who knew every inch of the Grasslands. He would be carried on a litter by six soldiers. After Mao dismissed him, Yang had a brief word with Deng Yingchao; her husband, Zhou Enlai, was too ill to see him.[1]

The Fourth Regiment marched through gravelly hills, still enfolded in yellow primroses, Indian paint (or its Chinese equivalent), carpets of violet-hued flowers, white starflowers and bursts of elderberries, their white fluff now turning into winy berries, a symphony of flowers. Not one word of this beauty can be found in the reminiscences of the Long March veterans. They had other matters on their minds. (But Zhang Guotao called the flowers "a magnificent spectacle.")[2]

With midafternoon the scene changed as the Fourth Regiment plowed ahead. Angry clouds covered the horizon. Winds cut swaths through the heavy grass, untouched for three thousand years, tugged at the thin tunics of the marching men, bit their bones. This floral paradise enjoyed only five frost-free days a year, the average annual temperature was just over freezing, the July mean 51 degrees Fahrenheit.[3]

In the words of Magistrate Wang Qiu, the Grasslands has no summer
—just an extended winter. It froze and froze hard every night the Red
Army was passing through. The route that Yang Chengwu and his men
followed was not a good one. There were no good routes. It was one
followed by Tibetan herdsmen. There were better routes to the east,
but the Red Army was blocked from them because of Zhang Guotao's
failure to capture Songpan. The route to the left (which Zhang Guotao
would follow) was also better, but it was farther west and lay through
Aba.

There were no guideposts on the trails except those put up by Yang
Chengwu and his men. There were no landmarks, just endless high
grass, high or higher than a man's waist, and water below. There were
hillocks firm enough for a man to stand on, but they were hard to
recognize under the grass. The water was often hip high over bean-curd
bog. Men who fell into the bog disappeared before their comrades could
pull them out. Rescuers vanished along with those they sought to help.

It rained. August and September are the rainiest season on the
Grasslands. There was no way to keep dry. No place to camp. Men spent
the night huddled on their knees on hillocks too small to stretch out on.

There was no food. The extra rations everyone had gathered, forty
jin a man, melted away. Men ate more; their exertions were heavy. But
they had no way to cook. No place for fires. No wood for fires. They
chewed raw, unmilled wheat. Bloody dysentery affected half the army.
The coarse seeds were tearing out their intestines.

But, said today's inhabitants, in late summer the air is filled with
birds—geese coming south from the Arctic, migrating ducks, plover,
every kind. Sometimes the air is black with them and the marshes rustle
to their presence. And as General He Long was to demonstrate when
his Second Front Army traversed the Grasslands a year later, the
treacherous water was filled with fish. A few moments a day with his
fishing rod kept his larder filled all the way across the terrible territory.[4]
Perhaps some of the tragedy of the Grasslands lay in the fact that the
Red Army men were not hunters or fishermen. Nor were they familiar
with the "weeds" now exhibited in the local museums to illustrate the
desperate diet they were forced to eat. In the showcases are plates of
succulent dandelion greens, bowls of nettles (which make excellent
soup), and other nourishing wild plants whose uses were not known to
the soldiers.[5]

That little butternut, the Woman Wei, probably saved the lives of
several women comrades. The Woman Wei had been doing propaganda

work with Tibetan women. When she came back to the hut, she found some mushroom broth left for her by her companions. She took a taste and put it down. It was too bitter. Her comrades were on the ground. She thought they were sleeping. She said: "Move over, let me have a place." They looked at her with open eyes. They could not speak or move. They were paralyzed. She got cold water, drenched them, shook them, and finally brought them around. She berated them: "Fine comrades you are. You ate all the mushrooms and left me the bitter soup." But it was the mushrooms that had paralyzed them.

Like the others in the Red Army, the Woman Wei had prepared food before entering the Grasslands. But there wasn't enough. She picked edible greens and ate roasted wheat. She and her friends ate the grains right out of the fire with their hands. The wheat was black with soot and soon their faces were black. "We all had beards and mustaches," the Woman Wei recalled.[6]

Food, food, food. Every day it was a problem. Zeng Xianhui, the old veteran who looked like Nikita Khrushchev, remembered the barley fields as they entered the Grasslands and emerged from them. No people were around. The men harvested the barley and he left IOU's for it.

As Mao Zedong told Edgar Snow in Bao'an in 1936: "This is our only foreign debt"—to the Tibetans for the food the Red Army took from them.[7]

To cross the Grasslands was a journey of five to seven days. Those who crossed first had the easiest time. They were able to follow the fragile, tenuous trails marked for them by Yang Chengwu's vanguard men. But each succeeding day it became more difficult. Heavy men and animals broke down the narrow paths and submerged them under water and grass so that a man could not tell where to place his foot. Yang Dinghua thought walking over the marsh was a bit like walking across a swinging bridge because your feet quickly penetrated to the quiverlike mass of grass roots that shifted with each step. The muck was not only slippery. It was like glue. Once in it, you sank deeper and deeper. The more you struggled, the faster you went down.[8]

Even the Tibetan guides had difficulty orienting themselves. All of the landscape looked the same. Only when the sun broke through the clouds could they correct the direction in which they were moving. Again and again they lost the trail.

Agnes Smedley discovered the diary of Long March veteran Mo Xu at Yan'an in 1937. He told of a comrade struggling in black mud and water. He helped him up but the man fell back into the water, clutching his rifle fiercely. Again he tried to lift the man but could not. The soldier was dying. Mo Xu tried to give him some parched wheat, but he could not chew it. Mo Xu carefully took back the parched wheat and put it in his pocket. The soldier died and Mo Xu went on, leaving the body huddled in the marsh. When he came to a halt he reached in his pocket and took out the wheat. As he held it in his hand, the image of his dying comrade came to his eyes. He could not eat the grain.[9]

Mao's bodyguard Chen Changfeng fell ill as the Army came down from the Snowies, recovered, fell ill again of malaria, got better, had a relapse as they entered the Grasslands. Mao made him rest, got him medicine, and he continued the march.

To him the Grasslands was: "A vast stretch of desolate marsh . . . Not a single human being . . . There were no houses. Wild grasses grew in profusion in the stagnant water. There seemed to be no end to it."[10]

People—the absence of human beings: everyone noticed it. "In eight days," Hu Yaobang, general secretary of the Chinese Communist Party, recalled, "I did not see a single human being. The villages were empty. I remember a few wild birds. When we got to Banyou there were a few animals. But the houses were empty."[11]

Often it was not possible to boil water for tea or to cook rice or grain. The ground was too wet, there were no dry branches (often no branches at all). The men munched uncooked hard wheat kernels until their teeth ached.

Older marchers tried to encourage the young. When they reached the river Hou, normally about three feet deep, now beginning to rise, the current strengthening, the Central Column backed up at the river crossing. Deng Yingchao, ill, worried about her husband, Zhou Enlai, and still being carried on a litter herself, was halted. Soldiers and officers crowded around. She asked a commander: "How deep is the river?" "Don't worry," he replied. "Everything will be all right." She called the young soldiers to her, told them to hold each other by the hands and they could wade over all right. Cai Chang, Mao's old friend from Changsha, wearing a Red Army tunic, rope sandals, a pistol in her belt, marched in the same column. Yang Dinghua didn't think you would know she was a woman from her dress. But the soldiers recognized her. They shouted: "Elder sister. Sing us a song. Sing the 'Marseillaise.'" Cai Chang smiled back. "O.K. Don't shout. I'll sing for you." And she did.

Yang Dinghua couldn't understand the words, but she lifted his spirits. Yang Dinghua was reminded of other women on the Long March; once he had seen Kang Keqing, wife of Zhu De, sit down on her bedroll, put her knapsack on her lap for a desk, and write out the order for the troops to cross a river. Yang, knowing as he did that when Kang Keqing joined the Red Army seven years earlier she was totally illiterate, enjoyed a moment of pride in the Revolution's achievements.

Mao's old Changsha teacher, venerable Xu Teli, was at the riverbank, his donkey beside him. Mao came up and asked why he wasn't riding the animal. Because, Xu Teli explained, it was carrying the belongings of three students who were ill. Xu was putting a patch on his worn trousers and wore a ragged fur cloak on his back. On his shoulders Xu Teli carried a sack containing eight jin of roasted wheat.

That evening, after all had crossed the river Hou, a great campfire was built. For once there was a dry riverbank and dry wood. Yang Dinghua and scores of soldiers gathered around, warming themselves, toasting their wheat, relaxing, their spirits reviving. Soon Mao Zedong and Peng Dehuai appeared and took places in the circle, looking as tired and muddy as the soldiers.

"Comrades," Peng Dehuai shouted, in his hoarse commander's voice. "Let's all ask Mao Zedong to tell us about something interesting." There was a burst of clapping. The well-known writer Cheng Fangwu turned up and sat with the group. Cheng told about his student days in Japan and Europe and how he had become a writer. Unfortunately, Yang Dinghua didn't jot down the stories Mao and Peng Dehuai told. This was the third night on the Grasslands. Four more lay ahead.[12]

Each day food grew more scarce. Especially for the men who followed in the path of the front units. There was little enough on the Grasslands, and what there was had been picked clean. Soon the men were boiling their leather belts and harness (when they could get water to boil), and eating them. Water was a problem. Much of the Grasslands water was poisonous. Soldier after soldier came down with violent cramps, dangerous diarrhea. Many died. The store of unhusked corn and unmilled wheat was running out. The men ate grasses that had no nourishment. Some grasses, too, were poisonous.

Ding Ganru served in the rear guard. He was part of the Fifth Army, and when it entered the Grasslands everyone else had gone before. Ding had joined the Red Army at the age of fifteen, in February 1932.

For Ding Ganru (in 1984 the retired PLA chief of staff in Chengdu), things began to go from bad to worse beginning with the Snowy Mountains. There was constant trouble from the minorities—the Miao, the Yi, and the Tibetans. There was a psychological barrier, Ding Ganru felt, between the Red Army and the minorities, and it had been accentuated by KMT propaganda.

The Fifth Army saw only very poor people. The rich and the landlords had long fled. If a Red Army man straggled, the minority people were on him in a flash, to strip him of his clothing and leave him to freeze to death. The Fifth Army had money to buy food. But there were no people to sell it, no food to sell.

"We had to eat what was left," Ding recalled. "Sometimes we found a pig. We always paid for it. But the country was picked clean. Sometimes we ate pig skin left behind by our comrades."

The Red Army, he said, was compelled to violate its rules in order to survive. It broke into Buddhist temples, smashed the huge idols, filled over the years with gifts of grain from worshipers, and devoured the wheat. "It was old and tasteless," he said, "but it was food."

The Red Army commands that preceded the rear guard suffered dreadful diarrhea and dysentery. The rough kernels of corn and wheat went through the bowels in a bloody discharge. Now the rear-guard men, faced with starvation, picked over the feces of the comrades who had gone before. They extracted the undigested grains of corn and wheat, as sparrows pick out the oat seeds from horse droppings, washed them, boiled them, and wolfed them down.

"The Grasslands was our worst trial," Ding said.[13]

Ji Pengfei, a onetime foreign minister, was seventy-three in 1984. He had been a paramedic on the Long March. Like most of his comrades, he felt that nothing matched the Grasslands for horror.

"It would look as though you were marching down a road," he said, "but after several columns had passed, it would turn into a water-filled ditch."

There was no place to camp. No dry place. No trees. Many men were weak and half sick when they reached the Grasslands. Some lay down in the muck and never rose.

"We lost more men at the Grasslands than in the Snowies," Ji Pengfei said. "Every morning we had to take a count to see how many were left. We found some who were not dead. Their eyes were open. But they could not rise. They could not talk. We got them to their feet and they slumped back into the bog—dead."

The high altitude of the Grasslands played a role. Many of the doctors were weak and ill. Many had to cross and recross the marshes, seeking out those who had fallen behind.[14]

Dr. Du Tanjin, in 1984 director of the Red Army Research Department, a tall, gray, distinguished man with horn-rimmed spectacles, spoke with precision and authority. He said that the rarefied air weakened the men. Everyone fell into the mud, everyone looked like the clay figures of the Xi'an archaeological treasure. The doctors administered camphor and smelling salts as the men grew faint. Some did not recover.

There was another factor, in the opinion of Dr. Dai Zhengqi, a sixteen-year-old in 1935, already a one-year veteran of the Red Army. He had started out as a propaganda worker, painting signs on walls and pasting up posters, but long before the Grasslands he had become a medical orderly. A thoughtful man, Dr. Dai had cast his mind back many times to the Grasslands experience.

In his view, there was no way of determining how many men died in the marshes. They did not die just of cold and lack of food or ambushes by the Tibetans. Salt was a cause. Lack of salt in the diet. They had had lots of salt on the March, but they hadn't bothered to carry it over the Snowies and into the Grasslands. There was no salt in the Grasslands and no salt in their diet. That took a toll. "I saw soldiers walking along," he said. "Suddenly one would collapse. By the time we got to him, he would whisper his home village and say, 'Tell my people I died.' And that would be the end."

Of course, the weather was changeable. The men were wet and they were hungry and they were cold. But this was not why so many died. They had all been wet and cold and hungry before. Nor was it just weakness. They had had a rest at Maoergai.

What was the reason?

"There were no people in the Grasslands," Dr. Dai said. "It was as simple as that. There were no people. None. You have to know us Chinese. None of us had ever had the experience of living in a world where we saw no people, heard no people, talked to no people. No one walked down the path. No houses. Alone. As though we were the last people on earth."

That was it, he said. That was what he thought was important. Men died of it.[15]

On the sixth day—August 27 for some troops—the First Army arrived at Baxi, a small Tibetan town at the northeastern edge of the

Grasslands. Mao probably arrived August 28. The vanguard, always moving more swiftly, got there a couple of days earlier. Others came considerably later.

Many troops went to Banyou or Axi or other settlements in the vicinity. It was important to scatter so as not to exhaust the meager food supplies of the villages. When Nie Rongzhen, political commissar of the First Army, and Lin Biao, its commander, were a day short of Banyou, they sent a wireless message to Peng Dehuai, commanding the Third Army just behind them.

They asked him to take a count of their casualties. They knew they had lost more than a hundred men and they had buried some. But more were left unburied, their bodies unfound. "Please bring tools and take care of this along the way," their message said.

Ten days later they got a report, signed by Zhou Enlai. The Third Army had found four hundred bodies and buried them.[16]

While the Right Column was arriving at Baxi and Banyou, the Left Column, under Zhang Guotao's direct control, was moving to Aba, located on a line about forty miles west and parallel to that being followed by the Right Column.

Then, on September 3, Zhang Guotao wirelessed the Right Column that he was halted at Aba. The floodwaters of the White River, the Gequ, would not permit his troops to proceed farther north. He proposed that the armies go south. The White is one of two sluggish rivers which in an almost imperceptible manner drain the Grasslands. The other is the Black River, the Muqu. Both flow into the Yellow River, the Maqu. These are all Tibetan, rather than Chinese, names.

Zhang Guotao's telegram was to precipitate the most serious political crisis of the Long March, one that again brought the Red Army to the brink of disaster. Its political effects would echo down through the years.[17]

26

DARK HOUR, BRIGHT GLORY

I T was, as General Yang Shangkun recalled fifty years later, a beautiful moonlit night. The rain had blown away. The fog had lifted. The moon was full, the sky star-spattered. He had no trouble keeping to the trail when he set out on his secret journey at 2 A.M.

The date was September 10. To Mao Zedong, speaking to Edgar Snow in 1960, it was "the darkest moment of my life," a moment when the fate of the Party "hung in the balance" and all that Mao had struggled for might be lost. On this night Mao believed that the Long March might blow up and that before dawn one part of the Red Army could be fighting another.[1]

Trouble had been building up. The talks between Mao and Zhang Guotao had gone badly. There were uneasy undertones. Rumors. Mao had taken the precaution of changing the codes. He had restricted communications among his troops to protect security.

The curious division of forces into Right Column and Left Column had not worked well. Mao marched with the Right Column, Zhang with the Left. Zhang's general, Xu Xiangqian, and his chief political officer, Chen Changhao, commanded the Right Column. Mao's men, Zhu De and Liu Bocheng, marched on the Left, as commander in chief, and chief of staff, of the GHQ. Neither Zhang nor Mao was accustomed to the other's command. There is a good deal of evidence that Zhang called the shots at "Unified Command Headquarters" in the Left Column, and that Mao (so far as he was able) was doing the same with his own armies in the Right Column.

At best, this made for a jerky, uneasy truce. At worst, it stimulated thoughts of conspiracy. The structure was a breeding place for friction and suspicion.

The Red Army was scattered along the fringes of the Grasslands in Tibetan territory. Zhang Guotao and the high command staff had gone to Aba, the biggest of the Tibetan settlements. Many of Zhang's troops were stalled on the west banks of the White River, which was in flood. They had to cross the White River if they were to continue northeast to a juncture with the Right Column in Gansu, as planned.

Right Column headquarters had been set up at Banyou, a not very appealing huddle of Tibetan yurts, some of them the conventional conical dwellings of felt stretched over a lattice crisscross, quickly taken down and put up as the Tibetans moved from one pasture to another. Others were permanent structures of clay smeared over dried yak-dung bricks. Round mounds of dried yak dung stood in filthy lanes between the huts, and dung was spread out on the wattle fences to dry in the summer months. It was used as both fuel and building material. Every Tibetan had fled and the yurts were empty of all possessions.

As the troops approached Banyou, there were jokes about spending the night "in foreign houses." To some Red Army men, this didn't seem funny. If they were going to sleep in foreign houses, they said, let them be Japanese.

To their relief, the troops passed by Banyou, moving on to Baxi, where there was a village with a hundred thatched-roof huts and a big lamasery, which reminded Yang Dinghua of the Charleston movie house in Shanghai. Plenty of roofs under which the Red Army could bed down, and the food supply was not bad. The temple boasted a great figure of Buddha. At his left and right were couples embracing in what Yang described as "sexual ecstasy." It was said to be a temple of love. Red Army men kept dropping in to have a look.

Right Column headquarters was set up at Banyou, not in the village —although several of the larger yurts were cleaned and used for meetings—but in a willow grove just beside the settlement. The grove still existed in 1984, clean and attractive, the Tibetan village then comprising about seventy families. It did not seem to have changed much since the Red Army saw it in 1935, except for a two-year school. There was still the sprawl of yurts, the mounds of yak dung, rubbishy lanes patrolled by fierce dogs, and on a snowy May 30, swarms of Tibetan-cloaked men and women and brightly clad children gathered for a horse fair and horse races in the rain, the riders carrying black umbrellas.[2]

It was here that Xu Xiangqian, Chen Changhao, Ye Jianying, and Yang Shangkun had their headquarters. Mao lived separately within a stone's throw, across a small river. The Third Army of Peng Dehuai was at Baxi, about four miles away. The First Army had pushed ahead to

Ejie, just across the line in Gansu, two days distant.

Mao divided his time between Banyou Headquarters and Baxi, where Zhou Enlai and Wang Jiaxiang, each improving but still bedridden, were being cared for by the Third Army.

The first sign of acute crisis had come September 3, when Zhang sent a wireless that he could not get over the White (Gequ) River because of flooding. He ordered all troop movement to halt and proposed abandoning the expedition to the north and east and going back to his original idea of the west and south.[3]

Zhang's telegram caused consternation in Mao's camp. It was seen as a maneuver to reverse the decisions of Maoergai and to put the whole Communist force under Zhang's control. Mao convened the Central Committee (the members were all committed to his viewpoint) and telegraphed Zhang, urging him to continue north and abide by the Central Committee decision. One telegram followed another. Yang Shangkun recalled one in which the Central Committee offered to come to Zhang's aid and help him cross the river.[4]

Tensions were heightened by fears of a Nationalist attack. In moving up to Banyou and Baxi, the Thirtieth Army, headed by Li Xiannian, had encountered elements of the KMT Forty-ninth Division of the Songpan commander Hu Zongnan, and dispersed them in the battle of Dajie temple at Baozuo. Hu Zongnan was seriously wounded[5] and a small stock of biscuits, canned goods, and cigarettes was captured. The cigarettes were sent to Mao and his companions, all heavy smokers. "They were delighted," Li Xiannian recalled. "It was better than eating chicken."[6] There was also a skirmish with a detachment of the fierce Moslem cavalry (KMT) of Ma Hongkui. This gathering KMT presence brought fears that if the Red Army did not get moving, Chiang Kai-shek would mount a major campaign against them. In turn, Zhang began to cite this possibility as an argument against advancing into Gansu and Shaanxi.[7]

Peng Dehuai's prison memoirs convey a sense of the growing fear of conflict between the two Red Army forces. Once Peng's Third Army reached Baxi, he said, he placed his Eleventh Regiment in a concealed position near Mao's residence—just in case—and began to visit Mao every day. He was worried about being out of contact with the First Army, which he said was stalled somewhere near Ejie for lack of a guide. Since the codes had been changed, he had no way of communicating. He made up a new codebook, entrusted it to a reliable

Party man, Mu Jong, a Korean, gave him a compass, and sent him forward to contact Lin Biao and Nie Rongzhen.[8] Nie Rongzhen recalled that the First Army knew nothing of what was happening. All it had received was a message to halt where it was.[9]

On the morning of September 9, Zhang Guotao sent a coded, secret message to his trusted political aide, Chen Changhao, at Right Column GHQ. The message was supposed to be deciphered personally by Chen. But he was busy attending a political meeting and making a speech. So the message was deciphered by a code clerk and handed to Ye Jianying.

Ye Jianying, reliable staff officer that he was, took the telegram unread to the meeting. Chen Changhao was on the platform; speeches were being made. Ye tried to deliver the message. "Later," Chen said. "Can't you see I'm busy."[10]

Since the message seemed to be urgent, Ye took a look at it. He immediately grasped its importance although, in Yang Shangkun's words, "he knew nothing of the conspiracy."[11]

The text of the message has never been published, although often cited by Chinese historians and possibly available in the Party archives for their inspection. Essentially, it ordered the Right Column to reverse its direction, recross the Grasslands, and join the Fourth Army for a conference to reconcile their differences. The message contained a critical phrase, which Li Xiannian recalled as instructing Chen Changhao to "uncompromisingly open up (expose) the struggle within the Party." The Chinese phrase used was *chedi kaizhan dangnei douzheng*. Taken as a whole, the words bear, as John Service has pointed out, a "definitely ominous, threatening implication." The term *douzheng* is that customarily used in the Party for violent struggles between opposing party lines, or in the term "class struggle."[12]

Ye excused himself, saying that he had to go to the toilet. Instead he went off to Mao's offices, a couple of hundred yards away, and showed him the message. Mao copied it and told Ye not to let on that he knew its contents.[13] Mao told Ye Jianying, "You have done a wonderful thing."

Ye went back to GHQ. Chen Changhao was still on the platform, the meeting still going on. Ye turned over the message to Chen Changhao's secretary.[14]

Peng Dehuai recalled that even before he heard about the telegram he had urged Mao to take precautions. Mao's units were dispersed. The First Army was two days away. There were two Zhang armies nearby.

"What will we do if the Fourth Army disbands the Third Army?" Peng asked. He urged Mao to "take some hostages to prevent the misfortune of Red Army troops fighting each other." Mao rejected the idea.[15] The smell of powder was clearly in the air.

In the afternoon of September 9, Mao met with Chen Changhao, probably at Chen's request. Chen Changhao briefed Mao on Zhang's orders. Yang Shangkun believes that Mao made a serious effort to win Chen Changhao over to his viewpoint, but, Yang said, Chen was "so absolutely obedient to Zhang that Mao could not move him."[16]

Mao then told Chen that if the Army was going to change course, he must consult his associates in the Central Committee. He pointed out that Zhou Enlai and Wang Jiaxiang were being cared for at Third Army headquarters. "Let Luo Fu and Bo Gu and me go to them for the meeting," Mao suggested. Chen Changhao agreed. Peng believed this was just a gambit by Mao to get away from GHQ and out of Chen's "sphere of influence."[17]

Mao Zedong hastened to Yanong, the hamlet beside Baxi where the Third Army was located. An emergency Standing Committee meeting agreed not to reverse course. A new wireless was dispatched to Zhang Guotao, asking him to join them and adhere to the original plan approved by the Central Committee. There was some talk about the relative strength of military forces—the Third Army had only four thousand men, the First Army about the same. Zhang had a vast preponderance, and Mao and his men believed he was likely to try to compel them to follow his will.

No time was to be lost. The Third Army would leave at 2 A.M. As a cover, Ye Jianying was sent to tell Chen Changhao that if the Army was to move back over the Grasslands, more food was needed. The whole force was being mobilized to cut barley in the fields at first light on the morning of the tenth. Chen had no objections.

"Chen Changhao was not worried," General Yang Shangkun said. "He saw no reason for special vigilance. Mao had so few men. He wouldn't dare go away by himself."

The most dangerous assignment was that of Yang Shangkun and Ye Jianying. They had to leave GHQ without rousing suspicions, and if possible, Ye had promised to bring maps and members of the Second Bureau, the intelligence bureau, which was made up of First Front Army men.[18]

Yang Shangkun had to make sure that as many as possible of his work team and Political Department got away to "harvest grain." Word was passed from person to person, Liu Ying remembered. She was awakened at midnight and told to get ready to leave immediately. No one knew what was up. Later Luo Fu passed word that Zhang Guotao was trying to split the Party and that they had to leave.[19] Yang Shangkun had a personal problem. His wife was not in Banyou. She had gone to Li Xiannian's Thirtieth Army to teach revolutionary songs to the soldiers. Yang couldn't send her an open message—that would have given the game away. He did manage to get word to her, but, as she recalled, she was under "a rather close watch" and could not leave.[20] She and her husband would be separated for more than a year, Li with the Fourth Front Army, Yang with the First.

At 2 A.M., Yang Shangkun and Ye Jianying slipped away from GHQ barracks. Ye had managed to get one map from those tacked up in the situation room; it had fallen to the floor. He brought it along in his luggage. Ye and Yang walked out of camp. They sent their bodyguards ahead with their gear, packed on mules. The Second Bureau and Political Department workers had gotten off at 1:30 A.M.[21]

As Yang and Ye walked along in the bright moonlight, they heard horses' hooves and darted into the shadows. A squadron of cavalrymen galloped past. They were looking for Ye and Yang, but assumed they would be mounted with an escort, as befit high officers. They never glanced at the men on foot in the shadows.[22]

At Third Army headquarters, Mao had wirelessed Lin Biao and Nie Rongzhen to stand by for a possible change in orders. Peng Dehuai was on tenterhooks, fearing Ye and Yang would not make their getaway. When they appeared at daybreak, he breathed a sigh of relief.[23]

Yang remembered seeing Mao, Zhou Enlai, Wang Jiaxiang, and Peng Dehuai waiting. "We were worried about you," Mao said.[24]

By this time, Chen Changhao had discovered that Mao's men had flown the coop. He completed several telephone calls, and with telephone receiver still in hand, looked over to the commander, Xu Xiangqian, and said: "A strange thing has happened. The First Army has pulled out. Shall we send troops after them?"

Xu Xiangqian replied in words repeatedly quoted in the last half century (particularly during the Cultural Revolution): "Have you ever seen the Red Army attacking the Red Army?" That was it. There was to be no attack. Chen Changhao might have given a different response.

"It was a very dangerous moment in the history of the Party," Hu

Hua, the Party historian, was to say in 1984. "Xu and Ye obtained credit for stopping a conflict. Both obtained credit."

By which he meant that Mao Zedong protected each from the worst excesses of the Cultural Revolution.

Instead of troops, Chen Changhao dispatched a delegation of students from the Red Army College and some Fourth Front Army men to Baxi. Among them was Li Te, chief of staff of the Fourth Front Army. Li Te, a returned student from the Soviet Union, had studied in Leningrad and had the habit of carrying a large revolver. He was known for his hot temper and his foul mouth. He was ultimately to die in the Soviet Union.

Mao decided to address the Fourth Army delegation, as well as any Fourth Army men left behind. The Third Army men were already well on their way to Ejie. They had been marching since 2 A.M.

The meeting was held at the "Charleston Theater," the Tibetan temple halfway up a hillside. Third Army headquarters was in the village beside it, overlooking the Baxi River (actually nothing more than a creek), a tributary of the White Dragon (Bailong) River.

The young Army students demonstrated in front of the temple, carrying banners proclaiming: "Oppose Mao fleeing." They chanted the slogan like a Buddhist sutra.

Mao told them that those who wanted to go south were free to do so; those who wanted to go north were free to do so. There was to be no coercion.

Then he invited sixty or seventy Fourth Front cadres to meet with him, Li Te among them. Otto Braun (Li De) had been put on the alert. He was tall and strong. He was to stand close and keep an eye on Li Te in case he pulled out his revolver and tried to shoot Mao.

Mao told the cadres that for the First Army to go south would lead nowhere. As for those who did not want to go north with the Central Committee, he said that "we go as an advance party."

"We will go ahead," he said, "and break new ground and get the job done and we will welcome you when you join us. I am sure that after a year you will come." (Mao was right, almost to the day.)

When Mao finished speaking, Li Te leaped to his feet, shouting that Mao was guilty of "escapism," of abandoning the Soviet base in Jiangxi and other crimes. Li De got worried. He thought Li Te was getting carried away. He grabbed him in a bear hug. Li Te struggled a bit, but could not break Li De's iron grip.

By 8 A.M. it was all over. The men who didn't want to go north streamed back to Banyou. Those who wanted to go forward headed north. It happened exactly as it had in the autumn of 1927 when Mao confronted the restive men at Jinggangshan and quelled the revolt by telling those who didn't want to come along to go home, then led the rest of his band upward and onward.

Yang Shangkun recalled his own moment of mock despair. The Fourth Army men took away all the cooks, porters, and support staff of his Political Department. He was left with a rice bowl but no one to fill it. He joined the Central Column and found a place at the mess with Xu Mengqiu, the historian, Lu Dingyi, the propaganda chief, and some others.

Within the hour, Mao was on his way. He did not take the trail with the others. Accompanied by his bodyguards and a few intimates (Zhou Enlai and Wang Jiaxiang on their stretchers), Mao came down the hill from the lamasery, crossed the Baxi River over a wooden bridge protected then (and now) from floods, destruction, and evil spirits by a yak's head hanging below its planks just above the water, strode straight up the facing mountain, Narizhai, and was on his own route across the country.

Whether the threat of attack by Zhang was real, as Mao thought, cannot be determined today. Possibly it was not. But Mao believed it was and was taking no chances. As he strode up the mountainside, he had arranged that rear-guard detachments be left behind at each pass, each strategic point, in case the Fourth Army came after him. "It was a very dangerous moment in the history of the Red Army," said General Yang Shangkun. "If conflict had emerged, I don't know where we would be today."[25]

Professor Xiang Qing, a conservative and careful student of the Long March, points out that no objective evidence, no written documents, have been found to support the theory that Zhang was prepared to use military action to bring Mao and his men to heel. Had this existed, he felt, it would have been presented in the case against Zhang Guotao made later on in Yan'an. It is true, he added, that Zhang had great ambition and that the point is still hotly argued by Chinese historians.[26]

General Qin Xinghan of the Military Museum agrees that no evidence Zhang was planning a military coup has been uncovered. He has not seen the famous telegram. He felt the fact that no such charge was made against Zhang in Yan'an was significant, yet he believed Zhang's ambition to take over was very real. Li Xiannian said that "at the worst it was an open attempt by Zhang to usurp the power of the Party."

Wang Nianyi, a Party historian, presented a careful analysis of the telegram (without, however, apparently examining its text) in *Materials on Party History Studies* 3 (1983). He concluded there was no "smoking gun"—that is, no positive evidence that Zhang made an overt threat of a "military solution." He concluded, however, that many in the Party believed such a threat was made or was implicit in Zhang's actions and that Mao's words in a footnote in Volume 3 of his collected works strongly implied that Zhang contemplated a "military solution."[27]

Wang Nianyi cites two authorities as stating flatly that Zhang contemplated a "military solution." One is Li Anbao, who in *Talking About the Long March* says positively Zhang "secretly ordered a military solution." The other is Lu Liping, who in his memoirs, *The Critical Moment*, told of being in the communications room while the duty officer, Chen Maosheng, was transcribing the "famous telegram." He claimed to have helped transcribe the message and said the telegram contained the words: "If they insist on pursuing the wrong ideas and move north, then a military solution is in order." However, after examining all of the official documents, Wang Nianyi concludes that there is no evidence that the telegram actually contained these words. He points out that no such charge was contained in any Central Committee document, nor was it cited at the proceedings in Yan'an or in the communiqué after Zhang Guotao fled Yan'an.

Zhang Guotao was enraged at Mao's actions. He pulled his troops back to Aba, making no offer to release the Mao men. He organized a mass meeting at the big Tibetan temple, its slogan: "Oppose the Mao–Zhou–Zhang (Luo Fo)–Bo Gu flight to the north." Zhang called on the Army cadres to denounce Mao and demanded that Zhu De make his position clear.

"Going to the north," said Zhu De, "was adopted as a decision by the Central Committee. I personally cannot go against that decision and I shall not lead the Red Army against it. To demand that Zhu reproach Mao would not have any effect on world opinion. The world knows Zhu-Mao as one person. As to deciding to go north, I have already raised my hand in approval and will not renounce my opinion."

"How can you be such an old diehard?" snapped Zhang Guotao.

The one-eyed dragon, Liu Bocheng, blazed up. "What do you mean by treating Zhu De like this?"[28] Very harsh language was directed at Zhu and Liu, in the recollection of Song Kanfu, a wireless and telephone operator at Zhang Guotao's headquarters, who attended the meeting. The Mao men were called "right opportunists" and "flightists."[29]

Someone shouted: "Down with Zhu De!"[30]

Soon Zhang Guotao began to move south. His Thirtieth and Fourth armies recrossed the Grasslands and joined him at Zhuokeji. Hou Guo-xiang, a rather heavyset, rather reticent, rather balding cadre of sixty-eight (but an eager twenty-year-old political worker in the Fourth Front Army in 1935, a member of Li Xiannian's Thirtieth Army), remembered that not long after Zhuokeji, the slogan under which the Army marched was changed. It had been: "Oppose the Right Opportunists—Mao, Zhou, and Bo Gu." Now it became: "March to Chengdu and eat rice."[31]

Zhang Guotao was going south; Mao was going north.

Mao assembled his armies at Ejie on September 12. They had reached a small, safe haven. This Tibetan area was controlled by Chieftain Yang, the nineteenth in a succession of Chieftain Yangs dating back to the Ming dynasty. His Tibetan name was Xie Dai. The first chief began paying tribute to the Ming emperor in the fourteenth century. Since then an unbroken succession of Yangs had ruled the region, paying annual tribute, secure in their own affairs. The nineteenth chieftain gave salt and food to the KMT and did the same for the Red Army. He was neutral, hostile to no one. He left his grain warehouses open for the Red Army men. There was no written agreement, but the First Army gave him some rifles, just as the KMT had done. The Yang line endures. The current Yang, the twentieth, was fifty-six in 1984 and vice-chairman of the provincial People's Congress. At twenty, he was made a lieutenant general by the KMT. But he cast his lot with the Communists.[32]

Mao and his fellow members of the Central Committee met for a day or two at Ejie. They reorganized the shrunken forces into a single grouping called, for propaganda reasons, the Shaanxi-Gansu Branch Force of the Anti-Japanese Vanguard Force of the Red Army. This reflected Mao's realistic acknowledgment of the small size of his group as compared with Zhang Guotao's formidable Fourth Front Army, further strengthened by Mao's Fifth and Ninth armies.

The Vanguard Force was commanded by Peng Dehuai. Mao was political commissar. There were three columns: the former First Army, still led by Lin Biao, with Nie Rongzhen as political commissar; the former Third Army, still commanded by Peng Dehuai concurrently with his overall command, with Li Fuchun as political commissar; and the former Military Commission column, commanded by Ye Jianying, with Deng Fa as political commissar. General Yang Shangkun became deputy director of the overall Political Department, which was headed by Wang Jiaxiang.[33]

The Ejie meeting approved a "Resolution Concerning the Mistakes of Comrade Zhang Guotao."[34] Mao resisted a proposal to expel Zhang from the Party,[35] and with its usual rush the Red Army set out for Lazikou Pass, whose narrow jaws—ten or twelve feet at the narrowest point—barred entry into southern Gansu. The Politburo meeting was held on September 12 and 13. On the morning of September 14, the Army was moving along the right bank of the White Dragon River toward Lazikou.[36] The White Dragon is a bouncy mountain stream that flows through a water-cut gorge at Maya, where a fine Tibetan house was found for Mao to spend the night. There also was the Wang Jang monastery, inhabited by four or five hundred monks. It was so clean the Red Army soldiers couldn't believe it. There were white and red plantings of chrysanthemums outside each of the dormitories. On the sunny side, morning glories, white and blue and purple, bloomed, and there were grape arbors. Yang Dinghua thought five or six thousand men could be accommodated in the building.[37] Many troops were given an extra day's rest at Maya.

But not the Fourth Regiment of the Second Division of the First Army, of which Yang Chengwu was still political commissar. At Maya, September 15, the shock regiment got its expected assignment—to attack and capture Lazikou and push on to Minxian in south Gansu. Lazikou was to be taken within two days. It was already dusk when the order came through. Everyone fell to, getting ready for the takeoff, and at 11 P.M., in a meadow beside the road, they assembled in the darkness. A whistle sounded and the commander called out to the troops: "Comrades! Now we begin. In two days we must conquer Lazikou!"

They marched off in the dark night along the White Dragon River, through a dark forest, over a mountain peak, through a sugar-candy snowstorm. ("How pretty! Let's eat sugar!" the men are said to have shouted.)[38] They ate a whopping big meal at 2 A.M., rested a bit, and marched on.

They skirmished with a battalion of the KMT Fourteenth Division, and scattered them. From prisoners they learned that Lu Dachang, commander of the Fourteenth, had built blockhouses at Lazikou. At about four in the afternoon of September 16, the advance guard got to the approaches of the pass over pleasant country, first the Nine Dragon gorge, then over a pass to the Lazi River, a small, swift-flowing mountain stream between narrow banks. The troops were dropping down from the high elevations now. There was subtropical foliage, heavy forests, some primeval, many ferns, rhododendron and azalea bushes; waterfalls spurted from the stone sides.

The pass itself was extraordinarily narrow. The walls of the valley closed in. The right side was a cliff that rose almost perpendicularly for a thousand feet. It couldn't be climbed by man or even by mountain goat. Only a bird could find a foothold on it. Across the pass, one hundred feet wide and narrowing to twelve at its throat, rose another cliff, not quite so high. It was jagged, not sheer. It could be climbed, perhaps, but not with machine guns looking down at you.

The Lazi River, hardly big enough for trout, flowed at the base of the sheer. The path led over a three-foot bridge of two logs to the wall of the sheer and continued along the wall on swinging bridges, riveted to the side of the rock wall by long iron bolts. The KMT had placed blockhouses so that they could rain fire down on anyone trying to cross the bridge and enter the narrow defile. Any madman trying to hitch his way up the cliffs looked straight at the gun nozzles.

The position, as anyone who observes it today can see, is impregnable.

Yang Chengwu assembled his men and said: "We must take Lazikou Pass. If we don't break through we must go back to the Grasslands!"

At 9 P.M. the Fourth Regiment began a succession of night assaults. Each failed. The KMT stood its ground. They opened up their machine guns and tossed hand grenades like fiery lollipops. A few men got across the bridge, but they could not climb the cliff. They huddled beneath the bridge as the battle raged.

There were three KMT regiments in the area and two battalions of possibly four to five hundred men assigned to defend the pass.[39]

Mao set up his command post three hundred yards back from the pass and directed operations all evening. Worry grew. Prisoners had told the Fourth Regiment that KMT reinforcements were en route.

At midnight Mao ordered the direct assaults halted. They had brought nothing but heavy casualties. A band of experienced mountaineers was assembled, with instructions to climb around the rear of the steepest sheer and attack the KMT from above. These men, thirty to sixty in all—about twelve of them Miao and other minority fighters—

gathered in the darkness. They carried only grenades and cold steel—daggers and short swords. They had no alpine climbing gear. They lashed together belts, roll puttees, and ropes to give them support over the dangerous crags. Silently the mountain men climbed up, quickly out of sight of the worried commanders. Fighting went on. Wrong signal guns were fired—red, not white. More failures. Toward dawn, as the commanders began to feel all was lost and that KMT reinforcements soon would arrive, there was a volley of explosions. The mountain men had reached the peak behind the KMT and were hurling down grenades. Within minutes the KMT soldiers were scrambling from their positions, toppling down the mountainsides, running for their lives. The battered remnants of the Fourth Regiment rushed in for the kill. Propaganda workers shouted in night-hoarsened voices the words of a battle hymn:

> Cannon shake the heavens—
> Bugles sound the attack.
> The decisive day is here.
> We will win victory in the battle
> And wipe out the hated enemy.

Soon the troops were pouring through Lazikou Pass. They would not return to the Grasslands, to washing feces and eating the undigested grains of wheat and corn. Already the Fourth Regiment was racing ahead. Next assignment: Hadapu. It was said to be a Han town, rich with food, very friendly toward the Red Army.[40]

27

HOME

THE Red Army marched into Hadapu at about ten-thirty on the morning of September 21, 1935. This was the main force, headed by Mao Zedong, Zhou Enlai (vastly improved in health), Peng Dehuai, Lin Biao, and the other top commanders. The vanguard had reached Hadapu, just inside Gansu, two days earlier.

The Red Army was home. It had broken out of the Snowy Mountains, the Grasslands, and the alien preserves of the Tibetans. It was back in Han China among the Hans—largely Moslem Hans, as it chanced. Hadapu felt like home to the Red Army men. The people looked as they did, they spoke Chinese. They *were* Chinese.

There would be a few more mountains to storm, a few more rivers to cross, a few more battles to fight, but no more starvation. No more retreats.

Hadapu turned out to welcome the tough, tired, thin men and women who had marched 24,000 li to the gates of this old town. They greeted the Red Army with cheers and smiles and food.

Every soldier got two shiny silver dollars from the treasure that had been lugged over the Snowies, the Grasslands, and through the jaws of Lazikou Pass. Mao made a speech: "Everyone should eat well."[1] They did. They could buy a hundred-pound pig for five dollars, a fat sheep for two, five chickens for a dollar. It was heaven. A dozen eggs for ten cents, one hundred pounds of vegetables for fifty cents. There was salt again and flour—the Red Army confiscated a ton of salt and six tons of flour, quantities of rice and wheat and millet. Every company slaughtered pigs and sheep. The soldiers ate three meat dishes and two of vegetables at every meal. Better than New Year's. Never had they eaten like this. There were even a few casualties. Some soldiers ate so much their bellies burst.

There was a fine Buddhist temple, where Zhou Enlai and GHQ set up shop, and an excellent merchant's courtyard house (still standing) for Mao Zedong. Two or three thousand people inhabited Hadapu on September 21, 1935 (the town has doubled in population in fifty years). The men of Hadapu were excited by the politeness, good conduct, and discipline of the Red Army men. "Very good soldiers!" they said. The women of Hadapu were surprised to see women soldiers—were they really women, these creatures with short hair, uniforms, pistols in their belts? They invited them into their houses and gave them a close inspection. They touched their breasts and followed them to the toilet. Once convinced, they wanted to hear stories of the women in battle.

Curiosity and hospitality are strong in Hadapu to this day. Fifty years later, the people lined the streets to cheer a party of foreign travelers. They had never seen Westerners before—strange white-haired beings with round blue eyes.[2]

Where was Mao leading his Red Army? He had arrived in Hadapu still without a clear idea. Yes, they were going north. To Gansu, to Shaanxi, perhaps even to Ningxia. They would fight the Japanese. But these were generalities, not fixed locations. As so often in the Long March, Mao knew in broad terms where he was going but lacked a specific goal.

In Hadapu at long last, thousands of li from his starting point in Jiangxi, that exact goal, that specific place, took real shape.

The Red Army vanguard had gone straight to the Hadapu post office, the first they had captured in a long, long time. There they found KMT newspapers, which Mao and his commanders devoured with excitement. The rumors they had heard as far back as the meeting with Zhang Guotao in Lianghekou were true! There was a Communist force in being in northern Shaanxi and a soviet base area. The papers revealed that Liu Zhidan, the daring commander of the Twenty-sixth Army, a friend of Mao's, a great folk hero, was alive and leading his army. So was Xu Haidong of the Twenty-fifth Army.

At last the great question was resolved. Ten days later, at Bangluezhen, Mao spoke openly of the plan to join forces with their comrades in northern Shaanxi. He assembled his troops. There were meetings of the Politburo and the Central Committee and the top commanders. Political workers spoke to the Army units and Mao himself addressed a 6 A.M. meeting of cadres and officers in a primary school building, talking about the problems of fighting the Japanese, of the north Shaanxi base, of political and economic conditions, and of improving basic discipline. The commissars spent the rest of the day carrying the message to the troops. More and more now, in the recollection of the memoirists, Mao was beginning to stress the line of fighting the Japanese.

Home. The Red Army was on the threshold of home territory and it was heading toward comrades and an established base. All that remained was to fight their way north for another thousand li—250 miles. True, they had had such hopes before the nightmare of the Fourth Front Army and Zhang Guotao. But somehow they felt this would be different. After all, they had survived the Fourth Army crisis. The Red Army was still an effective force in being. It had shrunk to six thousand men—but what men! They had fought and marched and suffered and died for a year. They had overcome every obstacle. They had spread word of the Red Army and the Communist cause to more than half of China.

No longer were they a ragged, quarreling band fleeing for their lives from Chiang Kai-shek's fine legions. They were turning the Long March into victory. No longer was it a retreat, ducking and dodging, not knowing where next to flee. All this had changed when they crossed the River of Golden Sands. No longer was the KMT dictating the terms of battle. Mao's force, compact, united, combat-hard, shared a spirit and purpose in common. By now the majority of the men were cadres. Not many ordinary soldiers left. These cadres would provide the nucleus for the revolution that all believed they would bring to China.

A hint of this feeling began to show in the rallies and in the speeches Mao would deliver in these last thousand li. As he said at Hadapu: "I believe that you, commanders and fighters, having crossed many thousand li in the Long March, under fire in battle, fearless of any hardship, will, thanks to your bravery and fighting experience, overcome all dangers and achieve our goal—to complete our march to the north and fight the Japanese occupiers."

The next morning, again at 6 A.M., with Mao and Peng Dehuai at the head of the column and Lin Biao and Nie Rongzhen at the head of what had once been the powerful First Army Group, the Red Army headed for the north. They set off for Tongwei. Here there was more political agitation. One evening, a gathering assembled in the central square. A platform had been put up, red flags flew, red bunting draped the square. All the troops in town assembled. There were talks by Yang Shangkun, security chief Deng Fa, chief of staff Ye Jianying. They sang the "Marseillaise" and had a banquet such as the town had never seen

—heaping dishes of pork, beef, and chicken. And entertainment—songs and magic tricks by Li Kenong and Yuan Xin.[3]

The Red Army raced north. They were harassed, but not seriously, by KMT forces, particularly the Moslem cavalry of the Ma clan. They crossed the Xi'an-Lanzhou highway, and climbed the eleven-thousand-foot Liupan Mountain in an afternoon and early evening, camping on the far side.

On October 14 or 15, just short of the Shaanxi border, moving out of Huanxian county on a narrow trail, Chen Changfeng, Mao's body-guard, as he tells the story, saw five horsemen galloping toward them, sturdy, young, carrying Mausers and wearing white turbans. They alighted from their horses and said: "Where's Chairman Mao?" Chen asked them who they were. One said: "We're sent by Old Liu to deliver a letter to Chairman Mao. Where is he?"

It was, as Chen reported, a deputation sent by Liu Zhidan, comman-der of the Twenty-sixth Army, and Mao's friend. Mao received the delegates, went over to some resting Red Army companies, and shouted that the deputies had come to welcome them from the Twenty-fifth and Twenty-sixth armies and that they were about to enter the soviet zone of northern Shaanxi.[4]

Ma cavalry was cutting in and out to harass the rear of the Red column. Peng Dehuai ordered the men to speed up. He didn't want straggling units to be killed by the ferocious Moslem KMT units.[5] The Red Army came up over Laoye Mountain, over the Ziwu Mountains into Shaanxi, and skirmished again with the Ma cavalry. The country-side was less rugged now, easier for horsemen. In the late afternoon of October 19, Mao's men walked up the brown valley of Toudaochuan into the dusty town of Wuqi, in the heart of Shaanxi's loess country. To their north was the Great Wall of China. To the south was the burial site of the Yellow Emperor, founder of China. They were home in the great loess plain below the Yellow River, the birthplace of the Chinese nation.

They were home in the barren town of Wuqi, with its cave dwell-ings. They would grow very used to cave dwellings in the months and years to come.

That evening Mao summoned his commanders. He proposed to "cut off the tail" of the enemy, the Ma cavalry, and get rid of the harassment the Red Army had been suffering for the last few weeks. On the twen-tieth, Mao positioned his men and guerrillas from the Wuqi area. Three rivers cut through the loess at this point. Mao put his men in a half-moon formation to lure the Ma cavalry up the valley of the central river, the Luohe. Early on the morning of the twenty-first, Mao took his place on the observation point atop Damaliang Mountain (the spot is still marked by a lone tree).

The Ma cavalry moved up to the attack—four regiments, about a thousand men in each. Mao had not many more. At 7 A.M. the Red Army opened fire on the leading Ma regiment. Within two hours it was fleeing the battlefield, carrying the other three regiments with it.

In the afternoon after the battle Mao met with two local leaders. After listening to their story, he summoned two trusted officers—Jia Tuofu and Wang Shoudao and sent them with a company of fast-moving men at full speed to Wayaobu. Their mission: to save the life of the Robin Hood leader of the Twenty-sixth Army, Liu Zhidan, and an unknown number of his comrades, who were awaiting execution at the hands of their fellow Red Army men of the Twenty-fifth Army.[6]

In the summer of 1929, a young man from Kansas City named Edgar Snow made a trip into the loess country south of the great bend of the Yellow River. Snow was twenty-four years old and he had come to look into reports of famine. Snow met another young Westerner on that trip, a New Zealander named Rewi Alley. Together they had a look at death in China. The loess land lay lifeless, baking in the sun and drought. No green. Trees barren, leaves stripped off, bark stripped off. Corpses thin as skeletons lay beside the roads, no flesh, bones brittle as eggshells; half-naked starving girls were being shipped in cattle cars to the brothels of Shanghai. No fleshy corpses. They vanished immediately. Six million Chinese died in the 1929–30 famine. The event rated half a column of inside space in *The New York Times.*

That terrible summer, Liu Zhidan hurried home to northern Shaanxi, to Bao'an, where his father was a minor landlord (old photos show the Liu house far less impressive than Mao's in Shaoshan). There were no crops. No rent from the tenant farmers. Liu Zhidan was twenty-six years old, handsome in the recollection of Yuan Yaoxiu, seventy-seven in 1984, Red Army veteran living in Wuqi who had served under Liu Zhidan, whom he remembered as a bit taller than average, a smiling face, pink cheeks, slim, a great talker, a voice loud enough so that he could address a throng of a thousand and everyone heard every word.[7]

When Liu Zhidan walked down the street, people paid attention.

When he spoke, he often talked for several hours. Everyone knew he came from a "rich" landlord family (landlords were not very rich in this remote dust bowl).

The landlords were putting up notices. Regardless of famine and drought, tenants must pay the rent. Liu's family asked him to draft a notice. Nonsense, he said. The people had nothing to eat, no grain to pay rent, no grain to pay taxes. He went to the tenants and organized a protest. "How long do you want things to go along like this?" he asked. Many of the Liu family tenants enlisted under his banner. The government was forced to declare a moratorium on rent and taxes.[8]

Liu Zhidan had been a member of the Communist Party since 1925. He had studied at Whampoa Military Academy. By 1929 he was a member of the underground Communist committee for northern Shaanxi.[9]

Liu Zhidan was a people's hero; everyone knew and talked of his exploits. They said he had expropriated his own family. They called him Old Liu. "He devoted himself to a search for the truth and for the liberation of the people," was the way soldier Yuan Yaoxiu expressed it.[10]

The career of Shaanxi's Robin Hood was stormy. Liu Zhidan was stronger in his feeling for the people than in dialectic politics. In 1931 he organized a revolutionary detachment, on which the Twenty-sixth Army was built, but within the year a man named Du Heng, political commissar and provincial party secretary, attacked Liu Zhidan for refusing to engage in large-scale battles with the KMT. Liu Zhidan was set aside; Du Heng, a follower of the "Bolshevik" line, took over and led the Twenty-sixth Army into a devastating defeat. Only Liu Zhidan and a few others managed to escape. Du Heng was captured by the KMT and turned traitor.[11]

Liu Zhidan made his way back to northern Shaanxi. Men surged to his side, and he quickly rebuilt the Twenty-sixth Army. Among those who joined him was another guerrilla commander, Gao Gang, who headed a band of a few hundred men.

Gao Gang became Liu Zhidan's political commissar. He was competent enough but had a reputation for "playing around" with women, as a Chinese put it. Liu Zhidan would not put up with this. Once there was a threat to execute Gao Gang for his loose conduct.[12]

In its second incarnation Liu Zhidan's Twenty-sixth Army had great success. By 1934 he had created a base area comprising all or parts of twenty counties. Liu had five thousand men in the Twenty-sixth Army and a small force euphemistically called the Twenty-seventh Army.[13]

But trouble was in the making. Three Central Committee representatives, all hostile to Liu Zhidan, straggled into northern Shaanxi and tried to oust him. They claimed he maintained clandestine contact with the KMT. In fact he was in touch with some secret Communists in the KMT.[14]

The Twenty-fifth Army, the one to which Zhou Enlai long ago in the spring of 1934 had sent Cheng Zihua, finally came in from the cold. After ten months in the wilderness, it arrived in northern Shaanxi.

Cheng Zihua arrived in northern Shaanxi on a litter. So did his co-commander Xu Haidong. Both had been carried on litters for months.

The odyssey of the Twenty-fifth Army and its commanders, Cheng Zihua and Xu Haidong, was an epic of human survival. Cheng Zihua, having made the hazardous trip from Jiangxi through Swatow, Shanghai, and Hankou, got to Henan in October 1934 and took over the Twenty-fifth Army. He led it to the remote mountains of Tongbai and Funiu in western Henan.[15]

In early spring 1935 the Twenty-fifth Army moved to nearby southern Shaanxi. One day they were holding a meeting at Yujiahe when Chiang Kai-shek's swiftest division, the Sixtieth, swept down from Zhuyangguan Pass and attacked from the rear. The fighting was ferocious. In 1930, Cheng Zihua had been wounded in the left arm, and he had the habit of holding the arm with his right hand. Now a bullet hit the left arm again, plowing through his right hand and crippling him. (Fifty years later, he had the use of only a clawlike right hand.) Xu Haidong, the political commissar, was struck by a bullet that pierced his head from the right side and emerged at the rear. He was unconscious for more than a month. Dr. Qian Xinzheng, twenty-four in 1935, a graduate of the German Tongji University in Shanghai, stood at the side of the commanders. He, too, was wounded, but not severely. He treated both men with Prontosil, a German precursor of sulfa drugs. Without it, he said, he did not believe he could have saved their lives.[16]

Cheng's wound became badly infected. His arm was operated on with an ordinary sharp-bladed knife. There wasn't even maotai to kill the pain. Hu Huanxian, a political commissar, took over command and somehow they managed to set up a base area in south Shaanxi. They knew that Liu Zhidan and the Twenty-sixth were operating to the north, but had no contact. In July 1935, while maneuvering toward northern Shaanxi—having heard from KMT newspapers that the First Front Army was headed that way—Hu Huanxian was killed. Cheng Zihua and Xu Haidong took over command from their litters, Cheng as political commissar, Xu as military commander.[17]

On September 18, in Cheng Zihua's recollection, the Twenty-fifth Army joined forces with the Twenty-sixth and Twenty-seventh armies at a place called Yongpingzhen in northern Shaanxi and the troops were consolidated into the Fifteenth Army Group. Xu Haidong, still on his stretcher, became commander-in-chief, Liu Zhidan, deputy commander, Cheng Zihua, political commissar, and Gao Gang, director of the Political Department.[18] Everything seemed fine. The combined forces fought a successful battle against a division of the Young Marshal's troops at Ganquan.

Then it happened. The Twenty-fifth Army had captured a KMT officer named Zhang Hanmin. Zhang said that he was an underground Communist and named Liu Zhidan as reference. They paid no attention and executed Zhang out of hand. Then the "Bolshevik" critics of Liu Zhidan convinced the Twenty-fifth that actually Liu Zhidan was an underground KMT man and that his Twenty-sixth Army was permeated with enemies. The arrests started. At first Liu Zhidan was left alone. He was sent off on a mission to take him away while the purge of lower ranks was in progress. But as he was riding down the road he met a young courier with a communication addressed to the Fifteenth Army leaders. The youngster gave it to Liu Zhidan. It contained a list of officers who were to be arrested including himself. Liu resealed the envelope, asked the messenger to take it to Xu Haidong, the Fifteenth Army Group commander. Then he made his way to the security bureau, put his revolver on the desk and said, "I know that you are looking for me." He expected that this would calm their suspicions. Instead, the security men threw him into a cell. It did not occur to them that a real KMT agent would have fled instead of turning himself in. Paranoia was in command.

In 1984 Liu Lizhen, daughter of Liu Zhidan, was a slight, appealingly eloquent woman of fifty-six. In 1935 she was five years old but she had not forgotten that September and October. She and her mother went to the prison. They stood outside, hoping for some sign of Liu Zhidan. There was none.

The authorities did not want people to know who was arrested. They kept Liu Zhidan's horse in prison so it would not be seen standing alone in the stable and start rumors. When the prisoners were led through the streets, hoods were placed over their heads. One day the five-year-old girl and her mother passed a column of hooded prisoners. One of them coughed and they thought they recognized Liu Zhidan.

Liu Lizhen has a small moon face, high cheekbones and an olive complexion. She talks with dignity of what happened half a century ago. A huge pit was dug near the gate tower of Wayaobu. She and her mother visited it. Some said the prisoners would be buried alive there, others that they would be buried in a common grave after being shot or beheaded.

Mao saved the life of Liu Zhidan and the lives of the other prisoners. Had he not arrived at the eleventh hour and sent his rescue mission to Wayaobu, Liu Zhidan and his comrades would have been killed. The death sentences had been approved, one more product of the hysteria that arises within a closed conspiratorial world.

Not until Zhou Enlai was sent to Wayaobu at the end of October were the men set free. By this time soldiers were saying that the whole Red Army would go in, if necessary, to release the prisoners. Mao did not wish to blame the Army men. He felt they had been ignorant victims of something they did not understand.[19]

Liu Lizhen saw her father only once after he was released from prison. "I felt strange," she recalled. "It took me some time to approach him."

He had been shackled, with his legs in chains, and had difficulty walking. Mao put him in charge of organizing and commanding the new Twenty-eighth Army and on February 10, 1936 he set out to fight the KMT in the Eastern Expedition. He was killed in battle at the age of thirty-four.

Liu Zhidan had no hobbies, his daughter said. He liked to smoke. To this day her mother, Tong Guirong, keeps a cigarette burning before his photograph. Tong Guirong at seventy-nine has lost none of the spunk of her north Shaanxi days. A wisp of a woman, she confessed that she had been ashamed to tell us that her marriage with Liu Zhidan was a traditional one, arranged while she was still at her mother's breast and consummated when she was seventeen and Liu Zhidan was eighteen. "I was afraid you would make fun of me," she said with a twinkle. She carried a cane but was strong as iron. She had been hospitalized with typhoid fever when Liu Zhidan died and was not present at the burial.

When in 1943 his body was placed in a memorial shrine at Bao'an, where he was born (the name has been changed to Zhidan in his honor), she had the coffin opened. She was pleased to see he was clad in the overcoat that she had made for him. At his death he had owned nothing but his pistol and his horse. She had asked that they be given to someone who needed them.

She touched her head with a wry gesture and said: "In those days the KMT put a price of two hundred silver dollars on my head." In her youth, she was, she asserts, a "political dropout." She paid no attention to politics until, in 1934, KMT troops came by and ransacked their home. "Then," she said, "I joined the Revolution. Someone said, 'Well, it's about time—what took you so long?'"

Tong Guirong and her daughter, Liu Lizhen, are proud of a snapshot Edgar Snow took of them in Bao'an in 1935, showing Liu Lizhen wearing a small Red Army cap with a red star sewn on by her mother.

When the Cultural Revolution came, the shrine at Bao'an (Zhidan), once smashed by the KMT, was smashed again by the Red Guards. Testimonial plaques from revolutionary leaders were defaced. The family was sent to the countryside. Tong Guirong reminded them: "It's nothing new. Just 1935 over again." Liu Lizhen said it was the same old persecution—this time from the Left. She is a doctor. She was made to work in the countryside. Her husband, Zhang Quan, now editor of the Xi'an newspaper, was sent to a production unit. Liu Zhidan's sister-in-law wrote a novel about him. Kang Sheng, Mao's chief of secret police, persuaded Mao it was a political document supporting Gao Gang (the alleged traitor). She and her husband were arrested and badly treated. So were close friends of the family.

Liu Zhidan's only heritage, his daughter said, her dark eyes intense and serious, was his spirit. To this day when her mother meets old comrades they burst into tears. They still cherish the memory of her father and his contribution to the Revolution.[20]

It was not all crisis in north Shaanxi. There was time for human things. More and more, Mao had been making jokes about Luo Fu and the petite Liu Ying. Since Liu Ying's work with the "Central Team," she and Luo Fu had become almost inseparable. This could hardly escape Mao's eyes. Luo Fu was secretary-general of the Party. He and Mao were together most of the time.

Once they had arrived at Wayaobu, Liu Ying and Luo Fu decided to marry. "We had drawn closer and closer ever since crossing the River of Golden Sands," Liu Ying recalled. "But we didn't start living together until we got to north Shaanxi."

They decided not to have a wedding party. "We were too poor," Liu Ying said. Mao came by. He was very happy about their marriage. He said they had to have a reception. So they did. But no feast.

Luo Fu stayed very close to Mao well into the Yan'an period, then gradually a separation became evident—nothing serious. Luo Fu became deputy foreign minister after the PRC was founded. Liu Ying became friendly with He Zizhen, Mao's wife, and went with her to Moscow in 1937. When Luo Fu became foreign minister, Liu Ying went into the foreign ministry.

The romance of Luo Fu and Liu Ying, he thirty-five and she twenty-seven, was one of the few on the Long March, and one that endured.[21]

There was tragedy, too, in north Shaanxi. Hardly had the Red Army arrived in Wuqi than the commanders of the famous shock regiment, the Fourth Regiment of the Second Division of the First Army, Yang Chengwu and Wang Kaixiang, fell ill of typhoid fever, Wang more seriously than Yang.

A few days later, Yang Chengwu was told that his comrade was dead. Wang Kaixiang had been running a temperature of 105 degrees Fahrenheit and went into delirium. He seized his pistol from under his pillow and put a bullet through his head. He had two favorite possessions, the pistol and a gold watch. All through the Long March he had each night polished his pistol until it gleamed.[22]

At almost the same time, Wang Jiaxiang, who had been carried on the whole March on a litter, took a sudden turn for the worse. General Yang Shangkun was staying with Wang Jiaxiang. He developed a high fever and fell unconscious; it was thought he would die.

Dr. Wang Bin, later to be head of the Army medical service, was caring for Wounded Wang Jiaxiang. Because of his severe stomach wound, a rubber tube had been inserted through which fluids were discharged. Only after Wang was on the verge of death was it discovered that the tube had degenerated and infected his wound. It was withdrawn, the wound was drained, his temperature dropped, and his life was saved.[23]

Wounded Wang Jiaxiang was sent off to Moscow as quickly as possible for treatment. It took the Soviet physicians half a year to close his wound and bring him back to something like normal health. They tried to get his weight up to 132 pounds but never succeeded. He became Chinese representative to the Comintern, taking over from Kang Sheng, who wanted to get back to China.

Home, Mao was home, but there was no end to conflict—conflict with the enemy, random and irrational conflict within the Red Army. But in this land of red dust, of winds, of gullies, of low mountains and dried-out rivers, Mao and the Communists would sink deep roots. They would make northern Shaanxi their home. Not for a week or a month or a year. But for many years. Mao spent only three days in Wuqi. Then he took the road for Wayaobu. Here he would stay until early in 1936, then on to the safe harbor of Bao'an, resting there until January 10, 1937, then on to Yan'an for nearly ten years more, the gestation period of the Revolution.

He had not yet completed the gathering of his flock. For the moment he had only the remnants of his own First Front Army and the quarreling Twenty-fifth, Twenty-sixth, and Twenty-seventh armies. But soon his legions would grow. Soon the Second Front Army of He Long and Xiao Ke, and the Fourth Front Army of the recalcitrant Zhang Guotao, with the remainder of Mao's own forces and the commanders Zhu De and Liu Bocheng, would find their way into the fold. Mao felt certain of this.

He pulled a wooden stool up to the deal table in his new cave at Wayaobu, had his bodyguard light the kerosene lantern that had accompanied him from the day the Red Army clattered over the pontoons at the Yudu River, took his ink stone out of his tin writing box, mixed some fine black ink, picked up his writing brush with its camel's hair tip, dipped it into the ink, and began to write on a strip of fine rag paper. The words flowed easily:

> The Red Army fears not the trials of the Long March,
> One thousand mountains and ten thousand rivers.
> The Five Ridges are but gentle ripples . . .
> Laughter in the thousand li of Minshan's snows
> And smiling faces when the last pass is crossed.

The Long March of 25,000 li, the *Chang Zheng*, the six-thousand-mile journey, had ended. How many lives it had cost would never be known. There had been 86,000 at the start. There were a scant 4,000 at the finish. But this did not tell the story. The ranks had been recruited and re-recruited along the way. By no means all those "lost" men had died. Many were dropouts.

Arithmetic was not the point. This was an epic in blood and courage, in victory and defeat, in despair and hope. Of this sacrifice and bravery would be woven the legend on which China's Revolution would be built.

28

THE GATHERING

IF in the company of the Red Army there existed a Damon and a Pythias, they surely were Xiao Ke, the slim, twenty-six-year-old commander of the Sixth Army, and He Long, the handsome thirty-six-year-old commander of the Second.

On October 22, 1934, the two generals brought their armies together at Muhuang in Yinjiang county in northeast Guizhou, close to the "Four Corners" of Guizhou, Sichuan, Hunan, and Hubei provinces. Four days later they crossed into Sichuan and held a victory feast at Nanyaojie.

Here the forces of the Sixth and Second armies formally united into what was to become the Second Front Army, and here what was to prove the close, enduring association of Xiao and He had its beginning.

There was a moving moment when Political Commissar Ren Bishi read out a telegram of congratulations from the Red Army's high command. Deep in the mountains neither Xiao Ke nor He Long knew that the telegram had come from a Red Army command already ten days into the Long March.[1]

The union of Xiao Ke and He Long aroused none of the psychotic suspicions of the meeting of Mao Zedong and Zhang Guotao. "When we joined He Long," Xiao Ke recalled fifty years later, "there was great joy. We needed him as much as he needed us."

In 1982 Xiao Ke was to write a poem celebrating that occasion. He recited it to a visitor in 1984, scrambling up from his knees, where he was studying a map of the Long March spread out on the floor:

> Eight thousand warriors march with
> Their swords pointing eastward
> With surging waves in the river Yuan and Li
> And vast prairies ablaze . . .

As I recall the past I cherish the memory of
The fallen at Fanjing Mountain.

Xiao Ke and He Long had met during the Nanchang Uprising in 1927. Now their lives would become entwined. They would marry sisters as the Long March was starting and each would have a child, He Long a girl in July or August 1935, Xiao Ke a boy toward the March's end.[2]

He Long made the big speech at Nanyaojie. They had, he said, no real base area. Now they must rely on three things: their feet, their mouths, and their guns. Yu Qiuli, a twenty-year-old very poor peasant with five years of the Red Army behind him, was leader of the military school team. He interpreted He Long as meaning they must keep on the go, use propaganda to win over the masses, and guns to hold off the enemy—a very important message, he thought.[3]

When Xiao Ke and He Long met at Four Corners in the autumn of 1934, He Long possessed a small, poorly defined base, sixty by thirty miles square, with a population of 100,000, too small to support much of an army. For most of their first year, He Long and Xiao Ke operated in and around this area, He Long's old stamping grounds. He was born in 1896 in Sangzhi county, close by Four Corners, in Hongjiaguan village, number three in a poor peasant family, with two elder sisters, one younger sister and a younger brother. He Ying, his oldest sister, had learned the martial arts, commanded a guerrilla outfit, and was killed by the KMT.[4] He Long's father was a tailor. They put their hopes on He Long to restore the family fortunes.

When he was ten years old He Long traveled nearly three hundred miles, bought a hundred horses, and sold them on the way back home, somehow keeping off the thieves. He studied in primary school, farmed for a year, and set up a caravanserai, but all this put him to thinking about the lives of the poor. A teacher, Chen Punan, was a disciple of Sun Yat-sen, and He Long signed up for Dr. Sun's Revolution. "I not only signed but I put my fingerprint on the paper," he remembered.

On the sixteenth day of the second moon of 1916, He Long committed his first revolutionary act. He led a band of peasants armed with big kitchen knives in an attack on a salt tax office, destroyed the office, captured some guns and the tax collector. They chopped off the collector's head.[5]

He Long had learned only a few Chinese characters, but could sign his name. When he gave an order, he wrote the characters of his name on the soldier's left hand. The soldier would go back to his unit, recite the order from memory, then raise his left hand to show He Long's genuine signature. After failure of the Nanchang Uprising in 1927, He Long began to teach himself to write and read. He possessed almost total recall. He would learn a text and repeat it until he knew the characters.[6]

He Long once told his colleagues his philosophy of life: "I believe in luck. You can't stop luck. You can't close a door on luck. And you can't bolt the door against it. It will always win out—if it is there."[7]

He never stood on ceremony. His feet bore deep cracks from walking barefoot or in straw sandals on the Long March. The Peking warlords in 1925 gave him the title of garrison commander and supplied him with a handsome uniform—gold braid and buttons, shoulder boards, gold-and-diamond orders, a handsome yellow sash. He had his picture taken and showed it to his revolutionary comrades. "My evil uniform!" he joked. (In the Cultural Revolution, that would be brought up against him as a display of "warlord mentality.")[8]

Chiang Kai-shek never stopped trying to get He Long back. He sent an old friend of He Long's to try to persuade him to return to the KMT. He Long cursed the man and had him shot. (This, too, was used against him in the Cultural Revolution—"illegal contact with the KMT.") At the same time, Chiang was trying to wipe out He Long's family. The KMT killed one hundred relatives, including his three sisters and his brother.[9]

It was an unlikely combination—He Long, veteran revolutionary, and Xiao Ke, ten years younger, men of contrasting style. He Long was flamboyant and mustachioed. He said he started to wear one at a time when only landlords and warlords did; he didn't see why peasants shouldn't have mustaches too. Helen Snow called him a Lochinvar.

He Long liked to play checkers with Guan Xiangying, his political commissar. Whoever lost had to shave off his mustache. It didn't happen often, but sometimes He Long's mustache would vanish.[10]

He Long, armed with kitchen knives, had raised the flag of revolt while Xiao Ke was an eight-year-old schoolboy. Xiao Ke was still very young to be leading the Sixth Army, but he was accurate, principled, and sure of his ground. He described himself as the son of a "petty intellectual" family, quite poor. Actually his father was a Confucian scholar of a decaying country gentry family. Xiao Ke was born in August 1908 in the Five Ridges of Hunan. Xiao Ke was a studious man, a fine

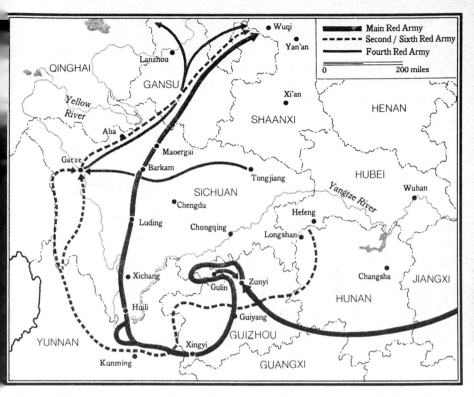

Route of the Second and Sixth Army Groups from the "Four Corners" of Guizhou, Sichuan, Hunan, and Hubei provinces to their juncture with the Fourth Front Army in northwest Sichuan and on to the final rendezvous with Mao Zedong in northern Shaanxi, 1934–36.

poet, slim, freckled, almost totally bald due to a childhood illness. He attended the Whampoa Academy in 1927. An older brother, he told Helen Snow, had been executed for "having relations with bandits."

The two men complemented each other—He Long outgoing, unable to walk down the street without attracting crowds, a fine popular orator; Xiao Ke a bit distant, didactic but possessing a beaver's determination to uncover every facet of a situation, strong in planning, resolute in execution. Both men acknowledged the political wisdom of their chief commissar, Ren Bishi, to whom Xiao Ke gave credit fifty years later for making the Second Front Army so formidable a force.[11]

"He was a fine general," Xiao said of He Long, his voice heavy with emotion as he spoke of his friend, dead more than fifteen years, a tragic victim of the Cultural Revolution. "He was a great revolutionary soldier. He was my dear old commanding officer."

Three weeks before He Long and Xiao Ke met, a remarkable observer had by chance joined the Long March, a foreigner who would (unwillingly) accompany the Red Army for eighteen months and later publish his impressions.

"One day," Xiao Ke explained, "we found ourselves in the old state of Guokong, east of the capital of Guizhou. We had defeated a band of local soldiers and captured the old county town of Huangping."

. In a Catholic church Xiao Ke's men discovered a large-scale map of China—about 36 by 36 inches. It was in French which none could read. Fortunately, said Xiao Ke, a "priest" at the church could speak some Chinese. The man, although Xiao Ke had long forgotten his name, was a Protestant, Rudolf A. Bosshardt, a Swiss of the China Inland Mission.

Bosshardt was brought to Xiao Ke's headquarters. After supper the two sat down at a square table, unfolded the map between them, and Xiao Ke pointed out locations. By the light of a small candle Bosshardt read out the names and together they worked out the Chinese equivalents. The two men spent all night over the map. To Xiao Ke it was an unforgettable occasion. His face lighted up as he spoke of it in the Military Academy.

"How happy we were now that we had a map of Guizhou available!" Xiao Ke exclaimed.

Bosshardt and a second missionary, Arnolis Hayman, spent many months with Xiao Ke, Hayman 413 days, to November 18, 1935, and Bosshardt 560 days, to Easter Sunday, April 12, 1936. They had been taken captive with their wives and Hayman's children but the women and children were swiftly released. Bosshardt's impressions are the only ones of an outsider on the Long March.

To Bosshardt, the day of union of the Sixth and Second armies was one of celebration. While bands played outside the house where he and Hayman were held prisoner he enjoyed his first day of rest since being captured. He and Hayman did their washing. He found that he had been discovered by what he called "China's millions," body lice.

He and Hayman bought two pounds of honey from a passing peasant and had a feast.

Bosshardt was becoming a bit knowledgeable about the Long March. He and Hayman walked in single file. Just ahead marched the color sergeant, carrying a red flag with a black star, in the center of which was a white hammer and sickle. The sergeant had made a waterproof cover for the flag, using the canvas of an oil painting depicting Christ in the manger surrounded by the shepherds and their sheep. The star of Bethlehem gleamed above. "At first," Bosshardt recalled, "it seemed strange to be following the Red banner, but when it was closed I was comforted by realizing that the star I was following was the Bright and Morning Star."

Sometimes the prisoners were roped. He and Hayman would be tied together or there would be a rope held like a dog leash by a guard who walked between them. Prisoners were brought in, interrogated, beaten if they were believed to be spies, then taken out and executed by teenagers wielding broadswords.[12] Along the trail in early morning, he often saw bodies of those executed. To each was pinned a piece of paper explaining the charges against the victim.

Xiao Ke's recollection of Bosshardt was warm. He felt he owed a debt to the missionary for his help with the map. Fifty years after the event, Xiao Ke set in motion a search for Bosshardt, who was found living in England, alive and hearty at the age of eighty-eight. He possessed an excellent recollection of what he had seen as "the second foreigner" on the March, to quote a page one article in the *People's Daily* in October 1984. (Otto Braun was the first foreigner.)

Bosshardt's first glimpse of He Long came in November 1934. The missionary was walking with some prisoners, including a rich young Chinese known as "Fatty Liao." A handsome man described by Bosshardt as "of fine bearing and with a black moustache" rode past and shouted to the prisoner: "Hey, Fatty, you had better hurry up and pay some more ransom or we'll chop off your head." This was He Long. Not long before Bosshardt's release, he was commissioned to crochet baby clothes for He Long's daughter, born at Sangzhi in August 1936. Bosshardt had taught himself to crochet and had gained a name for it, making sweaters, scarves, and mittens for Red Army men. Now He Long's aide appeared with yarn—black, brown, green, purple, and white skeins, German labels on some of the wool. Bosshardt thought it came from a mission. He was asked to copy two children's garments— a little inner Chinese gown and an outer, semi-foreign coat. He made paper patterns and started to work using a "beautiful crochet hook of stainless steel" which he was given.

The troops took to the road before Bosshardt could complete his task. He gave the baby things to He Long not quite finished.[13]

This was not the end of He Long's baby clothes problem. In Yan'an it was decided to send the child, now a year old, to Xi'an. She was called He Jiesheng, "Victoria"—her name means born at a time of victories. Kang Keqing contributed Zhu De's old underwear, very soft and worn, to make Victoria some underclothes.[14]

The prisoners with whom Bosshardt traveled were mostly held for ransom, to help finance the Long March, as Bosshardt thought. The missionary group was held for $700,000. In the end, ten thousand silver dollars were paid for Hayman, nothing for Bosshardt. But a good bit— referred to as "fines"—was squeezed out of the Chinese. Some Chinese were carted about for a year or more, their relatives occasionally paying something. Bosshardt had the impression that there were hundreds or even thousands of prisoners for whom fines were demanded. Landlords generally fled at the approach of the Red Army but often left an elderly relative or a trusted servant behind to keep an eye on their property. The Red Army arrested these people and held them until the landlords paid a suitable fine. When the fine wasn't paid the hostages were sometimes executed. This might also happen if they were too old or ill to keep up with the March.[15]

Bosshardt thought the reason he and Hayman were held so long was a bungled attempt to escape at Christmas 1934. Some missionaries fared far worse. Two Americans, John and Betty Stam, Presbyterians, and their three-month-old daughter were captured in Anhui on September 6, 1934. The Stams were executed and the baby left unattended until it was found twenty-four hours later. The child was called the "Miracle Baby" by the press. The Communists denied responsibility for this case. An elderly missionary named Fergeson of the China Inland

Mission was taken during the time of Bosshardt's captivity and never heard of again.[16]

In January 1936, after Hayman had been released, another missionary was taken prisoner at Shiquan, northeast Guizhou. This was a German priest, Heinrich Kellner of the Society of the Sacred Heart. Kellner was twenty-eight and had been in China two years. He was not sturdy. The forced marches, poor food, inadequate clothing, lack of decent footgear, and erratic routine took a toll. Sometimes Bosshardt and Kellner had horses or mules. More often they walked. Frequently they were housed in a landlord's granary and lay on the grain. But they slept on dirt floors too, usually with a plank for a bed.

Bosshardt's mission colleagues stubbornly sought his release, sending one delegate after another to negotiate. Kellner's mission made no moves to get his liberty.[17]

The Second Army was now moving across Guizhou from east to west, passing through Houchang (Monkey Town) near the river Wu, where a well-to-do householder told Bosshardt that a year earlier "General Zhu De's army" passed that way accompanied by two foreigners, very well dressed, believed to be Russians. One of them may have been Otto Braun. If there was a second, his identity remains a mystery.

Xiao Ke was glad to be moving west. Eastern Guizhou and southwest Hunan were so backward, so poor. Opium was the chief crop. It was not possible to recruit unless the Army accepted opium addicts. Everyone smoked. If a child caught cold the parents blew opium smoke up its nostrils as a cure. The Red Army had an iron rule: no opium smokers. But there was no one else to take. They put the addicts on a program of gradually reducing doses. Medics gave lectures and shots of sulfur dissolved in water. After a month most were able to kick the habit.[18]

Yu Qiuli, in 1984, was a robust, heavyset man with a broad face, hearty laugh, and wide gestures—one-handed because he had lost his left arm. Born in Ji'an county in Jiangxi in 1914, he grew up in an impoverished family that possessed 1.1 mu of land, 0.8 mu of it in rice paddy, 0.3 mu in sesame seed and peanuts (about one sixth of an acre in all). Not enough to feed his father, mother, brother, and himself. At fifteen he joined the Red Army.

As the Sixth moved southwest from Bijie, Yu Qiuli, who had risen to be political commissar of the Eighteenth Regiment, saw He Long and the high command standing beside a bridge on the road to Hezhang. He Long told Yu to take his regiment six miles down the path and set up a block so the army could pass without attack.

Yu found the KMT on a hill near the village of Zezhangba. He sent a platoon to attack them from the flank. It never came back. He ordered a frontal assault.

"I was shocked," he said, "to hear so much light machine gun fire. Then I realized that what I thought were light machine guns was machine pistol fire—twenty-shot machine pistols. We had never seen anything like that. It was state of the art. Top technology. We captured eight of them."

In his Red Army career Yu had never given a stand-or-die order. "That day I gave one," he said. The enemy almost overran his command post. He even mobilized the cooks for combat. At ten o'clock a machine pistol shell crashed into his left arm. It hung at his side. He could see the bone and white tendons.

Somehow he stayed on until nightfall, his arm wrapped in a towel, he gripping it to deaden the pain, bathing it in cold water and sweat. A doctor bound his arm tightly and his men carried him.

"I am a man who has gone through nine deaths," Yu said. Crossing the River of Golden Sands, his arm still bound, his raft overturned, plunging him into the water. A buoyant down quilt kept him afloat and saved his life.

When they joined the Fourth Front Army, doctors took off the bandage. Yu's wound was crawling with white maggots. They cleansed it with Merthiolate and wrapped it in a new bandage, and he was carried over the Grasslands. At Huixian in Gansu in late September, the surgeons amputated, using a Japanese razor to cut the flesh and a saw from the ordnance workshop for the bone. He was given a captured anesthetic. No one knew the proper dose. He almost died.[19]

Now the Army struck over the Wumeng Mountains, to which Mao dedicated a line ("And the majestic Wumeng Mountains roll by, globules of clay") in the poem he wrote on completing the Long March in October 1935.[20]

They stayed in the mountains, as Xiao Ke recalled, about two weeks and emerged March 23, fighting a fierce battle at Hutoushan near Xuanwei, defeating Yunnan commander Sun Du. Warlord Long Yun had just been named commander in chief for Guizhou and Yunnan and wanted his commander to make a showing.

The Red Army drove down to Panxian county, where they had some thought of setting up a soviet base, but around April 1, 1936, they got

a wireless from the Fourth Front Army instructing them to come north.
They were to time their move for March, April, or May, before the
upper Yangtze spring floods.

He Long and Xiao Ke had beefed up their force during their stays
at Bijie and Panxian. They now had about 18,000 men. They were being
followed, usually a day or two behind, by Commander Sun Du, who had
about 24,000 men. (Later, Sun Du said he had believed the Red Army
had 40,000 men.)[21]

He Long and Xiao Ke did not have a "walk-through" deal with Sun
Du or his boss, warlord Long Yun, but they hoped for a somewhat
neutral attitude.

In Bijie He Long met with a distinguished elderly man named Zhou
Suyuan, a former governor of Guizhou and an honored scholar of the
Qing dynasty. He Long asked why he hadn't run away. "Why run
away?" the scholar replied, pointing to the books on his shelves—works
of Marx, Lenin, and other Communists. "You are a Marxist and so am
I." He Long asked him to write warlord Long Yun and commander Sun
Du. The scholar did so. He told them the Red Army could not easily be
beaten, but it was not out to pick a fight. He reminded them of Chiang
Kai-shek's hopes to take over Yunnan and how Chiang had deposed
Wang Jialie in Guizhou.

The letter mentioned a story from the classic *Spring and Autumn
Annals (Jia tu mie guo)*, in which a big king "borrowed" the road of a
small king in order to attack a big enemy and then on the way back
gobbled up the little king. The scholar threw in a reference to the *Shi
You Ming Jian*—twenty lessons of history to be guarded against. The
Hunan warlord He Jian also sent Long Yun a quiet warning to watch
out for games Chiang Kai-shek might be playing.[22]

The warning of He Jian was particularly significant. A staunch anti-
Communist, He Jian had been alarmed by Chiang Kai-shek's success in
taking over Guizhou. He Jian sent a message through his son-in-law Li
Jue, cautioning his Yunnan colleague not to leave openings of which
Chiang Kai-shek could take advantage. The provincial forces, He Jian
emphasized, should look out for each other's interests and not worry
about Chiang's main army troops.

Warlord Long Yun was receptive. He told Li Jue that "probably we
will not catch up with the Red Army." Long Yun and the Hunan forces
did not cooperate with the KMT main forces. The KMT had difficulty
getting supplies and had to travel the rough path along the Golden

Sands River. The KMT troops were not permitted to approach Kunming because Long Yun feared they might turn on him.

"Let the KMT troops catch up with the Reds," Long Yun said. "If you want supplies, ask Chiang Kai-shek," he told them. Warlord Long Yun set his troops to building air raid shelters in Kunming. The Red Army had no planes. The KMT did.[23]

These intrigues did not give He Long and Xiao Ke a free passage to the Golden Sands—but they helped.

By the time Xiao Ke and He Long prepared to jump off from Panxian on their drive to join the Fourth Front Army, warlord Long Yun had the impression they were in bad shape.

So when they cut into Yunnan, planning to cross the Pudu River at a point about fifty miles north of Kunming by a suspension bridge, Long Yun sent a strong force to block them.

The warlord miscalculated. The Communist vanguard captured the suspension bridge April 6, and early in the morning of April 7 routed the special brigade of engineers guarding it.

But discovering the large force warlord Long Yun had mobilized, Xiao Ke and He Long called an emergency conference the night of April 7 and changed plans. They decided to feign an attack on Kunming in hopes of compelling Long Yun to draw back his men. Warlord Long Yun got the message. He pulled his men back to his capital in a hurry, the Red Army crossed the Pudu River near Fumin, and that was it so far as Yunnan was concerned. No more battles.[24]

Of these events, missionary Bosshardt had little knowledge. He knew they had plunged over the Yunnan border, crossing the (Wumeng) mountains, into a network of difficult trails. They were hard for him and much more difficult for Father Kellner, who was rapidly losing strength.

As they began to move over the plain, Bosshardt got hints he would be released. Finally Xiao Ke told him that he would be set free when the Army got close to Kunming, but Kellner would be compelled to continue on.

On Saturday afternoon, April 11, Bosshardt was given a banquet by Xiao Ke. There was easy talk. The general expressed surprise that someone educated abroad like Bosshardt could believe in God. "Surely," Xiao Ke said, "you know we came from monkeys."

Bosshardt told him evolution was only a theory. To his mind, it took "greater faith to believe we evolved from animals than to believe in an Almighty God."

Wang Zhen, then Sixth Army political commissar, now a Politburo member, told Bosshardt: "When you report to the newspapers you must remember we are friends. You have seen how good we are to the poor, how we work on principle and are not common bandits as we are slanderously reported to be."

Xiao Ke said he had no objection to Bosshardt's returning to China as a visitor. They would "even permit you to have a school if you will only refrain from drugging the scholars and the populace with this belief in God."

Father Kellner was present at the dinner. Later Bosshardt warned a man whom he called "Judge Wu," who was in charge of the captives, that unless the priest got better care he would die. He urged that an orderly be provided to make sure Kellner had water to drink and to bathe in, fuel for a fire, straw for a bed. Judge Wu promised to do better. They would see that Kellner got some coffee and cocoa.

Early next morning, the Red Army long since on its way, Bosshardt walked into Fumin. It was Easter Sunday. His ordeal was over.

Years later, Bosshardt learned that ten days after he was freed, the priest died. The Communists confiscated from a very rich landlord an elaborate coffin the man had prepared for his own funeral. Bearers were hired to carry the heavy coffin to a hillside and bury the priest. Then the Red Army marched on. The coffin was heavy, the men had been paid. They took their money and left the coffin on the hillside. Roving bandits spotted it and pried off the lid, expecting to find the silks and brocade a prosperous merchant would be buried in. Instead they found the priest's thin body clad in the cheapest black cotton soutane. Not worth their time. They threw down the lid and departed. That night the wolves came.[25]

It was a race. The Sixth and Second armies raced for the River of Golden Sands from Fumin, taking the main highway for Dali and the beautiful and famous Erhai lakes and on to Heqing and Lijiang, staging points for crossing the Golden Sands. They were 150 miles north and west of Jiaopingdu, where the First Front Army had crossed the river. They were closer to Tibet. The mountains were much, much higher, but there were good trails on both sides of the river and lower passes, not more than ten thousand feet. The Golden Sands ran swiftly at about

6,000 feet altitude. The great snow peak of Jade Dragon, crested with a fine glacier, loomed over the landscape at nearly 20,000 feet.[26]

But there was no opposition. Not a shot was fired. No one laid a hand on the Second Fronters as they tore up the highways. A few torpid KMT biplanes made observation flights.

When they got to Lijiang there was a celebration. People lined the streets. They cheered as the Red Army marched through their town of mixed Han and Naxi minority people. He Long and Xiao Ke were welcomed as conquering heroes. This was, of course, no accident.

In Lijiang there was, as there had been in Bijie, a famous Qing dynasty scholar, not Hanlin (top rank) but Jinshi (second rank), a man named He Songqiao. He Songqiao had been a Sun Yat-sen man. He consulted with Lijiang county magistrate Wang Fengrui. They decided to welcome the Communists as they passed through. Wang Fengrui went off to the mountains. After He Long and Xiao Ke left, he returned. He suffered no ill consequences. He was a protégé of warlord Long Yun. Wang Fengrui's career continued under the Communists. He rose to high office and was still alive at the age of eighty-four in 1984.[27]

Vanguard units picked crossing sites on April 25. There were five main crossing points over a forty-mile span of the Golden Sands. Most of the forces went over at Shigu, an easy section with comfortable sandy beaches. He Long started crossing on April 26. Xiao Ke got to Shigu April 26 after a forty-mile march and began crossing the next day. There were plenty of boats. By dusk of April 28, the eighteen thousand men were across. There had been not one Red Army man killed by enemy action. Seventeen were drowned when a boat was capsized by panicky horses. A bugler stood watch and blew his call every time a KMT plane flew over.

They moved north like clockwork. They had little trouble with the Yi but some with the Tibetans. "We paid for our food in silver dollars," Xiao Ke said. "We got grain and food and other supplies, and when we had sick and wounded, the minority people gave them horses to help out."

On June 30, He Long and his army arrived at Ganzi, now Garze, southwest of Aba, Fourth Army GHQ. A few days earlier, Xiao Ke had led his men in. "They were very friendly," Xiao Ke remembered. "We had just crossed the Snowy Mountains. Each of us got a warm sweater. The spirit was pretty good."[28]

29

RETURN OF THE PRODIGAL

NOTHING seemed to go right for Zhang Guotao, the self-important leader of the Fourth Front Army, after he split with Mao Zedong. (Naturally, he claimed that Mao split from him.)

Zhang's first act was to try to seize leadership of the Chinese Communist movement from Mao. He held a big anti-Mao rally at Aba and another in the lamasery at Zhuokeji. He proclaimed a new Special Independent Government of Nationalities. He declared the Party's Politburo and Central Committee illegal. On October 5, 1935, he announced a new Provisional Central Committee, of which he named himself secretary.*

Later on, he decreed, there would be a Party Congress to ratify this action. Meanwhile the new Central Committee and its secretary would be in charge.[1]

Zhang did not make public the names of his new Central Committee. He had not consulted those he had picked and did not want to embarrass them. It also spared him the embarrassment of public refusals. To this day the list reposes in the archives of his successful opponents, never published. Someone who has seen it has reported that among those whom Zhang did not name were Mao Zedong, Zhou Enlai, Luo Fu, and Bo Gu. But he kept most of the important military men, including Zhu De, Peng Dehuai, Lin Biao, and the top commanders of army groups. He also named Wang Ming, the controversial pro-Russian Politburo member so long resident in Moscow. Naturally, he put on the Committee all of his own top military and political associates.[2]

One of those named to Zhang's Central Committee knew that his name had been placed on the list. This was Zhu De, a captive general

*The proclamation was issued at Zhuomudao, about twenty-five miles from Maerkang.

in Zhang's entourage, technically commander in chief of all the armies but swiftly being reduced by Zhang to a figurehead.

For fifty years, controversy has simmered as to whether, in fact, Zhang Guotao attempted to eliminate Zhu—in plain words, to have him killed.

Conservative Party historians in Beijing say no. They doubt that anything so melodramatic occurred. As in the case of Zhang's threat to use military force against Mao, they contend no smoking gun has been found. "The only evidence we have on that is Agnes Smedley's statement," one of them said.

Agnes Smedley, the American radical, had what her friends called "a crush" on the big, bearlike general. She spent much time in Yan'an in 1937 collecting facts for her biography of Zhu De. She sometimes stayed with him all day in the Yan'an caves. She taught him to dance —she had a portable phonograph and records like "Crying for the Carolinas," "Fiesta," and "Siboney." Zhu De was quite light on his feet. She went into the field with him and accompanied him to the front.[3] She was hardly an unbiased witness. She says in her book *The Great Road* that Zhu De "never talked to me about the year he spent in Sikang as the virtual prisoner of Zhang Guotao." This may be a diplomatic disclaimer. Trouble with Zhang was being downpedaled when she wrote. She quotes an unnamed "Red Army political worker" extensively on Zhu De's year with Zhang. Could this be Zhu De himself?

Her source told her Zhang ordered Zhu De to denounce Mao and cut off all relations with him. Zhu De refused. Zhang then ordered Zhu De to renounce the Party decision to march north. Zhu De refused.

"Zhang Guotao said he would give Zhu De time to think things over, and if he still refused to obey these two orders he would be shot," the source told Agnes Smedley.

The source quoted Zhu De as replying: "That is within your power. I cannot prevent you. I will not obey your order."[4]

It takes only one look at the sturdy woman, sturdy in mind, sturdy in body, dressed in the traditional plain shirtwaist and men's-cut dark-brown pinstripe jacket and trousers of the Chinese women's movement, to sense that Kang Keqing has played a leading role in China's Revolutionary history. She made the Long March at Zhu De's side, a soldier-comrade ("I always called him comrade, not husband").[5]

Kang Keqing's antagonism toward Zhang Guotao has not dimmed

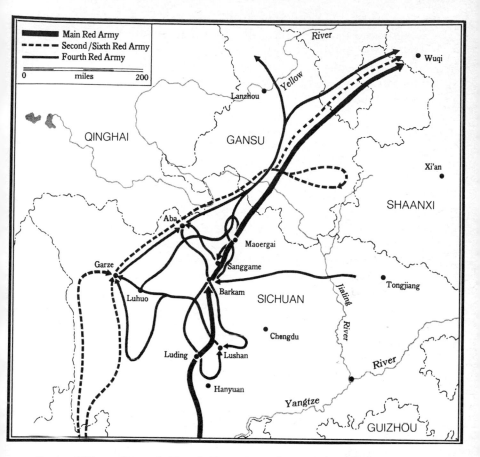

Route of Zhang Guotao's Fourth Front Army from northern Sichuan in spring, 1935, to northwest Sichuan, juncture with Mao Zedong's First Front Army and maneuvers finally leading to the arrival of the Fourth Army in Bao'an in December 1936.

with the decades. In the autumn of 1984, at age seventy-three, she was still convinced that Zhang had put "repeated pressure" on Zhu De, hoping to win him to his side.

"Zhang then played a petty trick on Zhu De," she said. "He had his horse slaughtered and he had his security detachment taken away. And he separated us so that we could not see each other."

Zhu De had spoken to her about that. He said: "These petty tricks are designed to kill a person without using a knife."

The killing of the horse and removal of the guards had occurred as the army was preparing to move from Aba. Zhu De had no animal to ride. He was ready to make the march on foot, but some soldiers found him another animal. The notion of the army's commander in chief walking down the road like an ordinary foot soldier had touched their consciences. Kang Keqing had the task of rounding up stragglers. She had been given a mule to help in her work. It was left behind—deliberately, in Kang Keqing's opinion. On another occasion, some wounded soldiers tried to take it from her.

Did Zhang deliberately try to kill Zhu De?

"I said these were petty tricks," she repeated sternly, lips tight, face serious. "Taking away the commander's horse and his guard troops are major moves."

There were more occasions when there was no horse and the commander had to walk. No longer was he served in the special GHQ mess. He had to organize his own food supply. Not always easy.

The experts might argue, but there was no doubt in Kang Keqing's mind of Zhang's intentions. Perhaps he did not contemplate direct action, but he deliberately put Zhu De at risk.[6]

Zhang Guotao and his men were "going to march to Chengdu and eat rice." The slogan was proclaimed after the meeting at Zhuokeji to denounce Mao. The soldiers liked it. Hu Zenggui was an ordinary soldier with Zhang's Ninth Army. He was sixty-three in 1984 and had joined the Army as a Red devil when he was thirteen. He painted slogans on village walls: "Rise Up and Defend the Homeland." "Go North and Fight the Japanese." He remembered there was a song: "Let's Fight for Chengdu." He liked that very much. No one was fond of the Tibetan country, Tibetan food, the Grasslands, and the Snowy Mountains.[7]

A soft-spoken man of sixty-eight named Ye Yingli had worked in the telephone team at Fourth Front Army GHQ and got a close look at

Zhang Guotao and his commanders. Zhang communicated with the army groups, Mao, and the Central Committee by wireless. Telephone communications were used within the Fourth Front Army. Zhang liked to make the calls himself. If they didn't go through, he was quick to fly into a temper. (Many high-ranking officers had quick tempers. When the dust settled they would be friendly again.) Operator Ye felt that Zhang and Zhu De stayed together, marched together, and ate together, but Zhu De had no real authority.[8]

Many soldiers were not aware of the friction at the top. But rumors spread about Zhu De—about his horse being slaughtered, his guards being taken away, about him and Liu Bocheng being under constraints. One soldier heard Zhu De was made to carry water for three days.[9]

General Yang Shangkun remembered Zhu De telling him that he had been "under a certain degree of restraint." Zhu De said he met and spoke with lower ranks of officers and men of the First Army down to company level. This made Zhang Guotao very uneasy.

General Yang did not believe that Mao or the Central Committee ever thought of rescuing Zhu De and Liu Bocheng. General Yang once proposed to Mao that he exchange a high Fourth Front officer for Liu Bocheng. Mao rebuked him.

"If you propose an exchange for someone else," Mao said, "he [Zhang] will probably have Liu Bocheng killed. Liu is safe and can live under present circumstances."

No personal messages were exchanged between Mao and the detained commanders.[10]

Zhang's drive on Chengdu started well. He had eighty thousand men with the addition of the First Front units. They trudged south from Zhuokeji in fine October weather. True, the winds were cold, many troops still wore summer uniforms, and food was not abundant. But there was little enemy opposition. They captured Danba, Maogong, and Dawei, routing some three thousand KMT troops and taking many prisoners.[11]

Fearing an attack on Chengdu, the KMT began to mass forces. They brought forward the Twenty-fourth KMT Army, the Twentieth, and the Twenty-eighth. The KMT "model division" defended Tianquan, a mountain pass on the approach to Chengdu.

Zhang started October 10 from Danba, heading toward Tianquan and Luding and the famous bridge. He was moving in reverse fashion over much of the route that Mao had followed in coming north.

On October 24, Zhang's central column, including the Thirtieth Army, the Thirty-first Army, and the Twenty-fifth Division of the Ninth Army, all under the command of Wang Shusheng, with Li Xiannian as the political commissar, crossed the Jiajin, the Great Snowy Mountain, and came down to assault Baoxing. The right column crossed the Dadu River and carried out a surprise attack on Tianquan, defeating the KMT model division. Zhang drove northeast to Lushan, getting closer and closer to Chengdu. He destroyed or captured about ten thousand KMT troops.[12]

The Fourth Army was now roughly sixty miles southwest of Chengdu, advancing on a main road. Zhang was full of confidence.

Chiang Kai-shek massed about eighty regiments—some 200,000 men—to defend Chengdu. He put his men in a rough semicircle north, east, and south of the advancing Fourth Army, which on November 16 took Baizhang. Three days later, the KMT counterattacked with possibly ten brigades, three miles east of Baizhang. They were supported by planes and heavy artillery. The attack came in waves, one wave of regiments after another.

Baizhang sat amid low hills and open level ground. No natural defenses. The contemporary traveler notes a large hill on the outskirts, possibly held by the KMT. The Red Army was driven back to Minshan Mountain in the south and Nine Peak Mountain in the north. In seven days, Zhang Guotao lost at least ten thousand men.

Zhang pushed Xu Shiyou, his Fourth Army commander, into another desperate encounter with Xue Yue, Chiang's best general. "I had never had a whole regiment of mine wiped out in one stroke by the enemy," Xu Shiyou recalled. "I was deeply shocked." Two thirds of his Thirty-fourth Regiment was destroyed. The commander and political commissar were killed.[13]

Fifty years later, Li Xiannian could not restrain his bitterness over Baizhang: "I was a commander in that operation. We didn't win. We lost. We had to retreat. Zhang's plans were impossible. We went north. The people were Tibetans. They didn't speak our language and we were there and we had to eat and we took their sheep and cattle—how could we have a good relationship?"[14]

Zhang had to pull his troops all the way back to Ganzi in Sikang, desolate Tibetan country, safe from Chiang Kai-shek but distant from any pertinent battleground. His combat strength by February 1936 was down to forty thousand. It was a low point. "To the Tibetans," he wrote, "the Red Army was just a hateful tribe that came to rob them of their food." The Living Buddha of Ganzi told him: "The Red Army is in a state of poverty. Its action in searching for food and other supplies is worse than that of Liu Wenhui [the KMT commander]."[15] There was no fighting. Survival was the problem.

Now, unexpectedly, a man from Moscow arrived on the scene. He was Lin Yuying, cousin of Commander Lin Biao. Lin Yuying had been in Moscow since 1932–33. He was the Chinese representative to the Profintern, the labor subsidiary of the Comintern, working with Wang Ming. Since Chen Yun's arrival in Moscow in August 1935, efforts to get back in touch with China had redoubled. It was not easy. One mission was sent from Outer Mongolia, disguised as a traders' caravan. It was carrying wireless apparatus. South of the Gobi, Ma cavalry or roving bandits wiped it out.

Lin Yuying was flown to Ulan Bator, capital of Outer Mongolia. He may have been parachuted over the border into northern Shaanxi. He carried no radio apparatus. No documents. No codebooks. No credentials. Nothing to give him away. He was disguised as a small trader.

He had memorized his instructions, particularly the text of the Comintern declaration of August 1 on the united front (which had supposedly originated with the Chinese Party), of which Mao knew nothing.

Lin arrived in northern Shaanxi in late November or early December. One day he was walking down a trail not far from Bao'an when, in a small village, he bumped into Luo Fu. Mao and Zhou Enlai were at the front. On their return, Lin submitted his report.[16]

There was much to tell. Isolated and preoccupied with the Long March and survival, cut off from the outside world, Mao knew little of the events that obsessed Moscow—the rise of Hitler, the convergence of Germany, Italy, and Japan, the danger of fascism and, as Stalin saw it, of a global offensive against the Soviet Union.

Stalin feared a two-front war—Hitler in Europe and Japan in the East. China suddenly occupied a key place. Stalin wanted a united front with Chiang Kai-shek, to hold off Japan. First there had to be a united front of Communists. There was no room now for a quarrel between Mao and Zhang.

The first step was to establish contact with Zhang Guotao. Mao and Zhang exchanged regular—if chilly—wireless messages by code. In late December or early January 1936 (according to Zhang's recollection), Mao wirelessed him of the arrival of Zhang Hao (this was Lin Yuying's

Party cover name) as head of a "Comintern Commission."[17] Zhang's reaction, in his own words, was "ecstatic." Mao sent a message from Lin, advising Zhang of the new united front resolution of the Comintern. Lin said he had hoped to come to Sikang, but "because of transportation difficulties" did not know whether he could make it.[18]

Lin was an old friend and associate of Zhang's and had his confidence. They had worked together in the labor movement as early as 1922, when Lin joined the Communist Party. A younger brother, Lin Yunan, had also worked with Zhang. Lin Yuying studied in Moscow before 1925 and held important posts in Shanghai, Hankou, and Harbin.

Lin worked hard to bring about reconciliation between Zhang and Mao. And he had other assignments. He told Mao that Moscow was agreeable that the Red Army go to Mongolia, if necessary, in order to survive. The same thing applied to Zhang—he could go to Xinjiang, on the Soviet border.

Lin Yuying brought a Comintern recommendation that the Chinese Communists establish international connections. No longer should they be a tiny reclusive band fighting in the deep recesses of China. This instruction may have opened the way for Edgar Snow to go to northern Shaanxi in the summer of 1936. Mao had been told specifically that he should establish "international" connections. Snow had been trying to get to the "Red areas" for some time. Once Lin Yuying arrived, Snow's permission soon came through, facilitated by Liu Shaoqi, who had just reestablished the Party's underground northern bureau at Tianjin.[19]

Lin's wireless diplomacy brought Zhang around. He quietly dropped his "Provisional Central Committee" in return for the promise —underwritten by Lin—of a Party congress to resolve all organizational questions. Mao agreed to acknowledge Zhang as head of the "Southeast Bureau" of the Central Committee. Actually, it was intended as the "Northwest Bureau," but there was a mistake in coding.[20]

By the time Xiao Ke and He Long had arrived at Ganzi, Lin's deal had been worked out. Zhu De had been returned to his post as commander in chief and the arrival of the Second and Sixth armies gave him more self-confidence. Liu Bocheng was back as chief of staff and Zhang was ready to take off to join Mao once again. Much of the bad atmosphere, Xiao Ke felt, had been dissipated.[21]

There was one catch. Zhang had wrested approval from Moscow for his long-desired expedition to the west—where, in Xinjiang province, if Zhang is to be believed, Stalin had promised a supply line. Zhang was to contend that Stalin favored a westward expedition to keep the Communists far from Chiang Kai-shek and avoid a collision.[22]

Zhu De, the grand old warrior, gave the order to cross, for the third time, the Snowies and the terrible Grasslands, which Xu Shiyou called the "death zone," and join up with Mao Zedong in northern Shaanxi. The armies did not move out until July 14, 1936, to give the Second Front Army a bit of rest.[23]

By August, the forces were circling south of Lanzhou on the approaches to Ningxia and the Yellow River when a dispute broke out. Zhang wanted to go north across the Yellow River to Ningxia, and then either north to the Mongolian frontier or west to Xinjiang—in either case to establish contact with the Russians. His political commissar, Chen Changhao, favored a base in southern Gansu, which would, in effect, be an extension of Mao's northern Shaanxi base.[24]

It was the first time Zhang and Chen Changhao had had a major dispute. In the end Chen agreed to go along with Zhang's decision, which in fact had the approval of Mao Zedong. There seems little doubt that Moscow had given its blessing to the Yellow River adventure as part of the package deal worked out by Lin Yuying.

Li Xiannian was shown a wireless message from Mao and Wang Jiaxiang specifically ordering Li's Thirtieth Army to cross the Yellow River. Li Xiannian recalled he read the telegram twenty times to be sure "to get the meaning deep in my memory."

Li Xiannian had no doubts: "This was a different case from the earlier efforts by Zhang to split the Red Army forces. The crossing was in conformity with specific orders of the Central Committee."[25]

Zhang tried to persuade other armies to join him—both the Second Front and the First. George Hatem, the American medic, happened to be with Zhang one afternoon in a little hut beside a dried-out lake. There were a lot of maps spread about and Zhang was trying to argue He Long into bringing his Second Front Army across the Yellow River. He Long refused. *"Qu ni ma di,"* he told Zhang. "Go fuck your mother."[26]

The order set up the worst disaster ever to befall the Red Army— the destruction of Zhang's Fourth Front Army. The Yellow River crossing was successful. It was made at what Li Xiannian called "Tiger Crossing," Hubao, not far from Jingyuan. There were only one hundred casualties. It was what came later that brought on tragedy.[27]

When 20,000 of Zhang's 35,000 men were across the river, a crack KMT division moved in, seized the crossing, and split Zhang's forces. The Ninth and Thirtieth armies, the Fifth Army (Mao's old-ironsides) and the headquarters detachments of Commander Xu Xiangqian and Political Commissar Chen Changhao (who actually ran the operation) had crossed to the west bank. Zhang Guotao, Zhu De, the Fourth and Thirty-first armies, the cadet school and staff were marooned on the south. They never got over.[28]

The annihilation of the forces north of the river was carried out by Ma cavalry. The Ma horsemen were savage and skillful, white-turbaned, armed with rapid-firing carbines, scimitars, whips. They rode like the wind. They could cover in two hours on their short-legged ponies distances it took foot-slogging Red Army men all day to traverse. The Mas were tall, heavy-bearded, almond-eyed, with Caucasian features. According to Edgar Snow, they bathed five times a day.[29]

The Ma forces blocked the Communists from going north, and after consultation with Zhang they moved west. Many years later, Li Xiannian said that had they gone west immediately, they could have taken western Gansu and Xinjiang without trouble. Now it was too late. The Ma horsemen had tasted blood. The Moslems wiped out the women's regiment. The two thousand women were killed, tortured, raped, sold in the local slave markets.[30]

Somehow the doomed force, the "west wing," as Zhang Guotao called it, struggled on, harassed by the attacks of the Moslem cavalry. Telephone operator Ye Yingli was in the Thirty-ninth Division of the Fifth Army. They were encircled at Linze, south of the Hei He River and north of the Qilian Mountains, but they broke out and joined remnants of the Thirtieth and Ninth armies.[31]

There was consultation with the Central Committee in Shaanxi. They still had a wireless. Shaanxi told them to try to fight their way back. This was impossible. They went on west. The Ma cavalry closed in. The last of the Ninth Army was destroyed. The political commissar was killed; the commander, Sun Yuqing, was put up to a cannon's muzzle and blown to bits. Li's deputy Xiong Houfa was killed.[32]

The survivors were disheartened. Broken units. No food. The commanders dead. "Only spirit got us through," Li Xiannian said. "If we didn't fight, we would have our heads chopped off."

A meeting was held. Chen Changhao displayed a telegram from the Central Committee calling him back to Shaanxi. He and General Xu Xianqian left March 16, 1937. Li Xiannian was put in command.[33]

They headed for the mountains. Again the Ma cavalry charged. Another meeting was convened in the lonely Kanglongsi temple, high in the mountains, a deserted spot. The enemy had been left behind. It was decided to split into small bands and try to slip through. One commander, Cheng Shizai, killed himself. Telephone operator Ye stayed behind in a unit that was supposed to provide cover for Li Xiannian and what was left of the Fourth Army. They dispersed into groups of four and five to make their way back to Shaanxi. Operator Ye got as far as Wuwei in Gansu, where he and many others, dressed as beggars, were rounded up by the KMT and put on roadwork. "They probably knew we were Red Army men," said operator Ye, "but they preferred just to let us work ourselves to death."[34]

Li Xiannian led his band over the high Qilian Mountains and down into the Qaidam salt basin in Qinghai. They had no maps. They computed their position by compass and the stars. They calculated they had reached Jiuquan Pass at the end of the Great Wall, coming up to Anxi, close to the ancient silk route that leads through the Buddhist sanctuary of Dunhuang, west to the oases of Hami, Qulja, Kashi, Samarkand, and on to Persia.

Then, as Li Xiannian said in 1984, shaking his head, he attacked Anxi. One more disaster. Hundreds of casualties. After that he had possibly a thousand men and women left. They were driven into the Gobi. No roads. No names. No food. No water. No hope.

One day a plane appeared in the western sky, circled, and landed. A man in brown leather flying togs tumbled out. It was Chen Yun, Party representative extraordinary, last heard of going off to Moscow to tell about Zunyi. He had been sent to Urumchi on a rescue mission. The plane picked up Li Xiannian, flew him to Lanzhou, and he came into Yan'an by truck, arriving January 1, 1938, the last man back home— except for his troops. Few more than a thousand arrived in the spring of 1938. They had been saved by the new era of KMT-Communist cooperation brought about by the Xi'an Incident—the kidnapping of Chiang Kai-shek, December 14, 1936.

When, as it finally did, the reunion of the Fourth Front Army of Zhang Guotao and the First Army forces actually came about in the old market town of Huining, eighty miles east and slightly south of Lanzhou, there was an American on hand to witness it.[35]

He was George Hatem, born in Buffalo, New York, educated at the

University of North Carolina and the American University at Beirut. He had a medical degree from the University of Geneva in Switzerland. He was twenty-six years old and he had bright brown eyes. There was not much he missed.

Troops of the Fifteenth Army of the First Front Army had broken into Huining October 2, 1936, through the west and north gates. There were eight hundred men in the assault force and only four hundred local defenders. The KMT tried to recapture the town October 5, but were defeated. More First Army troops, commanded by the veteran Chen Geng, moved into Huining, a fine old walled city with a population of about two thousand and handsome north, south, east, and west gates. Now only the west gate, refurbished in very handsome style in 1983–84, remains.

The town blazed with banners, slogans, and flags. When the Fourth Army men came in, commanded by General Xu Xiangqian, there were cheers, shouting, and jubilation. It was a glorious autumn day, sun shining, warm, no frost in the morning, a bit chilly at night. Perfect autumn weather.[36]

The harvest was in, grain piled up in sheaves, awaiting a freeze to harden the courtyard earth so that the flails could do their work. A few peasants were cleaning up the fields for winter. This was not wheat country. In 1936 they were growing millet, corn, buckwheat, for the most part. And potatoes, squash, pumpkins, all in from the fields, piled next to the plaster walls of the houses. Some strings of peppers still drying.

There was jollity on the night of October 8, and more the next day, when Zhang Guotao and Zhu De arrived with the headquarters detachment. Liu Bocheng was not present. He had been wounded crossing the River Wei.[37]

The big celebration was held October 10, outside the Confucian temple which still stands in the heart of Huining. In that time—but no longer—a great square extended before the temple. Here fairs were held several times a year.

Hatem, a short, energetic man, was just breaking in as a Red Army medic, having arrived in northern Shaanxi in the company of Edgar Snow a few months earlier. He sat on the platform in front of the temple with the big shots—Zhang Guotao, Xu Xiangqian, Zhu De, Peng Dehuai, Nie Rongzhen, Lin Biao, and all the others. He attracted a lot of attention. No one knew who he was, except that he was an obvious foreigner. Everyone knew the Comintern had had a hand in bringing about this reunion. Word quickly circulated. Hatem was the Comintern man.[38]

Zhu De spoke. No one seems to remember what he said. Telegrams of congratulation from the Central Committee in northern Shaanxi were read. The guests gorged themselves on newly slaughtered mutton, chicken, pork. There was *mingning jiu,* a local wine. Everyone laughed and smiled. There was no rush to leave this pleasant place. Most of the forces stayed until around October 20. He Long and Xiao Ke didn't arrive until October 19 and 20. Their troops had bypassed Huining.[39]

Hatem, not yet possessing his Chinese name of Ma [horse] Haide, jotted down his impressions: Of Zhu De: "Thin as a ghost but strong and healthy . . . a full growth of beard . . . does not look like a military commander . . . looks like the Father of the Red Army . . ."

Of Zhang Guotao: "The political commissar . . . fat, tall, and smooth. I wonder how he kept so fat while the others lost every ounce of excess weight . . ."

Of the day: "What a reunion . . . men threw their arms around each other, laughing and weeping."[40]

On December 2, Zhang Guotao, Zhu De, and Zhou Enlai rode into Bao'an. Lin Biao met them at the outskirts and led the way to the Red Army school. There stood Mao and his men in front of the academy. The students cheered. Mao Zedong and Zhang Guotao climbed up to a wooden rostrum. They made speeches. Each congratulated the other. The Long March had ended. The brethren again were as one. Mao and his armies had marched 25,000 li—6,000 miles. The others had marched at least as far. They had climbed the heights, crossed the rivers, fought the good battles, beaten back the enemy, and carried the word to the people.

Ahead lay a nation to make anew.

30

"COLD-EYED, I SURVEY THE WORLD"

A T the end of June in 1959, Mao Zedong made his way up the lovely mountain of Lushan, a 4,900-foot peak high over the valley of the Yangtze, well to the east of Wuhan, that great industrial city known as one of China's three "ovens." While Wuhan sweltered, cool clean air flowed about Lushan's crown of flowers, a favorite summer spot for missionaries. Mao loved it.

Mao had just visited his boyhood home of Shaoshan, near Changsha. The experience had moved him. In the years since he last saw Shaoshan before taking the road of revolution in 1927, there had been, as he wrote, "bitter sacrifice" and "bold resolve" to make the "sun and moon shine in new skies."

Now, sitting in a wicker chair on a terrace looking out on the valley of the great river, waiting for his comrades to join him, Mao again, as so often in the past, took brush in hand and with the bold strokes of his calligraphy wrote a poem, which he called "The Ascent of Lushan":

> I have leapt over four hundred turns to reach the green crest.
> Now, cold-eyed, I survey the world beyond the seas . . .[1]

Words to ponder as his comrades assembled on this perfumed peak a scant two hundred miles from Jinggangshan, which Mao had climbed with his ragged "Red bandits" in 1927, a hunted man, a price on his head, name unknown, faith burning like a coal in his breast.

Belief in his cause had taken him up Jinggangshan. It had carried him over the thousand mountains and the ten thousand rivers of the *Chang Zheng*. When his remarkable band assembled in northern Shaanxi, when all the armies had gathered—his own First Front Army, the Second Front Army of He Long and Xiao Ke, the Fifteenth Army

Group, and even the remnants of Zhang Guotao's Fourth Front Army —that faith had hardened to steel. The revolutionary company was complete. The cost of their March had been extraordinary in lives and sacrifice. Much more agony lay ahead. But the gains had been even greater.

The leading cadres and commanders had survived, and most would survive the battles still to come. The deepest losses had been among those left behind in southern Jiangxi. But even there a handful survived.

There had been fierce battles with Chiang Kai-shek and fierce battles among themselves. Thoughts of these struggles could not have been far from Mao's mind as he waited for his comrades to assemble for the Politburo meeting and the plenary session of the Central Committee that was to follow.

In the Long March not one leading revolutionary had gone over to the enemy. With every li of the 25,000 they had grown stronger, until Mao's leadership became unchallenged. The March had started amid a reek of suspicion, jealousy, intrigue, fears, with Mao on the sidelines. It ended with hard confidence. Mao had come to the fore and with pragmatic diplomacy won over his enemies. Only Zhang Guotao slipped away in 1938, to join Chiang Kai-shek, then on to exile in Hongkong and Canada. Bo Gu took over *Liberation Daily*, and was on the way to an important role in the Revolution that lay ahead when he died in the 1946 plane crash. Luo Fu and Wang Jiaxiang had become Mao's staunch supporters. Zhou Enlai, his most skillful rival, was now his brilliant chief of staff.

There was much for Mao to think about, sitting in his wicker chair, looking off into the blue horizon. Northern Shaanxi—who would ever have chosen it for a revolutionary base? Desolation, isolation, endless loess hills, brown, barren, no trees, no grass, no water, cruel winds that whipped the flinty sand into your face like shrapnel, the peasantry poor, illiterate, sparse, diseased. Xi'an, China's ancient capital of Changan, was a week's travel distant over mountain and desert. For generations, armed bands had made the hills their haunt, a land of anarchy, feudal clans, and secret societies.

Yet, as Mao well knew, it had proved an auspicious environment for the Revolution, particularly after the Xi'an Incident in December 1936, which led to a truce between the KMT and the Communists and a united front against Japan. In Yan'an, Mao had been able to think and write and ponder China's future. Here he had welded his movement into the elite revolutionary corps that won China. Here had been born out of the spirit of the Long March what came to be called the Yan'an spirit—the philosophy, the structure, the tactics from which Mao created his Communist state.

Mao and his men and women had gone forward under the banner of the Long March to win China. They had defeated Chiang Kai-shek and driven him from the mainland despite American support for the KMT and Stalin's effort to save for Chiang an empire south of the Yangtze. They had made their way in the world. They had fought the United States to a standstill in Korea, and as Mao well knew, they had been and still were fighting to create an economic, political, and social system that would bring China into the modern world.

It had all happened so swiftly. More swiftly than anyone had expected. More swiftly than even Mao had expected, although perhaps as he sat in the sunshine atop Lushan he had forgotten this.

George Hatem, the American doctor who saw China's Revolution from the inside after going to north Shaanxi in 1936 with Edgar Snow, was asked in 1984 if he had known Deng Xiaoping in Bao'an in 1936. Of course, he replied, everyone knew Deng Xiaoping. Did he ever think then that Deng might one day be the leader of all China? "Never," said George with his twinkle. "But I never thought Mao would either. We were not thinking then of the Revolution coming in our lifetime. We thought it would be in the next generation—the one after Mao."[2]

Now, as Mao sat on the mountain, his poem finished, waiting for his comrades, his mind would have focused on the problems of the present —the aftermath of his Great Leap Forward (backyard steel mills) and the drive to put all the peasants into communes (blue ants). His deep split with Russia and Nikita Khrushchev (atom bombs), and the views and attitudes of some of his own comrades (critical).

"Cold-eyed, I survey the world beyond the seas . . ." Mao had written in his poem. Cold-eyed . . . There would not be much poetry about this gathering of the heroes of the Revolution.

Tough old Pong Dehuai, China's commander in the war against the Japanese and in the war against the Americans in Korea, had been down in Hunan. He had gone to his native village of Wushi and to Mao's village of Shaoshan. He wanted to check on reports that something was

very amiss in the countryside as a result of the Great Leap Forward.*
Peng found a disaster. Peasants without food, fields unsown, industry
wrecked, officials in disarray, production figures cooked—exaggerated
again and again on orders from Beijing. No one was so blunt and honest
as Peng. He put his views into a letter to Mao. Mao reacted as though
Peng had put a bomb under his chair. Peng was removed from office,
exiled, shunned for sixteen years, and finally murdered. Nor was Peng
the only one. "This was the end," a thoughtful Chinese observer said.
"After the Hundred Flowers drive for 'free expression' by intellectuals,
whose heads were then figuratively chopped off, and after Lushan, no
one talked back to Mao. Everyone shut up. It was too dangerous. The
Hundred Flowers silenced non-Party people. Lushan silenced the
Party. It led straight to the Cultural Revolution."[3]

First Peng was sent away from Zhongnanhai, the leadership compound adjoining the Forbidden City. He was put into the Wu Family
Gardens in the western suburbs of Beijing. There he did manual labor.
As he wrote: "I never had so much as a moment of rest in my life as a
soldier. Now I have nothing to do in my old age except grow peaches."
In 1962 he sent Mao a letter of eighty thousand characters, in which he
set forth his life and his philosophy. (He sent parts of his draft for
safekeeping to Wushi village.) He had a reprieve in November 1965
when Mao sent him to Sichuan as deputy chief of military construction
(Mao feared the Americans were about to attack). The job didn't last
long. The Cultural Revolution was in the wings and soon Peng was in
the hands of the interrogators. Again and again he wrote out his life
story, believing that if he told the truth he would be released. He was
not. He was beaten and beaten and beaten. He was interrogated and
interrogated. He was knocked to the floor by heavy fists and kicked by
jackboots until his lungs were perforated and his ribs broken. He was
hauled through the streets on public display. He was sixty-eight when
this began and seventy-six before it ended. He was tough. He was
questioned 130 times. Finally he could no longer rise from his bed. He
was deprived of the right to sit up, to drink water, to go to the toilet,
to turn over in bed. His body collapsed and he died on November 29,
1974. He had not confessed a word.[4] General Yang Shangkun, his

---

*Some foreign specialists estimate ten to twenty million peasants died of famine in
the aftermath of the Great Leap. No official estimates have been made available.

friend, wrote: "Peng Dehuai was a man who dared to seek out the truth in an effort to save China."

What was the "crime" that Mao sought to beat out of Peng? That the old marshal had headed a "military club" which conspired to overthrow him. There was, of course, neither "club" nor conspiracy.

Cold-eyed, I survey the world . . . No longer was Mao drawing his Long March men close to him. Luo Fu had compared Mao to Stalin as "very strong-handed in rectifying people."[5] Mao showed Luo Fu his strong hand. A month after Lushan, Luo Fu lost his job as first deputy foreign minister and was sent to do economic work. Little Liu Ying, his wife, lost her foreign office job.

Liu Ying had faced the perils of the Long March without a qualm. At seventy-five, as she told of her husband's last days, she was close to tears, clutching her handkerchief and plucking at the cloth of her well-tailored gray jacket. They tried to fabricate an espionage charge against him: spying for the Soviet Union. "China has such feudal traditions," Liu Ying said, "that when the husband suffers, the wife does too." They wanted her to say her husband had spied for Moscow. He was put into prison. So was she. "You must tell about it," she was told. "It will be a sérvice to the Party." She wouldn't do it. Mao, she told her interrogator, believed in seeking "truth through facts." "So I was regarded as being unable to draw a clear line between my husband and my job," she said.

Luo Fu was hauled in front of the Red Guards for "struggle" sessions. Liu Ying was made to watch. On three days' notice, they were exiled at the order of Lin Biao to Guangdong, into the hands of a military command in the Zhaoqing area, west of Canton. For six years they lived there in protective custody. Luo Fu wrote economic papers—but who looked at them? His health went from poor to bad—hypertension, heart disease. He could not get permission to go to Beijing for treatment. He asked for a transfer to his home county near Shanghai. Refused. Instead he was sent to Wuxi, in Jiangsu. Medical treatment was inadequate. He died July 1, 1976, at the age of seventy-six. There was no memorial service. In 1978, he—along with Peng Dehuai and others—were "rehabilitated." Finally, a memorial service was held and Liu Ying, too, was rehabilitated. With the aid of Hu Yaobang, general secretary of the Party, she became a member of the Party Discipline Committee.[6]

Zhu Zhongli was twenty-three, "very young," as she explained, when she met Wang Jiaxiang—Mao's partner in the "litter conspiracy"

—in October 1938 at the Sixth Plenary Session of the Sixth Party Congress. She remembered the moment. She was a doctor, on duty at the meeting, and was standing at the door of the hall when Mao, Zhou Enlai, and Wang Jiaxiang entered. Mao made a pun about a "leather company" which she didn't understand and she blushed. "If you want to run that leather company," Mao said, "you're going to have to learn not to blush."

It must have been a pretty blush. Wang got an introduction and soon they were married. Wang Jiaxiang had just brought back from Moscow an important message in which Stalin and the Comintern recognized Mao as leader of the Chinese Party and told the Party to stop arguing about it. Nor, said Stalin, should the Chinese be afraid of being submerged in the sea of a Nationalist revolution as a result of the united front policy.

Wang almost didn't make it back to Yan'an. He was attacked by bandits south of Lanzhou. His bodyguard ran away. He was carrying a load of Party propaganda, some guns and a large supply of U.S. dollars. He managed to convince the bandits all he had was paper. Then between Xi'an and Yan'an his car tumbled over a cliff. No damage except loss of his spectacles.

Wang and Zhu Zhongli had no children. She had a miscarriage and then a hysterectomy. He had a son by his first wife, who had died in childbirth.

This man to whom Mao again and again had given credit for his recovery of power on the Long March in 1934 was in 1967 arrested, dragged to public platforms, cursed by Red Guards, spat upon by members of the "Department of Foreign Liaison," struck in the face by a foreigner who was assisting radical Chinese seeking to drive Zhou Enlai from power, knocked to the ground (he suffered a heart attack).

This was only the beginning. For eighteen months Wang was held in one room of his house, in total isolation and total darkness. Zhu Zhongli was permitted to cook his meals, but had to give them to a guard. She was not allowed to see or speak with her husband. Once a month he was permitted to take a bath. The water had been shut off and his wife had to borrow water from neighbors.

Zhu Zhongli was a doctor, but she was not allowed to treat her husband. Sometimes the guard would tell her Wang had a cold. She would give pills to the guard. Or the guard would say he had a fever. She would give the guard some pills. Wang Jiaxiang's health, never really restored from his terrible Long March wound, rapidly got worse. Red Guards tortured Wang's son to death.

In 1970, at the order of Lin Biao, Wang was moved out of Beijing to Xiangyang, in the remote Han River Valley northwest of Wuhan. His physical condition was low; his mental state was lower. He had saved many lives, including those of the navy commander Xiao Jingguang, husband of Zhu Zhongli's sister; Xiao San, author and childhood friend of Mao's; and possibly George Hatem, who secret police chief Kang Sheng thought was a spy. But now the life of Wang Jiaxiang was beyond saving. His wife did her best, but in January 1974 he died; he was seventy-three.

Cold-eyed, Mao surveyed his world . . . The first time Xue Ming, only twenty-two, very good-looking, a student in Beijing who had made her way to Yan'an, saw He Long was the evening of November 7, 1938, at a rally outside the south gate, a celebration of the twenty-first anniversary of the Bolshevik Revolution. She and some girlfriends, including one named Ye Qun, heard He Long would be there and rushed to the gate, carrying little paper lanterns. He spoke eloquently, in a loud voice. "I was full of admiration," Xue Ming recalled. "I regarded him as a hero."

As Xue Ming talked, a handsome woman of sixty-eight, her handsome daughter Xiaoming sat beside her. Xue Ming's father had died while she was a child and she was brought up by her mother, a dressmaker. They lived just outside Tianjin (Tientsin). "I wanted to help my mother," she said, "but my long-cherished desire was to become a boy."

She got into the student movement and there she met Ye Qun, whom with the years she came to hate with fierce passion. Ye Qun, she believed, had a bad past and may have been a KMT agent before she accompanied Xue Ming and other young women to Yan'an.

By 1942, He Long had started to appear quite often in the office where Xue Ming worked. He was separated from his beautiful Long March wife, who had left him for another man.[7]

The first conversation Xue Ming had with He Long had to do with Ye Qun and Lin Biao. "He Long," she said, "had apparently done some investigation of me." He told her that Lin Biao was courting Ye Qun and that Ye Qun was showing Lin Biao's letters to her friends. He Long said that if you liked a man you didn't show his letters around, and asked her to speak to Ye Qun about this. Soon Ye Qun and Lin Biao married. They didn't ask Xue Ming to the reception. Nor He Long either.

Xue Ming had developed admiration and respect for He Long, but she had some reservations. Men outnumbered women by about eighty to one in Yan'an. It was an unusual situation. She was a lot younger than the general. He was forty-six, she twenty-six. It was a big difference. "Schoolgirls don't marry men so much older," she said. "There was a saying among us girls: Old comrades are fine but they are not good lovers."

Still, she was attracted. He Long was very outgoing, but he lost his tongue when he was with her. Some of his older friends came to her— Ren Bishi, his political commissar, Lin Boqu, who had worked with Dr. Sun Yat-sen. "They said He Long was a good comrade," she recalled. "I felt under some pressure."

He Long and Xue Ming were married August 1, 1942, Army Day, the fifteenth anniversary of the Nanchang Uprising. They had a simple dinner at the northwest barracks outside Yan'an's south gate. "And we had a wonderful married life," she said wistfully. "One boy and two girls."

Upon the founding of the People's Republic, He Long became one of China's ten marshals. But in the Cultural Revolution his fall was swift. Xue Ming blamed Ye Qun and Lin Biao.

"He Long would have been an insurmountable obstacle in Lin Biao's assumption of power in the Army," she said. "So Lin Biao framed He Long."

Toward the end of 1966 Zhou Enlai warned them to stay away from their house because it was certain to be ransacked by Red Guards. Zhou feared this would be a serious psychological blow to He Long. So they went to the Western Hills. The Red Guards ransacked the He Long residence January 10–11, 1967, broke open his safe, and seized more than a thousand confidential documents. For a while He Long and Xue Ming lived fairly peacefully, but Zhou Enlai's power to protect them eroded. The Western Hills were under the control of the Army and that meant Lin Biao, Ye Qun, and secret police chief Kang Sheng.

Soon He Long was compelled to attend struggle sessions, but Kang Sheng decided He Long would be too difficult to struggle with. Better to use the "medical approach." He Long had suffered for years from diabetes and was on insulin. His condition had become critical. They halted the insulin and gave him glucose injections—a sure process of medical murder.

He Long and his wife were kept in a courtyard house. They were not permitted to go outside. Water was cut off. It was July and August.

Hot weather. Their only water was what they could collect from the roof when it rained.

Once in a while they would hear one soldier humming an old song about He Long. So they knew he sympathized even if there was little he could do.

Xue Ming was with He Long until six hours before his death, when he was taken away in an ambulance. She was not permitted to follow. "I have no idea of what the doctors did," she said. "This was the issue of the investigation before and during the trial of the Gang of Four."

It is known the hospital continued to inject large doses of glucose. No insulin. The official death certificate made no mention of glucose.

Xue Ming was held in custody for six years. She was sent to forced labor under false names in Guizhou. No one knew who she was. "I was the mysterious old lady of the mountains," she said. When Lin Biao and Ye Qun died in a crash of their escape plane in Outer Mongolia in 1971, Zhou Enlai got Xue Ming to Beijing. It took him some time to find her. Her youngest daughter, Liming, was with her in exile after being held for a time in a north Shaanxi reformatory for juvenile delinquents. Her son, He Pengfei, was imprisoned. Now he is a deputy chief of staff in the army. The elder daughter, He Xiaoming, was also put in prison. Xiaoming now is a history specialist in the Political Department of the PLA.[8]

He Long, said Xiao Ke sadly, was "a great revolutionary soldier, one of the founders and creators of the Red Army. He fought vigorously and endured hardships."

How, he was asked, could such a hero have been arrested, tortured, and murdered by medical means. There was a long silence. Then Xiao Ke began to speak:

"I could cite myself as an example. I took part in the Revolution at an early age. Even so, I was given unfair treatment during the Cultural Revolution. I was deprived of my position and subjected to political examination and sent to Jiangxi to do physical labor with my hands for two and a half years."

Xiao Ke spoke quietly.

"As I was being sent down to the country I wrote a poem," he continued. "I like to write poems."

He took a piece of paper and a pen and wrote:

> Trudging in straw sandals I left Jiangxi.
> Driving by car I am returning at full speed.

In my simple sacks are works of Marx and Lenin—
With an easy mind I am on my way to May Seventh Cadre School.
The yellow blooms on the old battlefields long withered,
As the bitter west wind howls in deep winter.
At Yunshan I write these verses of return—
An old steed in the stable still aspires to gallop.[9]

One-armed Yu Qiuli, PLA Political Department chief and Politburo member, jumped from his comfortable armchair to show how he had been forced to do "the airplane" by the Red Guards in the Cultural Revolution.

They put a knee to his back, forced him to a half-bowing position with his arm and his stump pulled back, something like an airplane about to take off. This was a Red Guard favorite.

"I had a relatively light time," he said, smiling. "I didn't give up resisting. I had had no political power. I never worked in the 'white' [KMT] areas. I had never been arrested. And I had never written any memoirs."

He was accused of being a protégé of He Long and a supporter of Peng Dehuai. They searched his house for three days, but found nothing. Later Mao said Yu had made mistakes but had been a good comrade. He could be corrected. His name was put on a list of those to be both criticized and protected.[10]

President Li Xiannian considered himself very lucky in the Cultural Revolution. He was not "pulled down," although it was a close thing. He was "set aside," protected both by Zhou Enlai—who often called him into conference just when he was supposed to go to a struggle session—and by Mao himself. Li Xiannian participated with several generals, including Nie Rongzhen, Ye Jianying, and Chen Yi, in a meeting in February 1967 which was critical of the Cultural Revolution—the "February reverse current," it was called. They were labeled "little lizards—not big dragons." Li was "set aside" from 1967 to 1970, and that kept him out of serious trouble. Later on, he said, he was again set aside, at a time when Deng Xiaoping was being criticized, and that spared him from calling Deng Xiaoping a "capitalist roader."[11]

Yang Chengwu, the daring commissar of the Fourth Shock Regiment, which stormed Luding Bridge, lost his footing in the dizzy politics of the Cultural Revolution. First he was its darling, replacing his chief, Luo Ruiqing, the PLA's chief of staff, who was crippled when he jumped or was pushed from a sixth-floor window; then he was "air-planed" along with General Yang Shangkun.

Yang Chengwu zoomed into alternate Politburo membership but swiftly fell victim to Lin Biao's intrigues and spent seven years in prison. He was accused of opposing the Cultural Revolution and of ordering someone to beat up Jiang Qing, Mao's wife.[12]

Xiao Hua, whose Long March poem was so admired by Zhou Enlai and Mao Zedong, quickly came under Cultural Revolution fire. He survived two fierce attacks as director of the PLA General Political Department. The third sent him to prison for seven and a half years and put his songs behind bars as well. His songs, his attackers said, had been written in praise of old Red Army commanders (almost to a man enemies of Lin Biao).

Xiao Hua was not permitted to hum his songs in prison. The guards were on the alert. "I could sing them only in my heart," he said. "The Gang tried in a thousand ways to put me and my songs to death. They did not succeed."[13]

General Yang Shangkun has a considerable distinction. He spent more time in prison than any other Long March commander. He was arrested after Lin Biao announced that "investigation" had disclosed that Yang had engaged in "underground" activities. The implication was that Yang Shangkun and others, including Luo Ruiqing and Peng Zhen, had been preparing a coup d'état against Mao. Lin Biao solemnly swore "Chairman Mao has not slept well for many days."[14]

General Yang was arrested in July 1966 and held until December 1978. He was condemned as a "black general," made to do the "air-plane" at mass struggle sessions of hundreds of thousands of Red Guards. He had, it was alleged, been a spy for the Russians over heaven knew what period and for the Americans through his friendship with the wartime American mission in Yan'an. Perhaps more serious, he had, or so it was whispered, tape-recorded Mao Zedong. General Yang did not mention the "airplaning" and torture. He spoke of it as an "enforced rest." But his wife, the diminutive, sparkling Li Bozhao, was made to clean toilets in a six-story building, up and down, on her hands and knees, damaging her back and her legs. For nine years Yang and his wife had no contact.*

*Li Bozhao died April 17, 1985, of a heart attack in Beijing. She had never regained her health after her torture during the Cultural Revolution. Xiao Hua died August 12, 1985, age 69.

"But I congratulate myself," he said with a shake of the head. "No one in my family was killed. Some of my comrades were not so fortunate. They were killed and their children were killed and maimed."

He has two sons and a daughter, both his sons educated, the oldest in the Army. His daughter was sent to the countryside. All the children were compelled to do forced labor.

"I was rather lucky," he said. He was seventy-six years old in 1984, robust, active, hearty, carrying a heavy load of work in the Military Commission, a close adviser to Deng Xiaoping.

Otto Braun left China in 1939. He started back to Moscow on the same plane that took Zhou Enlai and his wife, and Mao's brother Mao Zemin, out of Yan'an. Braun had tried for years to leave, but when Wang Ming came back to China in 1937 he warned Braun to stay put (it was the time of Stalin's purges). Braun gave up, applied for membership in the Chinese Communist Party, rid himself of his Chinese peasant wife, and married Li Lilian, a beautiful Shanghai actress. Zhou Enlai promised she could join Braun in Moscow. She never did. In Moscow, so Braun wrote in his memoirs, Mao Zedong tried to persuade Stalin to kill him; both Zhou Enlai and Mao Zetan testified against him. No Chinese contemporary historian believes this.[15] In fact, Stalin never again permitted Braun to handle Chinese matters. He probably was imprisoned for a while, sent into exile, and did not emerge to public view until the Sino-Soviet split in the early 1960s. He then popped up in East Berlin, and until he died in 1974 occupied himself in writing polemics against the Chinese.

Wu Xiuquan, Otto Braun's interpreter, went to Moscow in December 1949, when Mao Zedong and Stalin met for the first and only time. He became the Party specialist in relations with the Soviet Union and eastern Communist countries. He was arrested in 1967 as a Russian spy. "And also," he said wryly, "as a Yugoslav spy." He spent eight years in custody, six years of it in prison. He was still behind the bars, incommunicado, when President Nixon visited China in 1972.[16]

At the end of the Lushan meeting, Zhu De told his comrades: "To think that once we all ate out of the same rice bowl!"

In 1967 a big character poster appeared within Zhongnanhai, the leadership compound beside the Forbidden City. It called Zhu De a "black general." His house was ransacked by Red Guards. Kang Keqing, his wife, was paraded in the streets. Zhu De was charged with "shamelessly" calling himself a founder of the Red Army. In July 1976 he died, two months before Mao.

Hu Yaobang was not one of the most badly treated in the Cultural Revolution, nor was he one of the least. He was relieved of his duties as head of the Youth League in 1964 and sent to Shaanxi as Party secretary by Mao, who said Hu "needs some practical work." In less than two years Hu was back in Beijing, being criticized by Red Guards at struggle sessions. He was called one of the "Three Hus"—Hu Keshi, Hu Qili, and he had been the three top leaders of the Youth League. He was kept in isolation until 1974, then, probably at Deng Xiaoping's instigation, became director of personnel, then of propaganda, and then general secretary of the Party.

Chen Yi was China's foreign minister when he was attacked by rabid Red Guards seeking to seize the foreign ministry and depose Zhou Enlai. Once, at a struggle session of howling tormentors who placed a dunce cap on his head, Chen Yi begged permission to go to an appointment with the French ambassador. He removed the dunce cap and asked the Red Guards to keep it carefully. "I'm sure I'll need it again." Jokes could not save him. He lost his office, his freedom, his health. On January 8, 1972, Chen Yi died. The doctors' certificate said cancer. Two years later, his wife died. Whatever the medical verdict, his friends knew the two had died of an epidemic called the Cultural Revolution.[17]

Mao appeared at Chen Yi's services, clad in pajamas. Chen Yi, he muttered, "was a good patriotic person and an internationalist and a Marxist." What was going through Mao's mind on that occasion, none could say.[18] When Chen Yi led his men in the mountains around Ruijin, he had written a poem: "Broken Country and Death in the Family." There was no one to recite it on January 8, 1972.

In the compound of Zhongnanhai, the house of Liu Shaoqi, President of China, was next door to that of Mao Zedong. In July of 1966, Liu Shaoqi—belatedly—began to understand that the number one target of the Cultural Revolution was himself. Mao had just come back from his swim in the Yangtze on July 12. Liu strolled over to speak to his old neighbor. Guards barred the door. He telephoned. No one accepted his call. Liu's house had a window looking out on a path where Mao liked to walk. Liu sat from dawn to dusk, waiting for Mao. He never passed by.[19]

Liu Shaoqi had a big family. His sons and daughters were swept up in the Red Guard movement. Soon they began to be beaten up. His eldest son and eldest daughter were exiled to the Burma border, where the eldest son would die a tragic death and the daughter would be confined to a cowpen. His second son, Liu Yunruo, was jailed. His youngest daughter, Xiaoxiao, ten years old, was beaten by classmates and forbidden to attend school. His third son, Yuanyuan, and his friend, son of the persecuted mayor of Beijing, Peng Zhen, were penniless. They tried to sell their blood to a bloodbank. Permission was refused. Number three daughter, Pingping, was imprisoned.[20]

The indignity and torture to which Liu Shaoqi and his family were subjected would take pages to list. A whole book, perhaps. His children wrote a long letter listing the main items. It was published December 5, 1980, in the Beijing *Workers Daily*, very long, but much shorter than it had been written. His widow is writing a book about Liu Shaoqi, but she is confining herself to the forty-four days in 1960 he spent in Ningxiang, a Hunan village only twenty miles from Mao's. Liu Shaoqi, too, was trying to assess the state of the countryside and what was happening as a result of the Great Leap Forward, the communes, and the rest of Mao's policies.

For a time Zhou Enlai tried to keep in touch with Liu Shaoqi and his family by telephone. Then the Red Guards broke in and ripped out the telephone. Zhou warned the Lius not to step outside the protected zone of Zhongnanhai. But Red Guards lured Liu's wife, Wang Guangmei, out with a trick—they told her that her daughter Pingping had been badly injured and taken to a hospital. At a struggle session they dressed Wang Guangmei in a bizarre Chinese *changshan*, slit to her hips, and draped strings of pingpong balls around her neck. They slapped Liu Shaoqi in the face with the Little Red Book (of Mao's quotations) until his cheeks bled. They deprived Liu of sleeping pills. He lay awake all night.

They took Wang Guangmei to Qincheng high-security prison in the Western Hills of Beijing (where Jiang Qing, Mao's widow, and the Gang of Four are now confined).

One charge against Wang Guangmei was that her name meant "America" and that of her brother, Wang Guangying, meant "England"—obviously she was an American spy. Actually, the name Guangmei meant "beautiful girl of a glorious household"; Guangying meant "brave hero of a glorious household"—very elegant and traditional Chinese names. It was true that the Chinese in the mid-nineteenth century, trying to find flattering Chinese equivalents for America, called it *mei guo,* "beautiful country"; England was *ying guo,* "heroic country." There was in the Wang family another, special significance of the names. Wang Guangmei's father was China's minister of foreign trade. He was in England when Wang Guangying was born and in America when Wang Guangmei was born, and so the names contained this subtle reference.[21]

Liu Shaoqi, health deteriorating, awake all night, his room flooded by glaring lights (while his wife was kept in total darkness), was flown half-dressed and ill in October 1969, at Lin Biao's orders, to a maximum-security prison at Kaifeng in remote Henan. He was thrown on a basement floor, half conscious, suffering from pneumonia. His Beijing guards flew back to the capital, taking his medicines with them.

Lying on the cement floor, his hair uncut for months, a foot long, his mouth and nose deformed, blood on his chin, Liu died November 12, 1969. It was years before his death and its circumstances were publicly acknowledged.

Not long before the torture began, Liu, recuperating from an illness, had told his children:

"If only Marx will give me another ten years, we will be able to build China into a rich and strong country."

Chinese Communists often semi-seriously fantasized Marx in heaven, looking down over the world.

Liu Shaoqi and his comrades did not perceive that it was not Marx who was looking down upon them but, as he wrote, Mao, cold-eyed, surveying the world, on land and over the seas.

The question nags—why did Mao's eyes turn cold on Lushan's peak? Why did he savage his comrades of the Long March and shake China into anarchy? They had come so far, so long together.

No one in today's China has a simple answer but a wise survivor suggests that the answer may lie in Mao's powerful belief in destruction as the elemental method of social change. This was not a Marxian concept. "We are eagerly looking for the doom of the old world," Mao wrote in the margin of his copy of Friedrich Paulsen's *System of Ethics* which he studied in Changsha Normal No. 1 under Professor Yang Changji. "Its destruction will eventually lead to the establishment of a new one. And will it not be better than the old world?"

This principle entered Mao's thought during the intensive study of Buddhist philosophy which occupied him in 1920. It remained there. Destruction, he became convinced, was valuable in itself.

No Chinese of the Long March believes the chaos of the Cultural Revolution was accidental. None believes anyone other than Mao directed it. True, Lin Biao, Jiang Qing, and the Gang of Four played their parts but all were, essentially, acting within the parameters of Mao's design.

Nor do these men of the Long March accept the Western view that Mao launched the Cultural Revolution to regain personal power. He had never lost power—so they believe.

What happened, they feel, is that Mao grew impatient with his revolution. China was not changing fast enough or profoundly enough. Too much of the old persisted. The ideal society of his dream did not emerge. He began to strike out. He launched the Hundred Flowers campaign, the Communes, the Great Leap Forward. He tried—and failed—to get Nikita Khrushchev to join him in an atom-armed crusade for world revolution. Nothing worked. Frustration mounted. Mao was, his survivors declare, a *very radical* man. He grew more—not less— radical with the years. Evans Carlson, the American Marine officer and China hand, who came to know Mao and his Revolution well once said: "Mao is a dreamer, a genius, more than fifty years ahead of his time, but dangerous because he is impractical in many of his schemes."[22]

Mao drew one lesson from the failures; his comrades another. In the days before Lushan he, too, had gone back to his roots, had revisited his boyhood Shaoshan on June 25, 1959, for the first time in thirty-two years. Mao knew that all was not well in the countryside. He knew that Peng Dehuai, the blunt old soldier, had been down in Hunan too, taking a critical look. Perhaps the local authorities put on a show for Mao at Shaoshan. Whatever the cause, he came away writing of "heroes home-bound in the evening mist" and "cursing the long-fled past."

Peng Dehuai saw chaos and disaster. Mao saw a thousand rows of beans and flourishing rice paddies. He turned on his old comrades-at-arms with accelerating ferocity.

The parallel of Stalin's purges leaps to mind. Stalin wiped out the old Bolsheviks in the 1930s. Was the purge common to both Communist systems? Did it follow some corollary of Lord Acton's dictum that all power corrupts and that absolute power corrupts absolutely? The temptation to accept this explanation is great. Especially when one examines the paranoia characteristic of both Russian and Chinese revolutions. Stalin's suspicion manifested itself in his early days in his native Georgia. Mao carried out purges as early as Jiangxi.

But a Chinese who knew Mao well rejects paranoia. He agreed, as Luo Fu suggested, that Mao and Stalin were both strong "at rectifying people" but he did not believe that Mao suffered from a clinical form of paranoia. "He acted perfectly rationally," said Mao's associate, "on the basis of the information he received. It was the information that was twisted. Not Mao's mind."

Perhaps. Although this seems to let Mao down too easily. Certainly there were those who were quick to bring to Mao distorted and false accounts about his old comrades. Jiang Qing, his power-lusting wife, played a behind-the-scenes role at Lushan and increasingly thence forward.

Yet questions haunt the mind. Mao concluded his "Ascent of Lushan" with the words:

> Who knows whither Prefect Tao Yuanming has gone
> Now that he can till fields in the Land of Blossoms?

Mao was writing of the poet Tao, born a scant seven miles from where Mao sat on Lushan, then as now renowned for beauty. Tao, great-grandson of a famous general, turned his back on his prefect's career shortly after the year A.D. 405 and went back to Lushan to lead the life of a simple farmer, at peace with the world, contemplating nature, recording the passage of the seasons in his poetry.

Sitting in his wicker chair at Lushan, looking out toward Poyang Lake, Mao's eyes were cold and his mind rational. He had leapt over four hundred turns to reach the pinnacle, but who could say what lay ahead, what Lushan would bring? Perhaps like Tao he would soon put aside his official duties and turn back to Shaoshan, there to live as had Tao:

> Neither grieving and sorrowing in poverty or lowliness
> Nor in hot pursuit of riches or fame.

No longer would Mao live "imprisoned in a cage." He would return "once again to a life of careless freedom," as wrote Tao.

It was not a mood to last. With his victory at Lushan, Mao moved inexorably toward *luan.* In 1963 he wrote another poem:

> Seize the day, seize the hour . . .
> Our force is irresistible.
> Away with all pests!

And, on July 6, 1966, just before his famous swim in the Yangtze River, he wrote to Jiang Qing:

> Great disorder across the land leads to great order. And so once again every seven or eight years monsters and demons will jump out themselves.

The greatest *luan* of China's history was rolling forward. Mao had placed himself at its helm. His eyes were cold and sharply fixed upon his target—his old comrades—the "pests" with whom in Zhu De's words he had shared a common rice·bowl on the Long March, men whose revolutionary zeal, he felt, had faltered with the victory of their cause. Now, he would go forward into a new and greater revolution, single-handed if need be. This Revolution, the Cultural Revolution, would destroy the imperfect order attained thus far under an imperfect Communist rule and with it would destroy faltering and imperfect comrades of the Long March—a harsh and ruthless task, but one which would clear the way for the perfect social order, the vision of which now possessed the mind of Mao.

31

THE LITTLE MAN WHO COULD
NEVER BE PUT DOWN

I N late afternoon, as the parasol trees began to cast long shadows over the small courtyard of the unused commandant's residence in Xinjian county, northern Jiangxi, Deng Xiaoping would emerge from the red-brick house and begin to walk. Around and around the courtyard he walked at a brisk pace, head slightly bowed, deep in thought. Every day he walked, until his feet wore a path in the red soil.

From a window his daughter Maomao watched. Deng Xiaoping was in exile, under the constant supervision of guards. So was she.

"Watching his sure but fast-moving steps," she said later, "I thought to myself that his faith, his ideas and determination must have become clearer and firmer, readying him for the battles ahead."[1]

Fifty years have passed since those men in gray-brown uniforms, Deng Xiaoping among them, men with packs on their backs, rice bags slung over shoulders, Mausers in slings, straw sandals on their feet, and determination in their eyes, slugged their way over dangerous rivers and mountains, fought battle after battle, for the destiny of which they dreamed.

Nowhere does that destiny seem to be chiseled more sharply than in the quick mind of the man who has, most improbably (or perhaps inevitably), become China's leader—Deng Xiaoping.

The name of Deng Xiaoping did not then resound over the Five Ridges of Guizhou, the waters of the Golden Sands, nor the loess hills of northern Shaanxi. It did not reverberate around the world in the years of his imprisonment in the old barracks of Xinjian county to which he was confined in 1969.

But no man on the Long March possessed more spirit, and Deng had risen steadily through the years, almost spectacularly. No matter how often he was bowled from his feet, he got up again, ready for battle. After the Long March he served as political commissar for Liu Bocheng's 129th Division, which fought the KMT and the Japanese and, as the Second Field Army, drove Chiang Kai-shek from the mainland. Deng stood on the platform at Tiananmen Square on October 1, 1949, when Mao proclaimed the People's Republic and then became Mao's proconsul for the vast empire of southwest China. In 1952 he came to Beijing. He had a hand in everything. Party secretary, Politburo member—no responsibility seemed too heavy. He went to Moscow with Mao in 1957 for a showdown with Nikita Khrushchev, and on the job in China watched over agriculture, industry, and education.

Deng Xiaoping did not change. He was still blunt and honest. He perceived the disaster of the Great Leap Forward and spoke his mind. He was not one of those who came to Lushan Mountain with two speeches in his pockets, one to use if Peng Dehuai prevailed, one to use if Mao won out.

Trouble lay dead ahead. Deng (and Liu Shaoqi), so Mao later was to say, "treated me like I was their dead parent at a funeral." Or as Chen Boda, a Cultural Revolution leader, put it: "To discuss with Deng Xiaoping as equals is more difficult than to put a ladder against heaven."[2]

That was Deng. He fought back. He made a self-criticism, as he had years before when he got into trouble in Jiangxi. It did no good. He was called the "Number Two Capitalist Roader." Number One was Liu Shaoqi. After September 1966, Deng vanished from view. He was confined to his house, not permitted outside contacts. His children were dispersed, struggled with, sent to the countryside to do manual labor. His eldest son was shoved out a window by Red Guards and crippled for life, his back broken, paralyzed from the waist down and denied medical treatment. Deng, his wife, Zhuo Lin, and the stepmother who had raised him after the death of his mother were sent, in October 1968, to Jiangxi, where the Long March had started.[3] There, at a vacant infantry school outside Nanchang, Deng Xiaoping lived in a two-story house that once had housed the superintendent. The school was long since closed by the Cultural Revolution, like all schools in China.

For three years Deng lived a life like that of so many of the men of the Long March. He was sixty-five but he mopped the floor, split wood, broke up big hunks of coal for the stove to heat the chilly rooms. He had worked with his hands at the Renault factory in the days of the work-study movement in France. He had not forgotten his machinist's trade. Now he and his wife labored mornings in a tractor factory, he on the machines, she cleaning coils of wire. Armed guards escorted them back and forth on the twenty-minute walks over a slippery road where Deng sometimes took a tumble. They were not permitted to speak without permission.

Afternoons they worked in their garden. They raised chickens and vegetables. They saved their money, hoping they might bring their children to join them. Their youngest daughter, Maomao (Deng Rong), and their younger son, Deng Zhifang (his nickname was "little black man" because of his dark complexion), were working on production teams in the Shaanxi countryside.

Deng Xiaoping was not tortured. He had been permitted to bring some books from Beijing. Evenings he read—sometimes Marx or Lenin, sometimes Chinese history, sometimes Chinese or foreign literature. His stepmother did needlework. They listened to the evening news on the radio.

Slowly they developed friendly relations with their fellow workers. Did Deng play bridge during his long confinement? It seems unlikely. It would have been a three-handed game with his wife—often bedridden—and his stepmother, an elderly, energetic but illiterate woman. Deng, like many in Yan'an, had become fond of bridge. Some international bridge players rate him world class. Once he came into power, he played almost every day. He had for his partner Wan Li, Politburo member, vice-premier, onetime deputy mayor of Beijing, old friend and early victim of the Cultural Revolution. Sometimes, it was said, he played with General Yang Shangkun. Another player was Ding Guanglu, vice-secretary general of the People's Congress. Katherine Wei, a championship bridge player in New York, has played with Deng and calls him a fine competitor. He told her that bridge "keeps my mind sharp." He plays to win, but not for money. The loser must crawl under a table. When Deng loses, his partners always say, "Oh, you don't have to do that." He invariably responds: "Yes, I will. It is the rule of the game." And he crawls under a table, a bit easier for him because of his diminutive stature.[4]

Both bridge and poker were popular in Yan'an. Edgar Snow played poker with Mao Zedong night after night. Mao never wanted to stop. He was, in Snow's judgment, a "big gambler but a poor bluffer." He played for high—but fictitious—stakes. Helen Snow reported Mao often amused himself by playing solitaire and would play rummy by the hour.

In the Cultural Revolution, Deng's first consideration was for the welfare of his eldest son, so cruelly crippled. In 1971 he got permission to bring the injured Deng Pufang to Jiangxi. Pufang had been living under miserable conditions in a welfare center north of Beijing, flat on his back, weaving wire baskets to earn a little money. Deng, his wife, and the stepmother did their best to care for the young man without adequate medical facilities. Zhuo Lin nursed her son despite her own bad health. Deng gave the young man massages and helped him bathe. Deng began to petition authorities to send his son to Beijing for proper medical care. This did not come through until 1973 when Deng Pufang* was permitted to go to Beijing accompanied by his sister Maomao. Eventually Deng was able to send Deng Pufang to the United States for examination and diagnosis through the aid of Huang Hua then in New York to represent China at the United Nations. American doctors said Deng Pufang had been without treatment so long there was nothing to be done to restore his legs to normal.

On November 5, 1971, Deng and his wife were summoned to a meeting to hear a political report. This was the first time this had happened since their arrest in 1966. Both Maomao and Deng Pufang were now with their parents. When Deng and his wife returned with their armed guards, they said nothing. Then Zhuo Lin motioned to Maomao and she followed her mother into the kitchen. There the mother silently traced out four characters on her daughter's hand. They spelled "Lin Biao is dead."

In February 1974, Deng Xiaoping was called to Beijing. The long epoch of Mao was drawing to a close. The worst of the Cultural Revolution was over. Destruction had been worse than a war, industry brought to its knees, education wiped out, the Party a wreck. Liu Shaoqi and many, many others were dead. Mao's health was deteriorating, the state of his mind and emotions precarious. His wife, Jiang Qing, and her three fellow members of the Gang of Four were temporarily shaken but preparing a comeback. Zhou Enlai had cancer.

Mao turned again to the little man who could never be put down. Mao could have had Deng reduced to a pulp, as he did with Liu Shaoqi. Or murdered by doctors, as in the case of He Long. This Mao did not do. He brought Deng back and was to say of him: "Deng is a rare and talented man. Deng has ideas. He does not assault problems head-on without thought. He finds solutions. He deals with difficult problems with responsibility." Deng, said Mao, was a good fighter. He knew how to fight the Russians. A person like Deng was hard to find.[5]

*Deng Pufang now heads China's Federation for the Crippled.

As Zhou's strength declined, Deng took more and more matters into his hands. Some Chinese worried. He was, they said, going too fast. He was filled with impatience. He wanted to get China back on the track. He was obsessed with time. Better than anyone, he knew what had happened to the country. He knew who had been killed. He knew who had been tortured. He knew the able generals and administrators who lingered behind bars. He knew the price that had been paid by the people, as it had been paid in his own family. He knew the damage to the economy from insane slogans—"Make Revolution, not Production." He knew the disorientation in the Army, and the danger of the Four, still crouching close to Mao, filling the aging man's consciousness with poisonous thoughts.

Nimble and quick as he was, Deng could not speed up the clock. With the death of Zhou in January 1976, and the outburst of passion in Tiananmen in behalf of Zhou, the Gang pulled Deng down again. But not for long. In October 1976, after Mao's death, the Gang fell, and fighting, clawing, struggling, talking, persuading, bargaining, using every wile and strategy of a lifetime in Chinese politics, Deng came into command.

This is the man to whose hands China's future was confided. He wears for a time the mantle of heaven. To his task he brought not only his energy and originality but the concepts perfected as he strolled evening after evening in the courtyard at the infantry school in Xinjian county.

They were simple ideas. First get the country going again. Get the Gang of Four and their supporters under control. After all, they must have had the majority of the Party with them.

Get the army into shape. Get the factories working. Get the young people into school. Bring back the victims of the Cultural Revolution. Give them justice and a useful role in society.

Then move on to the goal of goals: Bring China into the twentieth century—by the twenty-first. Not many outside China—nor some in China—recognized the magnitude of this goal. It could not be achieved by cheap tricks or slogans like "Great Leap Forward." China needed *everything:* technology, science, education, distribution, consumer goods, food. It had to halt population growth before it drowned in a sea of babies. It had to make agriculture produce. No matter how. No matter the cost.

To these chores Deng Xiaoping brought an open mind. The Cultural Revolution had swept away every cobweb. He saw—and the men he brought with him saw—China without clichés. Their goals had been built on Marx and Mao. But now they began to say publicly that the Communist Manifesto was nearly one hundred fifty years old. Marx had studied a society that had been dead for a century and a half. Nor had he ever studied China. How could he possess the answers to a technological superworld that his nineteenth-century imagination could not conceive? Lenin knew World War I Czarist Russia. What did that have to do with China in 1985? Mao knew China's feudal peasant world before and after 1927, a long time in the past.

But the year was 1985. The world was moving at ultrasonic speeds. China had to have ultrasonic solutions. China had to look for answers where they existed. It could no longer live by catchwords and cant. As *Red Flag*, the Party ideological journal put it: "Marxist tenets must march with the times."

This was a heady brew. It was easy to jump to wrong conclusions. Older Party comrades could not comprehend the rhetoric of the "new Long March" as General Secretary Hu Yaobang called it. The military grew edgy as Deng Xiaoping carried on his campaign to retire the wonderful old men who had made the Long March.

But year by year, Deng picked up momentum. "My task," he said, "is to try to live longer." Not for himself, but for the sake of China. He felt "as fresh as a fish," he told his friends after taking a dip in the pleasant waters of Beidaiho, China's seashore resort on the Gulf of Bo Hai.[6]

Deng had a secret ally in his new Long March. It was the younger generation—particularly the younger generation of families such as his, which went through the Cultural Revolution. Never in China had the bond between the younger and the old been so strengthened by the commonality of their experience. Not only had the older generation, like Deng, been rethinking China's Revolution. The younger generation was bringing in new thoughts, new insights, many of them drawing on an unexpected source—the United States. Thousands of young Chinese were studying in the United States. If China's system is now receiving heavy injections of private enterprise, profit incentives, individuality and entrepreneurism, it is not an accident. Thousands of Chinese are going back to their homes and sharing with their parents firsthand insights into the West.

Along with the new Long March, China has embarked on what Deng Xiaoping calls the "open door policy:" an open door to ideas, to technology, to trade, to learning from other cultures, other ideologies, gaining from other nations techniques by which China can create a new order, ways of putting the West to China's use.

To many, China's "open door" sounds un-Chinese, incompatible with Chinese history and Chinese tradition. Not necessarily so. In the Tang dynasty (A.D. 618–907), when China's capital was still at Changan (present-day Xi'an), it boasted as many as ten thousand foreigners— experts, specialists, artists, businessmen, traders, scholars—the kind of men and women you would expect to find in the flourishing capital of a great empire. Isolationism, the closed door, xenophobia, the ban on foreigners, grew stronger and stronger with the decline of the last dynasty, the Manchu. The Chinese revolutionary movement was never inward-looking. It sought ideas and inspiration beyond China's borders, beyond the seas—in Japan, America, France, Germany, and Russia.

Therein, as Historian Li Rui has noted, lies the contrast between the approach of Mao and that of Deng Xiaoping. Mao "was not so interested in the West," his society was more closed in, more in the tradition of the Manchus. Deng is the opposite—greedy for new ideas, attracted to what China can gain from the West.

It is fifty years since the Long March ended. A trifle by the Chinese calendar. But already it has made indelible marks on the face of China, great changes in China's consciousness. It has bequeathed to the nation extraordinary unity and spirit unseen for many centuries. It has even proved powerful enough to overcome the terrible vagaries of the final years of Mao Zedong himself and move forward on a fresh new path— one which Mao would hardly have chosen. But the reckoning is far from complete. Perhaps, the Chinese would say, in a century or two we may begin to see the Long March in true historical perspective. For the present, we can view it as China does—an unparalleled act of collective courage, dedication, and hope.

NOTES

1. A Walk by Moonlight

1. This was told by Chen Yi to Wang Yanjian, a specialist in the Long March, a writer of film scripts and narratives about it, and associated with the August 1 Film Studio of the Red Army. (Personal interview, Beijing, 3/5/84). Chen Yi may have heard rumors of a pullout by the Red Army a bit earlier. (Zhong Shuqi, historical archivist, Ruijin Museum, to the writer, 4/11/84.) Chen Pixian, vice-chairman, Standing Committee, National People's Congress, and in 1934–35 aide to Chen Yi, confirmed the general accuracy of this account. So did three of Chen Yi's surviving children. (Personal interview, Beijing, 6/11/84.) Date of October 9, Chen Pixian, *Three Years of Guerrilla Warfare in South Jiangxi,* Beijing, 1980, ch. 1.
2. Zhong Shuqi, 4/11/84.
3. Helen Snow, *Inside Red China,* New York, 1979, p. 178.
4. Liu Ying, personal interview, Beijing, 6/14/84. Chen Changfeng, one of Mao's bodyguards, makes no mention of this in his *On the Long March with Chairman Mao.* The memoir, first published in 1959, and frequently reprinted, is marred by omissions and historical inaccuracies.
5. Excerpts from *Minguo Ribao,* 10/10/34, examined in Jiangxi Provincial Library, Nanchang. The building served as Chiang Kai-shek's headquarters in Nanchang. (Professor Dai Xiangqing, Party historian, personal interview, Nanchang, 4/14/84.)
6. Kong Xianquan, personal interview, Zunyi, 4/24/84. This was the only beheading of a Nationalist commander. On reflection, the Party decided it was bad propaganda.
7. Lin Jiachuan, director, Nanchang Museum, personal interview, 4/3/84.
8. This data is drawn from Wu Xiuquan, personal interview, Beijing, 3/28/84; and his memoirs. The order for the March was dated October 7, specifying that it would begin October 10. Units in the countryside began to move on different dates. The date of October 16 is usually used because on this date GHQ left the Central Area. Otto Braun (Li De's German name) sheds no light on the date in his memoirs. He states he first lived in a small house on the outskirts of Ruijin in a "barricaded zone" within which were located all the central institutions, the Central Committee, Provisional Revolutionary

Government, Military Committee, and GHQ. (Otto Braun, *A Comintern Agent in China, 1932–1939*, Stanford, California, 1982, pp. 31–33.)

9. Cheng Fangwu, *Memoirs of the Long March*, Beijing, 1977, pp. 18–21.

10. Wang Yanjian, personal interview, Beijing, 3/5/84; Wu Xiuquan, *My Experiences, 1908–1949*, Beijing, 1984, ch. 7; Chen Pixian, personal interview, Beijing, 6/13/84; Cai Xiaoqian, *The Jiangxi Soviet and the Red Army's Westward Flight*, Taipei, 1970, p. 201.

11. Ambassador Wang Bingnan, personal interview, Beijing, 3/20/84.

12. Detail on Mao's house, personal inspection, Yudu, 4/9/84; He Zizhen's pregnancy, Wu Jiqing, Mao's bodyguard, personal interview, Nanchang, 4/15/84.

13. Wu Xiuquan, *op. cit.*, ch. 7; Wu Xiuquan, personal interview, Beijing, 3/28/84.

14. The proposal to send Mao to the Soviet Union was sent to the Comintern in a telegram signed by Bo Gu and Li De after the Guangchang battle in April 1934. A reply was received sometime in May rejecting the idea because of Mao's importance to the Red Army and the Soviet zone. Wu Liangping, then state economics minister, was present when Bo Gu read the answer aloud. Li De was dejected, but Luo Fu favored acceptance of the Comintern decision. Wu Liangping, a well-educated young man, acted as Mao's secretary and also at times as an adviser to the Central Committee. He interpreted some of Edgar Snow's talks with Mao in 1936. (Hu Hua, personal interview, Beijing, 3/23/84.)

15. Mao's remark about Bo Gu does not appear in Snow's voluminous notes and papers. It was remembered by an old friend, who said he heard it from Snow. Mao's supporters have often claimed he was exiled to Yudu and kept under surveillance or house arrest. Li De takes the opposite view, claiming Mao went to Yudu to plot against Bo Gu and Li De with Lin Biao and other high military commanders.

16. Contemporary Chinese sources were unanimous in 1984 that Mao was not under house arrest at Yudu or earlier.

17. Peng Dehuai, commander of the Third Army Group, asserted that there was no discussion of the decision to leave the base area with senior military commanders, including himself. He said he had been told by members of the Central Committee (he was not a member) that they had not been consulted either. (Peng Dehuai, *Memoirs of a Chinese Marshal*, Beijing, 1982, pp. 189–91.)

18. Details of the conversation from Professor Hu Hua, People's University, Beijing, personal interview, 3/21/84; Zhang Demin, Yu County Museum, personal interview, 4/9/84; Nie Rongzhen recalled in his memoirs that the conversation occurred in Ruijin. He and Lin Biao had been advised that a "strategic maneuver" was to occur and that they should begin secret preparations. They were told they would be joining the Second and Sixth armies, but nothing more. Mao broke off the conversation by suggesting they go visit a new library started by Qu Qiubai, a former secretary of the Communist Party. (Nie Rongzhen, *Memoirs*, Beijing, 1983, ch. 8.)

19. Cheng Fangwu, *op. cit.*, pp. 18–21; Wu Jiqing, personal interview; Wu Xiuquan, *op. cit.*, ch. 7.

20. Wu Xiuquan estimated three thousand bearers were employed. Some estimates range as high as five thousand.
21. Zhong Shuqi, archivist, Ruijin Museum, personal interview, 4/11/84; Zhang Demin, 4/9/84; Chen Changfeng, *op. cit.*, pp. 24–25. Chen Changfeng says they left by the north gate and walked twenty li (about six miles) to the crossing. Zhang Demin states they left by the east gate and walked only a short distance.

2. The Rise of the Red Bandits

1. Galen's real name was V. K. Blyukher. He became Stalin's top commander in the Far East until he was executed in the purges in 1938. Chiang Kai-shek admired Blyukher, and as Li De told Helen Snow, tried to get him back in 1935 or 1936 as a military adviser. (Helen Snow, *My Yenan Notebooks.*)
2. Chiang was not, of course, aware that the new strategy of stand-and-fight was not that of Mao Zedong and Zhu De but was imposed on the Red Army by a new Comintern representative from Moscow.
3. The classic description is in Harold Isaacs' *The Tragedy of the Chinese Revolution,* Stanford, California, 1951, pp. 176–77. Also see Snow, *Red Star Over China,* pp. 75–76. Gu Shunzhang, by now chief of the Communist secret police, was arrested in Hankou, where he was performing as a street juggler, in the winter of 1930–31. He turned traitor and provided the KMT with information which led to the destruction of the Communist apparatus in Shanghai, Hankou, and other large cities. (Jacques Guillermaz, *A History of the Chinese Communist Party 1921–1949,* New York, 1972, pp. 221–22.)
4. Snow, *Red Star Over China,* p. 457.
5. Hu Hua, Party historian; Yan Jingtang, defense researcher, personal interviews, Beijing, 10/10/84.
6. Since 1949 the Grand Hotel has been the Museum of the August 1 Uprising.
7. Stalin's orders were conveyed in a telegram signed by Nikolai Bukharin, then running the Comintern but shortly displaced. In 1936, he was purged and shot. Lominadze delivered Stalin's message in Wuhan to Zhang Guotao, a member of the Communist Party Central Committee. Zhang delivered it to a five-man committee set up in Nanchang to conduct the uprising. Zhou Enlai was secretary and director. The other members were Li Lisan (soon to become general secretary of the Communist Party), Yun Daiying, Tan Pingshan, and Peng Pai. In the Museum of the August 1 Uprising at Nanchang, Zhang Guotao is not mentioned, but he is shown in a painting of a committee meeting on the eve of the uprising. (Lin Jiachuan, museum director, personal interview, 4/3/84.) Zhang Guotao describes his meetings with Lominadze and Zhou in his memoirs and says that while he had questions about the coup, in the end he gave it his complete support. (Zhang Guotao, *The Rise of the Communist Party,* Lawrence, Kansas, 1971, vol. 1, pp. 674–75, vol. 2, pp. 5–8. Lin Jiachuan quoted Zhang as telling his fellow committeemen: "You should not start this uprising unless you are certain you will succeed." Lominadze broke with Stalin in the late 1920s, and committed suicide in 1935. His threat that no Comintern advisers would be permitted to participate in Nanchang was an empty one. M. F.

Kumanin, one of the Soviet military advisers assigned to He Long, accompanied He to Nanchang and participated in the operation. He remained in China until 1928. (*Na Kitaiskii Zemle*, Moscow, 1977, pp. 149–59.) There probably were others.

8. The troops headed for Canton after leaving Nanchang, but never got there. Most were dispersed or wiped out. They did capture the port of Swatow (Shantou) and held it from September 24 to October 1, but Zhou fell ill and slipped away to Hongkong, where he was joined by He Long, Ye Ting, and Nie Rongzhen. Zhu De, Chen Yi, Lin Biao, and what was left of Zhu De's troops found temporary refuge with a friendly Nationalist general. (Details of Nanchang Uprising from Lin Jiachuan, 4/3/84. Also see Jacques Guillermaz, *China Quarterly*, July 1962, pp. 161–68.) Nie Rongzhen was recruited into the Communist Party by Zhou Enlai in 1921–22. Nie was then a student in technical-scientific studies in Belgium. He ultimately headed the Chinese nuclear armaments program.

9. All these men fell victim to Stalin's purges, Radek and Bukharin in 1936, then Mif in 1938. Mif's real name was Mikhail Aleksandrovich Fortus. He took the place of Lominadze as Stalin's "China hand."

10. Han Suyin, *The Morning Deluge: Mao and the Chinese Revolution, 1893–1954*, New York, 1972, pp. 173–79.

11. Mao's capture is described by Snow in *Red Star*, pp. 158–59. Han Suyin was told of the officers' plot at Jinggangshan in 1966. Mao told anyone who didn't want to accompany him to the mountain they didn't have to come, and gave them travel money. About one-fifth of his men left. (Han Suyin, personal communication, 8/19/84; see her *The Morning Deluge*, pp. 158–59, 175.)

12. He Changgong was alive in Beijing in 1984, vice-chairman of the Academy of Military Science. He had just published his memoirs, *Those Unforgettable Days*. On the Long March he was political commissar of the Ninth Army.

13. Several dates for the departure from Jinggangshan were given by authorities there, splitting about evenly between January 14 and 29. Different units left at different times, but the main departure was on January 14.

14. Snow, *Red Star*, p. 160. A few years later, Zhu De was to speak with nostalgia to Agnes Smedley about his talks with Wang and Yuan. He remembered their telling him about a bandit named Old Deaf Chu. Chu used to say: "You don't have to know how to fight; all you have to know is how to encircle the enemy." It was a principle Zhu De clung to all through his career. (Agnes Smedley, *The Great Road*, New York, 1956, p. 232.)

15. Han Suyin, *op. cit.* p. 206. While Peng Dehuai had left Jinggangshan in March 1929, long before the trouble over Yuan and Wang, his Fifth Army was in some manner involved in the execution order. When the big character poster appeared, Peng declared that if the Fifth Army was found to have profited by the elimination of Yuan and Wang (they were alleged to have seized the bandits' arms), he would ask to be executed. (Zhang Yuanyuan, letter, 8/14/84.) For a long time no one was willing to take responsibility for what was regarded as an "ugly and erroneous" decision, which

may be why there is no mention of it at the Jinggangshan Museum. The portraits of the two men are still displayed. Much of this detail is drawn from personal interviews with Gui Yulin, curator of the Jinggangshan Museum, at Ciping. The story of He Changgong and the capture of Yin Daoyi was related by Zhang Yen, deputy chief of the Jiangxi provincial foreign office, Nanchang, 4/6/84.

At the peak of the Cultural Revolution, more than 30,000 Red Guards a day arrived at Jinggangshan. Terrible problems of food, housing, sanitation, medical care, arose. The Red Army finally mobilized helicopters to bring in food and evacuate the ill. Peak numbers continued for more than two months until the government began to discourage the young people. Gradually the numbers fell to 20,000 a day, then to 10,000. No figures are available on loss of life. (Magistrate, Ciping, Jinggangshan Mountain, personal interview, 4/7/84.)

3. *On the Eve*

1. These are the figures of General Qin Xinghan of the Beijing Military Museum and represent his best approximation. (Qin, personal interview, Ruijin, 4/11/84.) There were many other estimates. Sometimes the total is given as high as 40,000, but all of these should be taken with the greatest reserve. General Chen Pixian, who worked with Chen Yi, gives a figure of 30,000–40,000. (Chen Pixian, *Three Years of Guerrilla Warfare in South Jiangxi*, p. 2.)
2. Zhong Shuqi, Ruijin Museum, personal interview, 4/11/84.
3. Chen Pixian, *op. cit.*, ch. 1; Wang Yanjian, Beijing, 3/8/84; Chen Pixian, personal interview, Beijing, 6/11/84.
4. Chen Haosu, Chen Yi's son, personal interview, Beijing, 6/13/84. Chen Pixian, his longtime friend and associate, said fifty years later: "I would liked to have seen Chen Yi carried on a litter [in the Long March]." (Chen Pixian, personal interview, Beijing, 6/11/84.)
5. Hu Hua, professor of Party history, People's University, Beijing, personal interview, 3/21/84.
6. Nie Rongzhen, *Memoirs,* ch. 10.
7. There has been controversy for fifty years about the strength of the Red Army. These are the actual figures of the muster rolls of October 8, 1934. They were listed in two columns; first, actual strength as of October 8, and second, the figure that would be reached when reinforcements were integrated into the armies as of October 12, 13, and 14. The first column total was about 70,000. The second column total, as given here, is 86,859. New recruits obtained in the intensive campaigns of 1934 had been placed in independent regiments together with local militia. These were now being assigned to the armies. The Third, Fifth, and Ninth armies each got two regiments. The Eighth Army which was formed only in September 1934 got one. The Seventh and Ninth armies were formed in October 1933. Few of those in the two central columns were combatants. Zhang Demin, of the Yu County Museum, Jiangxi, put total combat troops at about 70,000. This

seems reasonable. Inflation of the size of the First Front Army to 100,000 for propaganda purposes was consistent with Red Army practice. Numbers were constantly overstated. Unit designations were frequently changed to confuse the enemy. Many "armies" were properly corps or divisions. This became more and more true as attrition drew down the numbers. Yan Jingtang, Defense Ministry researcher and source of the archival figures, is convinced that the base line totals of October 8, 1934, were accurate. A "Front Army," in Red Army usage, meant a number of armies under unified command. The First Front Army at the beginning comprised the First, Third, Fifth, Seventh, and Ninth Army Groups. An "Army Group" simply meant an "army" under a military general and a political commissar (the two always shared command and usually the political commissar was the senior). These designations, more and more unrealistic, were maintained until almost the end of the Long March.

8. Yan Jingtang, senior researcher, Ministry of Defense, personal interview, Beijing, 10/24/84.
9. Wei Xiuying, personal interview, Nanchang, 4/15/84.
10. Documents, Jiangxi Memorial Hall, Nanchang.
11. Zeng Xianhui, personal interview, Guiyang, 4/18/84.
12. Zhong Shuqi, Ruijin, 4/11/84.
13. Data from Changgang Museum, 4/9/84.
14. Han Suyin, *The Morning Deluge*, p. 241.
15. Professor Dai Xiangqing, professor of Party history, Jiangxi Party school, Nanchang, 4/14/84.
16. Dai Xiangqing, 4/14/84.
17. Wu Xing, personal interview, Nanchang, 4/15/84.
18. Yang Chengwu, *Recollections of the Long March*, Beijing, 1982, pp. 7–11.
19. Wei Xiuying, 4/15/84.

4. The Man in Bleak House

1. Otto Braun, *Comintern Agent*, pp. 87–88. Wu Xiuquan was the interpreter for the Li De–Xiang Ying conversation. He did not recall Xiang's warning about Mao. He did recall Li De saying to Xiang: "I think you will come out alive with guerrilla warfare." (Wu Xiuquan, 3/28/85.)
2. George Hatem, personal interview, Beijing, 1984. Braun lived in Russia from 1939, when he left China, until after Stalin died in 1953. He was spared the fate of execution that befell most of Stalin's China specialists, but was forbidden to handle any Chinese matters. He lived in obscurity, possibly under police surveillance, and may well have been imprisoned or exiled for a period. His memoirs appeared first in *Horizont*, an East Berlin journal, in 1969 and posthumously in book form in 1974.
3. Much of this follows the impressions of George Hatem, who knew Braun intimately in Yan'an. It seems to have been Soviet practice at this time to send some agents out with passports in their own name on the theory that a "clean passport" provided better cover and less suspicion. Thus Richard Sorge, the famous Soviet spy, attached to military intelligence but originally

a Comintern man, was sent to Shanghai on a German passport carrying his own name. (F. W. Deakin and G. R. Storry, *The Case of Richard Sorge*, New York, 1966, p. 65.)

4. This route for sending funds was cut off with the rise of Hitler. The head of Red Help was arrested by the KMT and imprisoned. (Hu Hua, personal interview, Beijing, 3/21/84.) Ambassador Wang Bingnan expressed the opinion that the Comintern and the "Russian" faction had a great advantage over Mao Zedong because the Russians provided the Chinese Party "its leadership, its doctrine, its tactics, its financing—all of this. The Chinese Party was part of the Comintern." (Wang Bingnan, personal interview, Beijing, 3/20/84.)

5. Helen Snow, personal interview, 10/1/82.

6. Braun, *op. cit.*, p. 26; Steve Nelson, personal interview, 1/85.

7. Theodore Draper, personal interview, 10/81.

8. Deakin and Storry, *op. cit.* Peggy, wife of Eugene Dennis, and herself a Comintern courier, gives a picture of the Shanghai underground in late summer and early autumn 1934. She wrote that Dennis had visited the "Soviet provinces," but in personal conversation in January 1985, agreed that she was probably mistaken. Certainly he did not go to Jiangxi. Dennis sent a report on China to the Comintern via his wife, in violation of Comintern rules. He told her there was a row among the Comintern agents over the Jiangxi pullout and he could not forward his views through usual channels. It may have been that his wireless link had been broken. (Peggy Dennis, *The Autobiography of an American Communist*, Westport, Connecticut, 1977, pp. 82–84.)

9. Nelson, personal interview, 1/85.

10. Verle D. Johnson, *Legions of Babel*, University Park, Pennsylvania, 1967, pp. 125–26.

11. Braun, *op. cit.*, pp. 29–31.

12. If Braun was born in 1900, as stated in the introduction to his memoirs, he would have been only fourteen in 1914.

13. This comes from Wu Xiuquan, 3/28/84. In Braun's memoirs there is no mention of the Austrian army, of being a POW, of fighting in the Red Army in the Civil War, or of being a cavalryman. Wu Xiuquan believed, on the basis of his personal talks with Braun, that the street-fighting, escape-from-prison version was not correct. He said the interval between Braun's alleged arrival in Moscow in 1928 (in that version) and his appearance in China in 1932 was too short to enable him to enter Frunze and complete the course. Wu felt Braun's excellent Russian would have taken longer to acquire. He believed Braun's Austrian cover story was more or less true. In the text of his memoir, Braun claims he did train a Chinese cavalry division in 1936 on the basis of knowledge acquired at Frunze. He said he was not a cavalryman but was assigned to a cavalry division for a period in Tambov and participated in maneuvers in Byelorussia and the Ukraine. The English translation of Braun omits the reference to Tambov and in general is peppered with errors. (Braun, *Kitaiskiye Zapiskii, 1932–1940*, Moscow, 1974, p. 225; Braun, *Comintern Agent*, p. 167.)

14. This evaluation of Braun reflects the view of Wu Xiuquan and Hu Hua. Wang Yanjian provided the "dragon king" analogy.

15. Wang Yanjian, 3/5/84; Jerome Chen, *Mao and the Chinese Revolution,* New York, 1965, pp. 182–83.

16. Professor Hu Hua insisted that foreign descriptions of Bo Gu as "general secretary" were not correct. Xiang Zhongfa, he said, who was arrested and betrayed the Party in June 1931, was the last general secretary of the Party until Deng Xiaoping was elected by the Eighth National Congress in 1956.

17. Wu Xiuquan, *My Experiences,* p. 10.

18. This is based on the report of Interpreter Wu Xiuquan. Many, many years later, after the split between Moscow and Beijing in 1960, Moscow's propaganda was to take the same line. Mao, they insisted, was not a Marxist, China was not a Communist country. Mao was an "Asian Hitler" and China was run by "gangsters."

19. The slim pamphlet was published with the title *Red China: President Mao Tsetung's Report on Progress of the Chinese Soviet Republic, January 22, 1934.* It was issued in English translation by International Publishers in New York late in 1934, at a price of five cents. Hu Hua said in Beijing (3/21/84) that it had been so edited that only one paragraph of Mao's text remained. Examination of the English text seems to bear out Hu Hua. It is not a "report" to the Second Congress, but a propaganda text with segments extolling "Soviet Democracy," "The Financial Policy of the Soviets," "Marriage Under the Soviets," "The Anti-Imperialist Movement," "Soviet Labor Policy," etc. It reads like a pamphlet prepared for foreign distribution, not a speech made in Ruijin.

20. Wu Xiuquan, 3/28/84.

21. Lin Biao is presented in Beijing since his role in the Cultural Revolution, the plot against Mao, and his melodramatic death, as a supporter of Braun, but this may be a distortion. A Sino-French scholar, Chi-hsi Hu, cited an article written by Lin Biao and published in the Chinese Communist journal *Revolution and War* in July 1934, which contained what he regarded as a thinly veiled attack on Braun's strategy and implied support for Mao. (Chi-hsi Hu, *China Quarterly,* No. 82, June 1980, pp. 250–80.) Braun makes a rather condescending reference to Lin Biao's article in his memoirs, p. 74.

22. This is Hu Hua's evaluation on casualties. Zhou Enlai's estimate is from Snow, *Red Star,* p. 188. The comment on Guangchang from Peng Dehuai, *Memoirs,* pp. 189–92. The Liu Bocheng anecdote from Wang Yanjian.

23. Peng Dehuai, *op. cit.,* pp. 189–92.

24. Hu Hua, 3/23/84.

25. Peng Dehuai, *op. cit.,* pp. 189–92.

26. This is essentially the version of Wu Xiuquan. Some details from Wang Yanjian. Professor Hu Hua heard a more sinister version of this. He was told that Xiao Jingguang was deprived of his Army position on charges of "anti-leader" attitude and ordered to serve as one of the thousands of bearers on the Long March. He was not returned to command until after the Red Army reached Yan'an. However, Li Yimang, a Long March veteran, recalled Xiao as chief of the Cadres Battalion and said he went side by side

with him all the way to northern Shaanxi. (Li Yimang, personal interview, Beijing, 3/22/84.)
27. Hu Hua, 3/23/84.
28. Wang Yanjian, 3/5/84.
29. This is the conclusion of Professor Xiang Qing, personal interview, New York City, 1/14/85; some details from Wu Xiuquan and Professor Hu Hua.
30. Braun, *Comintern Agent*, p. 76. In spring 1936, Liu Changsheng arrived in northern Shaanxi from Moscow with a powerful wireless transmitter and a new codebook. The Moscow communications link was restored. A third member of the Central Committee underground Shanghai bureau, Huang Wenjie, was arrested in February 1935. He did not turn traitor. (Hu Hua 3/23/84.) Braun apparently thought the arrests were simultaneous. (Braun, *op. cit.,* p. 79.) Sheng Zhongliang ultimately came to the United States, where he published *The Chinese Revolution and the Sun Yat-sen University* (where he had studied during his stay in Russia).

5. First Moves

1. Wu Jiqing, personal interview, Nanchang, 4/15/84.
2. Wu Xiuquan, *My Experiences,* ch. 7.
3. This is the conclusion of Professor Dai Xiangqing of the Jiangxi Party School at Nanchang. Soviet sources are of no help. Most Soviet works simply say that the decision to leave was made in September 1934. There are some variations. *Ocherki Istorii Kitaya v Noveishee Vremya* (Moscow, 1959), edited by A. S. Perevertailo, says the decision was made by the Central Committee "in the summer of 1934" (p. 261). V. G. Sapozhnikov, in *Kitai v Ogne Voiny 1931–1950* (Moscow, 1977), says the decision was made by the Secretariat of the Central Committee on September 6, 1934, and that on September 8 there was a widened meeting of the Central Committee and the Military Council of the Red Army to discuss the planned breakout.
4. Wang Yanjian, 3/5/84; Zhong Shuqi, Ruijin Museum, 4/11/84; Wu Xiuquan, 3/28/84.
5. Xiao Ke, personal interview, Beijing, 3/9/84; personal communication, 6/11/84.
6. Cheng Zihua, personal interview, Beijing, 3/30/84.
7. Ningdu briefing, 4/13/84.
8. Peng Dehuai, *Memoirs,* pp. 182–83.
9. This account follows Hu Hua's reconstruction. Braun's comments from *Comintern Agent*, pp. 62–63.
10. Yang Chengwu, *Recollections of the Long March,* Beijing, 1982, pp. 14–15.

6. Stratagems

1. Smedley, *The Great Road,* New York, 1956, pp. 310–12.
2. Zhang Shengji, personal interview, Lanzhou, 6/4/84.
3. Peng Haiqing, personal interview, Bao'an, 6/8/84.
4. This information was supplied from Red Army archives by Yan Jingtang,

defense ministry researcher (personal interview, Beijing, 10/24/84, pp. 3–4). The code names were assigned by the Military Commission, October 13, 1934, to take effect October 15, 1934. They included: First Army Group, Nanchang; Third Army Group, Fuzhou; Fifth Army Group, Changan (present-day Xi'an); Eighth, Jinan (capital of Shandong); Ninth, Hankou. The First Military Column was called Hongan; the Second, Hongzhang. Within the First Army Group the three divisions had code names ending in "chang." They were: First Division, Guangchang; Second, Tienchang; Third, Duchang. In the Third Army, the division code names ended in "ou" —First Division, Ganzhou; Second, Suzhou; Third, Tingzhou. Each army group provided its own code names for regiments.

At the start of the March, deputy director of the Political Department and acting director in place of the ailing Wang Jiaxiang was Li Fuchun, an old friend of Mao's and married to Cai Chang, an even older friend.

The Army commands were as follows: First Army Group: commander Lin Biao, political commissar Nie Rongzhen; Third Army Group: commander Peng Dehuai, political commissar Yang Shangkun; Fifth: commander Dong Zhentang, political commissar Li Zhuoran; Eighth: commander Zhong Kun (later, when commander of the 115th Division, to desert to the KMT), political commissar Huang Xu; Ninth: commander Luo Binghui, political commissar Cai Shufan, later director of the Military Commission and political commissar of the Thirtieth Army. When the Red Army reached Zunyi, the Eighth Army was merged into the Fifth. The First and Second military columns were merged into one commanded by Liu Bocheng, political commissar Chen Yun, deputy Ye Jianying.

5. The Communist exit from the base area was not what Chen Jitang wanted; there is some evidence that he felt double-crossed. Otto Braun's account of this is confusing. He insists that Bo Gu consulted the Comintern and that this was the last message exchange with Moscow. (Braun, *Comintern Agent*, pp. 78–79.) Professor Hu Hua gave no credence to foreign rumors that the Communists paid Chen Jitang $50,000 for a free passage. (Hu Hua, 3/21/84.)

6. This information from Hu Hua. The transfer of wireless equipment was arranged through Wu Zhiping, a representative of Yang, and Xu Yixin of the Fourth Army, later to become China's ambassador to Pakistan. The transfer took place near Hanzhong. (Hu Hua, 3/23/80.)

7. Hu Yaobang, personal interview, Beijing, 6/14/84.

8. In January 1931, the Red Army captured a 16-watt transmitter, but it was not strong enough to reach Shanghai. (Hu Hua, 3/23/84.) The Red Army maintained two wireless bureaus, No. 2 for interception and decoding, and No. 3 for communications. Among those in Bureau No. 2 were Li Kehong, Zeng Xisheng, Fu Di, Cao Yingren. All were killed in action or dead by 1984. (Hu Yaobang, 6/14/84.) Li Qiang, later minister of foreign trade, was trained in Shanghai in cryptology and wireless techniques and ultimately invented a new kind of wireless antenna. Others who had a hand in it included Wang Zigang, later minister of posts and communications, Song Kanfu, later vice-minister of trade unions, and Zeng Xisheng, later first

secretary of Anhui province. Li Bai, another top specialist, lost his life in the closing days of the liberation struggle when he was killed in Shanghai. (Hu Hua, 3/23/84.)

9. Hu Hua, 3/28/85.
10. Li Yimang, personal interview, Beijing, 3/22/84.
11. *Minguo Ribao* files, Nanchang Provincial Library.
12. Chiang Kai-shek's intelligence failure may have been matched on the Communist side. In his unpublished manuscript *The Odyssey of a Fellow Traveller,* Philip J. Jaffe reports that the first issue of *China Today,* of which he was editor, appeared in October 1934. It featured an article on the Jiangxi soviet base. The chief source of *China Today*'s information was the underground Communist base in Shanghai. It was not until about two months later—that is, about December 1, 1934—that Jaffe and his associates received word from the Shanghai Communists that the Long March had started. (Jaffe, *Odyssey,* p. 127.)

7. The Conspiracy of the Litters

1. Edgar Snow, *Journey to the Beginning,* New York, 1967, p. 173.
2. Liu Ying, personal interview, Beijing, 6/14/84.
3. Zhong Ling, personal interview, Xi'an, 6/11/84.
4. Liu Ying, 6/14/84.
5. Hu Yaobang, 6/14/84.
6. Zhu Zhongli, personal interview, Beijing, 10/30/84; Liu Ying; Wu Xiuquan.
7. Hu Hua, 3/23/84.
8. Wu Xiuquan, 3/28/84.
9. Liu Ying, 6/14/84.
10. Braun, *Comintern Agent,* p. 88.
11. Han Suyin, *Morning Deluge,* pp. 10–11; Ross Terrill, *Mao,* New York, 1980, pp. 5–6.
12. Robert Payne, *Mao Tsetung,* New York, 1962, p. 30.
13. This perceptive analysis by Li Rui, deputy chief of the Organization Department of the Central Committee of the Chinese Communist Party, appeared in *Report on the Times,* dedicated to the ninetieth anniversary of Mao's birth, December 1983. It was published in English translation in *Peking Review* in April and May 1984. Li Rui estimated that Mao made one million words of notes in his five and a half years at Changsha Normal.
14. This reconstruction of Mao's reading and philosophy is largely based on the study made by Li Rui. Mao's notebooks were kept in a basket in his village home at Shaoshan. All but one were destroyed because of fear of reprisals in 1927, when Chiang Kai-shek turned on the Communists.
15. Translated (poorly) by Pearl Buck under the title *All Men Are Brothers* (New York, 1933).
16. This follows Li Rui. Mao told Edgar Snow about his mother's character. (Snow, *Red Star,* pp. 115–16.)
17. Xiao quote from Li Rui, *Beijing Review,* 4/30/84, pp. 23–24. Snow wrote that Mao "followed and studied" Washington's guerrilla tactics. This seems

an overstatement. Mao had no source for studying Washington's actual military operations. It seems more likely that he was inspired by Washington's success in fighting the British over many years with a small force, retreating in the face of superior military power, but keeping his movement alive and eventually triumphing. (Snow, *Journey*, p. 169.)

18. All of this follows Li Rui. Fang Weixia was chief instructor at Changsha Normal No. 1 and a friend of Li Rui's father. He joined the Revolution but was left behind in the Central Soviet Area when the Long March started and was killed by the KMT in 1935 in western Jiangxi. (Li Rui, personal interview, Beijing, 10/26/84.)

19. Li Rui, *The Early Revolutionary Activities of Mao Tsetung*, White Plains, N.Y., 1977, pp. 52–53.

20. Li Rui, *op. cit.*, p. 34.

21. George Washington was to be the role model of another Asian revolutionary—Ho Chi Minh.

8. *The Women*

1. Helen Snow, *The Chinese Communists*, Westport, Connecticut, 1972, p. 215.

2. Kang Keqing, personal interview, Beijing, 11/2/84.

3. Li Bozhao, wife of General Yang Shangkun, personal interview, Beijing, 6/15/84.

4. Snow, *op. cit.*, p. 173.

5. Wei Xiuying, personal interview, Nanchang, 4/15/84.

6. Liu Ying, 6/14/84.

7. Wu Xiuquan, 3/28/84.

8. Dick Wilson, *The Long March*, New York, 1979, p. 70.

9. Wu Xiuquan, 3/28/84.

10. Kang Keqing, personal interview, Beijing, 11/2/84.

11. Ding Ling, personal interview, Beijing, 3/23/84.

12. Helen Snow, *My Yenan Notebooks*, p. 46.

13. Helen Snow, *Inside Red China*, pp. 214–17.

14. Braun, *Comintern Agent*, p. 55.

15. Li Hong, *Guizhou Youth*, no. 2, 1983.

16. Han Suyin, *Morning Deluge*, p. 26.

17. Li Rui, personal interview, 10/26/84.

18. Li Rui, *Early Revolutionary Activities*, p. 334.

19. Li Rui, interview, 10/26/84.

20. Hu Hua, 10/84. Details of Yang Kaihui's death were reported by Suzanne Weiglan in *Eastern Horizon* No. 3, 1977. They were confirmed by Hu Hua, with minor differences. She gave Yang Kaihui's death date as October 26, 1930. This is probably the date of her arrest. In the intense Soviet-Chinese polemic after 1960, Moscow blamed Mao for the death of Yang Kaihui and Mao Zejiang. Moscow did not mention that Mao's attacks (there had been an earlier one, also unsuccessful) on Changsha had been initiated at instructions from the Comintern.

21. Poem translated in Willis Barnstone, *The Poems of Mao Tsetung*, New York, 1970. Many details of Yang Kaihui's children were reported in a big character wall poster during the Cultural Revolution. They are not necessarily accurate, but the story, in general, is confirmed from other sources including Hu Hua. The third Mao child had been placed with peasants and disappeared, only to be found years later, working as an accountant in a commune. The wall poster version is reported by David and Nancy Milton in *The Wind Will Not Subside* (New York, 1975, pp. 153–55). The existence of the third son is corroborated by Hu Hua. Ross Terrill, in *Mao*, says the children were saved by their grandmother and given the cover names of Yang Yunfu and Yang Yunshou. I was told in China in 1984 that Mao Anqing had several children. He was said to be unable to work because of brain injuries suffered either from a blow while begging in Shanghai or because of improper treatment by Soviet specialists. His wife was said to devote much of her time to his care.

22. *Journal of Revolutionary Relics*, No. 2, 1980.

23. An older brother, He Minxun, became a Communist cadre and in 1984 was serving on the Standing Committee of the People's Consultative Assembly and as vice-chairman of the Fujian Provincial Committee. He's mother escaped from Jiangxi with the aid of the Communist underground, made her way to Yan'an and died there of illness.

    Most of these details are drawn from a fascinating account of He Zizhen, published in issue No. 2, 1983, of the Guiyang journal *Guizhou Youth*. The article is signed by the nom de plume of Li Hong, daughter of a physician who treated He Zizhen in the Shanghai hospital where she spent much time in the last decade of her life. "Li Hong" interviewed He Zizhen on two occasions in 1978 and in autumn 1983. Most of these details had never before appeared in print in China. He Zizhen died in Shanghai April 19, 1984. A book of reminiscences was in preparation in Beijing in 1985.

24. Details of He Zizhen's pregnancy provided by Wu Jiqing, personal interview, Nanchang, 4/14/84; many Long March survivors, including some highly placed individuals, as late as 1984 had no knowledge of He Zizhen's experiences on the March.

25. Snow, *The Chinese Communists*, pp. 230–49.

26. Liu Ying, 6/14/84.

27. Liu Ying, 6/14/84.

28. Helen Snow, personal correspondence, 8/84.

29. Li Rui, 10/26/84.

30. Snow, *Inside Red China*, pp. 182–84.

9. The First Big Battle

1. These figures were supplied by Yan Jingtang, defense ministry researcher, from the archives, reporting Red Army weapons as of October 8, 1934, not heretofore disclosed. The figures are a bit smaller than the rough calculations of Otto Braun presented in *A Comintern Agent in China*, pp. 81–82. Braun was writing thirty years after the event, without benefit of notes. The

distribution of weapons was as follows: Rifles, etc.—First Army Group, 8,383; Third, 8,287; Fifth, 4,925; Eighth, 3,476; Ninth, 3,945; Military Commission, 1,987; Central Column, 2,240. Mortars—First Army Group, 8; Third, 9; Fifth, 2; Eighth, 2; Ninth, 2; Military Commission artillery battalion, 16.

The First Army Group had 546,649 cartridges and 612 mortar shells; Third, 482,736 and 680; Fifth, 213,661 and 93; Eighth, 180,351 and 104; Ninth, over 200,000 cartridges and 164 shells; Military Commission Column, over 70,000 cartridges and 880 shells; Central Column, 98,000 cartridges and no shells.

The Army started the March with 676 horses. The First Army Group had 338; the Third, 71; the Fifth, 49; the Eighth, 21; the Ninth, 29; the Military Commission, 34; the Central Column, 44. (Yan Jingtang, personal interview, Beijing, 10/24/84.)

2. Mo Wenhua's estimate is contained in *Velikii Pokhod*, Moscow, 1959, p. 158. *Velikii Pokhod* (The Great March) is the Russian translation of the Chinese-language *Recollections of the Long March of the First Front Army of the Chinese Workers and Peasants Army* (Beijing, 1958). It appears to be a verbatim translation. I use this rather than the original Chinese since I am familiar with Russian and not Chinese. Liu Bocheng, who offered the 400,-000 estimate (in *Recalling the Long March,* Beijing, 1978, p. 65), was hospitalized in 1984 in Beijing at the age of ninety-two. He was then the oldest surviving member of the Long March high command. Hu Yaobang offered his estimate in a personal interview,

3. Yu Qiuli, personal interview, Beijing, 10/31/84.

4. The question of the "corridor" is difficult to resolve conclusively in the absence of written evidence. It is not mentioned in the writings of Nationalist generals, although Xue Yue's cursory dismissal of the Xiang River battle has been cited as being indirectly supportive. There was intense antagonism between Bai Chongxi and Chiang Kai-shek, and an abortive rising by the Guangxi forces against Chiang in 1936. The Guangxi commander was equally opposed to the Communists. The evidence of Red Army commanders is confusing because the battle changed its character from the easy initial crossings to the desperate rear-guard actions. There was great variation between various locations. Xu Mengqiu's statements about the "arrangement" are unequivocal, but he also speaks of the ferocity of the battle. The declaration about the "arrangement" by Xu Mengqiu is cited by Professor Hu Hua. (Hu Hua, personal communication, 10/24/84.) In speaking to Helen Snow in 1937, Xu was not so clear. He spoke of a bitter five-day fight in crossing the Xiang, obviously the concluding phase of the battle. (Nym Wales [Helen Snow], *Red Dust,* Westport, Connecticut, 1957, p. 65.) In the introduction to the collection of Long March recollections he edited in 1938, however, Xu Mengqiu mentioned a "peaceful" crossing. Another Communist source, Miu Chuhuang, is cited by Jerome Chen as referring to Bai Chongxi's pullback of his forces, leaving the path for the Red Army clear to cross the Xiang. (Jerome Chen, *China Quarterly,* No. 40, October–December 1969, p. 32.)

5. Tan Zheng, *Velikii Pokhod*, pp. 166–67.

6. Wu Xiuquan, *Memoirs*, ch. 7.
7. Braun, *op. cit.*, p. 90.
8. Detail from Yang Chengwu, *Recollections of the Long March*, ch. 4. Yang's work was published with an introduction by Marshal Ye Jianying. The li approximates one-half a kilometer—between three and four to the mile.
9. Li Bozhao, personal interview, Beijing, 10/31/84.
10. All of this Eighth Army detail from Mo Wenhua, *Velikii Pokhod*, pp. 158–65.
11. Nie Rongzhen, *Memoirs*, ch. 8. Nie Rongzhen, Yang Chengwu and Peng Dehuai place the First Army Group on the right flank, Peng mentioning the First Army battling Hunan columns on "the extreme right." General Qin Xianghan and his associates say the Third Army was on the right, the First on the left.
12. Nie Rongzhen, *op. cit.*, ch. 8.
13. Mo Wenhua, *op. cit.*, pp. 158–65.
14. Nie Rongzhen, *op. cit.*
15. Liu Bocheng, *op. cit.*, p. 7; Qin, personal interview, 3/8/84; Xiao Hua, *The Difficult Years*, pp. 97–98.
16. Peng Dehuai, *Memoirs*, pp. 360–61.
17. Braun, *op. cit.*, pp. 89–90.
18. Wu Xiuquan was present at the scene as Braun's interpreter. He presents an account in his memoirs and added details in a personal interview. (Beijing, 3/28/84.) Wang Yanjian had a similar account. (Personal interview, Beijing, 3/5/84.) Braun offers a confused account, mixing up Zhou Zikun with Xiao Jingguang, later to become minister of the navy, with whom Braun had a running feud. (Braun, *op. cit.*, p. 91.)
19. Braun, *op. cit.*, pp. 89, 91.

10. *The Red Army Changes Course*

1. Kong Xianquan, personal interview, Zunyi, 4/24/84.
2. Dingyi in *Velikii Pokhod*, pp. 170–76. This is Lu Dingyi, a prominent Party cadre and propaganda official on the Long March. He rose steadily, entered the Politburo, became chief of the Central Committee Propaganda Bureau. He fell in the Cultural Revolution, was arrested and hauled before a Red Guard mob in the Workers Stadium of Beijing, along with General Yang Shangkun, Peng Chen, and General Luo Ruiqing, December 12, 1966. General Luo was already badly injured from a failed suicide leap (or a shove) from a sixth-floor window. Photographs show the men's arms being violently twisted by soldiers "guarding" them. On this or a later occasion, Lu Dingyi was hoisted by ropes tied to his arms and legs, swung about, and injured so badly Red Guards were unable to present him for further "trials." (Edgar Snow, *Red Star*, pp. 485–86; Edward E. Rice, *Mao's Way*, Berkeley, Cal., 1972, pp. 272–74.)
3. Zeng Xianhui, personal interview, Guiyang, 4/18/84.
4. Sun Ruikun, Party historian, Guizhou Museum, Guiyang, personal interview, 4/16/84.

5. Smedley, *The Great Road,* pp. 315–16.
6. Zeng Xianhui, 4/18/84.
7. Braun, *Comintern Agent,* pp. 92–93.
8. Wei Guolu, *On the Long March as Guard to Chou En-lai,* Beijing, 1978, pp. 6–8.
9. There is great variation in the estimates of the Chiang Kai-shek forces. Professor Hu Hua's figure of 100,000 is the lowest, but it applies specifically to the Nationalists in place in Hunan. General Wu puts the figure at 200,-000; Wang at 300,000; and General Xiao Hua at 400,000. The basic reason for the variation is differences over which regional troops are included in the overall total.
10. Most Chinese sources report that the meeting was held December 11. But Party historian Sun Ruikun believes it was held in the first ten days of December, probably December 10. He is the source of the information about Zhou's recollection, conveyed to him by Deng Yingchao, Zhou's widow. (Sun Ruikun, 4/18/84.)
11. Xu Mengqiu edited the volume *Record of Experiences with the Army on the Western March,* Shanghai, 1938, and wrote an introduction to it. Some of these materials were published in differing forms after the Chinese People's Republic was proclaimed, October 1, 1949. Helen Snow reported on Xu Mengqiu in *The Chinese Communists,* Westport, Connecticut, 1977, p. xix; Xu's later fate, Hu Hua, personal interviews, Beijing, 3/21/84, 3/29/84.
12. There are no substantial differences in the accounts provided by Professor Hu Hua (3/23/84); General Wu Xiuquan (3/28/84); Wang Yanjian (3/5/84); Sun Ruikun, personal interview, Guiyang (4/18/84); and Wu Dingguo, director, Cultural Department, Liping county (personal interview, 4/21/84). Otto Braun calls it a "short meeting." He says he suggested that they let the Nationalist troops move ahead, then slip behind them and head for the Second Army in northwest Hunan. No one seemed interested in this notion.
13. The Liping communiqué is dated December 18, and this date is generally used for the meeting. Sun Ruikun, and his colleagues at the Guizhou Museum, suggest a date of December 15–16. In not a few cases, official communiqués of meetings are dated a day or more after the actual meeting, reflecting a delay in composing or circulating the document. Professor Hu Hua calls it a Politburo meeting; Wang Yanjian calls it a Central Committee meeting; Sun Ruikun and his colleagues point out that the communiqué was signed in the name of the Central Committee and the Military Commission; Wu Dingguo calls it a Politburo meeting; so does Liu Bocheng. (*Recalling the Long March,* p. 8.)
14. Not until shortly before my visit to Guizhou and Liping in April 1984 did Chinese historians fix on the Xu merchant house as the site of the Liping meeting. The identification process had been under way for a long time. Local residents had been asked for ideas. Photographs of possible buildings were taken. These were then submitted to He Changgong, the redoubtable political commissar who won bandit Wang over to the cause of Mao Zedong; to Huang Hexiang; and to Fan Jinbiao, one of Zhou Enlai's body-

guards. The photographs were taken to Beijing in 1978. Fan Jinbiao recalled that the place where the meeting was held was next to a German Lutheran church. The church has since been torn down, but the only site that matched Fan's recollection was the shop and house of the merchant Xu. The building in 1984 was being restored to its 1934 condition. Information on the house was provided by Wu Dingguo.

15. Basic Liping details from Wu Dingguo, 4/21/84, and Sun Ruikun, Party historian, Guiyang, 4/18/84. Part of the original plan was to set up a base in southern Hunan. Li Yimang was named political commissar of a battalion for this purpose. The base was to be located beyond the Xiang River in a mountainous area where the Party was well organized. Perhaps it was envisaged as something like Mao's base on Jinggangshan. It was predicated on the theory that as the Red Army moved west, it would attract the KMT troops, pull them away, and leave the area free for the emergence of the new soviet regime. "Unfortunately," Li recalled, "it did not work out as we expected. We got there and had to disperse because the military situation was such that we could not operate." Hu Hua confirmed Li Yimang's account. He said the base was supposed to be a secondary operation and was not to be carried out until after the main force joined the Second and Sixth Army groups. Gong Chu, who was left behind in Jiangxi and who turned on the Communists and tried to capture Chen Yi, was involved in these plans, Hu Hua said. Gong wrote about them in a book which he later published in the United States as *The Red Army and I.* (Hu Hua, personal interview, Beijing, 3/23/84.) No one in Liping now remembered that foreigners had ever come there, although, of course, the Lutheran church showed that there had once been a foreign presence. The visit of our party brought a crowd of a thousand or more to the streets. Regular Army soldiers aided police in controlling it.

16. Sun Ruikun, Guiyang, 4/11/84.
17. Sun Ruikun, Guiyang, 4/11/84.

11. *Zunyi*

1. New Year's detail from Chen Changfeng, *On the Long March,* pp. 30–44. Order of the day cited by Han Suyin, *The Morning Deluge,* p. 277; the version published by (then) Air Chief Marshal Liu Yalou includes the phrase (probably added later): "and open up a new base for resisting the Japanese." (*Stories of the Long March,* Beijing, 1958, p. 11.) The order was signed by Zhu De, Zhou Enlai, and Wang Jiaxiang. (Yan Jingtang communication, 1/3/85.) General Qin Xinghan gives the date of the Politburo meeting as January 1, 1935, which presumably is the date of the order of the day. Qin adds that the order specified the setting up of a base in Guizhou. Braun recalls proposing to Mao that the Red Army halt and do combat with the three enemy divisions said to be advancing from Hunan. Braun dates this to the day after the crossing of the Wu. However, Chen Changfeng recalls Mao specifying the advance of the three divisions under Generals Xue Yue and Zhou Hunyuan as the reason they must hurry to the Wu. It seems likely

that the question of the three divisions arose at the protracted Politburo meeting. Braun wrote his memoirs with no notes, depending on his memory, a report he made in Moscow in 1939, and study of such documents as he could obtain in the U.S.S.R.

2. Fourth Regiment operations: Liu Yalou, *Stories of the Long March* (pp. 21–22); Sixth Regiment operations: Wang Chicheng, *The Long March: Eyewitness Accounts* (Beijing, 1963, pp. 22–28); bridge building: Huang Chaotien, *Recalling the Long March* (Beijing, 1975, pp. 26–32); capture of Zunyi: Tian Xingyong, director, Zunyi Museum, 4/24/84. There are slight discrepancies in dates. Completion of the bridge may have been on January 4; entry into Zunyi may have occurred January 5. The official chronology records the Red Army's capture of Zunyi as January 7 and the arrival of the command echelon, including Mao, as January 8. Authorities in Guiyang and Zunyi agree on the January 7 and January 8 dates. (Sun Ruikun, 4/18/84; Tian Xingyong, 4/24/84.) Entry to Zunyi: Wei Guolu, *On the Long March as Guard to Chou Enlai* (pp. 11–12).

3. Smedley, *The Great Road,* p. 315.

4. Nie Rongzhen, *Memoirs,* p. 10.

5. Description of the Bai Huizhang house, the residences of Mao and of Bo Gu, and the Catholic church, from personal inspection, 4/24/84; other details largely from Tian Xingyong, director, Zunyi Museum, personal interview, 4/24/84.

6. Sun Ruikun, Guizhou, 4/18/84.

7. Description of room at Zunyi, personal visit; seating arrangements, Wu Xiuquan. "The furniture now is somewhat modified," Wu said. ("Improved," commented one of those present at the interview.) The present-day chairs are an expensive set, dark wood, the backs woven bamboo, neatly arranged around the table, the whole scene bearing a ceremonial aura, like the set of a play. The rough iron stove that Braun was said to have kicked over in a fit of anger ("He didn't," Wu asserts) has vanished. The list of those present is from a Xinhua News Agency report of March 4, 1984, quoting the Committee for Collecting Party History Materials of the Central Committee, which discovered the Chen Yun report in April 1982. Chen Yun was said to have delivered it to the central column cadres about March 24, 1935, at the time of the Fourth Crossing of the Red (Chishui) River. Early versions had reported Dong Zhentang, commander of the Fifth Army, present. Detail on Wang Jiaxiang from Zhu Zhongli, his widow, personal interview, Beijing, 10/30/84. Wu Xiuquan presented some materials in his memoirs, some in a personal interview.

8. Wu Xiuquan, *My Experiences,* ch. 7 and interview.

9. Wu Xiuquan, *op. cit.,* ch. 7.

10. Wu Xiuquan, *op. cit.,* ch. 8 and interview.

11. Hu Hua, 3/23/84.

12. Wang Yanjian, 3/5/84.

13. Wu Xiuquan, 3/28/84.

14. Nie Rongzhen, *op. cit.,* p. 9; Wu Xiuquan, *op. cit.,* ch. 7; Hu Hua, 3/23/84.

15. Wu Xiuquan, 3/28/84; Braun, *Comintern Agent,* pp. 98–107.

16. Echelon Three was commanded by Ye Jizhuang, head of the Red Army Logistics Department. After liberation he became minister of foreign trade. Li Linkai, the political director whom Liu Ying replaced, is now dead. The echelon, Liu Ying recalled, was a big headache. It was very difficult to get new bearers to replace those who drifted away. They were fearful of reprisals and finally had to be hired for two- or three-day terms, which permitted them to return quickly to their homes. Chen Yun oversaw this reorganization. Most of the echelon's functions were absorbed into the Department of Public Work, headed by Li Weihan (Lo Man). (Liu Ying, personal interview, Beijing, 6/14/84.)

17. Wu Xiuquan, *op. cit.*, ch. 7.

18. Wu Xiuquan, *op. cit.*, ch. 7 and interview, 3/28/84.

19. Nie Rongzhen, *op. cit.*, pp. 10–11.

20. Hu Hua, interview, 3/23/84.

21. Braun, *op. cit.*, p. 103.

22. Wu Xiuquan, *op. cit.*, ch. 7, p. 5; Nie Rongzhen, *op. cit.*, p. 11.

23. Hu Hua, interview, 3/23/84.

24. Nie Rongzhen, *op. cit.*, p. 10.

25. Nie Rongzhen, *op. cit.*, p. 11.

26. Peng Dehuai, *Memoirs,* pp. 195–200.

27. The account of the Zunyi conference has been pieced together from many sources, but the chief reference throughout is Wu Xiuquan, his memoirs, and his expansion upon them in the long Beijing interview. Professor Hu Hua has filled in many important details. Wang Yanjian has added some tidbits, but their authenticity is not always provable. Braun's comments provide a counterpoint. His memory is not accurate and he was, as Wu suggested, like a prisoner in the box. His memoirs constitute a latter-day effort to justify himself and blacken the records of the men who opposed him, headed by Mao and seconded by Zhou Enlai. A few details have been added from remarks made by Wu Xiuquan at the fiftieth anniversary celebration of Zunyi, in January 1985, and from new documents published at that time. Contemporary Chinese historians confirmed that the text of the Zunyi resolutions which was published by Jerome Chen in *China Quarterly*, No. 40, October–December 1969, pp. 1–17 is an accurate one.

12. *Mao Takes Charge*

1. Sun Ruikun, Guiyang, 4/18/84.

2. Braun, *Comintern Agent,* p. 105.

3. Sun Ruikun, Guiyang, 4/18/84.

4. Yu Qiuli, 11/4/84.

5. Zhou Enlai was not present at the start of the Ningdu meeting but was summoned from the front when it was proposed that he be named political commissar of the First Front Army. The condensed stenographic report of the meeting of October 21, 1932, reads as follows:

    "About the military leadership of the front the comrades of the CC Buro at the rear propose that Comrade [Zhou] Enlai take overall responsibility for directing the war and Comrade [Mao] Zedong return to the rear to take responsibility for the work of the Central Government.

"Because Comrade Enlai insisted that Comrade Mao stay at the front and be responsible for directing the war and Comrade Enlai also stay at the front, being responsible for supervising the implementation of the general guidelines, the meeting finally approved that Comrade Mao take temporary sick leave and be allowed to return to the front when necessary."

The Ningdu meeting did not accept Zhou's proposal to keep Mao at the front. (Yan Jingtang, personal interview, Beijing, 11/3/84.)

6. Hu Hua, 10/29/84.
7. Hu Hua, 10/27/84.
8. Yang Shangkun, 11/3/84.
9. Yang Shangkun, 11/3/84.
10. General Yang Shangkun presented this evidence. He said that Stalin apparently was worried that the United States might intervene in China if Mao pursued Chiang across the Yangtze. Yang also thought that Stalin, through the Yalta agreements, might have been under some obligation to Chiang Kai-shek about which the Soviet leaders never—to this day—informed the Chinese. (Yang Shangkun, 11/3/84.) During these same discussions Mao made a request that the Russians permit Mongolia to return to the Chinese sphere of influence. Soviet dominance had been agreed to by Chiang Kai-shek after the Tehran conference but was repudiated by Chiang at the end of World War II. Mao's request was rebuffed. (Ambassador Ling Qing, 12/8/84.)
11. Departure date of 3/19/19 from Stuart Schram. Li Rui's analysis of Mao was based on deep study and personal observation. Li Rui was born in Hunan. His father was Li Jibang, also known as Xiao Xi, a native of Pingjiang county, Hunan, born in 1882, died in 1922, a member of the liberal intelligentsia in Changsha, a friend of Fang Weixia, chief instructor at Changsha Normal School No. 1, a supporter of Dr. Sun Yat-sen. Fang Weixia belonged to *Xinmin Xuehui*, the New People's Study Society, of which Mao was a founder in Changsha. He was a close friend of Yang Changji, the teacher who so strongly influenced Mao. Fang Weixia died in the guerrilla war of south Jiangxi and Guangxi. Li Rui worked in the 1940s and 1950s in the news media. He was a member of *Liberation Daily*'s staff in Yan'an, later became director of the Hunan Provincial Party Propaganda Department. In 1952 he came to Beijing and, having an engineering degree, was put in charge of hydroelectric development. During the Great Leap Forward he was Mao's secretary until the Lushan meeting of 1959, at which Peng Dehuai fell from power. Li Rui was dismissed and spent the next twenty years at hard labor, and in exile and prison. He served eight years in Qincheng prison in Beijing (where Jiang Qing is now confined). From 1979 to 1982 he was minister of electrical power. He then became deputy chief of the Organization Bureau of the Party Central Committee. He has now retired, devoting his time to studies of Mao and Party history. His classic study of Mao's youth was first published in 1957 in a book of 200,000 Chinese characters, then withdrawn. A new and enlarged edition of 300,-

000 Chinese characters was published in 1980. (Li Rui, 10/26/84; Yan Jingtang, 11/3/84.)

12. This summary was presented by Professor Hu Hua. Proliferation of committees and commissions has led to great confusion. The creation of the military troika came about, Professor Hu Hua said, after repeated problems in decision-making. Referring questions to the full Military Commission of twenty members was cumbersome. A controversy arose over whether the Red Army should attack or bypass a local warlord stronghold near Zunyi. The commission ordered the attack. Mao objected. The commission overruled him. Late at night, Mao came to Zhou and renewed the argument. He persuaded Zhou and the next day they put the question again to the commission, proposing a change to give the troika of Zhou, Wang Jiaxiang, and Mao the right to make daily decisions. This was approved.

13. Hu Hua, 10/14/84; Professor Xiang Qing, 1/14/85.

14. Xiang Qing, Party history specialist, Beijing University, personal interview, 3/16/84. Otto Braun says that Chen Yun had the mission of trying to persuade Moscow to provide military assistance to the Chinese Red Army. (Braun, p. 105.) The "million man" Red Army was an idea being propagandized in the Central Soviet Area by the "Bolsheviks" as early as 1932. It was completely divorced from reality.

15. The existence of the transmitter in Madame Soong's residence is attested to by two important Party historians, Hu Hua (personal interview, Beijing, 3/29/84) and Xiang Qing (New York, 1/14/85). However, Pi Pingfei, in Hongqi·(*Red Flag*, 4/16/84) said that the transmitter "Under Pan Hannian's leadership" was located in Rewi Alley's "residential compound." Rewi Alley had some years earlier spoken of the placement of the transmitter in the attic of his house. So there is still some uncertainty about the matter.

There seems to have been no foundation for the case against Pan Hannian. He was supposed to have been arrested by the Japanese when they occupied Nanking and to have been released after agreeing to spy for them. A close friend of Madame Soong's recalled being summoned to her house one Sunday in 1953. Madame Soong was extremely upset. "They've nabbed Pan," she said. After the Communists came into power, Pan was named deputy mayor of Shanghai under Chen Yi. Another man arrested on charges of Japanese espionage at this time was Liu Cunqi, in 1985 editor of the English language *China Daily*. He was exiled to the wild Manchurian border where he lived for twenty-five years before being released.

13. *A Needle Wrapped in Cotton*

1. Yang Shangkun, personal interview, Beijing, 11/4/84.
2. Yang Shangkun, 11/4/84.
3. Snow, *Red Star*, pp. 498–99.
4. Zhang Yunyi was commander of the Seventh and Yu Zuoyu of the Eighth. Zhang later became a senior general and president of the Guangxi provin-

cial administration and government. He died in the early 1970s. (Yan Jingtang, 10/27/84.)

5. Hu Hua, 10/28/84.
6. Hu Hua, 10/29/84.
7. Yan Jingtang, 10/24/84.
8. Hu Hua, 10/29/84.
9. Details from Yan Jingtang, 10/24/84; Hu Hua 10/26/84. Luo Fu told Edgar
   Snow that the total of "counter-revolutionaries"—that is, political prisoners
   as distinguished from "class enemies"—executed in the Central Soviet Area
   was "no more than 1,000." Between 400 and 500 landlords, and several
   hundred usurers (less than 1,000), were executed in Jiangxi, he estimated,
   and not more than 100 landlords and officials in the course of the Long
   March. (Edgar Snow, *Random Notes on Red China*, Harvard, 1957, p. 88.)
10. Yang Shangkun, 11/3/84.
11. Mao Zetan retained a post as political commissar of an independent army
    division but went to Yudu and stayed for a time with Mao Zedong. (Hu Hua,
    personal interview, 10/29/84.)
12. Hu Hua, 10/29/84.
13. The formal charges against Deng in Lo Man's article, "Struggle to Defend
    the Party's Line," were: (1) following an absolutely defensive line and
    opposing the Party's offensive line in military affairs; (2) opposing the policy
    of attacking large cities and of expansion of the Red Army to a strength of
    one million; and (3) distrust and lack of confidence in the Central Commit-
    tee elected at the Fourth Plenary and in the Comintern.
14. Details from Hu Hua, 10/29/84. Luo Ming and his wife started the Long
    March, but had to be left behind in Guizhou. Luo was seriously wounded
    by a bomb fragment in the Loushan Pass battle in February 1935, and his
    wife fell ill. (Hu Yaobang, personal interview, Beijing, 6/14/84.) When they
    recovered, they worked for a time for a landlord, he as a farmhand, she as
    a cook. Later they made their escape to Mei county in Guangdong and then
    to Singapore and Malaya, where they worked as teachers. After liberation
    they returned to China and Luo Ming became head of South China Univer-
    sity. (Zhang Yuanyuan, letter, 1/11/85.) Luo Ming was still alive in 1985,
    aged ninety, and was vice-chairman of the Guangdong People's Political
    Consultative Conference. General Yang Shangkun recalled meeting Luo
    Ming at the first National People's Conference in Beijing in 1950. A man
    came up, shook hands, and said: "You don't remember me. I'm the Luo
    Ming line." (Yang Shangkun, personal interview, Beijing, 10/28/84.)
15. Wang Yanjian, 3/5/84.
16. Wang Yanjian, 3/5/84.
17. Yang Shangkun, 11/3/84.
18. Yan Jingtang, 10/24/04.
19. The version of Deng being transferred at his own request is presented by
    Yan Jingtang. It conflicts with others, which place Deng as marching as a
    simple soldier, and with an account by Li Yimang, who says he traveled
    with Deng in the Cadres Regiment, each with a horse at his disposal. Yan
    Jingtang obtained his information from the Party Document Research De-

partment, which, in turn, obtained it by interviewing Long March com-manders. Details of Deng's early career remain somewhat fuzzy because of his reluctance to submit to biographical interviews. Professor Hu Hua believes that Deng's case as a follower of the Luo Ming line was handled somewhat leniently because of a division of opinion at the top: Zhou Enlai and Luo Fu favored leniency; Lo Man wanted severe punishment. (Hu Hua, 10/29/84.)

20. General Yang Shangkun has taken a lead in looking into details of Deng's role as secretary general of the Central Committee. The principal evidence of Deng's taking the post before Zunyi is his own recollection. This won support at the celebration of the fiftieth anniversary of Zunyi held in Beijing in January 1985. Deng Yingchao, Zhou Enlai's widow, came forward with a recollection that she had held the post until the Liping meeting, when she gave it up because of illness and it went to Deng Xiaoping. If her recollection is correct, the post must have been largely inactive, since she had been too ill before the start of the March and during most of it to carry on official burdens. As she wrote in *China Reconstructs* in 1984: "I was merely a sick camp follower in the convalescent brigade." The official roster of those who held the position, as now prepared by historical specialists in Beijing, is as follows: Cai Hesen and Wang Ruofei during the general secretaryship of Chen Duxiu; Deng Xiaoping, then twenty-three, under Qu Qiubai; Li Lisan under Xiang Zhongfa; "after the Central Committee move to the Central Soviet Area" in 1932, i.e., during Bo Gu's regime, Deng Yingchao; "after the Liping meeting," Deng Xiaoping; "after the Zunyi meeting" (actually probably after the Huili meeting), Liu Ying; "at end of 1937" (possibly as early as the Maoergai meeting in August 1935), Wang Shoudao, later to become minister of communications.

The role of Liu Ying as secretary-general was not known to Party historians until she mentioned it to the writer. Her recollection was confirmed by that of Kang Keqing (personal interview, Beijing, 11/2/84).

21. Wu Xiuquan, 3/28/84.

14. *Mao Skirts Disaster*

1. Tian Xingyong, director, Zunyi Museum, personal interview, 4/24/84.
2. Lian Chen (Chen Yun), *Velikii Pokhod,* pp. 66–67.
3. Tian Xingyong, 4/24/84.
4. The problem of "white" bandits was acute in this area after liberation. In one county they killed all but two members of the bandit suppression team. Regular PLA units had to be sent in to wipe them out. They were supported by the intricate clan structure and maintained contact with other KMT remnants in Guizhou and Jiangxi, like the KMT troops in the "Golden Triangle" of Burma, Laos, and Thailand. Bai Huizhang, the Zunyi KMT commander, came over to the Communists just before the PLA's victory and was enlisted to help the Commission for Wiping Out Bandits. However, caught passing information to the KMT soldiers, he was tried and executed

in 1951. Not until 1952 were the "bandits" wiped out. (Tian Xingyong, personal interview, Zunyi, 4/24/84.)

5. "Dr. Lian Chen," described as a former KMT physician who had been co-opted into the Red Army, published his recollections in the Long March reminiscences printed in Beijing in 1958, then translated into Russian and issued as *Velikii Pokhod* (The Great March) in Moscow in 1959. (This memoir and others in the collection were originally published individually in the period 1936–37.) The "Lian Chen" memoir is the first in the book and one of the most valuable. It breaks off after the crossing of Luding Bridge, when, the author explains, he was transferred to other duties. The identity of the writer, Chen Yun, was revealed only at the time of the fiftieth anniversary of the Zunyi meeting, in January 1985. In fact, Chen Yun broke off his account because at that point he was dispatched on a secret mission to Moscow to bring news of the Zunyi decisions to the Russians.

6. Tan Zheng, *Velikii Pokhod*, pp. 205–10.

7. Tian Xingyong, 4/24/84.

8. Wei Guolu, *op. cit.*, p. 24.

9. Ding Ganru, Deputy Chief of Staff, Chengdu, personal interview, 5/13/84.

10. Reported by Cheng Fangwu, *Memories of the Long March*, Beijing, 1977, pp. 53–55. Fifty years later, Kang Keqing minimized the danger: "It is possible that if we moved slowly we might be captured." In her judgment Qinggangpo was "a good battle." It had to be fought, otherwise the enemy would have overtaken the Red Army and the situation would have been worse. (Kang Keqing, personal interview, Beijing, 11/2/84.) Gu Yuping, a young bodyguard assigned to Zhou Enlai's wife, called the sudden move across the Red River a tactic to "confuse the enemy."

11. Details of the battle from on-the-spot inspection; from Tian Xingyong, Zunyi Museum, personal interview, 4/24/84; Sun Ruikun, Guiyang, personal interview, 4/24/84. General Qin was especially helpful in clarifying the conflicting and often contradictory details. Tan Zheng's account is the best that has appeared of the operations of Lin Biao and the Second Division. Li De's memoirs present an incoherent jumble. He reports that Mao twice visited Lin Biao's headquarters, but where and why are not made clear. No Chinese or foreigner's works touch on the battle. Even Lian Chen (Chen Yun) says not a word about Qinggangpo. It was not mentioned by Mao or anyone else to Edgar Snow in his Bao'an interviews of 1936. There were, actually, not a few recriminations about the battle, and after Mao turned on Peng Dehuai in 1959, efforts were undertaken to make him the scapegoat. Xiao Hua, then in the Political Department of the First Army Group, commented on Qinggangpo without mentioning it by name. "We did not do very well and suffered considerable casualties. The warlord troops, however, kept their strength practically intact." (*A Single Spark Can Start a Prairie Fire*, vol. 3, p. 83.)

12. Wu Jiqing, personal interview, Nanchang, 4/15/84.

13. Xiao Ke, personal communication, 6/11/84.

14. Liu Ying, personal interview, 6/14/84.

15. Ding Ling, personal interview, Beijing, 3/23/84.
16. Lian Chen (Chen Yun), *op. cit.*, p. 68.

15. *Holding Chiang Kai-shek by the Nose*

1. Karen Gernant, unpublished thesis, quoting *Ta Kung Pao*, Tianjin, 2/23/35.
2. Sun Ruikun, Guiyang, 4/18/84.
3. Peng Dehuai, *Memoirs*, pp. 365–66.
4. Personal observation, Loushan Pass, 4/25/84.
5. Qin Xinghan, Beijing, 3/6/84.
6. *Ta Kung Pao*, Tianjin, Gernant thesis, 3/6/35.
7. Zhang Aiping, *Velikii Pokhod*, pp. 230–32.
8. Kong Xianquan, 4/24/84.
9. Hu Yaobang, Beijing, 6/14/84.
10. General Yang Shangkun did not share Hu Yaobang's high opinion of Dr. Wang Bin, blaming him for poor treatment of Wang Jiaxiang, who had to be carried on the whole Long March because of his serious stomach wound. Wang Bin became head of Red Army medical services after the Long March. (Yang Shangkun, personal interview, Beijing, 10/26/84.)
11. Kong Xianquan, 4/24/84.
12. Qin Xinghan.
13. Kong Xianquan, 4/24/84.
14. Lian Chen (Chen Yun), *Velikii Pokhod*, pp. 70–77.
15. Lian Chen (Chen Yun), *op. cit.*, pp. 70–72.
16. Information from Liu family, 2/15/85.
17. Hu Hua, 3/23/84.
18. See Peng Dehuai, *op. cit.*, pp. 365–66. Some Chinese question whether Liu Shaoqi completed the Long March but Hu Hua believes he marched all the way to northern Shaanxi, participated in the Politburo meeting in December at Wayaobu, then went to Tianjin and Beijing to reorganize Party work and particularly to build on the December 9, 1935, student demonstration. (Hu Hua, 3/23.) This version is supported by Liu's widow, Wang Guangmei (personal communication 6/85). Many Western specialists remained skeptical for years about Liu Shaoqi's participation in the Long March but it has now been unequivocally established.
19. Sun Ruikun, Guiyang, 4/18/84.
20. Liu Bocheng, *Recalling the Long March*, p. 11.
21. Mao Tsetung, *Poems*, Beijing, 1976, p. 16.
22. Personal observation, 4/27/84; interviews, Qin Xinghan and Tian Xingyong, 4/28/84.
23. Kong Xianquan, 4/24/84.
24. Cheng Fangwu, *Recollections*, p. 59.
25. Qin Xinghan and Tian Xingyong, 4/28/84.
26. Wang Tianxi, *Historical Materials Collection*, Guizhou province, April 1963.

27. Chen Shiqu, *Velikii Pokhod,* p. 55.
28. Wang Tianxi, *op. cit.*

16. *Mao's Great Deceptions*

1. Wang Shoudao, *Velikii Pokhod,* pp. 281–86, on Ninth Army movements. Detail on wife of Luo Binghui from Snow, *Red Star,* p. 173, and Dr. Dai Zhengqi, 3/30/84.
2. Chen Shiju, *Velikii Pokhod,* pp. 255–60.
3. Nanjing, *Zhonqyang Ribao,* April 1936, quoted in Gernant unpublished thesis.
4. Kang Keqing, personal interview, Beijing, 11/3/84; Smedley, *The Great Road,* p. 316.
5. Smedley, *op. cit.,* p. 314.
6. Zhang Aiping, *Veiikii Pokhod,* pp. 267–68.
7. Braun, *Comintern Agent,* pp. 112–14.
8. Yang Chengwu, personal interview, Beijing, 3/15/84.
9. Deng Hua, *Velikii Pokhod,* pp. 271–80.
10. Zhang Aiping, *op. cit.,* pp. 271–75.
11. Lian Chen (Chen Yun), *Velikii Pokhod,* p. 69; Zhang Aiping, *op. cit.,* p. 274.
12. Yang Shangkun was wounded around April 27, 1935, according to KMT newspaper accounts. *Ta Kung Pao* of Tianjin mistakenly reported that First Army Political Commissar Yang Naikun [*sic*] was killed at Baishui. This report is unusual in its comparatively accurate information about a Red Army casualty. (Gernant, VIII, p. 25; Yang Shangkun, 10/26/84; Zhang Aiping, *op. cit.,* p. 287.)
13. Li Hong, *Guizhou Youth,* No. 2, 1980; *The Red Flag Waves,* vol. 24; "Random Thoughts on a Photograph of He Zizhen," *Journal of Revolutionary Relics,* no. 2, 1980. Gu Yuping, Deng Yingchao's attendant, mistakenly placed the scene of the bombing at a point near Zhaxi. He appears to have confused the site of the bombing with the location of the birth of He Zizhen's child.
14. Helen Snow, personal communication.
15. Zhong Chibing completed the Long March despite his wounds. He asked to be carried on a litter. When told men could not be spared to carry him, he asked for and was given a horse, which he rode despite his condition. (Yang Shangkun, Beijing, 10/26/84, p. 1.) Cai Shufan started the Long March as political commissar of the Ninth Army. In August 1935 the Ninth Army was reorganized as the Thirty-second Army and Cai Shufan became director of the Political Department of the Military Commission column; when the Red Army reached northern Shaanxi, he became political commissar of the Thirtieth Army. (Yan Jingtang, Beijing, 10/24/84.)

17. *The Golden Sands*

1. E. J. Kahn, Jr., *The China Hands,* New York, 1975, p. 57.
2. John S. and Caroline Service, personal interview, 12/2/84; Caroline Service correspondence, 3/84; Cyrus Carney to Peggy Darrow, 5/1/35.

3. Wang Yanjian, 3/5/84.

4. The story of Chiang and his wife fleeing in terror from Kunming has been endlessly repeated from the time of Edgar Snow's *Red Star Over China.* The couple did visit Kunming, but only after the fighting was over. They came in mid-June, as Caroline Service clearly recalled, after she got back from Tonkin and before the birth of her baby in July 1935. To the relief of local authorities, the visit came after the harvest of the opium crop (Chiang's "New Life" Movement disapproved of opium). (Caroline Service, personal interview, 12/2/84.)

5. Lian Chen (Chen Yun), *Velikii Pokhod,* p. 75; Wei Guolu, *On the Long March as Guard to Chou En-lai,* pp. 28–30.

6. Wang Shoudao, *Velikii Pokhod,* pp. 284–86.

7. Xu Jitao, Yunnan Provincial Museum, personal interview, 5/5/84.

8. Xu Jitao, 5/5/84.

9. Xu Jitao, 5/5/84.

10. Wang Zonghua, director, Party history research, Huili, personal interview, 5/7/84.

11. Xu Jitao, 5/5/84.

12. Xu Jitao, 5/5/84.

13. Wu Xing, personal interview, Nanchang, 4/15/84.

14. Xu Jitao, 5/5/84; description of terrain here and following from personal observation.

15. The principal details come from Zhang Chaoman, a surviving ferryboat man, interviewed at the Jiaoping site (5/8/84). There are minor discrepancies between his story and those of Mo Wenhua, *Velikii Pokhod,* pp. 281–84, a member of the vanguard Red Army detachment, and Xiao Yingtang in *A Single Spark Can Start a Prairie Fire,* vol. 3, Beijing, 1982. Some versions say the crossing was made in seven days. They contend the Cadres Regiment crossed the river May 3, not May 1, as the local authorities believe.

16. Personal observation. Details from Wang Zonghua, Huili, 5/7/84; Chen Changfeng, *On the Long March with Chairman Mao,* pp. 45–49. Li Yimang, chairman of cultural exchanges, came to the same conclusion as he reports in his reminiscences, published in *Velikii Pokhod,* under the name "I. Man." The cave was so hot and stuffy he moved out onto the ledge (pp. 303–22).

17. Xu Jitao, 5/5/84.

18. Mo Wenhua, *op. cit.,* pp. 290–99. Li Yimang found the extremely narrow path along the heat-radiating stone wall of the Mountain of Fire (where Monkey in the fairytale singed his tail) one of the most difficult and dangerous experiences of the Long March. So did we. (I. Man [Li Yimang], *op. cit.,* pp. 303–22.)

19. Zhang Chaoman, personal interview, Golden Sands, 5/8/84.

20. Wang Zonghua, 5/7/84.

21. The details concerning Long Yun were supplied by Xu Jitao, Yunnan Museum, 5/5/84. Many foreigners in Kunming in 1935 believed that Long Yun was eager to see the Red Army move swiftly northward into Sichuan; that he was fearful of Chiang Kai-shek's intentions toward him. Joseph Rock, the

eccentric American botanist and explorer, noted in his diary at the time: "If I were Long I would let them [the Communists] go and to hell with [the Kuomintang]. . . . Chiang is forcing the Communists to the south into Yunnan, closing their way to the north, but Long undoubtedly will play him the trick and let them slip west . . . and Chiang will be in the lurch and it will serve him right." Long Yun joined the Communist regime in 1949 as vice-chairman of the National Defense Council and of the Southwest Administrative Committee. (S. B. Sutton, *In China's Border Provinces: The Turbulent Career of Joseph Rock, Botanist-Explorer,* New York, 1974, pp. 246–48.)

18. *The Chicken-Blood Oath*

1. Local photographers took pictures of the burning of the houses. Some were preserved in the Huili Museum until it burned in 1982. Photographs of the Long March are almost nonexistent. No one carried a camera and only a few group pictures have turned up in local photographers' shops. There is nothing to show the great events except some crude sketches drawn by Huang Zhen.
2. Wang Zonghua, Huili seminar, 5/7/84.
3. Wang Zonghua, 5/7/84.
4. Braun, *Comintern Agent,* p. 117.
5. Yang Shangkun, *Memoirs of a Chinese Marshal,* p. 15.
6. Peng Dehuai, *Memoirs,* pp. 19–23.
7. Agnes Smedley, *Battle Hymn of China,* New York, 1943, pp. 167–68.
8. Peng Dehuai, *op. cit.,* pp. 9–10.
9. Wu Xing, personal interview, Nanchang, 4/15/84.
10. Helen Snow, *Inside Red China,* p. 62.
11. Braun, *op. cit.,* pp. 114–16.
12. Nie Rongzhen, *Memoirs,* ch. 8.
13. Peng Dehuai, *op. cit.,* pp. 368–69.
14. Liu Ying, 6/14/84.
15. Peng Dehuai, *op. cit.,* pp. 367–69.
16. Wang Zonghua, 5/7/84; Nie Rongzhen, *op. cit.,* p. 13.
17. Peng Dehuai, *op. cit.,* p. 369.
18. There is considerable dispute about this question. The judgment that no communications were exchanged in the period from mid-January until early June is that of Shan Guozheng, research specialist at the Sichuan Provincial Museum, Chengdu. (Personal interview, 5/19/84.)
19. Braun, *op. cit.,* pp. 117–18.
20. I. Man (Li Yimang), *Velikii Pokhod,* pp. 303–22.
21. Wen Bin, *Velikii Pokhod,* pp. 322–25.
22. Wen Bin, *op. cit.,* p. 325.
23. Wen Bin, *op. cit.,* pp. 324–25.
24. Lian Chen (Chen Yun), *Velikii Pokhod,* pp. 80–81.
25. David Crockett Graham, *Folk Religion in Southwest China,* Smithsonian Institution, Washington, D.C., 1961, pp. 75–79.

26. Lian Chen (Chen Yun), *op. cit.*, pp. 89–96.
27. Xiao Hua, personal interview, Beijing, 3/18/84.
28. Peng Haiqing, personal interview, Bao'an, 6/8/84.
29. Ding Ganru, personal interview, Chengdu, 5/18/84.

19. *Those Left Behind*

1. Professor Dai Xiangqing, Jiangxi Party School, 4/14/84.
2. Chen Pixian, *Three Years of Guerrilla Warfare in South Jiangxi.*
3. Li Bozhao, 6/15/84.
4. Chen Pixian, *op. cit.*, ch. 2.
5. Zhong Shuqi, Ruijin, 4/12/84.
6. Zhong Qisong, personal interview, Changgang, 4/10/84.
7. All these details are from Chen Pixian's memoirs. He does not give a date for the telegram. He says "in early February." Sun Ruikun of the Party History Section, Guizhou Museum, said (4/13/84) that a telegram had been sent to Chen Yi from Zunyi, informing him and Commissar Xiang Ying of the Zunyi decisions. This was the only message found in the archives; no other telegram to or from Chen Yi or Xiang Ying; Professor Dai Xiangqing said (4/14/84) that on February 12 or 13, Chen Yi and Xiang Ying sent the Central Committee a request for permission to go into guerrilla warfare. They waited all day February 13, and between 5 and 6 P.M. got an answer approving operating in small, self-sufficient groups, relying on local subsistence, no longer confined to the former Central Soviet Zone. This, he said, was from the archives.
8. Dai Xiangqing, 4/14/84.
9. Chen Pixian, *op. cit.*, ch. 2.
10. This is the version Chen Pixian gives in his memoirs. In speaking he said the message to the Central Command was sent after the Zunyi conference and that a reply had come simultaneously with word about the Zunyi meeting. (Chen Pixian, personal interview, Beijing, 6/14/84.) Zhong Shuqi, archivist at the Ruijin Museum, said (4/11/84) that the message from the Red Army command about Zunyi arrived "in early March." Liu Jianhua, officer of the South Jiangxi guerrilla group, confirmed that the "last message" came through to Renfeng in "February–March." (Personal interview, Nanchang, 4/15/84.) There is a clear conflict about the messages and dates, but the preponderance of evidence supports the version given above. Yan Jingtang found in the archives evidence that the First Front Army wirelessed Chen Yi on February 5, 13, 25, and 28, 1935. How many of these messages were received is not certain, but Yan is confident that the February 28 message did not get through. After Zunyi a platoon of soldiers is said to have been dispatched to bring Chen Yi information on the meeting.
11. Chen Pixian, *op. cit.*, pp. 15–19.
12. Liu Jianhua, personal interview, Nanchang, 4/14/84; some details from Dai Xiangqing, 4/14/84, and Zhang Demin, director, Yu County Museum, 4/10/84.
13. Chen Pixian, *op. cit.*, ch. 3. In the final breakout, in which He Chang and

so many others were killed, the KMT claimed they captured 1,400 men, 657 guns and 18 machine guns. By the end of March those captured numbered 5,700. The KMT offered no figures on killed. (Guo Hualun, *The History of the Chinese Communist Party*, Taipei, 1969, pp. 23–26.)

14. Chen Pixian, *op. cit.*, p. 20.
15. Chen Pixian, *op. cit.*, p. 20; Ningdu Museum staff, 4/14/84.
16. Yan Jingtang, Beijing, 11/3/84.
17. Information about the women comes from several sources. The names were provided by Zhong Shuqi, archivist, Ruijin Museum, 4/11/84, and Yan Jingtang, 11/3/84. Information on their fate comes from Zhong and Yan, with additional details from Hu Hua, communication of 1/11/85. The story of Huang Changjiao is from *Selection of Historical Materials of Jiangxi*, Nanchang, 1981. The list is obviously incomplete. The mother of Deng Yingchao, wife of Zhou Enlai, was left behind. She was a doctor. Her age and poor health kept her from the Long March. Separation from her mother was a cruel blow to Deng Yingchao.
18. *Selection of Historical Materials, op. cit.*
19. Yan Jingtang, 11/3/84.
20. T. A. Hsia, *China Quarterly*, No. 25, January–March 1966, pp. 176–212. Qu Qiubai's remains were removed to the Party's cemetery in Beijing, June 18, 1955, and Mao issued a statement declaring he had "died a hero's death." In the Cultural Revolution, his remains were rooted out and the grave destroyed. It has since been restored.
21. Zhong Shuqi, Ruijin Museum, 4/11/84.
22. Yan Jingtang, 11/3/84.
23. Zhong Shuqi, 4/12/84.
24. Li Rui, *Early Revolutionary Activities*, p. 5.
25. Information from Hu Hua, 10/24/84. Gu Bo was secretary of the Front Committee of the Fourth Army (the early designation of the First Front Army), then member of the Jiangxi Soviet Committee. He was killed in Yuanyangkeng village, Guangdong province, in March 1935. (Yan Jingtang, 3/1/85.) Xie Weijun, Division commander, also attacked in the Luo Ming affair, died in battle in northern Shaanxi.

20. *The Legion of Death*

1. Edgar Snow, *The Battle for Asia*, New York, 1941, pp. 127–29.
2. Liu Jianhua, personal interview, Nanchang, 4/15/84.
3. Chen Pixian, personal interview, Beijing, 6/13/84.
4. Snow, *op. cit.*, pp. 130–32.
5. Liu Jianhua, 4/15/84.
6. *Selection of Historical Materials of Jiangxi*, Nanchang, 1981.
7. Chen Pixian, *Three Years*, p. 30.
8. Hu Hua, 3/23/84.
9. Incident from Chen Pixian, *op. cit.*, ch. 5, pp. 23–27. Gong Chu's story in his book called *The Red Army and I.* (Hu Hua, 3/23/84.) Some details from article by Liu Jianhua.
10. Chen Pixian, *op. cit.*, ch. 11, pp. 44–50.

21. Luding Bridge

1. Luo Ergang, *History of the Taiping Heavenly Kingdom.*
2. Smedley, *The Great Road,* pp. 21–29.
3. Wen Bin, *Velikii Pokhod,* pp. 338–39; Smedley, *op. cit.,* p. 312.
4. Han Suyin, *The Morning Deluge,* p. 288.
5. Impressions of John S. Service's mother, Grace.
6. There is a new Luding Bridge, of standard reinforced steel and concrete, about half a mile downstream from the suspension bridge. A PLA soldier is stationed to guard it. He will not permit pictures to be taken. There is another at Anshunchang, and between Anshunchang and Luding there are fifteen individual pedestrian suspension bridges and another concrete bridge for motor traffic.
7. Yang Dezhi, *Recalling the Long March,* Beijing, 1978, pp. 79–81.
8. Xiao Hua, personal interview, Beijing, 3/16/84.
9. Snow, *Red Star,* p. 197.
10. Smedley, *op. cit.,* pp. 134–39.
11. Yang Chengwu, personal interview, Beijing, 3/16/84.
12. Zhang Fuchen, Anshunchang briefing, 5/22/84.
13. There are minor discrepancies in the accounts of the Dadu operation. Principal reliance is placed on Yang Chengwu's account as given in his personal interview and on data gathered at the scene from the local archivists. The Lin Biao telegram, which mistakenly gives the date for completion of the operation as May 25 instead of May 29, was published in *The Long March Eyewitness Accounts,* Peking, 1964, pp. 98–99, prior to Lin Biao's fall and death in 1971. It is omitted in subsequent versions.
14. Impressions of river from personal observation, 5/22/84.
15. This account is drawn from General Yang Chengwu's recollections as presented in his personal interview and in the account in *Recalling the Long March,* with minor additions from briefings at Anshunchang and Luding; from General Xiao Hua, and from personal observation. General Qin has made some suggestions.

22. The Great Snowy Mountains

1. Chen Changfeng, *On the Long March with Chairman Mao,* pp. 56–61; Wei Guolu, *On the Long March as Guard to Chou En-lai,* pp. 34–39.
2. Yang Chengwu, *The Long March: Eyewitness Accounts,* Beijing, 1962, pp. 99–111.
3. Chen Changfeng, *op. cit.,* p. 62.
4. Yang Chengwu, 3/15/84.
5. Zhang Guotao, *The Rise of the Communist Party,* vol. II, p. 361.
6. Li Xiannian, political commissar of Zhang's Thirtieth Army and in 1984 President of the People's Republic, corroborated Zhang's statement about the codebook. He said he knew it had been lost and that they feared Chiang Kai-shek might have it. Therefore, few transmissions were carried on before the start of the Long March and then none at all for a long period. (Li Xiannian, personal interview, Beijing, 6/15/84.)

7. Zhang Guotao, *op. cit.*, p. 362.
8. Zhang Guotao, *op. cit.*, p. 364.
9. Zhang Guotao, recollection from his memoirs, *op. cit.*, p. 372. Senior historical researchers in the Sichuan Revolutionary Museum at Chengdu could find no archival evidence that the two armies knew where each other was until sometime after the Golden Sands crossing, around May 10, 1935. (Shan Guozheng, Jia Ke, Sichuan Revolutionary Museum, Chengdu, personal interview, 5/19/84.) They found no evidence of any wireless messages exchanged after January 22, 1935, until Zhang Guotao sent a protocol message congratulating the Central Committee June 12 on the Red Army's crossing of the Great Snowy Mountains and its meeting with the Fourth Front vanguard. There was an acknowledgment on the same date by the Central Committee to Zhang. (Chengdu briefing.) Wang Yanjian, the Long March writer, believes Mao had only a general idea of Zhang's whereabouts until his troops reached the far side of Jiajin Mountain. (Wang Yanjian, personal interview, Beijing, 3/5/84.) Li Yimang believes Mao got a general idea of Zhang's whereabouts from rumors circulated among the peasants. (Li Yimang, personal interview, Beijing, 3/22/84.)
10. Li Xiannian, 6/15/84.
11. General Qin believes that at the time of the Golden Sands crossing, the Fourth Front Army was still in motion; that Mao was aware that it was moving to northwest Sichuan but could not have known its precise location. Mao did calculate (correctly) that Zhang was west of the Snowies. Establishment of many of these details is made difficult because of political antagonism between Zhang Guotao and Mao and other Party leaders. Zhang ultimately broke with the Party and joined Chiang Kai-shek.
12. Chiang Yao-hui, *The Long March: Eyewitness Accounts*, p. 110.
13. Chen Changfeng, *op. cit.*, p. 69.
14. Zhang Shengji, personal interview, Lanzhou, 6/4/84.
15. Dr. Dai Zhengqi, 3/30/84.
16. Dr. Du Tanjin, director of National Research, PLA, personal interview, Beijing, 3/31/84.
17. Yan Jingtang, 10/24/84.
18. Ji Pengfei, personal interview, Beijing, 3/14/84.
19. Chen Changfeng, *op. cit.*, p. 68.
20. Hsieh Fangtzu, *Recalling the Long March*, Beijing, 1978, pp. 106–8.
21. Ji Pengfei, 3/14/84.
22. Du Tanjin, director, Army Medical Research, personal interview, Beijing, 3/31/84.
23. Wei Xiuying, 4/15/84.
24. Ding Ganru, personal interview, Chengdu, 5/13/84.
25. Li Yimang, 3/22/84.
26. Zhong Ling, personal interview, Xi'an, 6/11/84.
27. Hu Yaobang, 6/14/84.
28. Yang Dinghua, *Velikii Pokhod*, pp. 358–59.
29. Chen Changfeng, *op. cit.*, pp. 67–70.
30. Wei Guolu, *op. cit.*, pp. 43–49.

31. Dr. Du Tanjin, 3/31/84.
32. Li Xiannian, 6/15/84.
33. Some sources give the date of the meeting of the First and Fourth Front armies as June 16, 1935. This is the date of exchange of official messages by the two commanders. (Qin Xinghan, 3/6/84.)
34. Zhou Guoqing, director, Xiaojin County Office, 5/25/84.
35. Li Xiannian, 6/15/84.
36. Zhou Guoqing, 5/25/84.
37. Yang Dinghua, *Velikii Pokhod,* p. 359.

23. *Reunion*

1. Zhou Guoqing, 5/27/84.
2. Shan Guozheng, Sichuan Provincial Museum, Chengdu, 5/19/84.
3. Shan Guozheng, 5/19/84.
4. There has long been confusion about the meeting of Zhang Guotao and Mao Zedong. There are two principal eyewitness accounts, that of Zhang and one presented by Agnes S :dley in *The Great Road,* pp. 328–32, which comes from Zhu De or o .: of his associates. The details of the rain, Zhang on horseback, etc., seem accurate and are confirmed by other sources, including Zhang. However, Smedley gives the date of the meeting as July 20 and the place as "Erhokou," possibly a mistake for Lianghekou ("er" and "liang" both mean "two"), where the meeting was held the next day. Zhang's account is loaded with ex post facto political arguments, but probably conveys his underlying emotions accurately. Much of the account here and on ensuing pages is based on contemporary Chinese historical and archival research and personal observation of the area.
5. Xu Lixin, *Zhang Guotao's Swerving and Awakening,* Taipei, 1981, ch. 6.
6. Li Qin, Xi'an, 6/6/84.
7. Shan Guozheng, 5/19/84. Cai Xiaoqian, an important Party cadre who later went over to the KMT, estimated the Main Red Army strength at the time of the reunion as seven to eight thousand. He believed Zhang Guotao had about 70,000 effectives, an advantage of ten to one. However, he rated Mao's cadres as far superior to Zhang's. (Cai Xiaoqian, *The Kiangxi Soviet Areas and the Western Flight of the Red Army,* Taipei, 1970, ch. 3.)
8. Wen Xingming, cultural secretary, Maerkang, 5/25/84; Han Suyin, *The Morning Deluge,* p. 293.
9. Zhang Guotao, *Rise of the Communist Party,* vol. II, pp. 378–79.
10. Braun, *Comintern Agent,* p. 123.
11. Shan Guozheng, 5/19/84.
12. Shan Guozheng, 5/19/84.
13. Wen Xingming, 5/25/84.
14. Zhang Guotao, *op. cit.,* pp. 370–72.
15. Wen Xingming, 5/25/84.
16. Wen Xingming, 5/25/84.
17. Wen Xingming, 5/25/84.
18. Peng Dehuai, *Memoirs,* pp. 335–36.

19. Li Xiannian, 6/15/84.
20. John S. Service, 3/6/85.
21. Hu Hua, 3/21/84, 3/29/84; George Hatem, 3/19/84.
22. Hu Hua, 3/23/84, 3/29/84. Zhu Guang was a worker in the Shanghai Central Bureau who came to the Fourth Front Army. Zhang did not trust Shanghai Central. He put Zhu Guang under arrest. Zhang executed Kuang Jixun, founder of the Hubei-Hunan base area, and chairman of the local soviet as a Trotskyite. Zeng Zhongsheng, chief of staff of the Sichuan-Shaanxi Military Commission, was carried along as a prisoner, hands bound, legs roped. In June 1935 he smuggled a letter to Mao Zedong asking him to intervene. Zhang learned of this. In July 1935 during a night march, Zeng Zhongsheng was thrown off a high bridge and drowned. Rumors were spread that he had escaped custody and vanished. Data on all these cases from Hu Hua.
23. Zhang Guotao, op. cit., pp. 378–79.
24. Otto Braun claims he attended one session of the Politburo at Lianghekou on June 28. He describes the meeting as "peaceful" and suggests that the principal decisions had been made earlier and were only being given pro forma ratification. He says he agreed with Mao's proposal to move north and west and adds that the question of anti-Japanese action was scarcely mentioned. No one else reports more than one Politburo session, or that Braun was present. It is likely that Braun, as so often, is mistaken as to the date. The remainder of his report seems consistent with the contemporary Chinese historical reports. (Braun, op. cit., p. 124.)
25. Zhang Guotao, op. cit., p. 383.
26. Zhou Guoqing, 5/27/84.
27. Zhang Guotao, op. cit., p. 380.
28. Hu Hua, 3/29/84.
29. It is probable that at this meeting or a subsequent one, agreement was reached on a demand by Zhang Guotao for the inclusion in the Central Committee of a number of his supporters. Xu Lixin asserts that at Zhang's initiative, Xu Xiangqian, Wang Shusheng, Zhou Chongquan, Zeng Zhuanliu, Li Xiannian, He Wei, and Li Te were named to the committee. Cai Xiaoqian adds the names of Fu Rong and Zeng Fu. Cadres of the main Red Army, he reports, were very dissatisfied. They felt Mao had made too great a concession to Zhang. (Cai Xiaoqian, op. cit., ch. 3.) Details of the meeting from Zhang's memoirs, Professor Hu Hua, Shan Guozheng (5/19/84) and Nie Rongzhen's Memoirs, ch. 3.
30. Peng Dehuai, op. cit., pp. 372–73.
31. Nie Rongzhen, op. cit., ch. 8, pp. 14–15.
32. Zhang Guotao reports a dinner with Bo Gu at which there was much talk and argument about the work of the Politburo, the Party line, the Zunyi conference, and other political matters. Bo Gu may have been the source of the troublesome reports that Nie Rongzhen mentions. (Zhang Guotao, op. cit., pp. 394–99.)
33. Delight there certainly was. But there were incidents. Li Qun, a veteran of the 276th Regiment of the 91st Division of the 31st Army of the Fourth

Front Army, recalled an angry controversy between First and Fourth Front men. The Fourth accused the First of slaughtering some of the Fourth's horses. Troops were deployed and some shots fired. But no one was injured and the quarrel was resolved. (Li Qun, personal interview, Bao'an, 6/8/84.) General Qin doubted that any shots were fired.

34. Zhang Guotao, *op. cit.*, pp. 398–493.

24. Back of Beyond

1. Many of these details from personal inspection and interviews. Alas, the yamen is now half in ruins, a haunt of chickens and strolling pigs, its carvings and decor long vandalized. Some details from Yang Dinghua, *Velikii Pokhod*, pp. 362–63, and from Cai Xiaoqian, *The Kiangxi Soviet Areas...*, pp. 348–49. In extended travel in Tibet in 1980, the author saw nothing to equal this remarkable structure. At the time of the Long March, Zhuokeji consisted of the yamen and associated buildings, a monastery, and a cluster of Tibetan houses. It was the scene of an important opium fair every autumn. It is now on the outskirts of Maerkang, a thriving industrial and administrative center of eighteen thousand, which contained nothing but a small lamasery and a few houses when the Red Army passed by.
2. Tian Bao, personal interview, Chengdu, 5/18/84.
3. Wen Xingming, 5/25/84.
4. Yang Dinghua, *op. cit.*, pp. 364–68.
5. Yang Dinghua, *op. cit.*, pp. 369–71.
6. Hu Hua, 3/29/84.
7. Dr. Sun Yizhi, Beijing, 3/31/84.
8. Li Xiannian, 6/16/84.
9. Wu Jiqing, 4/5/84.
10. Wei Guolu, *On the Long March as Guard to Chou En-lai,* pp. 50–54.
11. Nie Rongzhen says Zhou was not able to attend either the Shawo or Maoergai conferences. (*Memoirs,* ch. 8.) General Yang Shangkun recalls that Zhou presided over the Shawo conference but was too ill to be present at the Maoergai meeting. (Yang Shangkun, 10/26/84.) The account given by Wei Guolu, Zhou's bodyguard, leaves the impression that Zhou's illness was over in four or five days and that he was able to attend to his duties in the Grasslands crossing. (Wei Guolu, *op. cit.*, pp. 50–55.) This is simply not true. Zhou was too ill to meet Yang Chengwu at the start of the Grasslands crossing and not until some time after reaching Baxi did he begin to return to his duties.
12. Edgar Snow, *Random Notes on Red China,* p. 97.
13. Yang Shangkun, 10/26/84; Hu Hua, 10/29/84.
14. Li Xiannian, 6/16/84.
15. Yang Shangkun, 4/3/84.
16. Yan Jingtang, 10/24/84.
17. Yang Shangkun, 4/3/84.
18. Zhang Guotao, *Rise of the Communist Party,* vol. II, pp. 411–12. Otto Braun adds some confusion. He says there was a Politburo meeting at

Suomo at the end of June before Maoergai. Possibly he meant Shawo. He says he attended it. Peng Dehuai places the Politburo meeting at Heishui. (PengDehuai, *Memoirs*, p. 379.)

19. Nie Rongzhen, *op. cit.*, ch. 8, p. 15.

20. The resolution, in fact, was drafted by Wang Ming, the Chinese representative to the Comintern in June 1935. It was first made public in a Chinese newspaper in Paris in October 1935. (Xiang Qing, New York City, 1/14/85.) Chinese accounts published before Mao's death attributed the resolution and the stand for a united front to Mao's wisdom and foresight. These accounts emphasized the role of "going north to fight Japan" at the Maoergai conference. Actual materials on the meetings and memoirs of participants do not bear this out. Otto Braun, who was very sensitive to the issue (but who was strongly supportive of Mao's position at this time), said these reports simply were not true. (*Comintern Agent*, pp. 130–31.)

21. Hu Hua, communication, 2/4/85.

22. Details of troop disposal from Professor Hu Hua. This account is handicapped by conflicts between witnesses and imprecise information from contemporary historians and archivists. Zhang Guotao's account in his memoirs is confused, lacking in many details, polemic, and inaccurate. He makes no attempt to segregate what happened at the various meetings, omits times, dates, and other essentials. The account of Nie Rongzhen is superficial, that of Peng Dehuai equally so. The same is true of contemporary Chinese historians. The problem may be that the underlying archives (which contain a detailed account of these deliberations) have not yet been released for publication. Otto Braun was supplied these documents through Soviet sources and makes full use of them to supplement his memory. He dates the meeting to the "first days of August" and gives direct quotations from the communiqué dated August 5. It was extensive. It contained only a passing reference to the war with Japan, called for a march north to fight the KMT, the setting up of a Sichuan-Gansu-Shaanxi soviet area, ultimate formation of a Chinese Soviet Republic. It generally reflected Mao's views, with which Braun was in sympathy. Mao, Braun said, had the full support of the Politburo except for Zhang Guotao. (Braun, *op. cit.*, pp. 132–34.) Zhang Guotao gives the personnel at the "Shawo meeting" as: Mao, Zhu De, Bo Gu, Luo Fu, and himself, with Deng Fa (security chief) and Kai Feng (youth leader) as observers. Notes were taken by Wang Shoudao, whom he describes as "secretary-general of the Central Committee." (Zhang Guotao, *op. cit.*, p. 412.)

25. *A Magical Carpet*

1. Yang Chengwu, *A Single Spark Can Start a Prairie Fire*, vol. 3, Beijing, 1980, pp. 153–59.

2. Zhang Guotao, *Rise of the Communist Party*, vol. II, p. 420.

3. Wang Qiu, magistrate, Nuoergai, 5/27/84.

4. Wang Qiu, 5/27/84; Xue Ming, He Long's widow, personal interview, Beijing, 6/14/84.

5. Prefecture museum, Hongyuan, 5/27/84.
6. Wei Xiuying, 4/15/84.
7. Zeng Xianhui, Guiyang, 4/18/84; Snow, *Red Star,* pp. 203–4.
8. Yang Dinghua, *Velikii Pokhod,* p. 373.
9. Smedley, *The Great Road,* p. 338.
10. Chen Changfeng, *On the Long March with Chairman Mao,* p. 80.
11. Hu Yaobang, 6/15/84.
12. Yang Dinghua, *op. cit.,* pp. 378–85.
13. Ding Ganru, 5/13/84.
14. Ji Pengfei, 3/14/84.
15. Dai Zhengqi, 3/20/84.
16. Nie Rongzhen, *Memoirs,* ch. 8.
17. Hu Hua, 3/29/84.

26. Dark Hour, Bright Glory

1. This was Mao's response to questions by Edgar Snow in 1960. (Edgar Snow, *Red Star Over China,* rev. ed., New York, 1969, p. 432.) Yang Shangkun's description of the moonlit night, personal interview. Yang Dinghua described the weather at nearby Baxi that night in totally opposite terms: "very dark night . . . black clouds fully covered the sky . . . no moon . . ." (Yang Dinghua, *Velikii Pokhod,* p. 381.) Cai Xiaoqian said it was "pitch dark and drizzling" as they walked upstream along the Baozuo River. (Cai Xiaoqian, *The Kiangxi Soviet Areas* . . ., ch. 7.)
2. Descriptions from personal observation in 1984 and from the vivid picture painted by Yang Dinghua, *op. cit.,* pp. 378–89.
3. Zhang Guotao contended that a tributary of the White River blocked his path. Normally it was knee-deep, and the men had expected to splash across. It had suddenly risen to a depth of ten feet and a width of nearly a thousand feet. (Zhang Guotao, *Memoirs,* p. 421.) Most Chinese specialists consider this an exaggeration. Li Xiannian, then commander of Zhang's Thirtieth Army, conceded that the river was at flood stage, but said it would have receded within a few days. (Li Xiannian, 6/14/84.) There is no mention in Zhang's memoirs of the lively exchange of messages cited by Long March memoirists and contemporary Party historians. The texts of these telegrams have not been published.
4. Yang Shangkun, 4/3/84.
5. Yang Dinghua, *op. cit.,* p. 390.
6. Li Xiannian, 6/14/84. Yang Shangkun put the force defeated at Banyou as a brigade.
7. Yang Shangkun, 4/3/84.
8. Peng Dehuai, *Memoirs,* p. 375.
9. Nie Rongzhen, *Memoirs,* ch. 8.
10. Hu Hua, 3/29/84.
11. Yang Shangkun, 4/3/84.
12. Li Xiannian's report was offered in a personal interview, 6/14/84. The phrase "uncompromisingly open up" is a literal translation of the Chinese.

These words were used by Mao Zedong in discussing Zhang's telegram in a speech in Yan'an in March 1937. Li Xiannian did not hear the speech but read the text. Chinese specialists explain that Zhang's words conveyed the implication that the struggle within the Party between himself and Mao Zedong had not been decisive and that Zhang would now like the question between himself and Mao settled once and for all.

13. Yang Shangkun, 4/3/84.
14. Hu Hua, 3/29/84.
15. Peng Dehuai, op. cit., p. 376.
16. Yang Shangkun, 4/3/84.
17. Peng Dehuai, op. cit., p. 377.
18. Peng Dehuai, op. cit., p. 377.
19. Liu Ying, 6/14/84.
20. Yang Shangkun, 4/3/84; Li Bozhao, 6/15/84.
21. Yang Shangkun, 4/3/84; Hu Hua, 3/29/84.
22. Yang Shangkun, 4/3/84.
23. Peng Dehuai, op. cit., p. 377.
24. Yang Shangkun, 4/3/84.
25. Most details from General Yang Shangkun, 4/3/84. A curiously different version of this incident is offered by Cai Xiaoqian. He reports that about 10 to 12 miles from Baxi the marching column was suddenly confronted by a Fourth Front Army propaganda team, shouting: "Don't follow the Big Nose (Otto Bruan); turn around. The road north is a deadend; Southward is the way!" The main Red Army troops were upset by the demonstration and Mao and Peng Dehuai made an appearance to boost morale. (Cai Xiaoqian, op. cit., ch. 7.)
26. Xiang Qing, 3/16/84.
27. This account is based on an extensive interview with General Yang Shangkun in Beijing, and subsequent responses to specific questions, and upon an equally extensive interview with Li Xiannian in Beijing. Both were major participants in the events described. Professor Hu Hua, Beijing's leading Party historian, has provided a detailed record based on Party archives and his own research. Other details have been provided by General Qin Xinghan of the Military Museum and his research staff; Li Bozhao, wife of General Yang; Liu Ying, widow of Luo Fu, and others, in personal interviews. The memoirs of Zhang Guotao have been carefully scrutinized, as have those of Nie Rongzhen and Peng Dehuai. There are minor discrepancies in times, dates, places, and sequences. None are of consequence, except the major conflicts between Zhang Guotao and all the others. Most of these stem from Zhang's defense of his conduct and policies, and criticism of Mao. This portion of his memoir is polemicized and the factual framework of dates, places, messages, and acts is largely lost. Zhang contends that he knew nothing of the emerging crisis until he was informed of Mao's departure. He mentions no exchange of wireless messages and no word of what Li Xiannian called "the famous telegram." The account presented here would be improved if the Chinese Party archives keepers would release

texts of the relevant messages and documents. Much descriptive detail of terrain is based on travel over the region in 1984.

28. Hu Hua, 3/29/84.
29. Song Kanfu, Xi'an, 6/6/84.
30. Yang Shangkun, 4/3/84.
31. Hou Guoxiang, personal interview, Guiyang, 4/18/84.
32. Deputy County Magistrate Wei Donghai, Diebu, 5/30/84.
33. This is the conclusion of Yan Jingtang and contemporary military specialists. The changes may not have been effected until the columns reached Hadapu. Peng Dehuai in his memoirs (p. 380) says he and Ye Jianying commanded the force under the direct leadership of Mao. Otto Braun (p. 140) says Peng was made commander of the first column and Mao political commissar. Yang Dinghua (p. 391) said the march continued under command "of the highest leaders of the Red Army—Mao and Peng."
34. Nie Rongzhen, *op. cit.*, ch. 8.
35. Peng Dehuai, *op. cit.*, p. 379.
36. Yang Dinghua, *op. cit.*, p. 394.
37. Yang Dinghua, *op. cit.*, p. 397.
38. Yang Chengwu, *A Single Spark*, pp. 440–41.
39. Li Daoji, Lazikou, 5/30/84.
40. Detail from personal observation of Lazikou and the route thereto and briefings from Magistrate Li Daoji and his deputy Wei Donghai at Diebu, May 30–June 1, 1984. Details on the battle are from their briefings and the accounts of Yang Chengwu, leader of the Fourth Regiment, and Yang Dinghua, contained in *Velikii Pokhod*. There are some discrepancies over the size of the force defending Lazikou. The account here follows the local briefing. Yang Chengwu mentions three regiments, but this is obviously too large. Peng Dehuai makes it one regiment, under Deng Baoshan. (Peng Dehuai, *op. cit.*) The actual number appears to be two battalions. The local briefers' account of the suicide mountaineers is followed. Other accounts do not mention the minority men or Mao's orders. Some accounts published during the period of Lin Biao's ascendency stress his participation. None of the three main accounts relied on here mentions his name.

27. Home

1. Yang Dinghua, *Velikii Pokhod*, p. 455.
2. Mianxian seminar, 5/31/84; personal observation, 5/31/84.
3. Yang Dinghua, *op. cit.*, pp. 453–72.
4. This is the story told by Chen Changfeng in *On the Long March with Chairman Mao*. There are, as the narrative will make apparent, grounds for doubting his version.
5. Yang Dinghua, *op. cit.*, p. 498.
6. Yuan Yaoxiu, Wuqi briefing, 6/8/84.
7. Yuan Yaoxiu, 6/8/84.
8. Yuan Yaoxiu, 6/8/84.
9. Bao'an, Liu Zhidan memorial tablet, 6/8/84.

10. Yuan Yaoxiu, 6/8/84.
11. Professor Fang Chengxian, personal interview, Xi'an, 6/12/84.
12. Zhang Quan, husband of Liu Lizhen, daughter of Liu Zhidan, personal interview, Xi'an, 6/12/84. Gao Gang emerges as one of the most controversial participants in the Chinese Revolution. Early in 1949 he became chief of the special Northeast Region (Manchuria). He was arrested after the death of Stalin in 1953 and charged with conspiring to set up "an independent kingdom." He committed suicide in prison. There has long been suspicion he entered into a special relationship with the Russians. His entry in Moscow's *Bolshaya Sovetskaya Entsyklopedia*, second edition, was one of two which subscribers were invited to excise. The other was that of Lavrenti P. Beria, Stalin's secret police chief.
13. Fang Chengxian, Xi'an, 6/12/84.
14. Zhang Quan, 6/12/84. Guo Hongtao and Zhu Lizhi arrived from the underground northern Party bureau at Tianjin in 1934 and July 1935. A third, named Nie Hongjun, came a bit later. They claimed Liu Zhidan was following a "rich peasant line" and was not aggressive enough in his military operations.
15. Cheng Zihua, personal interview, Beijing, 3/30/84.
16. Qian Xinzheng, personal interview, Beijing, 3/30/84.
17. Cheng Zihua, 3/30/84.
18. Fang Chengxian, 6/12/84.
19. Wuqi briefing, 6/8/84. Gao Gang reported that some of those imprisoned were executed. "If the Central Committee had not halted this purge the future would have been unthinkable," he said. (Cited by Guo Hualun, *A History of the Chinese Communist Party*, Taipei, pp. 87–96.)
20. The complex tale of Liu Zhidan and the Twenty-sixth and Twenty-fifth armies is based on the testimony of Liu Zhidan's surviving family—his widow, Tong Guirong, his daughter, Liu Lizhen, and her husband, Zhang Quan—with some detail from the Shaanxi Party historians, Professor Fang Chengxian and Xu Angshao of the Shaanxi Normal University at Xi'an. Some details from Zhang Yuanyuan, Ministry of Foreign Affairs, Beijing. The story of the Twenty-fifth Army was provided by its commander, Cheng Zihua, and by Dr. Dai Zhengqi, physician attached to the Twenty-fifth Army. A confused version is contained in Snow's *Red Star Over China*, pp. 209–14. Snow met Tong Guirong and Liu Lizhen in Bao'an, but his information about the affair seems to have come from one of its instigators. Cheng Zihua did not have much involvement. The Twenty-fifth Army, by the time it reached northern Shaanxi, was under the effective control of Xu Haidong. Mao permitted no reprisals against either of them.

Gao Gang in a lecture which he later gave to political cadres in northern Shaanxi said the Party agitators claimed that Liu Zhidan was a "White Army officer" and "always a coward" and that Gao Gang was a "right opportunist." (Cited by Guo Hualun, *op. cit.*, pp. 87–96.)
21. Liu Ying, 6/14/84.
22. Yang Chengwu, *A Single Spark*, pp. 257–61.
23. Yang Shangkun, 10/26/84.

28. The Gathering

1. Xiao Ke, personal interview, Beijing, 3/9/84. Yu Qiuli, in 1984 Director General of the Red Army Political Department and in 1934 a Sixth Army political worker, first heard of the Long March, as he recalled, from a KMT newspaper, probably in December 1934. (Yu Qiuli, personal interview, Beijing, 10/31/84.)

2. Xiao Ke, 3/9/84.

3. Yu Qiuli, 10/31/84.

4. Helen Snow, *My Yenan Notebooks*, p. 47.

5. Xue Ming, He Long's widow, personal interview, Beijing, 6/16/84; Wang Qinghe, Lijiang military subdistrict, 5/1/84.

6. Shi Lueming, *Remembering He Long*, Shanghai, 1979.

7. Liu Gongjun, *What I Know About General He Long*, Beijing, 1983.

8. Xue Ming, 6/16/84.

9. Shi Lueming; Wang Qinghe, 5/1/84; *China Daily* reported, 7/1/84, that in 1984 a man named Yan Zhangyan, a language teacher in Wuhan, was sent to prison for seven years for fabricating the charges against He Long. Yan Zhangyan's father was the KMT official who sent Xiong Gongqing to He Long in December 1933 to try to persuade He Long to rejoin the KMT. In the Cultural Revolution, Yan Zhangyan wrote a letter claiming that He Long refused the offer because it didn't give him a high enough office, then had Xiong Gongqing executed to cover up the affair. Jiang Qing, Mao's wife, and Chen Boda, a Cultural Revolution chief, used this letter and Yan's testimony to fabricate the case against He Long.

10. Wu Song, Long March veteran, personal interview, Lanzhou, 6/4/84.

11. Xiao Ke, 3/9/84.

12. R. A. Bosshardt, *The Restraining Hand: Captivity for Christ in China*, London, 1935, pp. 24–35.

13. The mother of this child was Jian Xianren, only nineteen when she and He Long married. The couple split up later in Yan'an. Xiao Ke's wife was Jian Xianfo. (Zhang Renshi, Long March veteran, Lanzhou, 6/4/84; Ross Terrill, *The White-Boned Demon*, p. 151.)

14. Shi Lueming, *op. cit.;* Snow, *My Yenan Notebooks*, p. 47.

15. Bosshardt, correspondence, 1/24/85. One of the most important prisoners taken by Xiao Ke was General Zhang Zhenhan, commander of the KMT Forty-fifth Division, captured in early summer 1935. He was given extremely good treatment and Bosshardt got well acquainted with him. Zhang became an instructor in combat strategy at the Red Military Academy. (Xiao Ke, *Memoirs*, ch. 2, pp. 6–7.) He was released to return to the KMT 5/10/37. (Wales [Snow], *Red Dust*, p. 139.)

16. Bosshardt, correspondence, 1/24/85; Bo Gu told Helen Snow in 1937 there were no regular Red Army troops in the area where the Stams were killed, only "volunteers." (Snow, *My Yenan Notebooks*, p. 116.)

17. Bosshardt, *op. cit.*, pp. 179–82.

18. Xiao Ke, *op. cit.*, ch. 2.

19. Yu Qiuli, 10/31/84.

20. Mao Tsetung, *Poems*, p. 19.
21. The description of the movements and the wireless message to He Long and Xiao Ke was given by Wang Qinghe, deputy political commissar, Lijiang military subdistrict (personal interview, 5/1/84, p. 4). Professor Fan Shengyu, Northwest Teachers College, Lanzhou, said (personal interview, Lanzhou, 6/3/84) that the Second Front Army had sent out an uncoded wireless message addressed to the Central Committee and saying, in effect, "Where are you?" This was recorded by the Fourth Front Army but not by the First Front Army and the Central Committee. Thereupon, the message to the Second Front Army to come and join them was sent by Zhang Guotao and Zhu De. Some accounts claim that order was signed only by Zhu. Curiously, Zhang Guotao makes no mention of the wireless order in his memoirs and offers no explanation of how the Second Front Army came to join the Fourth.
22. Wang Qinghe, 5/1/84.
23. Wang Qinghe said the relevant documents are preserved in the archives. A number of the provincial generals sided with the Communists and stayed on the mainland in 1949. Lu Han, Warlord Long Yun's provincial military commander, joined the PLA and later became governor of Yunnan. Commander Sun Du stayed on the mainland. Li Jue, son-in-law of the Hunan Warlord He Jian, also stayed. So did Zhang Zhong, one of Warlord Long Yun's principal commanders. He became first Vice Chairman of Yunnan. KMT commanders Fan Songpu and Guo Rudong were the ones whom Long Yun and his men harried.

Despite his precautions Long Yun was ultimately tricked by Chiang Kai-shek into sending two divisions to Indochina in 1945 to accept the surrender of the Japanese. Chiang maneuvered a third division out of Yunnan and Long Yun fled to Hongkong, only returning to become a member of the National Defense Committee under the Communists. The Hunan Warlord He Jian died before liberation. (Wang Qinghe, 5/1/84.)
24. Wang Qinghe, 5/1/84.
25. Bosshardt, personal communication, 1/24/85.
26. Wang Qinghe, 5/1/84.
27. Wang Qinghe, 5/1/84.
28. Xiao Ke, 3/9/84.

29. *Return of the Prodigal*

1. Zhang Guotao, *Rise of Communist Party*, pp. 426–27.
2. Professor Hu Hua, who had a look at the list, pointed out that the whole procedure was in violation not only of Communist Party statutes but of normal Party policy. Had Zhang made contact with those he named to the Committee, many would have rejected his invitation. (Hu Hua, communication, 1/11/85.)
3. Helen Snow, *My Yenan Notebooks*, p. 61.
4. Smedley, *The Great Road*, pp. 330–31.
5. Snow, *op. cit.*, p. 48.

6. Kang Keqing forcefully expressed her views in a personal interview at Beijing. A typical view of historical specialists was given by Shan Guozheng of the Sichuan Provincial Museum at Chengdu (5/19/84). Shan insisted that Zhu De's guards had been given no orders to restrain his movements, that Zhu De was never under house arrest, that he moved freely among the various troop units, speaking to elements of both the First and the Fourth armies, and attended their basketball games. (Zhu De was a fanatical basketball player.) Shan minimized the question of Zhu De's horse.

7. Hu Zenggui, personal interview, Huining, 6/2/84.

8. Ye Yingli, personal interview, Xi'an, 6/11/84.

9. Li Qun, Bao'an, 6/8/84.

10. Yang Shangkun, 4/3/84.

11. Xu Shiyou, *My Ten Years in the Red Army,* Beijing, 1983, ch. 10.

12. Xu Shiyou, *op. cit.,* ch. 10.

13. Xu Shiyou estimated the KMT force at ten brigades; Shan Guozheng, of the Sichuan Museum, made the total four. General Qin confirmed the loss figure of ten thousand.

14. Li Xiannian, 6/15/84.

15. Zhang Guotao, *op. cit.,* p. 440.

16. Xiang Qing, 1/14/85.

17. Xiang Qing, 1/14/85.

18. Zhang Guotao, *op. cit.,* p. 444.

19. Xiang Qing, 1/14/85; Helen Snow, personal conversation; Wang Guangmei, Liu Shaoqi's widow, personal communication.

20. Hu Hua, 3/29/84.

21. Xiao Ke, 3/9/84.

22. Zhang Guotao, *op.cit.,* pp. 448–49.

23. Xu Shiyou, *op. cit.,* ch. 10.

24. Zhang Guotao, *op. cit.,* pp. 457–59.

25. Li Xiannian, 6/15/84.

26. George Hatem, personal interview, Beijing, 3/19/84.

27. Li Xiannian, 6/15/84.

28. Zhang Guotao, *op. cit.,* p. 461.

29. In the late KMT period, three Mas held important posts in the Moslem northwest territories. Ma Hongkui was governor of Ningxia; Ma Buqing was a former governor of Ningxia; Ma Bufang, son of a famous Moslem leader, Ma Keqin, and brother of Ma Buqing, was the principal military leader. One Ma was killed fighting the People's Liberation Army in Xinjiang, Ma Hongkui escaped to Taiwan and later became a horse breeder in the United States. Another Ma, improbably, became a Taiwan ambassador. (Li Xiannian, 6/15/84; Snow, *Red Star,* p. 322.)

30. One survivor was Zhang Qinqiu, later textile minister in the PRC. She was murdered in the Cultural Revolution. (Li Xiannian, 6/15/84.)

31. The Thirty-seventh Division, led by Dong Zhentang, had reached Gaotai, about twelve miles to the west of Linze. There it was wiped out. General Dong was killed. (Ye Yingli, 6/2/84.) The Thirty-ninth Division of the Fifth

Army was led by Sang Chao, a Zhang Guotao man. Li Zhuoran, political commissar of the Fifth Army who participated in Zunyi, was with them.

32. Li Xiannian, 6/15/84.
33. Li Xiannian, 6/15/84.
34. Ye Yingli, 6/11/84.
35. Smedley, *op. cit.,* pp. 343–47.
36. Li Yingchun, county magistrate, Huining, 6/2/84.
37. On this or another occasion, George Hatem watched Chinese doctors treat Liu Bocheng, who had been hit by a bomb tossed over the side of a plane by a KMT pilot. He was amazed to see them pop out the bomb splinters instead of extracting them with a probe.
38. Hu Hua, 3/29/84.
39. Li Yingchun, 6/2/84.
40. Smedley, *op. cit.,* pp. 344–47.

30. *"Cold-Eyed, I Survey the World"*

1. Mao Tsetung, *Poems,* p. 38.
2. George Hatem, 3/9/84.
3. Wang Bingnan, 3/20/84.
4. Peng Dehuai, *Memoirs,* pp. 1–11.
5. Terrill, *Mao,* p. 274.
6. Liu Ying, 5/14/84.
7. *Paris-Pekin,* No. 2, November 1979, p. 94.
8. Xue Ming, 6/16/84.
9. Xiao Ke, 3/9/84.
10. Yu Qiuli, 10/31/84.
11. Li Xiannian, 6/15/84.
12. Yang Chengwu, 3/18/84.
13. Xiao Hua, 3/16/84.
14. Edward E. Rice, *Mao's Way,* p. 243.
15. George Hatem, 3/9/84.
16. Wu Xiuquan, 3/28/84.
17. Chen Pixian, 6/13/84.
18. Li Xiannian, 6/15/84.
19. Letter of Liu Shaoqi's children, *Beijing Workers Daily,* 12/5/80.
20. Letter of Liu Shaoqi's children, 12/5/80.
21. Liu Pingping, 1/29/85.
22. Haldore Hanson, *Diary of a Trip Behind the Red Lines in the North,* started June 1938. Private publication, p. 25.

31. *The Little Man Who Could Never Be Put Down*

1. Deng Rong (Maomao), *Peking Review,* 9/3/84, pp. 17–18. *China Reconstructs,* No. 4, 1985.
2. Edward Rice, *Mao's Way,* pp. 184, 262.
3. Yang Shangkun, 11/3/84.

4. *China Daily,* Beijing's English-language newspaper, runs a daily column on bridge. Some people in Beijing joke that just as Mao made swimming popular (by his famous swim in the Yangtze July 12, 1966), Deng is making bridge playing popular.
5. Hu Hua, 10/27/84, Li Xiannian, 6/15/84.
6. Wu Xiuquan, 3/28/84.

A NOTE ON SOURCES

The materials on which *The Long March: The Untold Story* is based have been obtained in large measure through direct interviews with surviving participants, consultation with Chinese historical specialists, newly released archival data and personal inspection of the March route, the battlefield sites, the river crossings, the mountain ascents and the terrain along the 6,000-mile route of the main Red Army and substantial segments of the routes of the lesser forces.

The author owes a great deal to the assiduous cooperation of the Chinese authorities at every level and most notably to General Yang Shangkun, vice-chairman of the Central Military Commission, and Huang Hua, former Foreign Minister, who made every effort to facilitate access to sources needed in reconstructing difficult, obscure and never-before-revealed episodes and conflicts of the Long March. Without the decision of the Chinese government to open its archives and authorize Long March veterans and specialists, high and low, to speak frankly and to endeavor to answer every question, no matter how difficult or obscure, this book could not have been written. Literally thousands of questions have been responded to. When satisfactory answers were not obtained, historians and generals have gone back to the sources and searched again for the relevant data.

The writer is particularly indebted to General Qin Xinghan of the National Revolutionary Military Museum of Beijing and its vast resources, and to its research staff, especially Yan Jingtang, who have inspected their files repeatedly in the months the manuscript was being written to seek out more information and to clarify enigmas. General Qin and Yan Jingtang and his staff are often cited in the text as sources of new and startling information.

Second only to General Qin Xinghan and his staff have been the historians who assisted in the research, notably Professor Hu Hua of the People's University of Beijing, who has devoted his life to the study of the Long March and the Revolution. In searching for answers to my questions he sometimes discovered facts of which the official historians had no knowledge. His analysis and evaluation of often conflicting stories obtained from eyewitnesses and participants was invaluable. Professor Xiang Qing of Beijing University was another great help.

The advice, guidance and deep knowledge of China afforded by John S. Service, the former U.S. foreign service officer, born in China, gifted with an unparalleled background in the country and in the tangled skein of the 1930s and 1940s, was essential in assisting the writer through the thickets of puzzling evidence and interpretations. His services were beyond compare.

None of these specialists, I hasten to say, are in any way responsible for my narrative and conclusions but I am deeply grateful to them in guiding me and responding to the complex and staggering questions which arose at every step of the Long March.

No one has been of greater aid in enabling me to knit this story together than Zhang Yuanyuan of the Interpretation section of the Ministry of Foreign Affairs who served as interpreter for almost every interview in Beijing and along the Long March and who then undertook with the aid of the other specialists to comb the manuscript for factual errors, spelling, names, places and confusions which arose in translation, writing and collation. He bears no responsibility for this work but without his aid I could not have completed it.

This list of Chinese sources is voluminous. I want to name the more important of these but the roll that follows is by no means complete. First, come General Yang Shangkun and former Foreign Minister Huang Hua who assisted in locating and making sources available and themselves submitted to extensive personal interviews.

The sources include: Ambassador Zheng Wenjin in Washington; Ambassador Ling Qing of the United Nations Mission; those long-time friends of China and participants in its Revolution, Rewi Alley, the New Zealander, and Dr. George Hatem of American birth; General Xiao Ke, Long March commander, now President of the Academy of Military Science; State Counselor and Long March veteran Ji Pengfei; Wang Yanjian, writer and Long March specialist; General Yang Chengwu, Long March commander; General Xiao Hua, Long March commander; Ambassador Wang Bingnan; Li Yimang, chairman of cultural exchanges and Long March veteran; Ding Ling, famous woman writer; General Wu Xiuquan, Long March veteran, diplomat, head of the Institute for Strategic Studies; General Cheng Zihua, Long March commander; Drs. Qian Xinzhang and Dai Zhengqi, medical men on the Long March; Drs. Du Tanjin and Sun Yizhi, medical personnel on the Long March, now respectively PLA Director of Medical Research and Director of Logistics, PLA medical department; Hu Yaobang, Long March veteran and General Secretary, Communist Party of China; Li Xiannian, President of China and Long March commander; Xue Ming, widow of General He Long, Long March hero, and their daughter He Xuoming; General Chen Pixian, Long March commander; Beijing Deputy Mayor Chen Haosu, Chen Danhuai and Chen Shanshan, children of General Chen Yi, Long March hero; Liu Ying, widow of Luo Fu (Zhang Wentien), Politburo member and a director of the Long March; Li Bozhao, wife of General Yang Shangkun, and Long March heroine; Yu Qiuli, Politburo member, director-general, political department PLA, and Long March veteran; Li Rui, former secretary to and biographer of Mao Zedong; Zhu Zhongli, widow of Wang Jiaxiang, Politburo member and a director of the Long March; Kang Keqing, widow of Zhu De, Long March heroine and Chinese women's leader; Tong Guirong, widow of Long March hero, General Liu Zhidan, her daughter, Liu Lizhen and Zhang Quan, husband of Liu Lizhen; Wu Jiqing, bodyguard to Mao Zedong; Wang Guangmei, widow of Liu Shaoqi.

Also Assistant Director Nanchang Museum of August 1 (1927) Uprising Lin Jiachuan; Professor Dai Xianqing and Yu Boliu, specialists in Party history, Jiangxi Party school, Nanchang; Director Wang, Provincial Library of Nanchang; Red Army veterans, Nanchang: Wei Xiuying, Liu Jianhua, Wu Xing; Gui Yulin, curator, Museum, Ciping, Jiangxi; Zhong Qisong, Red Army veteran, Changgang, Jiangxi; Zhang Demin, director Yu county Museum, Jiangxi; Cheng Peng, director and archivist, Huichang county office, Jiangxi; Deputy Magistrate Huang Xian, Museum Director Yang Shizhu, and Archivist Zhong Shuqi, all of Ruijin.

Sun Ruikun, Party history section, Guizhou Museum; Liang Zhengqui, researcher, Party history, Provincial Military district, Guiyang, Guizhou province; Red Army veterans Zeng Xianhui, Hou Guoxiang, Guiyang; County Party Secretary Yang Chao, County Magistrate Cheng Yuan, director, Culture Department, Wu Dingguo of Liping county; Tian Xingyong, director, Zunyi house museum; Army veterans, Guizhou, Kong Xianquan, Wu Yisheng, Cai Shengjin.

Mu Rongxian, deputy prefect, Wang Qinghe, deputy political commissar, Lijiang Military subdistrict, Liu Runan, deputy secretary, prefecture, He Zegao, section chief, Yang Shugong, County political department, all of Lijiang, Yunnan province; Chen Zhangying, He Shuqian, Wang Lianhai, civilians at Shigu who assisted Red Army.

Wang Zonghua, director, Huili, Sichuan, County study/research department of Party history; Zhang Chaoman, Zhou Gilong, Chen Yueqing, Golden Sands River boatmen; Ding Ganru, deputy chief of staff, retired, Chengdu; Zhang Youjui, Long March artist; Tian Bao, Tibetan Long March veteran and member Party Central Advisory Commission, Chengdu; Jia Ke, director, Shen Guozheng, Gao Wenqing, Yu Jianzhang, research associates, Sichuan Provincial Museum, Chengdu; Zhang Fuchen, director, county cultural department, Shimian, Sichuan; Gong Wancai, Dadu river boatman; Zhang Jiafu, secretary of prefecture, Wen Xingming, prefectural cultural relics administration, Maerkang, Sichuan; Wang Qiu, magistrate of four autonomous Tibetan counties, Nuoergai.

County Magistrate Li Daoji, Deputy Magistrate Wei Donghai, Diebu, Gansu; Long March veterans Zhao Yongbiao, Tu Gubing, Diebu; Li Ling, principal, middle school, Jing Shengkui, director, County cultural center, Hong Tianshu, archivist, Minxian county, Gansu; County Magistrate Li Yingchun, Ding Junwu, county cultural committee, Song Zicheng, county relics department, Huining county, Gansu; Red Army veterans Yang Quan, Hu Zhenggui, Chen Lanxiang, Zhen Mingzang, Fu Juyou, Duan Xicheng; Fan Shengyu, professor, Northwest Teachers College, Qin Sheng, Party History department, Lanzhou, Gansu; Long March veterans Wu Song, Zhang Renshi, Zhang Shengji.

Wei Mingzhong, director, provincial foreign office, Xi'an, Shaanxi; Long March veterans Peng Haiqing, Li Qun, Xi'an; Long March veteran Yuan Yaoxiu, Bao'an; Long March veterans Zhong Ling, Ye Yingli, Xi'an; Professor Chen Hua, director No. 4 Army Medical college, Chen Jinzao, deputy director, Xi'an; Assistant Professor Sang Chengxian and Lecturer Xu Angshan, Shaanxi Normal University, Xi'an.

Special aid was given by Liu Pingping; by Han Suyin,Haldore Hanson, and Jerry Tannebaum.

Additional assistance was rendered by Sol Adler, one-time U.S. Treasury economist long resident in Beijing; Li Huming, Foreign Office secretary who made many arrangements; Yao Wei, now with the China International Trust and Investment Corporation; Li Zhengjun, Information Department, Foreign Office. Helen Snow proved an inexhaustible source of first-hand information on the Long March and its participants. Huang Bing, Mei Shan and Ben Yang provided translations as well as background information. Caroline Service, the Rev. R. A. Bosshardt, Peggy Dennis and Steve Nelson responded helpfully to numerous questions. Ruth Strauss again capably typed my manuscript. Simon Michael Bessie oversaw the whole project with customary wizardry. It could never have been completed without Charlotte Y. Salisbury who was at my side throughout and brought me through dark and difficult passages. And I owe a unique debt to Drs. Peter Schrag, Du Qiuhua, Chen Xiuliang and Chen Zhangyu.

The bibliography which follows consists only of materials directly employed. The slim file in the Chinese language was used only in translation. The writer does not, alas, possess any capability in Chinese. Of the various collections of first-hand accounts the most valuable is that translated into Russian in 1958 as *Velikii Pokhod (The Great March)* and extensively used in that version. English language translations of Long March stories are chiefly interesting for variations in editions—those published before and after the death of Lin Biao, before and after the death of Mao Zedong. On Mao Zedong the work of Li Rui, his former secretary, is outstanding, particularly that written after Mao's death and Li Rui's release from prison.

In English nothing approaches the many works by Edgar Snow and his wife of those times, Helen Snow. The American Agnes Smedley left an indelible account of the Long March as related to her by Zhu De. Edgar Snow first brought word of the Long March to the general public in his classic *Red Star Over China*. He was handicapped by the fragmentary and sometimes deliberately ambiguous account given him by Mao and Mao's associates who suppressed mention of political differences and some of the disasters. It is tragic that Snow himself did not carry forward his intention to write an account of the Long March. The only previous attempt at a Long March history is that of Dick Wilson, the English China specialist, first published in 1971 at a time when the Cultural Revolution had totally disrupted China and no access to source materials was possible. No comprehensive account has been published in China. For many years the only materials available there were a few popular collections of episodic (usually heroic) exploits. In the last two or three years, however, reminiscences of major leaders and generals have begun to be published, many of which, like the prison memoir of Peng Dehuai, shed great light on the March and particularly on its political aspects. There is every indication that the publication of such materials will increase, in part due to the stimulation given to Long March studies by Chinese response to the writer's free-wheeling inquiries.

BIBLIOGRAPHY

Works in Chinese

Cai Xiaoqian, *The Kiangxi Soviet Areas and the Westward Flight of the Red Army (Jiangxi su qu he hong jun xi guan)*, Taipei, 1970.

Cheng Fang Wu, *Memoirs of the Long March*, Beijing, 1977.

Chen Pixian, *Three Years of Guerrilla War in Southern Jiangxi*, Beijing, 1982.

(Chen Yun) Shi Ping, "The Heroic Western March," *Comintern Journal*, Moscow, February, 1936.

"Chen Yun's Report Has Clarified Some Facts Concerning Zunyi Conference," Xinhua, Beijing, March 4, 1984.

Guo Hualun (Warren Kuo), *The History of the Chinese Communist Party (Zhong gong shilun)*, 3 vols., Taipei, 1969.

Huang Changjiao, "Declaration": *Selections of Historical Materials of Jiangxi*, Nanchang, 1981.

Li Bozhao, *The Long March*, Beijing, 1951.

Li Bozhao, *Women CPC Members*, Beijing, 1979.

Li Hong, He Zizhen, *Guizhou Youth*, no. 2, 1983.

Li Rui, *The Early Revolutionary Activities of Comrade Mao Zedong*, rev. and supp. ed., Beijing, 1980.

Lue Liping, *Star of the Western Frontier*, Chengdu, 1984.

Luo Ergang, *History of the Heavenly Kingdom*, Peking.

Luo Ronghuan, *Growth in Battle*, Beijing, 1981.

Nie Rongzhen, *Memoirs*, Beijing, 1983.

"Pioneers and Models of Revolutionary Women," *Outlook* (Liao Wang), nos. 11, 12, 1984.

"Random Thoughts on a Photograph of Comrade He Zizhen," *Journal of Revolutionary Relics*, no. 2, 1980.

Shi Lueming with Zhang Xia and He Xiaoming, *Remembering He Long*, Shanghai, 1979.

A Single Spark Can Start a Prairie Fire, Selected ed., vol. 3, Beijing, 1980.

Wang Tianxi, "The Awkward Performance of Chiang Kai-shek in Guiyang as the Central Red Army Went Through Guizhou," *Historical Materials Collection of Guizhou Province*, April, 1963.

Wang Yinian, "Questions About the Telegram of Zhang Guotao for 'a military solution' of the Central Committee," *Material on Party History Studies,* vol. 3, 1983.

Wang Yuonan, *The Difficult Path,* Beijing, 1983.

Wu Xiuquan, *My Experiences, 1908–1949,* Beijing, 1984.

Xiao Feng, *Long March Diary,* Shanghai, 1979.

Xiao Hua, *The Difficult Years,* Shanghai, 1983.

Xiao Hua, *Songs of the Red Army,* Beijing, 1972.

Xiao Ke, *Memoirs,* Beijing, 1983.

Xu Lixin, *Zhang Guotao's Swerving and Awakening (Zhang Guotao de panghuang yu juoxing),* Taipei, 1981.

Xu Shiyou, *My Ten Years Experience in the Red Army (Wo zai hungjun shinian),* Beijing, 1983.

Yang Chengwu, *Reminiscenses of the Long March (Yi chengzheng),* Beijing, 1982.

Yang Liangshen, *The Red Army Crosses Sichuan During the Long March,* Chengdu, 1980.

Yuan Guang, *The Stormy Years,* Beijing, 1983.

Zhou Chunlin, *The Violent Battle Along the Hexi Corridor,* Beijing, 1984.

Files of *Minguo Ribao,* Nanchang Nationalist Daily, 1934–35.

Collected Documents on the Zunyi Conference, Beijing, 1985.

Works in English

Bai, Shouyi, ed., *An Outline History of China,* Beijing, 1983.

Barnstone, Willis, *The Poems of Mao Tse-tung,* New York, 1972.

Bonavia, David, *Verdict in Peking,* New York, 1982.

Borisov, Oleg, *From the History of Soviet-Chinese Relations in the 1950's,* Moscow, 1982.

Bosshardt, R. A., *The Restraining Hand: Captivity for Christ in China,* London, 1936.

Braun, Otto, *A Comintern Agent in China 1932–1939,* Stanford, California, 1982.

Buttinger, Joseph, *Vietnam: A Dragon Embattled,* New York, 1967.

Chang, H. C., *Chinese Literature 2. Nature Poetry,* New York, 1977.

Chang Kuo-t'ao, *The Rise of the Chinese Communist Party 1928–1938,* 2 vols., Lawrence, Kansas, 1972.

Chapple, Geoff, *Rewi Alley of China,* London, 1980.

Chen, Jerome, *Mao and the Chinese Revolution,* New York, 1965.

Chen Chang-feng, *On the Long March with Chairman Mao,* Peking, 1972.

Clubb, O. Edmund, *Twentieth Century China,* New York, 1964.

Deakin, F. W., and Storry, G. R., *The Case of Richard Sorge,* New York, 1966.

Dennis, Peggy, *The Autobiography of an American Communist,* Westport, Connecticut, 1977.

DeWoskin, Kenneth J. (tr.), *Doctors, Diviners, and Magicians of Ancient China: Biographies of Fang-shih,* New York, 1983.

Dimond, E. Grey, *Inside China Today,* New York, 1983.

Dittmer, Lowell, *Liu Shao-ch'i and the Chinese Cultural Revolution*, Berkeley, California, 1974.
Elegant, Robert S., *Mao's Great Revolution*, New York, 1971.
Gernant, Karen, "The Long March," unpublished thesis, University of Oregon, Eugene, 1983.
Giles, Herbert A., *A History of Chinese Literature*, New York, 1923.
Graham, David Crockett, *Folk Religion in Southwest China*, Smithsonian Miscellaneous Collections, vol. 142, no. 2, Washington, D.C., 1961.
Granich, Manny, Unpublished notes for a memoir.
Guillermaz, Jacques, *A History of the Chinese Communist Party, 1921–1949*, New York, 1972.
Hanson, Haldore, *Diary of a Trip Behind the Red Lines in the North*, privately published, n.d.
Han Suyin, *The Morning Deluge: Mao Tsetung and the Chinese Revolution, 1893–1954*, New York, 1972.
Han Suyin, *Wind in the Tower: Mao Tsetung and the Chinese Revolution, 1949–1975*, Boston, Massachusetts, 1976.
Hsin, Chi, *Teng Hsiao-Ping*, Hong Kong, 1978.
Hsueh, Chun-tu, *Revolutionary Leaders of Modern China*, New York, 1973.
Huang Zhen, *Sketches on the Long March*, Beijing, 1982.
Isaacs, Harold R., *The Tragedy of the Chinese Revolution*, Stanford, California, 1951.
Jacobs, Dan B., *Borodin*, Cambridge, Massachusetts, 1981.
Jaffe, Philip J., *Jaffe: The Odyssey of a Fellow Traveller*, unpublished mss.
Johnston, Verle B., *Legion of Babel*, University Park, Pennsylvania, 1967.
Kahn, E. J., Jr., *The China Hands*, New York, 1975.
Kau, Michael Y. M., *The Lin Piao Affair*, White Plains, New York, 1975.
Kim, Ilpong J., *The Politics of Chinese Communism: Kiangsi Under the Soviets*, Berkeley, California, 1973.
Li Jui (Li Rui), *The Early Revolutionary Activities of Comrade Mao Tsetung*, White Plains, New York, 1977.
Liu Po-cheng (Liu Bocheng), and others, *Recalling the Long March*, Peking, 1978.
The Long March: Eyewitness Accounts, Peking, 1964.
Mao Tsetung, *Poems*, Peking, 1976.
Mao Tse Tung, *Red China*, New York, 1934.
Milton, David and Nancy, *The Wind Will Not Subside*, New York, 1975.
Nelson, Steve, Barrett, James R., and Ruck, Robert, *American Radical*, Pittsburgh, 1981.
North, Robert C., *Moscow and Chinese Communists*, Stanford, California, 1963.
Official Guide to Eastern Asia: vol. 4, China, Tokyo, 1915.
Payne, Robert, *Mao Tse-Tung*, New York, 1969.
Peng Dehuai, *Memoirs of a Chinese Marshal*, Beijing, 1984.
Rice, Edward E., *Mao's Way*, Berkeley, California, 1972.
Rinden, Robert, and Witke, Roxane, *The Red Flag Waves: A Guide to the Hung-ch'i p'iao-p'iao Collection*, Berkeley, California, 1968.

Roots, John McCook, *Chou: An Informal Biography of China's Legendary Chou En Lai,* New York, 1978.

Schwartz, Benjamin, *Chinese Communism and the Rise of Mao,* Cambridge, Massachusetts, 1958.

Service, John S., *Lost Chance in China,* New York, 1974.

Siao-Yu, *Mao Tse-tung and I Were Beggars,* New York, 1959.

Smedley, Agnes, *Battle Hymn of China,* New York, 1943.

Smedley, Agnes, *China Fights Back,* London, 1938.

Smedley, Agnes, *Chinese Destinies,* New York, 1933.

Smedley, Agnes, *The Great Road,* New York, 1956.

Snow, Edgar, *The Battle for Asia,* New York, 1941.

Snow, Edgar, *Journey to the Beginning,* New York, 1967.

Snow, Edgar, *The Other Side of the River: Red China Today,* New York, 1962.

Snow, Edgar, *Random Notes on Red China,* Cambridge, Massachusetts, 1957.

Snow, Edgar, *Red Star Over China,* 1st rev. and enl. ed., New York, 1968.

Snow, Helen, *The Chinese Communists,* Westport, Connecticut, 1972.

Snow, Helen Foster, *Inside Red China,* New York, 1979.

Snow, Helen (Nym Wales), *My Yenan Notebooks,* Madison, Connecticut, 1961.

Snow, Helen (Nym Wales), *Red Dust,* Westport, Connecticut, 1972.

Snow, Helen, *Women in Modern China,* The Hague, 1957.

Snow, Lois Wheeler, *Edgar Snow's China,* New York, 1981.

Stories of the Long March, Peking, 1958.

Strong, Tracy B., and Keyssar, Helene, *Right in Her Soul: The Life of Anna Louise Strong,* New York, 1983.

Sutton, S. B., *In China's Border Provinces: The Turbulent Career of Joseph Rock, Botanist-Explorer,* New York, 1974.

Terrill, Ross, *Mao,* New York, 1980.

Terrill, Ross, *The White-Boned Demon: A Biography of Madame Mao Zedong,* New York, 1984.

Thornton, Richard C., *The Comintern and the Chinese Communists, 1928–1931,* Seattle, 1969.

Vishnyakova-Akimova, Vera Vladimirovna, *Two Years in Revolutionary China, 1925–1927,* Cambridge, Massachusetts, 1971.

Wang Ming, *China: Cultural Revolution or Counter-Revolutionary Coup?,* Moscow, n.d.

Wang Ming, *Mao's Betrayal,* Moscow, 1975.

Wei Kuo-lu (Wei Guolu), *On the Long March as Guard to Chou En-lai,* Peking, 1978.

Willoughby, Charles A., *Shanghai Conspiracy,* New York. 1952.

Wilson, Dick, *The Long March,* New York, 1982.

Wilson, Dick, *Zhou Enlai,* New York, 1984.

Witke, Roxane, *Comrade Chiang Ch'ing,* Boston, 1977.

Wolf, Margery, and Witke, Roxane, *Women in Chinese Society,* Stanford, California, 1975.

Zhelokhovtsy, A., *The "Cultural Revolution": a Close-up,* Moscow, 1975.

Periodicals

Charles, David A., "The Dismissal of Marshal P'eng Teh-huai," *The China Quarterly*, no. 8, October–December, 1961.

Ch'en, Jerome, "Resolution of the Tsunyi Conference," *The China Quarterly*, no. 40, October–December, 1969.

Chen Rinong, "Ruijin—Where It Started," *China Reconstructs*, no. 6, May, 1984.

Deng Rong (Mao Mao), "My Father Deng Xiaoping's Years in Jiangxi," *China Reconstructs*, no. 4, April, 1985.

Deng Rong (Mao Mao), "My Father's Days in Jiangxi," *Beijing Review*, September 3, 1984.

Garavente, Anthony, "The Long March," *The China Quarterly*, no. 22, April–June, 1965.

Goldstein, "Zhou Enlai and China's Revolution: A Selective View," *The China Quarterly*, no. 96, December, 1983.

Heinzig, Dieter, "Otto Braun and the Tsunyi Conference," *The China Quarterly*, no. 42, April–June, 1970.

Heinzig, Dieter, "Otto Braun's Memoirs and Mao's Rise to Power," *The China Quarterly*, no. 46, April–June, 1971.

Hsia, T. A., "Ch'u Ch'iu-pai's Autobiographical Writings," *The China Quarterly*, no. 25, January–March, 1966.

Hu, Chi-hsi, "Hua Fu, the Fifth Encirclement Campaign and the Tsunyi Conference," *The China Quarterly*, no. 43, July–September, 1970.

Hu, Chi-hsi, "Mao, Lin Biao and the Fifth Encirclement Campaign," *The China Quarterly*, no. 82, June, 1980.

Hua Chang-Ming, "Revolutionnaires au Foyer: Les Femmes à Yan'an, 1935–1946," *Paris-Peking*, no. 2, November, 1979.

Hu Yaobang, "The Best Way to Remember Mao Zedong," *Beijing Review*, January 2, 1984.

Li Chuang, "Snow Mountain and the Marshy Grasslands," *China Reconstructs*, no. 11, November, 1984.

Li Rui, "Mao Zedong in His School Days," Part 1, *Beijing Review*, April 30, 1984.

Li Rui, "Mao Zedong in His School Days," Part 2, *Beijing Review*, May 7, 1984.

MacFarquhar, Roderick, "The Tsunyi Conference," *The China Quarterly*, no. 41, January–March, 1970.

Selden, Mark, "The Guerrilla Movement in Northwest China," Part 1, *The China Quarterly*, no. 28, October–December, 1966.

Selden, Mark, "The Guerrilla Movement in Northwest China," Part 2, *The China Quarterly*, no. 29, January–March, 1967.

Simmonds, J. D., "P'eng Te-huai: A Chronological Re-examination," *The China Quarterly*, no. 37, January–March, 1969.

Truscott, Alan, "Calling a Bluff," *The New York Times*, March, 1981.

Truscott, Alan, "A China Hand," *The New York Times*, April, 1984.

404   BIBLIOGRAPHY

Weiglan, Suzanne, "The Martyrdom of Yang Kaihui," *Eastern Horizon*, no. 3, March, 1977.

New York Times files for 1934–35.

China Daily files for 1983–85.

Works in Russian

Braun, Otto, *Kitaiskiye Zapiskii, 1932–1940*, Moscow, 1974.

Burlatskii, Fedor, *Mao Zedong*, Moscow, 1976.

Chudodeev, Yu. V., *Na Kitaiskoi Zemle: Vosmominaniya Sovetskikh Dobrovoltsev, 1925–1945*, Moscow, 1977.

Delyusin, L. P., ed., and others, *Komintern i Vostok*, Moscow, 1969.

Grigoriev, A. M., *Revolyutsionnoye Dvizheniye v Kitai, 1927–1931*, Moscow, 1980.

He Gan-Chzhi, *Istoriya Sovremennoi Kitaiskoi Revolyutsii*, Moscow, 1959.

Martynov, A., ed., *Velikii Pokhod*, Moscow, 1959.

Perevertailo, A. S., ed., *Ocherki Istorii Kitaya v Noveishee Vremya*, Moscow, 1959.

Sapozhnikov, B. G., *Kitai v Ogne Voiny, 1931–1950*, Moscow, 1977.

Tikhvinskii, S. L., ed., *Novaya Istoriya Kitaya*, Moscow, 1972.

Titov, A. S., *Iz Istorii Borby i Raskola v Rukovodstve KPK*, Moscow, 1979.

Ulyanovskii, R. A., ed., *Komintern i Vostok: Kritika Kritiki*, Moscow, 1978.

Vasilev, L. S., *Problemy Genezisa Kitaiskogo Gosudarstva*, Moscow, 1983.

Vladimirov, O., and Ryazantsev, B., *Stranitzy Politicheskoi Biografii Mao Zedong*, Moscow, 1980.

INDEX

412   INDEX

ABOUT THE AUTHOR

Harrison E. Salisbury is a product of Minnesota where he was born, grew up and went to school and had his start in journalism. His earliest ambition was to go to China and work there as a newspaperman but instead his career took him in the opposite direction.

He worked for United Press International in Chicago, Washington and New York. In World War II he became a foreign correspondent in London, the Middle East and Moscow. He was assigned to Chungking but before he could reach his post was brought back to New York as foreign editor of UPI. He joined the *New York Times* in 1949 and became their Moscow correspondent, serving for many years in the Soviet Union, traveling widely in Siberia, Central Asia and Outer Mongolia along China's borders.

From 1959 onward his attention turned more and more to China and Southeast Asia, stimulated by his discovery in Outer Mongolia of the first signs of the great rift between Soviet Russia and Communist China. He spent much time in the Far East and in 1966—at a time when China was closed to Americans—made a complete orbit of her borders, surveying the country from the periphery.

Beginning in 1972 he has made frequent trips to China and has traveled extensively along the Sino-Soviet border, the extreme Northwest of China, Tibet, along the rocky road from Lhasa to Katmandu and in 1984 7,100 miles along the routes of the Long March.

Catalog

If you are interested in a list of fine Paperback
books, covering a wide range of subjects
and interests, send your name and address,
requesting your free catalog, to:

McGraw-Hill Paperbacks
1221 Avenue of Americas
New York, N.Y. 10020